United Artists

United Artists

The Company Built by the Stars

Tino Balio

The University of Wisconsin Press

Published 1976

The University of Wisconsin Press
Box 1379, Madison, Wisconsin 53701

The University of Wisconsin Press, Ltd.
70 Great Russell Street, London

First printing

Printed in the United States of America

For LC CIP information see the colophon

ISBN 0-299-06940-0

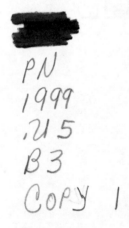

For Diana, Andrew, and Julia

Contents

	Illustrations	ix
	Preface	xiii
1	*Artists in Business: 1919*	3
2	*Starts and Fits: 1919-1924*	30
3	*Joe Schenck's Reorganization: 1925-1931*	52
4	*Adjusting to the Talkies: 1928-1932*	75
5	*Depression and Monopoly: 1932-1934*	95
6	*Schenck's Last Years: 1932-1935*	110
7	*Without a Leader: 1934-1936*	127
8	*The Goldwyn Battles: 1936-1941*	142
9	*Facing the War: 1941*	161
10	*Worsening Strains Within: 1942-1944*	186
11	*Coming Apart at the Seams: 1944-1948*	202
12	*The End and the Beginning of UA: 1949-*	230
Appendix 1	*Releases: 1919-1950*	245
Appendix 2	*Producers*	260
Appendix 3	*The Walt Disney Cartoons*	280
Appendix 4	*Income History*	283
Appendix 5	*Record of Dividend Payments*	284
Appendix 6	*Capital Stock Purchased by the Company*	287
	The UA Collection: A Descriptive Inventory	289
	Notes	293
	Index	305

Illustrations

The Big Four   4
Mary Pickford   15
Charles Chaplin   17
Douglas Fairbanks   19
D. W. Griffith   22
The signing of the certificate of incorporation   27
Fairbanks' *His Majesty, the American* (1919)   31
Lillian Gish and Richard Barthelmess in D. W. Griffith's *Broken
    Blossoms* (1919)   32
Fairbanks' *Robin Hood* (1923)   38
Fairbanks' *The Thief of Bagdad* (1924)   46
Pickford's *Rosita* (1923)   47
Norma Talmadge   53
Joseph Schenck   55
Chaplin's *The Gold Rush* (1925)   57
Gloria Swanson   59
Belle Bennett in Goldwyn's *Stella Dallas* (1926)   67
Keaton's *The General* (1927)   69
Samuel Goldwyn   70
Ronald Colman and Lilyan Tashman in Goldwyn's *Bulldog Drum-
    mond* (1929)   80
Noah Beery and Norma Talmadge in Schenck's *The Dove* (1928)   81
Swanson's *Sadie Thompson* (1928) with Raoul Walsh   82
Walter Huston in Art Cinema's *Abraham Lincoln* (1930) directed by
    D. W. Griffith   86
Chaplin's *City Lights* (1931) with Harry Myers   90

Fairbanks and Pickford in *Taming of the Shrew* (1929)   92
United Artists doing its part for the NRA   98
"The greatest selling organization in pictures"   107
Paul Muni and Ann Dvorak in Hughes' *Scarface* (1932)   111
Walt Disney   114
UA poster for *Mickey's Good Deed* (1932)   115
The Big Bad Wolf in *Three Little Pigs* (1933)   115
Darryl Zanuck   119
Fredric March in 20th Century's *Les Miserables* (1935)   124
Chaplin's *Modern Times* (1936)   131
Charles Laughton in Korda's *The Private Life of Henry VIII* (1933) 133
Alexander Korda   135
Mary Pickford and Walter Wanger   139
Douglas Fairbanks, Alexander Korda, Mary Pickford, Murray Sil-
    verstone, Charles Chaplin, A. H. Giannini, and Samuel Goldwyn   143
William Wyler, Samuel Goldwyn, Bonita Granville, and Merle
    Oberon on the set of Goldwyn's *These Three* (1936)   148
Laurence Olivier and Merle Oberon in Goldwyn's *Wuthering
    Heights* (1939)   156
Burgess Meredith and Lon Chaney, Jr., in Roach's *Of Mice and
    Men* (1940)   162
Chaplin's *The Great Dictator* (1941)   163
Ernst Lubitsch and Jack Benny on the set of *To Be Or Not To Be*
    (1942)   173
Andy Devine, George Bancroft, and John Wayne in Wanger's
    Stagecoach (1939)   175
Fredric March and Janet Gaynor in Selznick's *A Star Is Born*
    (1937)   178
Joan Fontaine and Judith Anderson in Selznick's *Rebecca* (1940)   180
David O. Selznick   183
Xavier Cugat and orchestra in Lesser's *Stage Door Canteen* (1943) 189
Cagney's *Johnny Come Lately* (1943)   192
Jane Russell in Hughes' *The Outlaw* (1946)   204
Jennifer Jones, Claudette Colbert, and Shirley Temple in Selznick's
    Since You Went Away (1944)   207
Chaplin's *Monsieur Verdoux* (1947) with Martha Raye   211

Montgomery Clift in Hawks' *Red River* (1948)   218
Laurence Olivier in *Henry V*   221
Gradwell Sears and Loew's, Inc., president Nicholas Schenck   228
Mary Pickford and husband Buddy Rogers (1949)   231
Charles Chaplin and wife Oona O'Neill Chaplin (1950)   236
Press conference in Arthur Krim's office, October 1951.   238

Preface

In April of 1968, I met with Arnold Picker at United Artists headquarters in New York. He was then executive vice president of UA, and I wished to discuss with him an invitation from the Wisconsin Center for Theatre Research to establish a collection of corporate records documenting the history of the company. The Center is an archive of primary source materials relating to theater, film, and television located at the University of Wisconsin—Madison. As director of the Center, I was interested in United Artists not only because it held a prominent position in the motion picture industry but also because it had been organized and owned for many years by four of the most illustrious names in the business—Douglas Fairbanks, Mary Pickford, Charles Chaplin, and D. W. Griffith.

United Artists was founded in 1919 as a distribution company for independent producers: those actors, directors, and producers who were constitutionally opposed to the studio system and who risked their own money on custom-made pictures that reflected their special talents. Since this breed of showman was rare, UA released no more than fifteen to twenty pictures a year, often fewer, but they were consistently among Hollywood's finest.

Many great filmmakers, including Sam Goldwyn, Joseph Schenck, Alexander Korda, David O. Selznick, Darryl Zanuck, Howard Hughes, Walt Disney, Walter Wanger, and Hal Roach, were associated with the company at one time or another.

From a position of enormous prestige and financial success in the thirties, UA declined in the forties to the extent that it was spared from bankruptcy only when Arthur B. Krim and Robert S. Benjamin took over the management of the company from the two remaining stockholders, Pickford and Chaplin, in 1951. Benjamin and Krim revitalized UA and managed to transform it once again into one of the most successful organizations in the industry. United Artists became a publicly held company in 1957, and in 1967 it became a subsidiary of Transamerica Corporation.

In making my presentation to Arnold Picker, I fully realized that motion picture companies regarded their business affairs as closely guarded secrets. Understandably, Mr. Picker wanted time to consider the matter. Later in the week, I received a message from his office asking that I contact Robert Schwartz, then UA's director of administrative services. I did so and was elated to learn the decision: United Artists would donate to the Center its corporate records up to 1951, when the present management took over. They were located in a warehouse in Queens and were available to us at our convenience. Although we were free to take everything, he added that we would probably want to make a judicious selection since, in total volume, the materials occupied about 5,000 cubic feet of space! I agreed, since stack space in the manuscripts library of the State Historical Society of Wisconsin, where the Center's collections are housed, was limited.

For the selection process, I needed the assistance of a trained archivist, which the Society gladly provided in the person of Jack Jallings, assistant state archivist for the Society and a specialist in corporate records. I returned to New York with Jallings. After a week of surveying the material, it became apparent to us that a full examination would take a great deal of time, far more than we cared to spend in the warehouse, and so we shipped the bulk of the records to the Society in Madison. Although it would take two additional years to complete the processing and inventory the material, we knew then that the Center had acquired a collection of exceptional research value.

It was only after surveying the hundreds of cartons of materials in Madison that we realized the magnitude of the job. Our major problem in cataloging was to discover the structure of UA and to determine the extent to which the diverse materials documented the operations of the company. We knew less about UA as a corporation than about any other major film company. As a privately held company, UA was not required to file documents with the Securities and Exchange Commission describing its history, capital structure, holdings, mode of operation, management, financial statements, and other data. Nor had much been written about UA in the few economic histories that had been published. UA was the smallest company among the so-called Big Eight, and economists have focused on the behavior of the giants, principally Paramount, Warner Brothers, Twentieth Century-Fox, and Loew's—those corporations which made the greatest impact on the marketplace. United Artists operated a business, not an archive. When papers were no longer needed for reference, they were simply packed in cartons and sent to the warehouse. There was no useful inventory of the materials in storage, nor were the materials arranged in any order.

The process was a slow and halting one, at first, gradually increasing in speed and efficiency as we began to fit the materials into an organized pattern. As it turned out, we devoted more than a year just to initial processing, that is, sifting through the contents and establishing an overall design for the collection. And it took two full-time archivists and several part-time student assistants to get this much done.

The collection documented all facets of the company's operations through its various departments—domestic sales, foreign sales, advertising and publicity, accounting, and legal, among others. The range was broad: minutes of the board of directors, executive correspondence, producers' contracts, financial journals and ledgers, litigation files, exchange correspondence, and income-tax returns. The collection did not contain production information pertaining to United Artists pictures, it should be noted. Such materials as shooting schedules, scripts, budgets, artists' contracts, and artwork belonged to the company's independent producers. The collection describes the life of a film in its UA distribution phase only.

Despite the vastness of our acquisition, however, it eventually became apparent that there were gaps in the materials:

1. The collection contained little about the most glorious years of the company during the twenties. It was distressing to discover that the records describing the sales campaigns for UA's releases had been discarded, no doubt long ago.

2. Materials from the thirties were more numerous, although far less complete than those of later years. In general, however, there was a positive correlation between the volume of materials and the magnitude of the company's operations at any one time.

3. Documents written by the founders numbered only four or five dozen in all. I have incorporated in the text the most important of these, while wishing that more had been written or preserved.

4. There was a paucity of correspondence of the principal pre-1940 officers. This was especially disappointing in the case of Joseph Schenck, who was president and chairman of the board from 1925 to 1935 and the man most responsible for the rapid development of the company during that period.

Nonetheless, we were able to trace the history of the corporation. The collection contains all the minutes of the board of directors' meetings and stockholders' meetings. As records of the results of the meetings—motions that were made and either passed or defeated—they are invaluable in developing an accurate chronicle of the movements of the company. They do not, however, record discussions, arguments, nuances of feelings, or friction among participants. In addition, the files of UA's legal counsel until 1951, the firm of O'Brien, Driscoll, and Raftery, came to us intact. They are the heart of the collection and document virtually every legal matter in which the company was involved.

After the initial processing was completed in the summer of 1969, United Artists offered to increase its gift. Over the remainder of the year, it added the following materials: pressbooks, still negatives, and photographs of United Artists releases; the Warner Film Library (1913-1950), 50 silent features, 800 sound features, 1,500 short subjects, 300 cartoons, scripts, still negatives, and pressbooks; the RKO Film Library (1929-1954), 700 sound features; the Monogram Film Library (1931-1946), 200 sound features, still negatives, and pressbooks; the Ziv Television Library (1948-1962), 2,000 episodes from 38 television series, shooting scripts, and still negatives; and 200 Popeye cartoons, Eagle-Lion still negatives, Film Classics still negatives, and starheads. It may seem strange that there were no United Artists films in the gift to go along with the corporate records, but the company had none to give; UA's pictures were owned by the producers and reverted to them after the distribution period.

The acquisition of this gift and its importance for film scholars led us to rename our organization the Center for Film and Theater Research.

This collection—the first of its kind ever donated to a research institution by a major film company—has made possible the construction of this history. It covers the years 1919-1951, the period in which the original owners controlled the company. At the outset of my research I was able—through the good offices of Arnold Picker—to secure an interview with Charlie Chaplin at his home in Vevey, Switzerland. During that interview, he advised that I focus the story of United Artists on the purposes of the owners rather than on the business of the company. "If UA's history is written from a human point of view," he said, "I think it would make a very interesting history."

Although I would have liked to follow his advice, the records of a personal and human nature were too scant to permit me to present a sustained insight into the behavior of the owners throughout the history of the company. There were enough records, however, to reveal the behavior of the owners at crucial points in the company's history and how their decisions affected the course and fortunes of United Artists. Chaplin, Fairbanks, Pickford, and Griffith have been known primarily as filmmakers. Now we will see them as business partners. Theirs was an uneasy alliance of headstrong artists who, though seldom united, managed despite their differences to sustain a motion picture enterprise for the benefit of the independent producer in an era dominated by big business and an oligopolistic market structure. Theirs was a unique company whose story deserves to be told.

The willing cooperation of many people is reflected in this work. My thanks must go first of all to United Artists Corporation, and especially to UA vice presidents Herbert Schottenfeld and Robert Schwartz, both of whom gave generously of their time from the very conception of this history, through the many stages of its research, and continuing until its publication. Throughout my long and close association with these officers of UA, I was deeply impressed with their serious concern that the history be written accurately and in the best traditions of scholarship. Their interest and encouragement helped sustain me throughout the course of my project, for which I am grateful.

I am also indebted to those people whose insights enabled me to interpret the corporate records with greater perspective and understanding. I received interviews with (in addition to Chaplin) Arthur Krim, Arnold Picker, the director Lewis Milestone, former UA vice president George Bagnall, and, most significant, Paul O'Brien, a UA counsel for more than fifteen years and a member of the law firm of O'Brien, Driscoll, and Raftery. (Miss Pickford, with Chaplin the other remaining principal, has not received interviewers in recent years and was not approached for this purpose.)

Important in my research, also, were those graduate students in the Department of Communication Arts who took my research seminars on the history of the motion picture industry and who explored with me the rich resources of the collection.

An absolute prerequisite to any research endeavor is the easy accessibility of materials, and to Stephen Masar and Susan Dalton, who cataloged the United Artists Collection, I am especially grateful. Both are archivists on the staff of the Center for Film and Theater Research, Masar as curator of the United Artists corporate records and Dalton as film archivist. Their diligent and intelligent efforts facilitated not only my work but also the research of the hundreds of students and scholars who have come, and will come, to Madison to use the collection.

In the preparation of the manuscript, I am greatly indebted to C. V. Cook of Delray Beach, Florida, who shared with me his expert knowledge of motion picture business procedures. I thank Elizabeth Uhr, who edited the manuscript with expertise and sensitivity, and who offered many sound suggestions for its improvement. And thanks must surely go to Mary Beth Schlagheck, who typed the manuscript in all of its stages with dispatch, rare competence, and unwavering good humor.

I would also like to thank the Graduate School of the University of

Wisconsin—Madison, which awarded me a research grant during the academic year 1970-1971, and the American Film Institute, which awarded me a Louis B. Mayer Research Associateship at the Center for Advanced Film Studies in 1972.

The acquisition and maintenance of the United Artists Collection have been a collaborative effort with the State Historical Society of Wisconsin, and I wish to express my gratitude to its staff, in particular to James M. Smith, Richard A. Erney, Barbara J. Kaiser, Josephine L. Harper, F. Gerald Ham, Jack K. Jallings, Eleanor McKay, and George Talbot.

Last, my special thanks to Frederick W. Haberman, former chairman of the Department of Communication Arts, for his encouragement and counsel.

Tino Balio

Madison, Wisconsin
March, 1975

United Artists

1   *Artists in Business*
[1919]

THE MOVIE INDUSTRY IN 1919

It is January, 1919. A convention of the First National Exhibitors Circuit is meeting at the Alexandria Hotel in Los Angeles. On the mezzanine floor, in Parlor A, the seven members of the executive board are in session. Below them, in the lobby, the atmosphere among the sages, kibitzers, and gossipers is fraught with excitement. Rumors, conjectures, and guesses about mergers fill the air: mergers that aim to control the industry; mergers that spell the death of the star system; mergers that eliminate the small fish of filmdom. A. H. Giebler of *Moving Picture World* surveyed the scene and said:

> Did Dave Griffith eat a little snack of lunch with Sam Goldwyn, a merger was seen in the offing. Did J. D. Williams stop Adolph Zukor in the lobby and say, "Dolph, this certainly beats New York for climate," the nucleus for a new combination was born.
>
> Did Winnie Sheehan shake hands with Hiram Abrams and ask him politely for news from Broadway, the name of William Fox was written large on the dope sheets. . . .
>
> Did those two mysterious strangers from the East, Hiram Abrams and Benny Schulberg, parade their slow and solemn way along the length of the lobby, eyes were rolled in their direction and bated voices asked: "What have those two wise birds got up their sleeves . . . ?" "The First National will control all the stars." "The First National is going to form a combination with Famous Players, Artcraft, Goldwyn, Metro, Fox, and after that they'll tell the stars just where to get off in the matter of salary."
>
> "Doug has signed up with First National." "Doug has done no such of a thing." "Charlie's going to Europe. . . . Mary will renew her contract with First National." "Mary will not." "Mary may, but Charlie won't." "See me in the morning, and I'll give you the whole story." "Don't quote me, but here's the right dope. . . ."
>
> Thus it went on all day long, from getting up time until hay time—everywhere—all over the big hotel, upstairs and down, in parlor, bedroom and bath, lobby, grill, tearoom, candy shop and barber shop, until voices grew husky and imaginations were worn to a frazzle.[1]

An adjustment of industry conditions was clearly imminent. Just before the convention, Richard A. Rowland, president of Metro Pictures, proclaimed that "motion pictures must cease to be a game and become a business." What he wanted was to supplant the star system, which forced companies to compete for big names and pay out-of-this-world salaries for their services. Metro, he said, would thenceforth decline from "competitive bidding for billion-dollar stars" and devote its energies to making big pictures based on "play value and excellence of production."[2]

Other moguls felt the same way. The industry had been in the grip of the star system for ten years, ever since audiences began to recognize individuals from among the uncredited players on the early screen. People began to ask, for instance, who was that little girl with the blonde curls? Or who was that little man with the funny mustache? Thereafter, as the audiences decided that they preferred this actress to that one, and as millions of fans flocked to theaters to see their favorites and stayed home when their favorites failed to appear, the balance of power shifted from the businessman to the employee. And did the salaries skyrocket: $100, $500, $1,000, and for the brightest and most illustrious, Pickford and

The Big Four

Chaplin, $10,000 a week. Negatives that before World War I cost $10,000 to $30,000 were now requiring expenditures of $50,000 to $100,000 and more, depending on the magnitude of the star. "Acting," as Benjamin Hampton said, "historically one of the most precarious of all professions, suddenly found itself among the best paid on earth."[3] Mary Pickford, John Bunny, Francis X. Bushman, and Bronco Billy Anderson were the first to benefit from the new idolatry. Then Chaplin, Douglas Fairbanks, William S. Hart, Theda Bara, Mae Marsh, Lillian Gish, and a whole constellation of others.

There were other reasons for the rise in production costs. Audiences had come to prefer feature-length pictures to the one- and two-reelers and wanted stories having more than rudimentary plots. More money was needed for plays, novels, and scenarios, for better sets and more expensive costumes. Nevertheless, the consensus in Hollywood, concurred in by supporting actors, was that too much of the gross was going to the star.

The industry was in the throes of a titanic struggle for control. There were two main protagonists: on one side stood Adolph Zukor's Famous Players-Lasky Co., the world's largest producer and distributor of feature films; on the other stood the First National Exhibitors Circuit, an association of powerful theater owners from around the country who banded together to curb Zukor's growing dictatorial powers by financing productions of top stars and distributing them among themselves.

EARLY STRUGGLES FOR CONTROL[4]

The Motion Picture Patents Company

The struggle had its antecedents in the days of the Motion Picture Patents Company, a patent-pooling combination that held monopolistic control of the industry from 1908 to 1912. When the Trust, as it was called, was formed in September, 1908, motion-picture business was robust and flourishing. Movies had graduated from their novelty stage when they were typically fifty feet in length and photographed anything that moved, whether parades, trains, dancers, or fire engines. Now they told gripping stories with relatively well-developed plots and characters—containing dramatic tension in lengths of about 1,000 feet, and taking about fourteen minutes of screen time. Overwhelming audience acceptance of the medium had placed the industry on a sound commercial basis. There were more than a hundred small companies engaged in producing pictures or importing them from Europe. Between 125 to 150 film exchanges distributed the pictures to nearly 10,000 nickelodeons, those theaters in storefronts and rented halls most often found in the slum neighborhoods and poorer sections in every industrial city. From 1895, when motion pictures were first exhibited in the United States, to 1908, business was wide open and free wheeling.

With the founding of the Motion Picture Patents Company, however, conditions changed. It was formed in a peace settlement between two hostile factions—one led by the Edison Manufacturing Company and the other by the American Mutoscope and Biograph Company—that had been fighting each other to establish the hegemony of their respective patents. Together, they held all the important patents on motion-picture film, cameras, and projectors, and secured a stranglehold on the industry for over three years. There were ten constituent members of the Trust, virtually every leading producer and manufacturer of equipment. In addition to Edison and Biograph, the others were Essanay, Kalem, Kleine Optical Company (a film importer), Lubin, Selig Polyscope Company, Vitagraph, and two French companies that had branches in America, Gaston Méliès and Pathé Frères.

The Trust issued licenses to produce pictures only to its members. Eastman Kodak colluded with the Patents Company in an attempt to drive all other producers out of the field by granting it the exclusive right to purchase film stock. On the distribution level, members agreed to lease pictures only to those exchanges that dealt in licensed film entirely and at stipulated prices. These exchanges in turn could rent pictures only to exhibitors using licensed projectors.

In addition to its licensing function, the Trust undertook a royalty-collecting operation on behalf of its members. From manufacturers of projectors, it exacted a five-dollar fee per machine. From exhibitors, it demanded two dollars a week for the right to operate each licensed projector, and on the condition that it be used solely to exhibit films produced by one of the ten licensed companies.

To enforce its regulations, the Trust filed lawsuits by the hundred, employed private detectives to search for evidence of patent violations, and called upon federal marshals to arrest offenders, confiscate their equipment, and throw them in jail. Nonetheless, outlaw producers continued to make pictures and somehow managed to find outlets for them, owing to the seemingly unlimited demand on the part of exhibitors. Independent exchanges also continued to operate; even the licensed exchanges, succumbing to the temptation of quick profits, defied Trust regulations. Independent producers, by the way, helped to establish Hollywood rather than New York as the production center of the industry. To evade the Trust, they had fled to Cuba, Florida, and Southern California. The Los Angeles area, with its proximity to the Mexican border, temperate climate, and cheap labor, was found to be the ideal location.

These conditions spurred the Patents Company to go into distribution. In 1910, it organized the General Film Company as a subsidiary, which bought out fifty-eight exchanges nationwide. Others were driven out of business by such expedients as cutting off the supply of films, price-cutting, discrimination, and so forth. Within a year, only one of the former exchanges remained, and with this exception, General Film was the sole distributor of motion pictures in the United States. The one exception, however, was partly instrumental in the Trust's undoing. William Fox, who then operated theaters and an exchange, called Greater New York Film Rental Company, in New York City, refused to sell out. Instead, he went into film production and instituted a lawsuit against the Patents Company under the provisions of the Sherman Antitrust Act, charging unlawful conspiracy in restraint of trade. The suit went to trial in January, 1913, and resulted in the dissolution of the Patents Company by the courts five years later. By then, however, the Patents Company had long since disintegrated.

Resistance to the Trust

Despite its strong-arm tactics to control production, formidable strength in distribution, and ingenious schemes to regulate exhibition, the Patents Company stimulated competition rather than stifling it. Outlaw production companies mushroomed, finding sympathetic allies among the thousands of exhibitors who bitterly resented the weekly two-dollar levy on their projectors. At the time the government filed its antitrust suit in mid-1912, a strong and well-organized independent movement had come into existence, offering the Trust stiff competition. Among the early producers were Fox, Independent Motion Picture Company (IMP), Keystone, Thanhouser, Rex, and dozens of others. Mutual and Universal were the important distributors. By 1914, literally hundreds of new firms had entered the business.

The competition engendered by the independents had far-reaching effects on the content of the film as well as the structure of the industry. The Patents Company, in attempting to regulate commerce, considered the motion picture as merchandise to be mass-produced at low cost in standard lengths of 1,000-foot reels and sold at a flat rate regardless of the quality of the picture, the actors, or director. In fact, the policy was to keep the names of players secret, so that public acclaim could not inspire demands for greater salaries. Thus, the objective was to manufacture a commodity—film—to fill the weekly playing schedule of theaters. That the motion picture had enormous potential as a medium of mass entertainment was beyond the comprehension of the Trust.

Successful Innovations—Stars and Feature Films

Independents, on the other hand, experimented freely to please the public. For example, Carl Laemmle, the head of IMP, created the first movie star in the person of Florence Lawrence of Biograph. Due to Trust policy, she had been known only as "the Biograph Girl" to her admirers. Laemmle hired her away from the company with an offer of a larger salary, rechristened her "the Imp Girl," and in a daring publicity stunt, revealed her name to the public. He planted a story in a St. Louis newspaper stating that the former Biograph player, Florence Lawrence, had died in a streetcar accident. Soon afterwards, he took out an ad in the newspaper declaring that the story was a false rumor spread by the Trust. She was alive and well, the ad continued, and she would be featured in forthcoming IMP productions.

Thus began the star system of motion-picture production. Other independents followed suit by publicizing the names of their players. The star craze hit the industry like a storm and forced even the conservative members of the Patents Company to change with the times, although by then, most of their most promising actors had been stolen by independents. How the star system affected the economics of the industry will be told later in this chapter.

Another innovation introduced by independents was the feature film. Before 1911, a few longer films—two, three, and even four reels in length—had been imported from Europe and found an enthusiastic reception in the exchanges. But once again, the Trust's rigid policies regarding standardization stood in the way of the production of this type of film in the United States. Exhibitors had been clamoring for better and longer films, ones that told well-developed and dignified stories that could attract a more intelligent clientele. These demands were met by the argument that better-quality pictures would necessitate increased production costs, higher rentals from theaters, and the raising of admission prices at the box office above the prevailing level without increasing consumer demand. The Trust believed that audiences did not have the mental capacity to understand, let alone appreciate, longer films. It would pay heavily for this insensitivity.

Zukor and Famous Players

It is here that Adolph Zukor enters the story. Like other nickelodeon owners of the day, he observed a growing unrest with the usual movie fare and thought that audiences would be receptive to feature films. There was no steady source for this kind of picture, so Zukor went to the heads of the Patents Company to persuade them to revamp their production policy.

After receiving a humiliating rebuff, Zukor decided to risk his savings in production on his own. As a beginning, he experimented with the imported French film *Queen Elizabeth,* starring Sarah Bernhardt. His hunch proved correct. The longer film would go over with the public, especially if it had a star. Thus, with Daniel Frohman, one of the biggest theatrical producers, Zukor formed Famous Players in 1912 and signed up Broadway stars: first James O'Neill and James K. Hackett, then Lillie Langtry, John Barrymore, and Fannie Ward.

The first feature produced and distributed by Famous Players was *The Prisoner of Zenda,* starring James K. Hackett. This picture as well as the others that followed at monthly intervals were distributed on a "states-rights" basis, by which is meant that exhibition rights to pictures were sold to distributors operating within a particular metropolitan or geographical area. A national distribution network did not yet exist to handle feature films; Mutual, Universal, and Fox still sold programs of short subjects that changed daily or every other day. Feature films required special and individual promotional effort and the states-rights method had to suffice until a better one could be perfected, which occurred in 1914.

W. W. Hodkinson, a progressive exhibitor with overwhelming faith in quality pictures, organized Paramount Pictures Corporation. This was a distribution company consisting of eleven regional states-rights buyers who joined forces to advance a steady stream of capital to producers that would enable them to make a regular supply of features. Zukor's Famous Players was brought into the scheme, as well as Bosworth, Inc., Jesse L. Lasky Feature Play Co., Morosco Photo Play Company, and others. These companies signed franchise agreements granting Paramount the exclusive right to distribute their pictures for a period of years at the fee of 35 per cent of the gross sales.

Zukor and Paramount

The formation of Paramount was a death blow to the Patents Company. Paramount had geared itself to deliver 2 features a week, 104 a year. Theater owners and audiences enthusiastically endorsed the plan, which assured the company success from the start. Gross rentals soon reached the unprecedented amounts of $100,000 to $125,000 per picture. Other companies got on the band wagon, among them Lewis Selznick's World Film Corporation, Triangle Film Corporation, Goldwyn Pictures Corporation, Metro Film Corporation, and Fox Film Corporation. And a wave of theater construction began in the principal cities to contain the growing audiences. In the midst of the feature film revolution, the Patents Company and General Film gradually faded away.

This tremendous expansion of the movie business convinced Zukor that Paramount and its producers should merge not only to effect economies of scale in production but also to enable him to share more equitably in Paramount's burgeoning profits. Famous Players in its third year of existence earned over $1 million in profits and had become the mainstay of Paramount's operations. Yet, 35 per cent of its revenues remained in Paramount's tills as distribution fees. Moreover, because Famous Players was not a stockholder in the distribution company, Zukor was powerless to influence the course of its operations. Hodkinson vetoed the idea, arguing that the three branches of motion pictures—production, distribution, and exhibition—should be kept separate. Better pictures, better distribution, and better theater management would result if a lively independence existed among them.

But Zukor was not to be denied. He went to work on Paramount's board of directors and persuaded a majority to see things his way, with the result that in 1916, Hodkinson was deposed, Paramount, Famous Players, and Lasky were merged, and Adolph Zukor assumed the presidency of the $25 million Famous Players-Lasky Corporation. Paramount now became a Zukor subsidiary. This marked a turning point of major significance for the industry. The independent movement that grew up in opposition to the Trust was coming to an end; the vertical integration of production, distribution, and exhibition would continue until by the twenties, a new form of monopoly would control the motion-picture business.

Zukor would not go into exhibition so long as he could maintain a strategic hold on the market with his stable of stars. He had long since abandoned his original plan to use personages from the legitimate stage. Trained primarily to use the voice rather than pantomime as the main instrument of communication and often too old and too heavy to photograph well, theater idols had proven unsatisfactory for the silent screen. Zukor thereafter gathered together in his organization players and artistic talent on whom the movie public had conferred stardom. His greatest prize was Mary Pickford; others in his illustrious stable were Douglas Fairbanks, Gloria Swanson, William S. Hart, Fatty Arbuckle, Pauline Frederick, Blanche Sweet, Norma and Constance Talmadge, Nazimova, and directors Cecil B. De Mille, D. W. Griffith, and Mack Sennett. With approximately 75 per cent of the best talent in the industry under his control, Zukor could dominate the field.

Now at the reins of Paramount as well, Zukor implemented the next stage of his thinking. Before the year 1916 ended, he increased film rentals sharply and introduced block booking to the Paramount distribution system. Block booking was not new to the industry, but it had never been particularly effective until Zukor used it. Zukor had greatly expanded his production program, so much so that by 1919, Paramount distributed 139 features. Despite the fact that Famous Players-Lasky had the greatest array of talent around, a major portion of its output was decidedly second-rate. But by using the distribution practice of block booking, Zukor assured that these pictures would be rented to exhibitors at a profit.

Resistance to Zukor—First National

Paramount's seasonal output was arranged in blocks of up to 104 pictures, enough to fill the entire playing time of a theater if it changed its bill twice a week. Each block would be sprinkled with a few specials containing top-name stars and maybe even a Mary Pickford super special. The bulk of the block, however, consisted of pictures which if offered individually would rarely find takers. Zukor's block-booking system worked because of the enormous drawing power of Mary Pickford and his other stars and also because these blocks were offered to exhibitors on an all-or-nothing basis. If an exhibitor rejected Paramount's rental terms, his patrons would likely desert him in favor of a theater down the street featuring the Paramount stars.

Exhibitor resentment to the imperial Zukor climaxed in 1917 with the formation of First National Exhibitors Circuit. The brainchild of Los Angeles theater owner Thomas L. Tally, this organization was created to act as purchasing agent for twenty-six of the nation's largest first-run exhibitors located in key cities, that is, those cities where national distributors had their regional exchanges. Their objective was to acquire outstanding pictures made by independent producers. First National would not waste money buying or building studios; rather it would use its considerable purchasing power to capture the biggest box-office names. The twenty-six franchise holders agreed to put up financing in return for the right to exhibit the picture and then to distribute it among theaters in their respective territories.

First National proved its determination by plucking Charlie Chaplin from Mutual and then Mary Pickford from Paramount with $1 million contracts in 1918. By then, the franchise holders controlled nearly 200 first-run houses and approximately 60 subsequent-run houses, as well as over 350 theaters controlled under subfranchise agreements. First National was indeed becoming an aggressive opponent.

Thus, rumors of a merger between Famous Players-Lasky and First National early in 1919 were bound to give stars pause. The addition of hundreds of theaters to Zukor's empire and the dissolution of the most attractive outlet for independent production would indeed spell the end of the star system as it then existed.

THE STARS UNITE TO FORM A COMPANY

Thomas L. Tally, spokesman for First National's executive committee, denied all of the rumors. He said that his company was not planning to merge with Famous Players-Lasky, Goldwyn, Metro, or any other concern. Charlie Chaplin, for one, believed otherwise. He had gone before First National's board during the convention to request an increase in his production budget and had been turned down. Not only that! He had been treated with indifference as well. He, Chaplin, who was earning millions for First National. In analyzing the situation, Sydney Chaplin, Charlie's brother and business manager, became suspicious and conferred the following day with Mary Pickford and Douglas Fairbanks. They too were perturbed because their contracts were about to run out at First National and Famous Players-Lasky, respectively, and they were not receiving the customary offers from the big companies. To get to the heart of the matter, the three of them hired a detective. Chaplin, in his autobiography, tells the following story:

> We engaged a very clever girl, smart and attractive-looking. Soon she had made a date with an executive of an important producing company. Her report stated that she had passed the subject in the lobby of the Alexandria Hotel and had smiled at him, then made the excuse that she had mistaken him for an old friend. That evening he had asked her to have dinner with him. From her report we gathered that the subject was a glib braggart in an esurient state of libido. For three nights she went out with him, staving him off with promises and excuses. In the meantime she got a complete story of what was going on in the film industry. He and his associates were forming a forty-million-dollar merger of all the producing companies and were sewing up every exhibitor in the United States with a five-year contract. He told her they intended putting the industry on a proper business basis, instead of having it run by a bunch of crazy actors getting astronomical salaries. That was the gist of her story, and it was sufficient for our purposes. The four of us showed the report to D. W. Griffith and Bill Hart, and they had the same reaction as we did.[5]

The stars decided to stage a revolt on their own, and Sydney called a meeting at his house on Tuesday, January 14, to discuss strategy. The ubiquitous Giebler claimed he was there and gave an eye-witness account of events:

> Of course, Charlie was there, and Doug and Mrs. Charlotte Pickford, who represented Mary because Mary was ill with the flu, and Bill Hart and D. W. Griffith. It was a most enthusiastic little gathering, and it lasted until late at night but when it was all over, film history had been made, and every slate that had been written on the possible results of the week needed a wet sponge.
>
> Wednesday the news of the meeting began to sift through here and there. Telephones were busy; corridor conferences were held; vociferous denials were made.

I got to the Fairbanks studio right in the thick of things. Doug was sizzling around like a bottle of old-fashioned soda pop.

"Happiest man in the country," he said. "We are doing what we have all wanted to do for years. This meeting of the First National and all the talk of combinations and mergers and controlling the stars as though we were chattels to be bought and sold, has brought it to a head. We are going to make pictures, and make them as we want to, without the hampering restraints of set dates of release, and we are going to put the distributing profits into the pictures, where they belong."

Sydney Chaplin came in just then with an important looking paper in his hand. Three signatures were already on the document, the names of Fairbanks, Griffith and Hart.

"All ready?" asked Doug. "Come on. Let's go. Let's get it all finished."

Syd buttoned the paper on the inside of his coat, and Doug, telling me to "come along and get this thing straight," four of us, Doug, Syd, Bennie Ziedman [Fairbanks' press agent] and I piled into the machine—and off.

We stopped at Charlie Chaplin's house first, and at this point I am sorry to say that Benny [*sic*] eloped with the car to do some necessary phoning to a newspaper that was waiting for authority to set a seven-column display head and spread red ink all over its front pages in announcing the combination.

But before the ink of Charlie Chaplin's name was dry on the paper, Doug had borrowed Henry Bergman's car and we were on our way to the home of Little Mary.

And in fifteen minutes, at 2:45 P.M., on Wednesday, January 15, 1919, Mary Pickford's name completed the five signatures to the articles of agreement entered into by the United Artists' Association.[6]

This was the statement they signed and released to the press:

A new combination of motion picture stars and producers was formed yesterday, and we, the undersigned, in furtherance of the artistic welfare of the moving picture industry, believing we can better serve the great and growing industry of picture productions, have decided to unite our work into one association, and at the finish of existing contracts, which are now rapidly drawing to a close, to release our combined productions through our own organization. This new organization, to embrace the very best actors and producers in the motion picture business, is headed by the following well-known stars; Mary Pickford, Douglas Fairbanks, William S. Hart, Charlie Chaplin and D. W. Griffith productions, all of whom have proved their ability to make productions of value both artistically and financially.

We believe this is necessary to protect the exhibitor and the industry itself, thus enabling the exhibitor to book only pictures that he wishes to play and not force upon him (when he is booking films to please his audience) other program films which he does not desire, believing that as servants of the people we can thus best serve the people. We also think that this step is positively and absolutely necessary to protect the great motion picture public from threatening combinations and trusts that would force upon them mediocre productions and machine-made entertainment.[7]

Hollywood was too cynical to take the revolt seriously. "Film magnates and a number of lesser stellarites in celluloid," said *Variety,* saw Adolph Zukor behind the whole affair in just another attempt to weaken First National.[8] Others prophesied that the all-star combination would soon be riven by jealousies and never get off the ground. And then there came Richard Rowland's famous wisecrack, "So the lunatics have taken charge of the asylum." A more accurate assessment, however, came from Arthur Mayer, who said, "The founders of United Artists displayed the same brand of lunacy as Rockefeller, Morgan, and du Pont."[9] A review of their careers up to 1919 suggests Mayer was closer to the truth.

Mary Pickford

Mary Pickford's movie career began in 1909, when D. W. Griffith hired her for five dollars a day at Biograph. Although only sixteen, she was a trouper with three years' experience on the stage, and a position in David Belasco's eminent theatrical company. Her special appeal was soon evident on the screen. Long before her name appeared in movies, audiences began to identify her as "the girl with the long curls" or as "Little Mary," the character name most often used in her films. So with a foresight that would characterize her entire career, she went to the Biograph executives to suggest that they capitalize on her drawing power by releasing her name to the public and by building her up in the press. The studio bosses refused.

But Carl Laemmle, a scurrying independent producer, had a hunch that Little Mary could be made into a star. An offer of $175 a week lured her to his Independent Motion Picture Company in December, 1910, and the name Mary Pickford was revealed to the movie public. Production standards at IMP were too low for Miss Pickford's tastes, however, so she left the company within a year. After an even briefer stint with Majestic, she returned to Biograph in 1912. Finding that the stodgy mentality still prevailed at Biograph, Miss Pickford resumed her stage career with Belasco in 1913. While performing in the Broadway production of *A Good Little Devil,* she caught the attention of Adolph Zukor, who soon convinced her to join his Famous Players.

Mary quickly became Zukor's most effective box-office attraction, and her starting salary of $20,000 a year was raised to $1,000 a week. With *Tess of the Storm Country* in 1914, Mary Pickford became a household word.

Her meteoric fame and salary caused trade practices of the industry to be revamped. Famous Players had been releasing through Paramount. Theater owners contracted for the entire Paramount program, which in-

Mary Pickford

cluded the Pickford pictures, in a block-booking arrangement. Although this practice was standard in the industry, it changed, when Mary's mother heard that salesmen were saying, "As long as we have Mary on the program we can wrap everything around her neck"—that is, exhibitors would buy the entire Paramount output to get the Pickfords. If her daughter's neck was that strong, she reasoned, Mary was entitled to more money.

Zukor passed the problem on to Paramount's president, W. W. Hodkinson. Mrs. Pickford's demands would have to be met, he decided, and Mary's weekly salary was raised to $2,000. The money would not come from the Paramount coffers, however, but from the exhibitors. Hodkinson proposed selling the Pickford pictures as a "series," and charging more for them than for the regular Paramount program. This apparently slight departure from the program system eventually broadened into a completely new method of distribution. "It made possible the high salaries that were to come to actors, the increase in admittance prices to the great theaters that were to be built, and the enthusiastic endorsement of both by the public."[10]

Hodkinson's distribution plan proved so successful that in the following year, 1916, Charlotte Pickford suggested that her daughter's salary could be boosted still further. Her logic could not be denied. To accomplish this Mrs. Pickford proposed that Mary become an independent producer (until then she had been a contract player). Thus, in partnership with Adolph Zukor, the Mary Pickford Corporation was formed. Zukor became the president and Mrs. Pickford, representing Mary's 50 per cent interest, became treasurer with the authority of approving all expenditures. In addition to receiving half of the profits on her pictures, Mary was to earn $10,000 a week, to be paid every Monday of the year. The number of pictures she would make each year was reduced from ten to a minimum of six to enable her to improve their quality. A separate distribution company, called Artcraft, was formed to handle the Pickford features, which thereafter were to be sold individually rather than in a series. On June 24, 1916, Mary Pickford became the first star to become a producer of her own pictures and to win a considerable degree of control over her work.

The Artcraft pictures that followed marked some of the greatest achievements in Miss Pickford's career. Among these were *The Pride of the Clan* and *The Poor Little Rich Girl*, both directed by Maurice Tourneur; two Cecil B. De Mille films, *A Romance of the Redwoods* and *The Little American*; and *Rebecca of Sunnybrook Farm*, *A Little Princess*, and *Stella Maris* by one of her best directors, Marshall Neilan.

Despite her popular success and enormous salary, Miss Pickford was dissatisfied. She wanted complete control over her work, including script approval. Moreover, Paramount's salesmen, she discovered, were forcing exhibitors to rent other pictures in order to get hers. Knowing that Miss Pickford's contract expired in 1918, First National made an unprecedented bid for her services.

Here was the offer: First National would pay her $675,000 for three negatives, plus 50 per cent of the profits. To Mrs. Pickford, for her good offices, $50,000. Equally important, Mary would have complete authority over her productions, from the selection of the script to the final cut of the release print. First National would top Artcraft's distribution, Tally and the others assured her, so that her net revenue would be $1 million, perhaps even $2 million, a year. This type of competition was too much even for Adolph Zukor, so with tears in his eyes and a lump in his throat, he bid Mary Pickford farewell.

Charlie Chaplin

Charlie Chaplin had caught the eye of Adam Kessel while touring America with Fred Karno's English pantomime company in 1913. Kessel signed him up to work in Mack Sennett's Keystone comedies at a starting salary of $150 a week, three times what he had been making as an acrobat, pantomimist, and clown in Karno's program, "A Night in a Music Hall."

In a single year's time at Keystone, Chaplin made thirty-five pictures. "Popular acclaim was immediate; nothing like it had ever been seen before," said Edward Wagenknecht. "Chaplin swept first America, then the world. This was not anything that had been expected or planned for by the motion-picture industry or by Chaplin himself; both indeed were greatly surprised by it."[11]

Charles Chaplin

Sennett tried to keep his star in quarantine at the studio, but, as the story goes, an agent from Essanay got to Chaplin by hiring out as a cowboy extra. Yes, Chaplin would switch—for $1,250, nearly ten times his Keystone salary, and the right to direct his pictures. "Comedians could be very serious when talking about money," said Hampton.[12] Essanay promoted the pictures vigorously and the Chaplin craze intensified. After only two years in movies, he had become the top drawing-card in the business. Essanay earned well over $1 million on the Chaplin series.

Chaplin went over to Mutual on February 26, 1916. With his new salary of $670,000—$10,000 a week plus a bonus of $150,000—he had once again multiplied his earnings of the previous year by ten. Not bad for a young man of twenty-six, who just three years earlier had been an obscure vaudevillist. The twelve pictures Chaplin made for Mutual, all two-reelers, were masterpieces. Among them were *The Floorwalker, The Count,* and *Easy Street.* Along with increasing fame came visits from such world-famous figures as Paderewski, Leopold Godowsky, Nellie Melba, and Harry Lauder. Even the intellectuals took notice and began to write appreciations of Chaplin's art.

Mutual wanted Chaplin to make a second series of twelve pictures and offered him $1 million to stay on. This money was to be straight salary; Mutual would bear all production costs. Chaplin, however, rejected the proposition and instead signed with First National. Money was not the major consideration in this decision. The First National contract paid Chaplin $1 million plus a $15,000 bonus for the act of signing. It called for the delivery of eight pictures within eighteen months. Chaplin was to pay his own production costs from the $125,000 advanced for each negative. Since First National agreed to share the profits equally, Chaplin stood to make more money from this deal than from Mutual's. The clincher, though, was that it provided Chaplin the opportunity for going independent. As a spokesman for First National said:

> There are no conditions in that contract which permit us to interfere in the least with him as a producer. He is an independent manufacturer, owning and operating his own producing company and the studios in which it works. He can take any length of time he feels is essential to quality in his releases. He is free to choose his own stories. He is not harassed by telegrams and long-distance telephone calls, urging haste in the completion of a picture to make a certain release date. He is entirely independent of any one or any other concern of any character. His contract with us provides for distribution of his output and that, to Mr. Chaplin, is First National's only function and part in his activities.[13]

Douglas Fairbanks

Frank Case, proprietor of the Algonquin Hotel, told the story that when Harry Aitken offered Douglas Fairbanks a chance to join his Triangle Film

Corporation, Doug balked. Case noted that the $104,000 offer "was not hay," to which Doug replied, "I know, but the *movies!*" As a matinee idol with some fifteen years' experience, Fairbanks shared in his fellow actors' disparagement of the theater's "bastard child." But Doug, like many in his profession, put his artistic principles aside and succumbed to the irresistible attraction of quick money.

Douglas Fairbanks

Aitkin's Triangle company, formed in 1915, became the industry's most spectacular scheme to capitalize on the talents of the stage. The star system was then in vogue, and Aitken and his partners conceived the plan to capture the brightest theater talents and to translate their greatest plays for the screen. Triangle had three master directors, D. W. Griffith, Thomas Ince, and Mack Sennett. In addition to appealing to the upper classes, Aitken's scheme attracted Wall Street financiers, whose money he needed to engage the cream of theater, vaudeville, and musical comedy. In all, he hired nearly sixty players, among them Sir Herbert Beerbohm Tree, Mary Anderson de Navarro, Weber and Fields, De Wolf Hopper, Billie Burke, and Dustin Farnum.

Although Doug Fairbanks was one of the less-celebrated stars, Aitken chose Fairbanks' *The Lamb* to open the first Triangle program at the Knickerbocker theater in New York on September 23, 1915. This theater was taken over by Aitken to be the metropolitan home of his company and its pictures were presented there at the standard Broadway price of two dollars. Doug's debut was well received, at least by *Variety,* which said, "After viewing 'The Lamb,' it is no wonder the Triangle people signed up Fairbanks for a period of three years at any salary within reason. . . . He registers on the screen as well as any regular film actor that has ever appeared in pictures and more strongly than most of them."[14] After the picture was released, Aitken doubled his $2,000 weekly salary.

Part of *The Lamb*'s appeal lay in Doug's acrobatics and stunts—he let a rattlesnake crawl over him, tackled a mountain lion, and ju-jitsued a bunch of Yaqui Indians. Griffith, however, was not impressed and suggested that Doug's acting style was better suited to Sennett's comedies. With that, Griffith shunted Fairbanks to the care of Frank Woods, who "acted as a sort of cowcatcher to Griffith productions, sweeping accumulated embarrassments away from the path of the Master."[15]

As coordinator of productions, Woods guessed that the rambunctious Doug would probably have much in common with two others on the Triangle payroll, director John Emerson and scenarist Anita Loos. It was this precocious girl, still in her teens, who had the insight to realize that acrobatics were an extension of Doug's effervescent personality; if they continued to be written into his scenarios, he would develop into an immensely entertaining screen character. She was correct, for after *His Picture in the Papers,* Fairbanks' third Triangle picture, the public accepted him as a new kind of popular idol.

Fairbanks made thirteen pictures for Triangle. By the time his contract expired, Aitken was paying him the princely sum of $10,000 a week. With the exception of Doug, Aitken's high-priced stars were inglorious failures. He learned too late what Zukor had discovered at the outset of his Famous

Players venture, that most actors trained for the stage could not communicate on the silent screen. Audiences stayed away from their pictures, and exhibitors refused to pay the high rentals Aitken had to ask to meet his astronomical payroll.

Sensing that Triangle was on the verge of collapse, Zukor moved to pluck its prize box-office attraction. He would help set up Doug as an independent producer and distribute his pictures under the Artcraft banner, just as he had done for Mary. No longer having qualms over making movies, Doug accepted. The Douglas Fairbanks Picture Corporation was formed at the end of 1916.

To perfect the formula developed at Triangle, Doug hired Emerson and Loos. They collaborated with him on four of the five pictures he made in 1917; in 1918 he made seven more pictures, all satires on contemporary mores. As Richard Griffith described his output, "He spoofed Couéism, the new and growing octopus of publicity, psychoanalysis, social snobbery, pacifism, and practically anything else that came along to snatch the momentary interest of the American people."[16] By the time United Artists was formed, Douglas Fairbanks was idolized as "the ideal twentieth century American . . . a mentor, a model for growing boys, a homespun philosopher of the generation after Will Rogers."[17] He was also a multimillionaire.

D. W. Griffith

D. W. Griffith had the singular distinction of being the only director whose name above the title had greater drawing power than any actor in this star-crazed era. When his *The Birth of a Nation* was released in 1915, "the most important single film ever made was thus given to the public." Said Iris Barry in her appreciative essay for The Museum of Modern Art:

> The response was overwhelming: people had not realized they *could* be so moved by what, after all, is only a succession of photographs passed across a screen. All depends, they found, upon what is the order and manner of that passing. *The Birth of a Nation*, which had cost about $100,000 to make, grossed $18,000,000 in the next few years. Even more important, it established the motion picture once and for all as the most popular and persuasive of entertainments and compelled the acceptance of the film as art.[18]

Griffith had presented himself to Biograph as a scenario writer and actor in 1908 only because he was a thespian "at liberty." His new employment, which paid $5 a day, would be temporary, he hoped, until something, anything, became available for him in the theater. Griffith was soon asked to try his hand at directing. Biograph was in a precarious condition and needed more and better product to strengthen its competitive position. On the basis of his initial effort, *The*

Adventures of Dollie, Griffith was given other movies to direct, and on August 17, 1908, he received a contract. His salary was $50 a week plus a commission of not less than $50 based on the footage he turned out. In his first year, Griffith directed 130 pictures; in his second, 100; and in his third, another 95. Biograph now owed its financial strength to Griffith's output, but his salary was still a ridiculously low $75 a week. Although royalties brought Griffith's income to about $3,000 a month, he was still essentially an employee.

D. W. Griffith

For his fourth contract, Griffith insisted on receiving Biograph stock. The shrewd Jeremiah Kennedy refused and also turned down Griffith's request for 10 per cent of the company's profits. By the end of 1912, Griffith had made 423 films. He complained about the commission arrangement; nonetheless, as long as he could control his artistic destiny, he remained with the ungrateful Biograph.

But Biograph would not even grant him that freedom. Griffith wanted to make longer films, even features, rather than the one-reelers that were Biograph's staple. Why tamper with success, he was told; one-reelers were earning handsome profits at the box office. Griffith replied that the length of the film should be determined by the requirements of the story rather than by arbitrary restrictions. Kennedy gave in only to the extent that if Griffith felt an urge to go over the one-reel limit, he would have to secure Kennedy's special permission.

For the first time, according to Robert Henderson, Griffith saw his directorial prerogatives threatened. "The freedom that he had enjoyed at Biograph, the absolute control over his acting company, over the selection of stories to film, and the entire creation of his films, had led him to regard the Biograph executives as merely salesmen and paymasters. This assertion of administrative control was both frustrating and frightening to him."[19]

Griffith broke with Biograph in September, 1913, to join Harry Aitken's Reliance-Majestic Company, which distributed through Mutual. Here too, Griffith made program pictures, but Aitken gave him the independence of filmmaking, including budgeting, that Biograph had denied him. Moreover, Griffith was given the opportunity of making two independent films a year. One of these was *The Birth of a Nation*. When Mutual's board of directors became increasingly distressed over the mounting costs of the picture, however, Aitken and Griffith ended up producing and distributing it on their own. Even so, after the profits from *Birth* were spread among its many investors, Griffith's cut was not as great as one might expect—about $1 million.

The sensational box-office returns of *Birth* did not vindicate Aitken in the eyes of Mutual's board, of which he was president. In a fit of jealousy, his associates ousted him from their ranks. Undaunted and riding high on the success of *Birth*, Aitken formed Triangle Film Corporation, taking with him Mutual's principal assets in the persons of Ince, Sennett, and Griffith.

Griffith soon became totally preoccupied with his most ambitious directorial project—the making of *Intolerance*. As each day this project grew in scope and expense, it began to tax even Aitken's ability as a money raiser. The result was that Griffith assumed control of the picture by forming his own companies to finance and distribute it. Griffith became the largest investor by pouring into the venture his profits from *The Birth of a Nation;* the fifty others who helped put up the $2 million for the production costs included Aitken and his brother, Roy, Lillian Gish, and Mae Marsh. *Intolerance,* as we know, became a *succès d'estime;* Griffith's prestige was enhanced, but his production venture was bankrupted.

Griffith switched to Zukor's Artcraft in 1917. Although the fate of *Intolerance* at the box office was yet to be determined, Griffith foresaw Triangle's downfall. His objective now was to own and control his own studio so he could make his films without interference. Joining Artcraft was but a first step on the road to independence.

UNITED ARTISTS TAKES SHAPE

Choice of UA's President

W. S. Hart, although in on the early planning stages of United Artists, no longer figures in the narrative. He decided that discretion was the better part of valor, and remained with Famous Players-Lasky rather than take the risks of going independent. Zukor helped him to reach this decision by offering him $200,000 per picture to stay put. The others, meanwhile, were conferring with the man they hoped would agree to head the new distribution organization, William Gibbs McAdoo. He had been head of the Federal Railroad Board during the war, Secretary of the Treasury before that, and was a son-in-law of President Wilson. Pickford, Fairbanks, and Chaplin had come to know McAdoo well during the Third Liberty Loan drive when the three toured the country selling millions of dollars worth of bonds to support the war effort. Late in 1918, McAdoo had announced his resignation from government service, effective January 17, 1919, and now was in Santa Barbara for a rest before returning to his Washington law practice. When his private railroad car pulled into Los Angeles, a band serenade and a grand reception at the station greeted him, courtesy of Doug Fairbanks.

McAdoo declined the invitation to become UA's president, but suggested that if Oscar Price, his former assistant on the railroad board, were named instead, he would gladly serve as counsel for the company. This satisfied everyone; McAdoo, in the words of an editorial in *Moving Picture World,* would bring "prestige second to that of no other businessman in the country . . . his association marks another step in the progress of the business side of the screen, and it goes without saying his voice will have large influence in many quarters where large influence sometimes is very necessary."[20] For a while, anyway, the skeptics would be silenced.

The Origin of the Idea

Who first suggested the organization of artists that became UA is a matter of dispute. Film historians from the twenties to the present day have credited Benjamin P. Schulberg with the original idea.[21] Their conclusions were evidently based on a 1920 court case in which Schulberg brought suit against UA's general manager, Hiram Abrams, for a share of his commissions.

When this suit was filed in the Supreme Court of New York on September 8, 1920, the press gave it wide coverage.[22] Schulberg's story as taken from the complaint was that while employed as vice-managing director of Famous Players-Lasky, he "devised and developed certain ideas" concerning a distribution plan for pictures produced by ranking artists. In November, 1918, he described this plan to Abrams, the managing director, after which they agreed to resign from Famous Players-Lasky and go to Los Angeles for the purpose of convincing Pickford, Fairbanks, Chaplin, and Griffith to adopt Schulberg's scheme. During "numerous and extended conferences," Schulberg alleged, he prepared and presented to the artists an extended prospectus setting forth the details of the plan and describing its profit potential. In February, 1919, Schulberg and Abrams "succeeded in interesting the said artists in the said plan, and obtained their consent to the adoption and carrying out of the same. . . . Thereupon the said artists caused to be organized . . . the United Artists' Corporation."

The claim for a division of Abrams' commissions was based, said Schulberg, on an oral agreement with Abrams making them equal partners in all ventures they engaged in. Since it was by no means certain that United Artists would succeed, Schulberg did not ask to become a party to Abrams' contract, so that he could devote "part or all of his time to ventures and activities for their joint benefit."

This in summary was the case of Schulberg the plaintiff, and historians have accepted it as fact. But they did so by ignoring the case for the defense. On balance, it should be noted that Abrams denied all of the allegations in the complaint. In a deposition dated May 15, 1922, he testified that "plaintiff had nothing in the world to do with the organization of the United Artists Corporation, and did not at any time confer with any of the witnesses named or influence them in any way in respect to the formation of the United Artists Corporation, and that as a matter of fact, the witnesses named were unwilling and indisposed at anytime to consider the plaintiff in any way in connection with the United Artists Corporation." A brief submitted in Abrams's defense described Schulberg's complaint as "an ingenious fiction." And Dennis O'Brien, who represented Abrams, politely summed up his opinion of the case when he said,

"Schulberg has the tendency of writing, talking, and claiming too much."[23]

On which side does the truth rest? The issues, unfortunately, were not tried in court. Both parties consented to discontinue the action on December 15, 1922, after reaching an out-of-court settlement for an undisclosed amount of money.

When the declaration of independence was released, Miss Pickford made the following explanation: "We are on the defensive, and many people have asked us why we didn't do this thing long ago. The answer to that is that we were never forced to do it until now. But now, with the possibility of the merger of distributors looming before us, a combination that threatens to dominate the theatres of the United States, it becomes necessary for us to organize as a protection to our own interest."[24]

That their fears were justified was borne out when the Federal Trade Commission in 1927 completed its investigation of Famous Players-Lasky for alleged infringement of antitrust laws. In one of its findings, the FTC stated that Adolph Zukor, in 1919, "endeavored to form a combination with First National by which the latter would produce no films, exhibit no films other than those produced by Famous Players-Lasky Corporation, and finally become subsidiary to or merge with, Famous Players-Lasky Corporation."[25] The merger did not go through, as it turned out, but that did not stop Zukor. After failing to lure First National's officers to his company, he continued to struggle for control of the industry by attempting to acquire First National theater franchises. And this battle he won.

Even without this threat, the founding of United Artists was inevitable. A distribution company to fully market and exploit their pictures was but the next step for these artists in achieving autonomy. Pickford, Chaplin, Fairbanks, and Griffith each started out as employees under contract. With star status came the right to form independent production units, which meant more artistic control and a share of the producer's profits. By becoming their own employers, they now would receive all the profits from their pictures. To be sure, they would have to provide their own financing, but a distribution company managed by a topflight salesman would certainly minimize risks. And it is precisely for this reason that Hiram Abrams was brought into the company as general manager. Acknowledged by all to be the greatest salesman in the business, he was described by *Moving Picture World* as a pioneer who "made the history of this industry's development so colorful."[26] From the time he started out as a successful distributor in the Boston area until he became one of the original organizers of Paramount and its second president in 1916, he worked in turn as salesman, booker, exchange manager, exhibitor, and head of a great distributing company. Now that he was no longer associated with Zukor, United Artists could put Abrams' wide range of experience to good use.

Structure of the Company

The actual formation of the company was the result of the handiwork of the lawyers, most notably Dennis O'Brien, the counsel for Pickford and Fairbanks. The other lawyers involved were Nathan Burkan for Chaplin and Albert Banzhaf for Griffith. Two sets of contracts were drawn up and signed on February 5, 1919. The first set established the corporation. The four principals agreed to become associated with each other in the marketing of motion pictures and to set up a company with headquarters in New York having the name United Artists Corporation.

The stock issue consisted of two classes: preferred, in the amount of 6,000 shares, subscription price $100 per share and redeemable at 105 per cent of par; and common, in the amount of 9,000 shares, no par value, 1,000 shares of which were issued to each of the four principals in consideration of their signing exclusive distribution contracts with the corporation. McAdoo was to be issued 1,000 shares in consideration of his becoming general counsel.

The signing of the certificate of incorporation—D. W. Griffith, Mary Pickford, Albert Banzhaf, Charles Chaplin, Dennis O'Brien, Douglas Fairbanks

The common stock had cumulative voting power, enabling each of the stockholders to elect his own representative to the board of directors. Thus control of the management and policies of the company actually rested with the stockholders and not the directors. Nine thousand shares were authorized in the event that other well-known artists could later be induced to join the venture.

Financing the company's operations—opening exchanges, hiring salesmen, and the like—was to be borne by the four producer-owners. Each subscribed to $100,000 of the preferred stock and agreed to pay on demand up to 20 per cent of the subscription every thirty days if needed.

To prevent the company from slipping out of the hands of the owners, the agreement contained a clause giving the company prior right to repurchase the common stock in the event that a stockholder wanted to sell his interest in UA to an outside party. Another clause prevented the stockholders from forming partnerships with each other, so as to ensure complete equality among the parties. And to further stimulate the cooperative spirit of the venture and as a gesture of mutual trust, the owners decided to adopt an unwritten law stating that no proposal, policy, or decision could be effected without unanimous consent.

In the second set of agreements, the artists turned over to the company, upon the completion of their present distribution contracts, the exclusive rights to handle their pictures for five years. Each agreed to deliver nine pictures to the company; Griffith was required to direct his, and the others were to play the leading roles in theirs. Originally, the distribution contract was for the United States and Canada, but later it was amended to cover world rights.

The distribution fee was set at 20 per cent of the gross in the United States and 30 per cent elsewhere. If in the future the company gave one owner better terms, a "most favored nation" clause guaranteed similar adjustments in the other contracts. These fees were well below what Famous Players-Lasky and First National had been charging, because United Artists was conceived of as a service organization rather than an investment that would return dividends. Profits would accrue to the owners as a result of the company's securing the best possible rentals for their pictures. With this in mind, the owners reserved the right to approve through their representatives in the home office all contracts with exhibitors.

A key feature of the distribution contracts stipulated that each picture was to be sold and promoted individually. Block booking was out. In no way could one United Artists release be used to influence the sale of another UA product. Merit alone would determine a picture's success or failure.

On April 17, 1919, UA's certification of incorporation was filed with the secretary of the state of Delaware. The board of directors consisted of Albert Banzhaf, Nathan Burkan, Dennis O'Brien, Mrs. Charlotte Pickford, and Oscar Price, who represented the interests of Griffith, Chaplin, Fairbanks, Mary Pickford, and McAdoo, respectively. Price was named president; O'Brien, vice president; and George B. Clifton, secretary and treasurer.

The law firm of McAdoo, Cotton and Franklin became the general counsel for the annual retainer of $50,000. Price's salary was $18,000 plus a small percentage of the gross. As the man in charge of sales, Abrams received 2 per cent of the domestic gross and 1 per cent of foreign sales in excess of $500,000. Headquarters were established in New York, at 729 Seventh Avenue, where the company is housed to this day. In a matter of weeks, Abrams had opened exchanges across the country. United Artists was in business.

2

Starts and Fits
[1919-1924]

INITIAL ARRANGEMENTS, PRODUCTIONS AND PROMOTIONS

Abrams geared the company to release one picture a month; each of the four owners was to contribute three a year. The weekly overhead of $25,000 necessitated such a schedule. But at the outset, UA faced a production shortage. Chaplin had five pictures to go at First National and each seemed to take longer to make than the one before. Miss Pickford was working as fast as possible to complete the two remaining features on her First National contract, but these could not be rushed. Nor could Abrams look to Griffith for product. Within days after the company's founding, Griffith also became a First National producer by signing a three-picture contract for $285,000 plus a share of the profits. He informed his partners that he needed the money to meet his UA commitments. Only Fairbanks was free to work for the new company.

To spur the completion of these outside contracts and to ensure a steady flow of pictures thereafter, the owners entered into an escrow agreement on July 5, 1919. Each thousand-share block of common stock was placed in escrow to be issued to each owner in nine installments as he delivered the pictures called for in the distribution contract. Dividends were also to be escrowed, so that a producer could not share in the dividends resulting from profits of other producers' pictures until he delivered pictures of his own.

UA released its first picture, Fairbanks' *His Majesty, the American,* on September 1, 1919. Its New York premiere on October 24 opened the newly constructed Capitol, the world's largest theater. A tumultuous reception for both the picture and the theater gave the company a well-publicized start. The next UA release, on October 20, was a surprise entry, Griffith's *Broken Blossoms.* It had been made originally for Famous Players-Lasky, but Zukor, thinking the subject too poetic for audience tastes, was more than happy to get rid of it. Guessing UA's plight, he drove a hard bargain—$250,000 for a picture that had cost him only $88,000 to make. United Artists had no choice but to advance the money to Griffith in return for the distribution rights. The deal turned out to be a good investment, however; *Broken Blossoms* was acclaimed a masterpiece, grossed $600,000 in the United States alone, and eventually earned a profit of $700,000.

Fairbanks' *His Majesty, the American* (1919)

Lillian Gish and Richard Barthelmess in D. W. Griffith's *Broken Blossoms* (1919)

The Fairbanks-Pickford Union

Fairbanks' second picture, *When the Clouds Roll By,* appeared in December; Miss Pickford's UA debut, *Pollyanna,* followed in January. On March 28, 1920, the two postponed production work to become Mr. and Mrs. Fairbanks. "The wooing and wedding of the two great motion picture stars was a romance that the most hectic scribbler of scenarios might have hesitated to tap off on his wheezy typewriter," rhapsodized *Photoplay Magazine.* "It is one of the great love stories of all time. . . . Telegraph and cable wires ticked the details across the world. . . . Astonishing newspaper headlines shrieked out the story in giant type. . . . In every home mothers, fathers, sisters and brothers chatted over the precious news. . . . It was not hard to imagine President Wilson pausing in the midst of his breakfast egg and remarking to the first lady of the land: 'Think of that, Mary Pickford and Douglas Fairbanks are married.'"[1]

Doug and Mary had taken a calculated risk. This was the second marriage for each of them. Doug had been married to the former Beth Sully, socialite daughter of "Cotton King" Daniel J. Sully and mother of Douglas Fairbanks, Jr.; Mary to the actor Owen Moore, one of Griffith's leading men at Biograph. They met each other for the first time in 1915 at a party celebrating the success of Fairbanks' motion-picture debut in *The Lamb*. Although they were linked romantically, Doug did not seek his divorce until 1918 and Mary did not get hers until 1920. Both knew that in shedding their spouses to come together, they risked alienating their public and shattering their careers permanently.

For a moment, it seemed that they had lost the gamble. Mary had obtained her divorce in Nevada in March, 1920. Moore, by the way, had tried to extort a large sum as a price for acquiescence, but was in turn threatened by leaders of the industry, who warned that he would never again work in motion pictures unless he backed off. She moved to Nevada in February and declared her intention of becoming a resident of the state. Within a few weeks after the decree was granted, she and Fairbanks married in Los Angeles, even though the period of residency in Nevada was far short of the year then required for the granting of a divorce. There were a few murmurs of criticism, but these had died away when, unexpectedly, the attorney general of Nevada, capitalizing on the growing movement to reform Hollywood, filed suit to set aside the decree on the grounds that Miss Pickford had not been a bona fide resident of the state. Thousands of Americans had done just what Miss Pickford had done without encountering difficulties, but professional reformers apparently could not pass up the chance to attack the two stars. This was grossly unfair, since Doug and Mary's personal lives could bear comparison with the manners and morals of husbands and wives in any other sphere of activity. Fortunately, the suit was ignored by the public and, amazingly, by the press. The suit, nonetheless, did wend its way through the courts until the Supreme Court of Nevada in 1922 sustained Miss Pickford's divorce.

By the middle twenties, American parents were holding up the Fairbankses to their offspring as the sort of ideal marriage to which all should aspire. Pickfair, their home in Beverly Hills, became, in the words of Richard Griffith,

> the Buckingham Palace of Hollywood, the place where all official industry functions and important entertainments took place as a matter of course, and where Mr. and Mrs. Fairbanks extended hospitality to a literally endless stream of house guests, from the Duke of Alba to such truly distinguished celebrities as Albert Einstein and Bernard Shaw. On their days off from the studio (one sometimes wonders how they found time to make pictures at all) they were summoned from one end of the USA to the other to lay cornerstones, cut ribbons, crown festival queens, and march in bond-selling parades. They were, in all but name, unelected officials of the U.S. Government, and they shirked none of it.[2]

All of this, of course, added prestige to the United Artists name.

Purchase of Romance

The Fairbankses were not expected to complete their next pictures until the summer of 1920, so to fill in its program, UA secured the distribution rights to Mack Sennett's *Down on the Farm* by guaranteeing an advance of $200,000. Since additional product was needed to get through the spring, Griffith came to the company with this proposal: An opportunity had arisen to purchase the motion-picture rights to Edward Sheldon's recent Broadway hit, *Romance.* Doris Keane, its star, was also available. If he could get help with the financing, he would gladly produce the picture for UA release.

To protect the company's meager assets, the owners, including McAdoo, each decided to put up a $70,000 note to furnish collateral for the production loan. Griffith offered the use of his studio rent free and arranged for Chet Withey to direct the picture under his supervision. The profits were to be divided six ways, with two-sixths for Griffith. But there were no profits; *Romance* lost $80,000. With $150,000 going for the story and Miss Keane's salary, the production cost went $100,000 over budget.

Ouster of McAdoo

In one respect the *Romance* venture proved instructive; the four artists learned the extent of McAdoo's commitment to the company. When the contracts were being drawn up and final arrangements made for the production loan, McAdoo got cold feet. Although he agreed to sign his promissory note, he asked for release from his pledge if production costs went over $350,000. Moreover, he wanted the proceeds from the sales distributed among the backers before the bank loan was paid in full. In essence, McAdoo's position was that he wanted to share the profits but not the liabilities. Said Dennis O'Brien, "It is very surprising to me and shows how far you can rely upon Mr. McAdoo's association in an enterprise."[3]

After the picture was released, the UA board let McAdoo off the hook by assuming his interest in the production. The board did so only because McAdoo had resigned from the company on April 9, 1920. He was paid $25,000 for his stock. Oscar Price followed him out to head for a short while a distribution company patterned after UA called Associated Producers, Inc. This distribution company consisted entirely of independent producer-directors—Allan Dwan, Marshall Neilan, Maurice Tourneur, King Vidor, and others. In 1921 it merged with First National to become known as Associated First National.

The episode served as an excuse to get rid of McAdoo and Price. Relations between them and the four artists had already deteriorated. The main cause was a rather pretentious theater project that Price had attempted to engineer, involving the Du Pont interests, the Brady brothers, Joseph Godsol, and a consolidation with Goldwyn Pictures Corporation. "McAdoo wanted to expand the activities of the owners . . . into motion picture activities, which they did not have the capital for or the organization. Apparently, [McAdoo] thought he could use his time and talents and prestige in larger fields," explained Dennis O'Brien.[4] Charlie Chaplin gave a different reason for the resignations: "The use of McAdoo's name [in forming the company] was enough. Mary Pickford and Douglas Fairbanks said we didn't need to pay salaries to these men. We got rid of them."[5]

McAdoo and Price had done little for the company. O'Brien and Nathan Burkan had handled the legal affairs while McAdoo was spending most of his time at his Washington law firm. And Price only got in Abrams" way at the home office. O'Brien's law firm took over as counsel and Abrams was elected president in Price's place.

FINANCING DIFFICULTIES

UA's first season closed in June with Mary Pickford's *Love Light* and Fairbanks' *The Mollycoddle.* By now it was obvious that Abrams' production quotas would have to be revised downward; at most, he could expect two pictures a year from each of the owners. One reason for the slowdown was that the owners had to do their own financing. Because banks considered independent production a highly speculative enterprise, loans were practically impossible to procure. This in itself made producing for United Artists a hazardous affair. But the company's sales policy further compounded the risks. UA's product could not be sold a season in advance of production, as was the output of the larger corporations using the block-booking method of distribution. Because pictures were sold to exhibitors separately on an individual contract, not only was a greater effort required of the sales staff, but also it took longer to exhaust the market for each picture. A UA producer would be well into his third picture before he could hope to recoup his investment on the first. In short, the owners did not have the unlimited capital with which to furnish the company its requirements.

For UA's competitors, on the other hand, conditions were different. Such producers as Famous Players-Lasky, Fox Films, Goldwyn Pictures, First National, and Universal Pictures had established impressive profit records during the post-World War I boom, and now because the industry showed promise of exceptional growth, bankers and financiers looked to these companies as investment possibilities.

Until the twenties, motion-picture companies, in general, had to finance their operations from within. Business was conducted on a cash-in-advance basis, which under the block-booking system meant that exhibitors had to pay 25 per cent of the rentals upon signing the contracts and the remainder as each picture was delivered. Conventional bank loans to movie companies during these years were rare.

A. H. Giannini, working for his brother, A. P. Giannini, the founder of the Bank of Italy (later renamed the Bank of America), pioneered in this field by making small loans to producers as early as 1909, and in 1918 made a then unprecedented loan of $50,000 to Famous Players-Lasky. In 1919, after he assumed control of the East River National Bank in New York, he continued the policy inaugurated in San Francisco. By advancing First National $250,000 for the financing of Chaplin's *The Kid,* he made history. The loan was repaid in six weeks, which may possibly have disappointed Mr. Giannini at the small amount of interest the bank received, but was certainly a vindication of his business judgment.[6]

That same year marked a whole new phase of growth of the industry. In the autumn of 1919, the Wall Street banking firm Kuhn, Loeb and Company offered a $10 million issue of preferred stock of Famous Players-Lasky Corporation to finance the expansion of the company into the exhibition field. This was by no means the first motion-picture stock offered to the public. Zukor's company with assets of over $37 million had been listed on the New York Stock Exchange and Loew's stock was being traded on the curb exchange, for example. What it signified was that from the point of view of Wall Street, the motion-picture industry had reached maturity. Afterwards, banks began to make available to the leading companies both commercial and long-term credits on customary trade terms. Investment houses underwrote stock issues which by 1926 would bring the invested capital of the industry to over $1.5 billion.[7] By 1927, the preferred and common stocks of seven motion-picture companies would be traded on the New York Stock Exchange.

To retain control over its own affairs, United Artists refused to go public, which closed one avenue for production financing. Another, utilizing conventional loans from banks, was also closed to it because the company had yet to turn a profit and lacked the necessary collateral for this type of financing.

Griffith attempted to solve this problem by forming a public company, D. W. Griffith, Inc., on June 30, 1920. It was capitalized at $50 million with 500,000 shares of fully participating preferred stock and 375,000 shares of nonvoting common. The initial offer consisted of 125,000 shares of the preferred at $15 a share. The entire issue of the common stock went to Griffith in return for his investment in the land, studio, and equipment at Mamaroneck, N.Y.; his rights in certain past productions; and his UA stock, optimistically described by the prospectus as an "extremely valuable asset." According to Griffith's estimate, his company would earn more than $1.5 million the following year and could, as a result, guarantee a 10 per cent dividend on the preferred, which in any case had to be paid before any dividends applied to his stock. Control of the new company, because it was public, was vested in a board of directors. Griffith as president became its employee. Ironically, in trying to gain his independence from the industry, Griffith tied himself to investment bankers.

Pickford and Fairbanks turned to exhibitors for assistance. Since Abrams knew what their pictures fetched at Paramount, he could go to a theater owner and say, "I'll give you the next Doug Fairbanks release providing you help finance it by paying your rental now." These monies were advanced to the producers without interest on a weekly basis. But in order to protect itself, UA agreed to advance to its owners no more than $200,000 on each picture, which meant that they still had to invest heavily in their own productions.

Doug and Mary could not rely on this method of financing for long. The exhibition field was in a state of flux. More and more theaters were being acquired by the big chains or were forming alliances to secure better terms. Abrams, as a result, had to cajole, plead, and haggle to keep sales from slipping. To those exhibitors threatened by the likes of Zukor, Abrams, in a nationwide campaign, said:

Sit tight and look the thing squarely in the eye. Here is what confronts us.

Big distributor interests are seeking to tie up your theatres. WHY? Because their product is of uneven quality and they dare not try to sell it exclusively on a basis of merit. How are they trying to tie up your theatres?

By forcing you to sign long-term and exclusive contracts.

If you sign these contracts, you shut your house to all the splendid offerings of the independent producers and are compelled to play a program of uncertain quality in competition with the biggest attractions of the screen. You've got no chance to win.

If you don't sign the contract, these would-be monopolists offer to buy a controlling interest in your theatre. If you sell, they run your business. Again you've got no chance to win.

If you don't sign the contract and won't sell out, what then? They try to frighten you with threats of building a house next door to yours, if need be.

Suppose they build. Let them run their programs while you have the pick of the whole independent field and you'll close them up.

Theatre men, if you will only think a moment, you'll realize that it is a monumental bluff that is being shown. These distributor-interests can't control the theatre situation unless they can control productions. Thank Heaven, producers are getting freer every day and the dominant factor in the rental business today is not the old line monopoly, but the independent producers.[8]

Arguments such as these did not dazzle exhibitors nor did they guarantee acceptance of UA's policies. For example, Sydney Cohen, president of the Motion Picture Theater Owners of America, openly charged that Abrams was "hostile and arrogant." Exhibitors wanted UA's pictures, but not under the condition of having to pay full rentals at the time of booking. A more equitable arrangement, he said, would be to pay 25 per cent down and the balance a week before the playdate. Abrams refused to entertain either that proposition or another suggesting that UA accept checks. It would be cash on the line. Retorted Abrams in a letter to *Moving Picture World,* "I am running a business organization [which would be] impossible to run without ample security for the fulfillment of obligations."[9]

This imbroglio took place during the summer and fall of 1920. And there were many others, which meant that in its early days, UA's pictures played in many second-rate theaters. In some areas of the country, the company was shut out completely.

Since returns were being threatened, UA eventually had to modify its sales policy. It would have had to change its methods in any event, because the owners began producing on a grand scale, particularly Fairbanks.

Fairbanks' *Robin Hood* (1923)

Encouraged by the reception of *The Mark of Zorro,* he determined his métier was costume spectaculars. *The Three Musketeers, Robin Hood,* and *The Thief of Bagdad* were among those that resulted. Production costs rose accordingly: Fairbanks' *His Majesty, the American* (1919) had cost $300,000, whereas *Robin Hood* (1923) cost $1.5 million. Nor was he the only producer with mounting costs. Miss Pickford's *Pollyanna* (1920) cost $300,000, and *Dorothy Vernon of Haddon Hall* (1924) cost $750,000; Griffith's *The Love Flower* (1920) cost $300,000, and the budget for *Way Down East* (1921) reached $1 million.

To recoup these growing investments, rentals had to be raised. There was a limit, though, to what exhibitors would pay even for the most sought-after pictures. Abrams, as a result, introduced a percentage method that called for a guaranteed base rental and a split of box-office receipts over a specified figure, depending on the picture, theater, and town. This method worked best for the first-run houses, and boosted sales. However, because much of the earnings could not be collected until after the playdates, the percentage method did not solve the problem of production financing.

Slowly, the attitude of banks changed. Loan officers were beginning to discover what theater owners had known all along, namely, that a Mary Pickford feature or a Chaplin comedy warranted a triple-A rating. So, in 1923, when UA did not have sufficient funds to advance Miss Pickford $150,000 for the completion of *Rosita,* she could turn to the Mutual Bank in New York. UA negotiated the loan for her, which carried an interest rate of 6 per cent. As security, Mutual demanded not only a first lien on the producer's share of the gross, which was to be expected, but also that UA deposit its operating funds with the bank for the duration of the loan.

But UA's resources were modest; it could do little to nurture the owners' productions, let alone those of outside producers. John Barrymore stayed away from the company for this reason. And negotiations with Alla Nazimova and others during the early days of the company got nowhere until they could be persuaded to take the risks of independent production.

OPENING FOREIGN MARKETS

In the meantime, UA faced the task of establishing a worldwide market for its pictures. In signing the original distribution contracts, the founders gave the company the right to handle their productions in the United States and Canada only. Each producer was to make his own arrangements abroad. But to capitalize on the United Artists name and to maximize profits, the artists agreed in principle that their pictures should be marketed together in foreign countries.

Distribution deals came in from all over the world, but they were all rejected straight off, save one. In October, 1919, Morris Greenhill, a London exporter, submitted a most appealing proposition. He offered to distribute the UA product abroad at a charge of 40 per cent of the gross. For the Pickford and Chaplin pictures, he would guarantee minimal earnings of $225,000; for Fairbanks' and Griffith's, $200,000. Moreover, he would provide an advance of $125,000 for each picture, to be paid in New York upon delivery of the negative.

After checking out Greenhill's credentials and credit rating, the owners accepted his proposal on July 20, 1920. Greenhill was given ninety days to carry out all provisions of the contract: to found a distribution company in Great Britain to be called United Artists, Ltd.; to float a stock issue; to execute all necessary contracts to market the pictures in foreign markets; and to deposit $1 million in security with banks in New York. As evidence of good faith, Greenhill was required to put up $100,000 as a nonreturnable deposit.

To help his project along, Doug and Mary decided to make a goodwill tour of England as part of their honeymoon. Thousands greeted them in Southampton, shrieking as Doug with Little Mary on his right shoulder ran down the gangway and into the thick of the crowd. "Mary kissed a tiny ragamuffin and Doug hauled a newsie out of the mob and bought his bundle of papers. They did exactly what the crowd wanted them to do—gave themselves up to it and kept their good nature intact," reported *Moving Picture World*. [10] In London, an even larger crowd welcomed the Fairbankses, and five thousand fan letters awaited them when they finally reached the hotel.

The news releases describing their reception no doubt leaned toward the hyperbolic, but not without cause. In a 1947 article on the independent producer, Donald M. Nelson said that on this trip and subsequent good-will tours Pickford and Fairbanks were acclaimed by literally millions of ardent fans and "were most instrumental in creating the foreign appetite for American film fare." [11] This foreign market would provide up to 40 per cent of the total gross income for their pictures.

Despite Doug and Mary's reception, Greenhill ran into trouble. The British stock market turned bearish, making it impossible for him to find underwriting for the stock issue. Greenhill was given extensions but to no avail. He defaulted on his contract, and UA's hopes for beginning foreign distribution in 1920 were dashed.

United Artists now had the option of either distributing abroad through existing companies or opening exchanges of its own. In England, for example, the Goldwyn Corporation, Paramount, Fox, and First National were well established. While it would have been practical to associate with one of these, UA could not seek help abroad while proclaiming independence at home.

So, with the $100,000 that Greenhill forfeited, UA set up in England its first foreign subsidiary, the Allied Artists Corporation, Ltd. (the United Artists name had been contracted away to Greenhill and only later, when it was proved that this original company was inactive, was the name changed to United Artists Corporation, Ltd.). Getting started proved frustrating, as Dennis O'Brien indicated in this letter to Doug's business manager and brother, John:

> Our old friend, Lord Beaverbrook is active again. He seems to be another Hearst using his newspapers to influence public opinion in favor of his private interests. His representative here wanted to negotiate relative to a corporation that Lord Beaverbrook would control marketing our pictures in England. The cables from Mr. Berman, who is one of the three men we sent over, indicate that it is practically impossible to hire competent men over there without agreeing to pay them tremendous sums. They all insist upon our paying their income tax besides their salaries. This has been more or less brought about by the propaganda that has been circulated among the trade that we are going to ask exorbitant prices for our pictures.[12]

When the British company opened with *Pollyanna,* business was terrible, "due somewhat to existing conditions, but more particularly to the fact that the people running the Palace Theatre put the picture on shamefully," reported Sam Berman.[13]

To gain a foothold on the Continent, UA for lack of capital borrowed the producer's share of the rentals in England from *Pollyanna* and *The Mark of Zorro* and established Les Artistes Associés. From this office in Paris, exchanges were opened in Sweden, Norway, Belgium, Switzerland, Denmark, and Spain. Expansion into Germany, Italy, Australia, Latin America, and the Orient followed, giving UA a worldwide market by 1926. Distribution in the Orient was particularly costly because its principle office in Tokyo had to handle the whole territory. The head salesman there often had to go all the way to Bombay, six weeks' journey by boat, to sell pictures.

Aggravating the problems inherent in foreign expansion was the lack of cooperation the company received from Chaplin and Griffith. (First National controlled only the domestic rights to the Chaplin pictures.) When Allied Artists was being formed, for example, Griffith withheld *Way Down East* until his brother, Albert Grey, who was vice president of D. W. Griffith, Inc., had had an opportunity to inspect the setup for himself. Grey did not have confidence in the new company and was vocal about it. According to Berman, he also said that if the British subsidiary handled the picture, Griffith would be carrying Pickford and Fairbanks. This comment was passed on, of course.

Straining relations further, Griffith decided to distribute *Orphans of the Storm* on his own, which brought this response from Doug and Mary:

> We have learned that you have held back the *Two Orphans* from release abroad. At the last meeting of the Board of Directors in New York you voted upon opening more foreign offices. You must appreciate that in the majority of foreign countries, in order to make it at all profitable to operate branch offices, it is necessary to have considerably more product than we have at present. In view of this situation, you can readily understand what it means for us not to have your productions in all countries. It places us in a precarious position and our overhead will be tremendous under these circumstances. If we are to succeed, we must all work together for the good of the organization. [14]

When Miss Pickford asked Chaplin to sign this letter, he refused, saying that since he had not obligated himself to release through UA abroad, it would be wrong for him to pressure Griffith. An incensed Miss Pickford complained to Dennis O'Brien that she and Fairbanks were shouldering all the responsibilities for the foreign operations. If Griffith and Chaplin were going to equivocate about giving the company their pictures for foreign release by withholding *Way Down East* and *The Kid* and selling them to the highest bidder, leaving UA such "mediocre output" as *The Idle Class* and *Dream Street,* then, she added, their foreign distribution fee should be raised from 30 per cent to 40 per cent. The moderating voice of O'Brien prevailed, and no alternative distribution scale was suggested for the recalcitrant partners.

THE STRUGGLE FOR PRODUCT

Nonetheless, UA was in a bind. Chaplin was still at First National and although pictures of the other owners were setting records, their output could not sustain the expanding company. In 1921, for example, UA had three big hits on its roster: Griffith's *Way Down East,* Fairbanks' *The Three Musketeers,* and Pickford's *Little Lord Fauntleroy.* These pictures were to gross $1.8 million, $1.5 million, and $900,000, respectively; yet the deficit continued to grow, reaching $213,000 by the end of the year. As a result, the distribution fee had to be raised to 22.5 per cent in 1922.

The company had to find means to secure more product. Offering stock participation to other stars would have been one answer, but no one could state with certainty whether UA had a future. Besides, the owners felt they were in a class by themselves and did not want to tarnish the company name by bringing in partners of lesser achievement.

Allied Producers and Distributors

Abrams was convinced that many good people in the business wanted the opportunity to go independent and suggested that a subsidiary be formed to handle their pictures. UA's prestige would remain inviolate, he said, since the parent company would distribute the four founders' pictures exclusively. More important, such a subsidiary could generate enough revenue to cover the operating expenses of the entire organization. No longer would the owners have to pay a distribution fee.

Accordingly, on the occasion of its third anniversary, UA announced the formation of Allied Producers and Distributors. Pickford, Fairbanks, Chaplin, and Griffith each subscribed to $12,500 of stock to provide the capital. Since the subsidiary would operate out of UA's exchanges, this modest investment met the necessary requirements. Allied Producers would have its separate sales staff, however, to dispel any idea that exhibitors would have to rent pictures of lesser quality in order to get the UA product.

But the anticipated rush to Allied Producers never materialized. Among the few who used the company were Charles Ray, Max Linder, and Jack Pickford. The cause, once again, was financing, a problem Jack Pickford obviously did not have, because his three pictures were bankrolled by sister Mary's production company. But John Robertson, George Fitzmaurice, and other filmmakers were not as fortunate. O'Brien and Abrams were always willing to give advice on how to secure backing, but when the company was asked to guarantee bank loans, as it inevitably was, negotiations usually came to an end.

Associated Authors, Inc.

UA's deficit grew to $300,000 in 1923. Now, Doug and Mary took a turn at finding product. They proposed setting up a production company for three well-known screenwriters, Frank Woods, Elmer Harris, and Thompson Buchanan. Woods had been a respected film critic for *The Dramatic Mirror,* story editor at Biograph for Griffith, and his assistant in the preparation of the screenplay for *The Birth of a Nation.* Harris, a friend of the Pickford family, had written the adaptation for Miss Pickford's *Tess of the Storm Country* in 1922 and the scenario for Jack's *Garrison's Finish* in 1923. Buchanan had a long list of credits at Famous Players-Lasky. All three had production experience.

The plan called for a three-picture deal and distribution through Allied Producers. Each was to be written by one of the principals and produced at a cost of not more than $100,000. To ensure strict economies, a top business manager would be brought in as a partner. If production advice was needed, the Fairbankses would be there to give it. Doug and Mary had offered to guarantee the financing themselves, but their enthusiasm prompted Griffith, Chaplin, and Nathan Burkan to participate as well.

With a $300,000 loan from the Bank of Italy, the new company, now called Associated Authors, Inc., began production. The first picture was Woods' *Richard the Lion-Hearted* with Wallace Beery as Richard, a role he had played in *Robin Hood.* Buchanan's *Loving Lies* followed, starring Monte Blue, and after that Harris' *No More Women* with Matt Moore and Madge Bellamy. Interest on the loan, print costs, cost overruns, and distribution fees boosted the break-even point for the package to $675,000, not much by UA's standards. However, the three pictures were dreadful. Only an extraordinary sales effort saved the backers from having to pay more than $11,000 when the time came to settle up.

An unexpected irritant was the bank's attitude toward the project. The Bank of Italy was fast becoming the largest banking institution in the United States and a major financier to the motion-picture industry. In 1923, however, it had not yet worked out a satisfactory arrangement with movie people. The agreement with Associated Authors stipulated that the loan was to be made in three $100,000 installments as each picture went into production. The producers endorsed the notes, and Pickford, Fairbanks, and the other backers guaranteed repayment within fifteen months. But shortly after the final picture went into production, the bank gave notice that it was calling in the three notes. This action, said the bank in its deathless prose, was "made necessary on account of the deposit balance of the Associated Authors, Inc., being almost nothing, $10.00 to be exact, and also, the account of the individuals endorsing and the guarantors of the notes amounting to very little and not at all commensurate to the loans."[15]

If the bank foreclosed, all it could do was to take over the pictures, two of which were still in production. Woods pointed this out to Bank of Italy head A. P. Giannini but to no avail. Probing into the matter, Doug and Mary learned from Joe Schenck, a director of the bank, that Giannini was disturbed, first, because the 7 per cent interest rate was too low for the risks involved and, second, because the backers had not been required to carry a minimum cash balance in the bank as a consideration for the financing. "The Bank has no justification whatever for its attitude," said Miss Pickford's business manager. "We will have to do the best we can to handle an unpleasant situation. Of course, it would be highly inadvisable for Miss Pickford or Mr. Fairbanks to put any money in the Bank of Italy; it is unlikely that either of them will be inclined to do any business with that institution."[16] Resolving the controversy, Schenck stepped in to convince Giannini to hold to original conditions for the loan.

Rejection of Outside Product

The handling of outside product had by now thoroughly tried the patience of everyone at UA. Charles Ray had withdrawn in a huff, claiming that Abrams was not pushing the Allied Producers pictures, and Mack Sennett wailed that *Suzanna,* his latest picture, did poorly because it was not sold properly. The trade press played up these incidents, endangering UA's relations with exhibitors. Pickford and Fairbanks were particularly distressed. After conferring with Chaplin, they concluded that United Artists should revert to its original policy and cut costs by reducing the staff of the exchanges. They reached this verdict despite the fact that outside pictures had grossed $3.5 million by 1923, providing the company with nearly $1 million in revenue.

Griffith was duly informed of the decision by Mary Pickford, who threatened that if he did not go along with it, she, for one, might make arrangements to distribute elsewhere at the expiration of her UA contract. Expressing her will even more forcefully to Dennis O'Brien, she said that Griffith was likely to be sentimental about the matter and that if he voted against the decision, they would change the policy anyway.

The company, Mary felt, was certain to prosper now that Chaplin, at long last, had completed his First National contract. UA could expect a picture soon because Chaplin was thoroughly frightened, according to Miss Pickford, and realized that he had to get down to business if he hoped to keep in public favor. Moreover, Fairbanks predicted that his next picture, *The Thief of Bagdad,* would be more popular than *Robin Hood,* which was doing phenomenal business and eventually grossed over $2 million. As for herself, Miss Pickford believed that *Rosita,* her forthcoming release, would mark a new phase in her career. In it she departed from her adolescent roles by playing a Spanish street singer.

Chaplin's first United Artists release, *A Woman of Paris,* was probably different from what Miss Pickford expected. Chaplin directed the picture to be sure, but he did not appear in it except for an uncredited bit as a porter; Edna Purviance was the star. Nor was it a comedy. It was an intimate, sophisticated drama, Chekhovian in style, about a peasant girl who becomes the mistress of a worldly Parisian. The picture received great critical acclaim from the intelligentsia but only tepid response from Chaplin fans. "It was a courageous experiment," said Theodore Huff—but "too adult for the general film audience."[17] *A Woman of Paris* opened on October 1, 1923, and grossed domestically $634,000, about the same amount as the least successful releases of the other owners.

The Chaplin picture aside, Miss Pickford's appraisal misjudged realities; it underestimated the company's product requirements and

Fairbanks' *The Thief of Bagdad* (1924)

ignored the problems straining the relations not only among the owners but with Abrams as well.

Roadshowing

A case in point was the matter of roadshowing. Originally, the term meant exhibiting pictures before the general release in legitimate theaters at prices comparable to those charged for stage productions. In the twenties, after the movie palaces were built, it meant playing a picture before general release in a first-class theater on an extended basis and at top admission prices, usually about two dollars. Griffith started the practice at United Artists with *Way Down East,* against the advice of Abrams. Roadshowing the picture, said Abrams, would alienate the smaller exhibitor who always made good money on these big pictures. And it would affect rentals during the first run by exhausting the market in metropolitan areas. Abrams further observed that if all the owners were to roadshow their pictures, the company might as well go out of business, because these engagements were handled by the producer exclusively.

Doug and Mary had also opposed Griffith and demanded that the board of directors force him to comply with the terms of his distribution contract. Griffith stood firm, however, insisting that because he did not personally appear in his pictures, he needed this prestigious form of exploitation to maintain box-office appeal. His partners had no choice but to modify the distribution contracts.

Subsequently, they took up the practice that they had condemned. Fairbanks roadshowed *Robin Hood* at Grauman's Egyptian theater in Hollywood, playing there for so long that all first-run possibilities in the Los Angeles area were destroyed. Chaplin personally handled *A Woman of Paris* in Los Angeles, and Miss Pickford handled *Rosita.* Not only was the company being deprived of revenue, but Abrams, whose salary was set at 2 per cent of UA's share of the gross, was losing money as well. Only when the owners agreed to pay the company 10 per cent of the gross from all roadshow engagements was the controversy resolved.

MOUNTING DISSATISFACTIONS

The distributor's dilemma is that, try as he may, he cannot please both the producer and the exhibitor. He is destined by the conditions of motion-picture marketing to bear the animus of one or the other and sometimes both. Such was the case of Abrams. The owners expected him

Pickford's *Rosita* (1923)

to sell their pictures for as much as possible while the exhibitors tried to buy them for as little as possible. Although Abrams was acknowledged to be one of the finest salesmen in the business, his employers were seldom satisfied with his performance.

Fairbanks was his most outspoken critic. When he was not trying to subvert Abrams' position by placing one of his men on the payroll to oversee distribution, he was asking O'Brien to investigate his work. A report submitted by Abrams during one of these investigations describes his efforts to sell the Fairbanks spectaculars:

> *Three Musketeers* played Baltimore, Md. two of the best weeks in the season, i.e., October 31st to November 12th, 1921. They paid $7,500 for the picture and made $148.60 profit, claiming that if they had played any other picture, which they could have bought for much less money, they would have made a good profit these two particular weeks.
>
> I tried to sell *Robin Hood* in Baltimore to Whitehurst and Bernard Depkin. The best offer I could get from Whitehurst was $5,000, and the best offer made by Depkin was $8,000 for three runs in the city of Baltimore. After negotiating for about two months, and not being successful in making a sale in Baltimore, I went to Philadelphia and convinced Al Boyd that he could lease the New Theatre from Whitehurst, buy *Robin Hood* from me, and make some money. I got him to pay $12,000 and feel sure that I robbed him. . . .
>
> I sold *Three Musketeers* in Camden, N.J. for $1,200. They played the picture two days and had to pull it off. Douglas is not liked very well in this particular city. They bought the picture for a week and grossed less than $500. . . .
>
> I tried to sell *Three Musketeers* to the two best theatres in Atlantic City and was not successful on account of the price I was asking. A Mr. Elliott came in to see me one day and said he would like to buy *Musketeers* to be shown in Atlantic City. I asked him if he had a theatre there and he said he had not, but that he was willing to buy the picture and take a chance that he could secure a theatre for this great big production. I saw that he was very much interested in the picture and charged him $2500 for it. After he purchased *Musketeers* he could not get a theatre in which to show it. He finally succeeded in playing a theatre on percentage and he lost all the money that he paid me for the picture.[18]

Responding to Fairbanks' complaint, *Variety* stated that he could "find little sympathy among exhibitors. . . . The Fairbanks specials always have been costly to the exhibitors in their estimation. Exhibitors say Fairbanks was among the very first who ran up the rental cost of super pictures. Most of the exhibitors felt they had to pay the Fairbanks rental figure to keep his pictures away from the other fellow."[19] And so it went.

Mary Pickford too began questioning Abrams' sales policy when he kept *Little Lord Fauntleroy* out of cities for two years because his terms were not met. In response to her demand for an investigation, O'Brien, ever the conciliator, replied, "Each of the principals will have reason to be disappointed with results from time to time, as the organization is but human."[20]

As this explanation did not satisfy Miss Pickford or Fairbanks, they instructed O'Brien to appoint Maurice Cleary, their business manager, vice president to "assist" Abrams. An informal meeting was held at Griffith's Mamaroneck studio in October, 1923, to consider the matter. Abrams stated that without full authority to select employees, he could not control the sales force; people hired at the insistence of one of the owners tended to resist his supervision, sometimes causing the corporation to incur large losses.

Griffith also spoke against the Cleary nomination. He already felt isolated because Chaplin, Pickford, and Fairbanks, who were together in Los Angeles, more often than not acted as one; the election of Cleary as vice president would only serve to further his separation from the others. If the corporation needed another officer, Albert Grey, his brother, was his choice.

Responding to Griffith's reference to isolation, O'Brien said that according to Miss Pickford it was Griffith who received special attention from the home office because he was right there in New York. Griffith's answer was that he would never give Abrams advice on how to sell pictures. Chaplin said that he tended to take Griffith's side, and with that, the Cleary campaign and the meeting came to an end. But not Griffith's growing displeasure with the company.

Griffith's Departure

On February 21, 1924, shortly after the original distribution contract had expired, *Variety* reported that the Griffith organization was "aroused against the sales method employed in the organization, having obtained affidavits from exhibitors in various parts of the country indicating that a certain amount of favoritism was displayed in favor of some other attractions that the organization was releasing as against the Griffith pictures. . . . Whether this difficulty with the Griffith organization can be adjusted or not remains to be seen." To counteract rumors of a split, UA issued a press release on March 28, the occasion of the annual meeting of the stockholders, stating that the owners had "unanimously decided to not only carry out their existing contracts, but to renew and extend their contracts for a period of three years, except Charles Chaplin who has 8 pictures still to deliver to the Corporation."

Griffith, who later described the statement as "meaningless window dressing," on June 10 secretly concluded a $250,000 deal with Adolph Zukor to produce three pictures for Paramount, an arrangement his UA partners learned about, after the fact, from a news story. As Griffith was abroad shooting *Isn't Life Wonderful,* his lawyer, Albert Banzhaf, had to do the explaining when Doug and Mary called an emergency meeting in their suite at the Ritz. Banzhaf told them that Griffith considered the March press release merely a publicity piece to quell rumors about dissension within the company. Everyone else assumed that Griffith had signed a legal document clearly expressing his intention to remain with United Artists.

Not satisfied with Banzhaf's explanation, Fairbanks sent off what Griffith called an "antagonistic wire" to get to the heart of the matter. In response, Griffith described his dissatisfaction with the company:

> Through exhibitors reports I have information that my picture [*The Love Flower*] has done much bigger business as a whole throughout the country than *Suds* and other United Artists pictures. . . . Yet receipts on my picture have been absurdly low. Have felt for some time that I was in a hopeless minority. . . . It has been spoken through United Artists booking offices that Griffith pictures were not even priced as high as some others. . . . Knowing what I can do with my own pictures with my own handling and having good proof of what the booking offices can do with my pictures, would like very much to withdraw entirely from United Artists. . . . Do not see why it could not be done and each go our own way and still be good friends as business is one thing and friendship another. . . . Am willing to meet any arrangements that you may consider along this line and in a generous fashion you can take this matter up with your people there.[21]

United Artists was reluctant to take legal action to force a showdown, even though Paramount dared the company to try. Griffith was too valuable to risk losing completely. The company's deficit in 1924 had grown to over $500,000 and there was little hope of reversing the situation without Griffith. He had been the first to fulfill his distribution contract, having delivered his ninth picture, *Isn't Life Wonderful,* in November, 1924. At the end of the year, his pictures had a cumulative domestic gross of nearly $8 million, comparable to Fairbanks' eight pictures, but $1 million more than Pickford's eight and $7.5 million more than Chaplin's one and only contribution.

But if Griffith did go, UA's interests were going to be protected. A settlement was reached granting UA the right to distribute Griffith's first Paramount picture, *Sally of the Sawdust.* Griffith agreed to place his UA stock in escrow for the life of the new contract; if he decided against returning to UA, his stock would revert to the company; if UA declined to give him a new distribution contract, the stock would be returned to Griffith.

Griffith accepted these conditions to preserve friendships and to resolve his desperate financial condition. What he refrained from telling his UA colleagues, but they may have suspected, was that D. W. Griffith, Inc., was foundering. All its productions, save one, had lost money. The exception, *Way Down East,* eventually earned a $1 million profit, but this was not enough to carry the overhead expenses of the fully equipped Mamaroneck studio and its huge staff. And since his company's credit had been fully extended, the Paramount deal was Griffith's last hope.

Temptations from Paramount

Zukor had removed a major prop from United Artists, perhaps for good. Losing Griffith intensified the perennial product crises, and the company was not in a position to attract other producers. It was only a matter of time, according to the trade press, before Pickford and Fairbanks would follow Griffith's lead and the insatiable Paramount would swallow up UA.

Joining the Paramount organization would enable the stars to concentrate on their production work, the reasoning went. Because Zukor had built up the greatest roadshow organization in the business, Doug and Mary would get maximum returns from the specials, which were all they now made. In turn, Zukor needed Pickford and Fairbanks to protect his position in the industry. Marcus Loew's recent addition of the Goldwyn organization to his Metro production company and theater chain presaged a threat to Zukor's dominance of motion-picture production, distribution, and exhibition. As a result, he would offer the most attractive terms to lure Pickford and Fairbanks from their company. These may have been rumors inspired by the representatives of the Famous Players-Lasky organization, as Hiram Abrams claimed, but Zukor certainly hoped for Doug and Mary's return. His stockholders obviously did; in anticipation of their possible switchover, the Famous Players-Lasky stock reached its 1924 high of 84.

But Pickford, Fairbanks, and Chaplin were not yet ready to give up their independence. The problems their company faced were serious, but not insurmountable. Besides, they were resourceful people. Once they had found someone with the know-how to reorganize the company, they could return to devoting their talents to making pictures. And there was never any question in their minds as to who that person should be.

3 Joe Schenck's Reorganization
[1925-1931]

JOSEPH SCHENCK TAKES THE HELM

Joseph Schenck, producer and entrepreneur, was known throughout the industry for his business acumen, fair play, and generosity. His rise to prominence had been swift. He began by working in an amusement park with his brother Nicholas in the Washington Heights section of New York City. In 1910, they joined the fledgling Marcus Loew Theatrical Enterprises, Joe as head of film and vaudeville bookings and Nick as secretary. While working to build the Loew theater empire, the brothers developed the Palisades Amusement Park in New Jersey, a venture that made them both wealthy men. Joe resigned from the Loew organization in 1917 to promote the career of his new wife, Norma Talmadge. With the help of the best directors, writers, and designers that money could buy, he turned her into a highly successful star. Her career reached its peak in the twenties when she was releasing through First National. For that company she made some of her best-remembered pictures—*Yes or No?, Smiling Through, Ashes of Vengeance, Secrets,* and *Camille,* among others.

Schenck, in the meantime, purchased a controlling interest in the United Studios in Hollywood and a large block of stock in West Coast Theaters. He also expanded his production activities by taking on Fatty Arbuckle and then members of the talented Talmadge family—Norma's sister Constance and their brother-in-law, Buster Keaton, husband of Natalie, the youngest of the three sisters. Bank of Italy head A. P. Giannini was quick to recognize Schenck's grasp of the entertainment business, so when his bank decided to go into production financing, Joe was made a member of the board with the responsibility of advising the bank on all matters relating to the movie industry.

UA had first approached Schenck in 1920 in an attempt to lure the Talmadge sisters from First National. His explanation for not budging indicated the kind of competition the company faced in acquiring product:

Norma Talmadge

After listening to the arguments and proposition of the First National people
. . . I am strongly inclined to renew my contract with them for both Norma and
Constance pictures. They have a strong claim on my consideration, and I intend
to fulfill it.

In my first deal with the First National Exhibitors' I have sold them my pictures outright. Later on when I represented to them that conditions in the picture business had changed and my contract with them would not permit me to

make any money, they changed my contract and let me have the amount of money that I sold my pictures for outright as an advance, and distributed my pictures on a percentage basis, thereby really making me a present of about a million and a quarter. This has all been pointed out to me clearly, and I feel that I am bound to give them first consideration.[1]

The second attempt to capture Schenck succeeded, but it took five days of conferences at Doug and Mary's studio in Hollywood to thrash out a deal. Chaplin was there, of course, as well as Abrams and Dennis O'Brien. UA's past, present, and future were discussed in detail, the meetings sometimes lasted for ten hours. An agreement was reached on November 22, 1924. Schenck was brought in as a partner and elected chairman of the board with the authority to reorganize the corporation.

In return for his thousand shares of common stock, Schenck agreed to deliver six Norma Talmadge features. He had the right to release six other movies each year on the condition that he allowed his UA partners to invest equally with him in financing them.

The board of directors was reorganized to give the partners equal representation. The directors and corporate officers then were Schenck as chairman; Hiram Abrams, president; Dennis O'Brien, first vice president representing Pickford and Fairbanks; Arthur Kelly, second vice president, representing Chaplin; and Albert Grey, representing Griffith. Griffith was made a party to the agreement even though he did not participate in the discussions.

The matters of organization were disposed of during the conferences. Later, when it came to drafting new distribution contracts and formulating a financing scheme, however, the negotiations hit snags. It was Chaplin and not Schenck who created the problems. To enable the company to generate more revenue, Chaplin reluctantly voted in favor of raising the domestic distribution fee, to 25 per cent. But he balked at the proposal to extend the owners' distribution contracts by six more pictures. The intent of the extension was to guarantee that Pickford, Fairbanks, and Chaplin would remain with the company during the period the Talmadge pictures would be in release. Chaplin could not agree to this. In fact, he was dissatisfied with his present contract. It will be recalled that when the company was founded, each partner agreed to deliver nine pictures. Chaplin's contract differed from the others in that it specified two- or three-reelers rather than features, which averaged eight to ten reels in length. Chaplin's first UA release, *A Woman of Paris*, was feature length, and since he planned to continue producing this type of picture exclusively, he wanted his commitment reduced to six features. His partners went along with him for the sake of harmony and, to an extent, from a sense of fairness, because the production costs of the features would be as great as nine shorts.

Joseph Schenck

Another troublesome matter for Chaplin was UA's foreign department, which he did not consider an efficient operation. He insisted on the right to market pictures abroad as he saw fit should the financial returns from his forthcoming production be unsatisfactory in his "sole and absolute judgment."

These concessions were made to conciliate Chaplin, but when it came to the most crucial aspect of the Schenck deal, Charlie's partners prevailed. Chaplin opposed any arrangement for the financing of outside pictures. Since he financed his pictures on his own, he felt that producers coming into the corporation should do likewise. It took four days for the others to convince him that if they did not provide financing, they might not get enough product to survive. At the same time, they all realized the potential danger of accepting outside capital—that control of the company could slip into other hands. A safeguard was placed in the contract, as a result, stating that if financing were to be provided to UA producers, it would have to be done through a separate corporation in which Schenck's interest would be larger than any non-UA party's.

The Schenck agreement preserved the cooperative setup of United Artists. Schenck was to receive his common stock in the prescribed manner, namely as he fulfilled his distribution contract. Like his partners, he invested in the corporation by subscribing to a $100,000 block of preferred stock. And he accepted the position of chairman of the board as a co-adventurer. Schenck agreed to defer any salary consideration until the company showed a profit. His agreement stipulated that he would serve without pay until January 1, 1927, at which time the board by a majority vote was to determine the compensation he deserved for services rendered and to fix his compensation thereafter.

THE ART FINANCE CORPORATION

Schenck attacked the product crisis by organizing a finance company called Art Finance Corporation on April 24, 1925. It was capitalized at $625,000 in this manner: Schenck and his associates put up $300,000; Pickford, Fairbanks, and Chaplin each subscribed $25,000; and the banking combine of Lehman, Lasker, and Paul Block supplied $250,000. Art Finance, in turn, organized Feature Productions, Inc., to release pictures through United Artists. To give the new company a well-publicized start, Schenck assigned to Feature Productions his contract with Rudolph Valentino, the star of *The Four Horsemen of the Apocalypse, The Sheik, Blood and Sand,* and *Monsieur Beaucaire.* Valentino was making a comeback after a brief retirement from the screen as a result of quarrels with Adolph Zukor and uncompleted pictures for Famous Players. Although the Valentino craze was still strong, his first UA release, *The Eagle,* on November 8, 1925, was only a moderate success. His next picture, however, was a spectacular if not a ghoulish triumph. *The Son of the Sheik* was released at the time of Valentino's princely funeral in September, 1926. Within a year the picture grossed $1 million worldwide. Eventually, it more than doubled that amount.

Feature made a third picture with Art Finance money, the Roland West production of *The Bat,* based on the popular stage mystery by Mary Roberts Rinehart and Avery Hopwood. Then, in 1926, Art Finance was absorbed by a larger organization—Art Cinema Corp.

THE ACQUISITION OF GLORIA SWANSON

Meanwhile, the prospects of United Artists were beginning to brighten. In 1925, it released Josef von Sternberg's *The Salvation Hunters,* William S. Hart's *Tumbleweeds,* Fairbanks' *Don Q, Son of Zorro,* Pickford's *Little Annie Rooney,* and the great Chaplin hit, *The Gold Rush,* which in a matter of a few years grossed over $4 million worldwide, earning the company $1 million and Chaplin a profit of $2 million.

In that year as well, United Artists scored two coups; Schenck brought in Gloria Swanson as a partner and signed Sam Goldwyn to a five-year distribution contract. Miss Swanson had been Paramount's strongest box-office attraction. "To get one of the four to six pictures she made annually, an exhibitor would have to book at least six other Paramounts, and for the most part he didn't particularly care which six," said Richard Griffith. "Her hold on both metropolitan and small-town audiences was

Chaplin's *The Gold Rush*

so strong that seemingly she could star in any kind of script, or no script at all, and still fill the movie houses to their rafters. Nobody else, not even Mary Pickford, not even Garbo, more thoroughly demonstrated the money value of star glamour."[2] When Miss Swanson's contract had come up for renewal, Paramount knew that she would be more expensive the second time around and offered to double her $6,500 weekly salary if she continued making four pictures a year. She declined this offer and also rejected the company's further offers of $18,000 weekly and a flat $1 million a year.

Her decision to leave Paramount was the result of cold self-appraisal. To sustain her career, she would have to make fewer and better pictures and exploit them with care. Independent production seemed to be the answer, despite the risk. Joe Schenck, and Doug and Mary, no doubt, gave her the encouragement she wanted, pointing out the advantages of joining United Artists: she would receive all the profits from her productions. As a partner, she would benefit additionally from the distribution of earnings the company was certain to make. Financing would be no problem, because Art Finance stood ready to back her. Gloria Swanson signed a six-picture distribution contract on July 25, 1925, subscribed to $100,000 of preferred stock, and thereupon formed the Swanson Producing Corporation. She became an independent producer and gambled on her future.

ACQUISITION OF SAM GOLDWYN

If goodwill and a sense of paternalism characterized the negotiations with Swanson, apprehension and mistrust best describe those with Goldwyn. Goldwyn had been dissatisfied with the returns from his First National pictures and approached United Artists, at Chaplin's urging, to arrange distribution for his future productions. He wanted a straight distribution contract. He did not need financing.

Doug and Mary were hesitant. Goldwyn was sure to make trouble, they said. Abrams concurred, stating that Goldwyn would be on his neck all the time telling him how to sell pictures. These predictions were based on a realistic assessment of Goldwyn's history in the industry. He was indeed shrewd, aggressive, and stubborn, traits that had enabled him to survive many a bloody corporate battle. But there was another side to his reputation. Sam Goldwyn was also regarded as a first-rate producer with a sense of daring and a passion for quality.

At the beginning of his career, he had equated quality with the prestige of the stage. For example, in 1915 he and his partners in the Jesse L. Lasky Feature Motion Picture Company produced *Carmen* with opera star

Gloria Swanson

Geraldine Farrar. To the surprise of the industry it made money. Under Cecil B. De Mille's direction, Miss Farrar brought to life on the silent screen the role that made her a favorite at the Met. And in 1916, after organizing the Goldwyn Pictures Corporation with Arch Selwyn, he brought to his studio playwrights Bayard Veiller, Avery Hopwood, and Margaret Mayo; stage celebrities Maxine Elliott and Jane Cowl; and designers Robert Edmund Jones, Hugo Ballin, and Everett Shinn. (His original name was Goldfish, but he liked the composite name of the corporation so well that he adopted it as his own.)

Next, in 1919, Goldwyn conducted an experiment to make story value the supreme element in the film. He formed a special unit in his company called Eminent Authors, signed up many of the established writers of the day, and gave them carte blanche to translate literature into film. Gertrude Atherton, Mary Roberts Rinehart, Robert Hughes, Gouverneur Morris, Basil Kind, and Rex Beach responded to Goldwyn's call. That the project ultimately failed was not the fault of Goldwyn's aspirations, but because his writers ignored the advances made in cinematic technique. Their pictures were static, shot to resemble plays seen from the middle of the house.

As another experiment in 1919, Goldwyn imported the German expressionist masterpiece *The Cabinet of Dr. Caligari.* It was acquired against the advice of his business associates, by the way, who thought the picture was too advanced for American tastes. They were correct. Audiences "considered it to be so advanced as to be entirely out of sight," in the words of Richard Griffith. "They booed the film and demanded their money back. . . . *Caligari's* initial failure at the box office was complete. But the critics, and many of importance besides the critics, hailed it as the first artistic masterpiece of the movies and praised its American sponsor for his courage. . . . *Caligari* was the kind of failure which contributed to the growing prestige of the Goldwyn name."[3]

These ventures did little to endear Goldwyn to his backers, who would have preferred that he confine his efforts to more profitable schemes, making program pictures, for example. As Goldwyn's tastes and company policy did not mesh, the stockholders ousted him as president in 1922. In the settlement, the company purchased his stock for $1 million. With this money for capital, Goldwyn decided to go it alone. He thereafter financed and supervised his own films from script to screen, unhampered by the opinions of a board of directors.

Goldwyn signed with United Artists on August 25, 1925. Schenck persuaded his partners to give Goldwyn a distribution contract by reminding them that, more than anything else, UA needed product. Goldwyn's pictures did well at the box office. His production company had a formidable array of talent—George Fitzmaurice and Henry King comprised the directorial staff and Vilma Banky and Ronald Colman were his leading stars. Besides, Goldwyn did not come in as a partner. His contract, however, was the same in all respects as those of the owners, and included what he could not get from First National—the right to approve exhibition contracts.

SCHENCK'S ATTEMPT TO MERGE WITH MGM

Schenck's principal concern was to prevent United Artists from losing money. Adding producers to the lineup was one way to reach the break-even point; another was to streamline the operations of the company. UA's worldwide distribution system would always be costly to maintain because the number of pictures in release would be relatively small. If Schenck could cut the overhead, or better still, discover an alternative method of distribution, the company could begin to reap handsome profits.

Schenck lighted on such a solution after conferring with his brother Nick, who was now vice president and second in command at Loew's. The brothers realized that their companies had complementary problems. United Artists had the prestige that the Loew's subsidiary, Metro-Goldwyn-Mayer, needed to bolster its image in the marketplace; MGM had the efficient distribution system. Why not combine, they said, everyone's doing it.

The Schencks proposed forming a new corporation having the name United Artists—Metro-Goldwyn-Mayer, Inc., with the sole function of distributing the UA and MGM product. the Schencks were not contemplating merger per se; United Artists would retain its corporate identity by releasing its product separately. The proposal called for UA and MGM to transfer their assets to the new corporation in exchange for equal shares of voting stock. The liabilities of the companies, up to $300,000, were to be assumed in the process. Since the new stock issue was to be considered paid in full, UA stood to benefit by over $500,000 at the outset, according to Joe Schenck. The new corporation would own and operate the exchanges and charge a distribution fee of 35 per cent. United Artists could deliver up to twenty films a year; MGM up to fifty. Both companies were guaranteed 1 per cent of the distribution gross of the new corporation. The decision as to who should head the new company was postponed for the moment.

When the deal was presented to United Artists in November, 1925, Chaplin was the only one who would not agree to it. Pickford and Fairbanks had certain reservations at first, but Joe Schenck persuaded them to trust his judgment. Chaplin objected to the duration of the contract, which tied UA to the new corporation for fifteen years. Should it incur losses, he would be held liable, he feared. Also, Chaplin had little respect for MGM, which he referred to at the time as "three weak sisters." In attempting to overcome Chaplin's objections, Nick Schenck proposed that the term of the contract be changed to five years and that the corporation guarantee to make up all deficits incurred during that period. As an added inducement, he said that if UA wanted to drop out afterwards, the corporation would purchase its stock for $1 million.

But Chaplin remained adamant and the deal had to be called off. According to *Variety,* Chaplin did not want to be associated with a "trust." The so-called merger, it reported Chaplin as saying, "would have been but a club for Metro-Goldwyn to force exhibitors into line, using the 'block booking' as a means to foist its film 'junk' on the exhibiting market."[4]

Schenck's public explanation was different. Negotiations ended, he said, because

> a storm of protest arose from exhibitors all over the world. These protests were based on the mistaken premise that there was to be something in the nature of a trustification of the motion picture industry. Nothing could have been further from the facts, but realizing our inability to dispel this impression, we have decided that our independence and integrity before the exhibitor is paramount to any economy we might effect in the face of adverse, if mistaken, criticism. Both companies are in complete accord in this decision.[5]

In truth, it was Goldwyn who manipulated Chaplin to oppose the merger. According to Schenck, Goldwyn "felt that he might not have as good a position in the United Artists Corporation for the distribution of his pictures if the deal was effected: and convinced Chaplin to veto it." Schenck went on to say that "the deal could have been made without the consent of Chaplin, but when Charlie came over to me and told me he would be very unhappy if the deal was made, I felt that we, as partners, had no right to make Charlie unhappy and therefore called the deal off with the approval of Mary Pickford and Douglas Fairbanks as neither one of the three of us wanted to make our partner unhappy."[6]

Once again, Chaplin had sorely tried the patience of his partners. Fairbanks, for one, was livid and called Chaplin a "kicker," to which Charlie replied that Doug was nothing but a "jumper." Looking back ten years later, Schenck said that if United Artists had amalgamated with MGM, it would have earned a minimum of $5 million a year.

THE STRUGGLE FOR FIRST-RUN THEATERS

To keep United Artists alive and well, Schenck had to do more than cut operation costs. The film industry was undergoing a series of major adjustments to which United Artists had to accommodate itself or perish. The post-World War I period saw the consolidation of the production, distribution, and exhibition branches of the business.[7] Fewer and fewer companies were assuming more and more control. Overall, they were taking vertically integrated shapes. Zukor had begun the trend during the rise of the star system when he merged his Famous Players-Lasky production company with the distribution forces of Paramount. First National Exhibitors Circuit continued it by financing producers and then by building a giant studio in Burbank in 1922. Zukor countered the First National threat by going into exhibition. With $10 million in cash from a Kuhn, Loeb bank flotation he terrorized First National's ranks by buying options, intimidating theater owners, and awing local bankers from New England to Texas. His biggest victory in a long series of battles with First National occurred in 1926, when he acquired controlling interest of Balaban and Katz, which operated ninety-three theaters in and around Chicago and was First National's tower of exhibiting strength. Zukor now owned or controlled over a thousand theaters, which he wrapped together and called Publix Theatres Corporation.

Marcus Loew, meanwhile, who had a chain of a hundred theaters and whose Loew's Inc. was a $25 million company listed on the New York Stock Exchange, had bought an impoverished producer-distributor company called Metro in 1920. Going deeper into production in 1924, he purchased first the Goldwyn Pictures Corporation and then the Louis B. Mayer unit.

The trend continued. Fox Theaters Corporation, one of the most important chains in the country, embarked on a spree calling for the construction of thirty first-run theaters each seating between four and five thousand. The Pathé exchange contracted with the Keith-Albee and Orpheum vaudeville circuits to ensure exhibition of its product. About 1930 the battle ended and the smoke cleared away to reveal five fully integrated corporate giants.

During the years of consolidation, the power struggle focused first on the star, then on the producer-distributor, and finally the theater. The acquisition of theaters began when Zukor realized that of the $800 million taken in by the movies, more than $700 million remained in box-office tills. The retail branch had become the steadiest earner in the industry. It was not inherently speculative like motion-picture production, because the public had come to regard the movies more as a necessity than a luxury. By 1925 theater attendance rose to about eighty million per week, or nearly once a week for every person in the United States.

The expansion of theater holdings followed a specific pattern: The Loew chain was concentrated in New York State; Publix in Canada, New England, and the South; First National (later to be merged with Warner) in Pennsylvania and New Jersey; Fox on the West Coast; and so on.[8] Only in the thirty or so metropolitan centers did the majors compete with each other. In these key cities, the majors fought to acquire the largest theaters or vied for the best downtown locations to build their deluxe movie palaces. These theaters were the first-run houses and their importance was enormous. Their proximity to large concentrations of population meant they received the bulk of the business. No picture could earn a profit without a first-run showing at one of them. Typically, a producer received up to 50 per cent of the total rental from these theaters, usually within six months after a picture's release. Further, a successful first-run showing became the greatest selling point for distributors in dealing with the thousands of small theater managers throughout the country. In short, control of these theaters meant control over access to the screen.

The implications of this theater build-up were not lost on United Artists. The company was never in danger of being shut out completely from key cities; quality pictures were always in demand. But a power shift had been occurring in the negotiations over rental terms. As a company acquired more first-run houses, its bargaining position improved. It could ask for and get scaled-down terms. Thus, when the Stanley Corporation, which controlled first-run theaters in Philadelphia and many cities in the Middle Atlantic states, took over the Strand theater in New York, it informed United Artists that the previous rates would no longer prevail. If it wanted to book the Strand for its Broadway release house, UA would have to do so on the theater's terms. Conditions similar to this existed in Los Angeles, Chicago, and Pittsburgh.

United Artists Theatre Circuit

To cope with this threat, UA had no choice but to go into the theater business. Its requirements would be met nicely by a small chain of first-run houses in the larger metropolitan areas. But once again Chaplin stood in the way of expansion. He did not roadshow his pictures or rely upon first runs to reach his audiences; therefore, he saw little reason for investing in a scheme that would benefit the other owners primarily.

So without Chaplin, but presumably with his blessings, Schenck, Pickford, Fairbanks, and Goldwyn formed United Artists Theatre Circuit, Inc., in June, 1926. They paid in $1 million and received 80 per cent of the common stock. Then, through the banking firm of J. & W. Seligman & Co., $4 million of convertible preferred stock was sold to provide capital for theater acquisitions. The UA producers acted as individuals in the formation of the Theatre Circuit; United Artists Corporation was not a party to the deal. The only connection between the two was a ten-year franchise that granted Theatre Circuit the preferential right to exhibit United Artists pictures, except Chaplin's, of course. United Artists was supposed to supply about thirteen pictures a year.

Each would be released simultaneously in all the theaters and play about four weeks. To reach mass audiences, the pictures were to be run continuously each day at a box-office price of no more than one dollar. This departed from the usual roadshow practice of showing films twice a day at up to two dollars.

The terms of the franchise were unique in the theatrical world. Typically, an exhibitor paid a guaranteed rental to secure outstanding pictures. In the apportioning of the box-office gross, the rental cost had to be paid first, before the overhead expenses. The remainder, if any, was profits. The franchise with the Theatre Circuit reversed this order: box-office receipts went first to pay operating costs and thereafter to the distributor on a basis of 30 per cent to the distributor and 70 per cent to the theater. It was thought that such an arrangement would allow both companies to prosper.

Control of the Theatre Circuit rested with the UA producers: Schenck was chairman of the board and president; Dennis O'Brien, vice president, represented the Fairbanks and Pickford interests; and Bertram Nayfack, Goldwyn's lawyer, represented him as secretary and treasurer. Lee Shubert, the Broadway producer and head of the Shubert theatrical enterprises, bought a substantial interest in the company and was made vice president. Louis Anger, a long-time Schenck associate, became general manager. The other members of the board included William Philips, partner in the Seligman company; Harry Buckley, UA vice president; Nathan Burkan; and Joseph Moscowitz.

It was the intent of the Theatre Circuit to own all of its houses, but the board soon decided to go into partnership with other companies as conditions warranted. Too many first-run theaters in any locality would mean less profits for everyone. Only in Detroit, Chicago, and Los Angeles did the Theatre Circuit own houses outright. In Pittsburgh, Baltimore, and Louisville, it purchased half interests in seven theaters owned by Loew's. In New York, it bought into the highly profitable Rivoli and Rialto theaters owned by Paramount. In the Northwest and California, it went into partnership with West Coast Theaters. In Hollywood, it became associated with Sidney Grauman's Chinese and West Coast's Egyptian.

Compromise with the Majors

In establishing a theater chain, United Artists proved to the industry that it would fight if pushed. The majors, as a result, chose to accommodate this spunky little company rather than encourage further theater expansion. All the affiliated chains needed UA's product because, first, no producing company released enough first-class pictures to fill the playing time of its important houses; second, the UA name enhanced the prestige of such houses in cities where competition was the keenest; and third, the UA product could help meet the high overhead of the new movie palaces. United Artists thus gained greater access to the first-run exhibition field than the Theatre Circuit could provide by itself.

Loew's and Publix were the first to make deals with the company. On February 3, 1928, they signed franchise agreements that obligated them to play a specific number of UA pictures each year for ten years in their important houses. The terms were mutually beneficial: for each engagement, United Artists was guaranteed a basic film rental determined by a sliding scale related to the production cost of the picture. The next call on box-office receipts was to pay the theater's operating expenses. Thereafter, the profits were to be split, fifty-fifty. Similar agreements, but for shorter periods, were negotiated with Warner Brothers and RKO in 1930. By this time, the industry had stabilized, dominated by five giant corporations—Warner Brothers, Loew's, Fox, Paramount, and RKO. Schenck had created for United Artists a niche in which it could function unmolested until the industry itself underwent another upheaval twenty years later.

UNDER SCHENCK'S MANAGEMENT

Art Cinema Corporation

There still remained the product crises, nonetheless. UA released a mere eight pictures in 1926, not enough to fill the playing time of even the Theatre Circuit. Norma Talmadge had not yet completed her contract at First National and Swanson was still preparing for her debut as an independent producer. Among the releases were Fairbanks' *The Black Pirate,* and Mary Pickford's *Sparrows.* And then there was the Valentino vehicle, *The Son of the Sheik.* Sam Goldwyn saved the year by delivering three pictures: *Partners Again, Stella Dallas,* and *The Winning of Barbara Worth,* the last two of which were solid hits.

Although the shortage of pictures in 1926 was anticipated, United Artists, namely Schenck, did not intend to be caught short again. He signed a second distribution contract, whereby he would deliver up to ten additional pictures a year for ten years. (It will be recalled that Schenck's first contract required him to deliver six Talmadge pictures in return for common stock. When production problems delayed Miss Talmadge's work at First National, the contract was amended to give Schenck stock for the two Valentino pictures and *The Bat.*) Schenck had expected to receive financing for his expanded production program from Art Finance, but the Paul Block group balked at the high cost. So Schenck personally

Belle Bennett in Goldwyn's *Stella Dallas* (1926)

bought out their common-stock holdings and turned for help to Seligman & Company, the underwriter for the Theatre Circuit stock offering. Seligman decided to participate in the production venture, but on the condition that Schenck assign his distribution contract with United Artists to a new finance company which Seligman was to help organize. Schenck agreed for the consideration of $90,000.

In July, 1926, Art Cinema Corporation was formed to take over the assets of Art Finance. The new company had an authorized capital of $5 million, $1.8 million of which was subscribed to immediately. Seligman and Schenck became the heaviest investors, owning respectively about $1 million and $400,000 of the preferred stock and proportionate shares of the common. William Philips, as nominee of the bankers, assumed the chair; Schenck ran the corporation as president and general manager.

Art Cinema established its production headquarters at the Pickford-Fairbanks Studio in Hollywood. A subsidiary corporation had been formed to acquire a ten-year lease on the land and to make improvements.

Art Cinema purchased two-thirds of the stock of the subsidiary, and Pickford, Fairbanks, and Goldwyn, the balance. An administration building was constructed along with new stages, dressing rooms, film vaults, shops, and bungalows for the stars. When the $1 million in improvements were completed, four pictures could be produced simultaneously on the lot, now called, appropriately enough, United Artists Studio.

Howard Hughes

Art Cinema, however, did not hit its stride until 1928. It released only three pictures in 1927: John Barrymore's *The Beloved Rogue;* a Duncan Sisters' vehicle, *Topsy and Eva;* and the Herbert Brennon production of *Sorrell and Son.* To cover the shortage, Schenck gave a distribution contract to a brash young man by the name of Howard Hughes, who delivered *Two Arabian Knights* and captured the 1927 Academy Award for comedy.

Buster Keaton

Schenck also yanked his star Buster Keaton from MGM and signed him to a three-picture distribution contract. Then at the height of his creative powers and rivaling Chaplin's comic genius, Keaton made three masterpieces for United Artists, *The General* and *College* in 1927 and *Steamboat Bill, Jr.* in 1928. Brother Nick was no doubt miffed at the switch, but Joe had UA's interests to protect.

Abrams' Death

Schenck in the meantime had to take on added responsibilities at the home office when Hiram Abrams died of a heart attack on November 15, 1926—some say having literally worked himself to death. To keep the company functioning, Schenck created an executive committee of three vice presidents to take over the work Abrams had done singlehandedly: Al Lichtman, former head of Paramount's sales force, headed domestic distribution; Arthur Kelly, UA's treasurer and close friend of Chaplin's, took charge of the foreign department; and Harry Buckley, who formerly managed Fairbanks' roadshows, managed physical operations. Schenck headed the committee as president, a post he was elected to in April, 1927, while retaining the position of chairman of the board.

Deficits

United Artists had yet to turn the corner. Although its income had more than doubled since Schenck joined the company, from $6.6 million in 1924 to nearly $14 million in 1926, so had its overhead. In 1927, United

Keaton's *The General* (1927)

Artists was facing an accumulated deficit of more than $1 million, despite a two and a half per cent boost in the domestic distribution fee. Because of this, the balance of the pledges for preferred stock was called to enhance the company's cash position.

To get through the year UA was forced to sell more of its capital stock. Schenck suggested that Art Cinema subscribe to $100,000 worth of preferred stock, which it did, but only in return for a partnership in the company. Since Art Cinema was expected to play an integral role in the company's future, the stockholders readily consented.

Goldwyn as Partner

Correctly observing that Art Cinema's pledge would not bail out the company, Goldwyn approached Schenck with a deal of his own. He would gladly subscribe to a block of preferred stock if he too were made a partner. To Doug and Mary, the prospect of Goldwyn as a partner was appalling. Take his money for the capital stock, but postpone giving him

Samuel Goldwyn

the common, which carried voting rights, until his pictures had proven themselves, they said to O'Brien.[9] Viewing the matter more realistically, O'Brien counseled them that if they took Goldwyn's money they had to admit him as a partner.

Doug and Mary had yet to hear Goldwyn's conditions: he demanded a five-year distribution contract; the right to vote his common stock in perpetuity should he decide at the completion of the contract to distribute elsewhere; an option to sell back the preferred if he left the company; and a revision of the by-laws to require all policy matters to be decided by a unanimous vote. Concerning the last condition, Doug and Mary said:

> [We] cannot under any circumstances consent to a unanimous vote which would give any shortsighted selfish member . . . the opportunity to demand a greater benefit for himself than that which others would obtain and we feel very strongly that we have had a sufficient experience to convince us that the trouble is not one of mental attitude but inherently due to selfishness and stupidity which we feel are inborn characteristics and cannot be changed.[10]

If Goldwyn had to be brought in, the Fairbankses added, he would have to bring Vilma Banky and Ronald Colman with him on a binding contract for the entire distribution period. Schenck concurred and insisted on this point during the protracted negotiations. Describing these by way of understatement, O'Brien said, "Sam Goldwyn is not an ordinary person to deal with."[11]

Goldwyn became a United Artists partner on October 11, 1927. He was granted no special concessions; Schenck was no ordinary man to deal with either. The contract ran for three years, to be extended to five when Goldwyn "proved" himself. To receive the stock, Goldwyn had to deliver six pictures starring Colman and Banky either together or separately. Up to five additional pictures a year could be delivered, but a quality clause prevented Goldwyn from using the company as a dumping ground for inferior product. How Goldwyn responded to the implication that he would make anything but first-class pictures is not recorded. Another clause stated that if Goldwyn should discontinue producing or distribute through another company at the termination of his contract, he would be required to exchange his common stock for nonvoting shares or allow the company to redeem his preferred and common stock for $100,000. In other words, Goldwyn could participate in the affairs of the company only while he contributed pictures to it. Since United Artists was a cooperative organization, this was a reasonable clause, but only Goldwyn's contract had it. Goldwyn knew this, of course, but so long as the others remained active as producers, he did not make an issue of it.

Profits

Schenck's reorganization made its impact in 1928. United Artists began the year with a $1 million deficit and ended it with a $1.6 million surplus. As a testimonial to this achievement, the UA board voted Schenck a $100,000 honorarium and fixed his salary at $2,000 a week. Net profit for 1929 came to $1.3 million. The money makers during these seasons were Chaplin's *The Circus;* Fairbanks' *The Iron Mask* and *The Gaucho;* Pickford's *Coquette;* the Pickford-Fairbanks production of *Taming of the Shrew;* Goldwyn's *Bulldog Drummond;* and Swanson's *The Trespasser.* Each of these pictures grossed over $1 million. The hits of 1930 were Goldwyn's *Whoopee* and Hughes' *Hell's Angels.* In that year UA paid its first dividends on common stock—$160,000. In 1931, it released Chaplin's *City Lights,* which brought in additional millions. By 1932, UA actually had a surplus of $2.5 million and this was the amount remaining after the company retired all of the preferred stock. Each stockholder was paid back his investment in the company together with cumulative dividends and a 5 per cent bonus.

Not all of the stockholders were carried along on the wave of United Artists' prosperity. Schenck's reorganization served to expedite production and to ensure access to the marketplace, but it could not guarantee either critical acclaim for UA's releases or financial stability for the producing units. As always each picture was tested on its own merits. It was up to each producer to satisfy evolving audience tastes and assimilate technological changes in the industry.

THE PROPOSED MERGER WITH WARNER BROTHERS

His success in reorganizing United Artists was trifling compared to what Schenck envisioned. Given the forces within the industry towards amalgamation, it was only natural for him to propose combining the distribution company, Theatre Circuit, Art Cinema, and the UA production units into one integrated organization. More surprising, however, was his proposal, in January, 1929, to merge with Warner Brothers as well.

The new company, according to Schenck, would be called United Artists Consolidated and have an authorized capitalization of $15 million in preferred stock, $10 million of which would be issued outright and exchanged for the UA, Theatre Circuit, and Art Cinema preferred stock that remained outstanding. The common-stock issue was to consist of two million shares, one-half going to Warner at $20.50 a share, raising $20.5 million in cash, which, along with the other million shares, would be divided among the UA groups in return for their entire business. (Swanson and Griffith did not figure in this deal for reasons that will become apparent in chapter 4.)

Warner and UA Consolidated would retain separate identities in the merger. However, to economize on distribution costs, their sales forces would operate out of common exchanges. The UA stockholders would be asked to sign new contracts obligating each of them to deliver two pictures a year for an initial period of five years. In so doing they would become employees of the company. Joe Schenck at the helm, according to the revamped production policy, would control costs and oversee budgets. Under this arrangement, the producers would be paid modest salaries, but, Schenck promised, they would stand to make millions on increased profits and dividends.

To finance UA's end of the deal, Schenck approached the Wall Street banker Blair & Co. In his pocket he carried some interesting figures. The combined earnings for the UA group in 1928 came to $5.5 million. The $1.6 million profits of United Artists resulted from a world gross of $20.6 million, up considerably from the $6.6 million gross in 1924, when Schenck became executive head. Art Cinema and Theatre Circuit each earned only $500,000, but as Schenck explained, profits would increase now that the two companies had passed the developmental stage. More fascinating, however, were the tallies for the Pickford, Fairbanks, and Chaplin production units; during the previous five years, their average annual profits, after federal taxes, came to $300,000, $665,000, and $650,000, respectively. These figures attested to the popularity of the UA stars, to be sure, but they also vindicated the whole United Artists idea. Goldwyn certainly must have thought so, because during the two years he had been with the company, his average annual profit was $630,000. In comparison, Schenck's figures for the Norma Talmadge productions showed that her ten First National pictures released during the 1923-1927 period earned the respectable, but less average, annual profit of $385,000.

Warner Brothers was in the midst of solidifying its position in the industry. By taking the lead in the conversion to sound and as a result of the phenomenal success of *The Jazz Singer,* the company was raking in profits. But as the owner of only a few theaters, it had been in a vulnerable position. Once the big studios made enough talkies to fill the screen time of their chains, Warner could have found itself squeezed out of the market. To forestall this possibility, Warner went on a spending spree, the likes of which had never been seen even in the movie business. It began in September, 1928, with the purchase of the Stanley chain of three hundred theaters and a one-third interest in First National. Now it was looking over the United Artists group. By 1930, it would control all of First National as well as circuits belonging to its affiliated members and boost its assets from $16 million in 1928 to $230 million.

United Artists did not become a part of the Warner empire, nor did it subscribe to Schenck's plan to consolidate the UA group. The extant corporate records are silent on these matters, but if the reports in *Variety* are accurate, it was Chaplin who again obstructed the deal. His immediate response was that if the merger with Warner took place, he would withdraw from the company and distribute his pictures on his own.[12] His partners argued that the contemplated arrangement would net him between $10 million and $15 million within five years. Chaplin replied that he could earn over $20 million working for himself by producing two pictures a year. But given Chaplin's UA record—three pictures in seven years—this was as farfetched as the idea that he could market his pictures independently. Schenck intimated that the merger just might go through without Chaplin. Soon, however, Pickford and Fairbanks began to waver when it became obvious that as a result of the underwriting for the consolidation, control might pass to the banking interests, leaving them without a voice in the company they helped create. Schenck, thereupon, had to call off the negotiations. United Artists would remain what it was founded to be, what Chaplin doggedly insisted on its being, a distribution company for independent producers.

4

Adjusting to the Talkies
[1928-1932]

THE INTRODUCTION OF SOUND

Sound technology created an enormous upheaval in the motion picture industry.[1] When American Telephone and Telegraph salesmen first made the rounds of the major producers they found no takers for their new equipment. Prudent studio heads were not about to tamper with the existing order. Business was flourishing. Producers had extensive inventories of silent pictures. Their studios were designed only for the production of such pictures and the theaters throughout the country were built and equipped for them. Actors in whom producers had made huge investments were trained in making silents. The change to sound would involve not only scrapping millions, but the investment of corresponding amounts in sound equipment. Moreover the Western Electric sound system of AT&T was far from perfect. But the companies soon found they had no choice.

Warner and Fox as Innovators

The Warner brothers—Sam, Harry, Albert, and Jack—had by 1925 succeeded in establishing a small production company in Hollywood. They solved the problem of distribution by purchasing the Vitagraph Company with its nationwide system of exchanges. Business was good; profits for 1924 came to $1 million. Yet their future looked bleak. The battle for theater control had reached a climax and Warner, now fully extended, found itself without the resources to acquire a first-run theater chain of its own.

The bulk of its business was done with small independent circuits and struggling neighborhood houses. If Warner could equip these theaters with sound, they could be made to compete with the opulent downtown movie palaces. Sound, in the form of synchronized musical accompaniments for features and shorts, could provide a cheaper equivalent of live full-size pit orchestras. What the Warner brothers decided to do then was to produce entertainment programs for smaller exhibitors comparable in quality to those presented by the best metropolitan theaters. Accordingly, in April, 1926, Warner formed the Vitaphone Corporation with Western Electric to make sound motion pictures and to market sound-reproduction equipment.

The premiere of *Don Juan* at the Warner theater in New York on August 6, 1926, marked the first step in the strategy of Warner Brothers. This film, starring John Barrymore, had a synchronized musical background played by the New York Philharmonic Orchestra. The clarity of sound reproduction met with an appreciative response and the demand for Vitaphone slowly began to build.

On October 8, 1926, almost a year before *The Jazz Singer,* Warner presented its second Vitaphone feature on Broadway, *The Better 'Ole,* starring Charlie Chaplin's brother, Sydney. The shorts on the program introduced two popular vaudeville stars to the screen, George Jessel and Al Jolson. After hearing Jolson sing "The Red, Red Robin," "April Showers," and "Rocka-Bye Baby," Mordaunt Hall, of the *New York Times,* said "this Vitaphone [short] assuredly destroys the old silent tradition of the screen."[2] Later in the season, after the opening of *When a Man Loves,* Warner simultaneously had three hits on Broadway in the first three theaters wired for sound.

By the end of 1926, Warner had made more than one hundred shorts and in 1927, over two hundred more were produced. Made under the supervision of Brian Foy, these films provided a testing ground for the development of new sound-recording techniques and production methods. Still, despite the widening popular appeal of these pictures, acceptance of sound on the part of the industry was by no means unanimous. In fact, MGM, Universal, First National, Paramount, and Producers Distributing Corporation signed a contract in February, 1927, to adopt a wait-and-see attitude. The "Big Five" Agreement, as it was called, recognized that there were several sound systems then on the market, but because the equipment was not interchangeable, wide distribution of pictures would be hindered. These companies, therefore, agreed not to adopt any system unless their specially appointed committee certified that a particular system was best for the industry. Further, they decided not to employ any sound system unless it was made available to all producers, distributors, and exhibitors on reasonable terms, and that for one year none would adopt sound unless all did. Even Warner remained cautious. Vitaphone was kept separate from the rest of its operations, so that if sound proved just a fad, the company could immediately return to silent production.

Besides Warner, only the Fox Film Corporation had shown any interest in sound. Its head, William Fox, had investigated the sound-on-film system of the Case Laboratory, and found it to be a great improvement over the cumbersome disk-recording system developed by Western Electric. The result was that he purchased the Case patents and founded the Fox-Case Corporation on July 23, 1926, to exploit the system commercially. Soon after, the Fox Movietone Corporation went into production, following Warner's example of making comedy and vaudeville shorts with synchronized accompaniments and then, taking a different course, sound newsreels.

Fox scored his first successes in May, 1927, when a Movietone newsreel showed Charles Lindbergh's takeoff at Roosevelt Field, Long Island, for his historic transatlantic flight. Subsequently, the welcome-home ceremonies held for Lindbergh in Washington, D.C., were also photographed by Movietone's sound cameras on June 12. The newsreel recorded Coolidge's speech of introduction and Lindbergh's remarks.

By now, the public reaction to sound was unmistakable; after the premiere of *The Jazz Singer,* on October 6, 1927, it was overwhelming. The picture cost $500,000, which brought Warner's investment in sound to $5 million. Had the sound venture failed to excite audiences, Warner Brothers would have gone under. But *The Jazz Singer,* in the words of Ben Hampton, "proved to be one of the plays that have occasionally shaken the movie world like an earthquake, people crowding into houses to see it, and leaving the theaters completely converted to the talkies. The Jolson production was the final act in closing the doors of the silent film era and sweeping theaters and studios into a whirlpool of 'all-talkie' productions."[3] *The Jazz Singer* was not a talkie, though; it was planned as a full-length film drama with music and songs by Al Jolson.

The Industry's Shift to Sound

Warner's gamble had paid off. In the spring of 1928, Paramount, Loew's, and First National began wiring their studios and theaters for sound. United Artists, at the same time, signed an agreement to use its best efforts to encourage the UA Studio and UA Theatre Circuit to install Western Electric equipment. Universal and Columbia fell into line that summer. The Electrical Research Products, Inc. (ERPI), a Western Electric subsidiary that had taken over from Vitaphone the exclusive marketing rights to the Western Electric sound system, could not begin to fill orders fast enough to keep up with the demand, and exhibitors grew frantic because of delays in turning their silent screens into talkies. It took nearly a year before the majors began to add dialogue to their pictures. In the meantime, Warner stock skyrocketed from 39 to 139 a share. Warner Brothers released the sensational *Lights of New York,* the first all-talking feature, and a second Al Jolson vehicle, *The Singing Fool,* constructed their third sound stage, and rose from among the least to among the greatest of all movie companies.

The speed with which the industry accommodated to the sound revolution was truly remarkable. By the autumn of 1929, the conquest of the talkies was so nearly complete that a silent picture could not be found above the rank of third or fourth run. During this year, all the producers, with a harrowing outlay in nerves and money, caught up with Warner Brothers by transforming themselves from silent to talkie. Enormous technical problems were overcome; studios were sound-proofed, armies of technicians were hired to service the delicate equipment; theaters were wired; scriptwriters who had trained themselves to think in visual terms were replaced by playwrights skilled in the writing of dialogue; actors without stage experience took voice lessons (those with foreign accents, or faulty diction, or unpleasant voices found themselves unemployed); and, most significantly, the art of the silent screen was replaced by a new film aesthetic.

ERPI's Hold on the Industry

The industry had entered another boom period, so great was the public's infatuation with the talkies. Warner's profits soared from $2 million in 1928 to $17 million in 1929; Paramount's jumped to $7 million; Fox's to $3.5 million; and MGM's to $3 million. The company that stood to make the most money, though, was AT&T, who through its subsidiaries, Western Electric and Electrical Research Products, captured the entire market for sound equipment. All the important film companies signed with ERPI during the spring and summer of 1928 to make the conversion to sound. Their Recording License Agreement amounted to a stranglehold on the entire industry. In order to get the sound equipment they needed to survive, the film companies had to agree to pay a royalty fee on every negative reel produced. The licensees were required to distribute their pictures only to theaters with Western Electric sound systems. Should a company want to distribute a picture recorded on another sound system and for which a royalty had been paid, it had to pay a royalty to ERPI, nonetheless (the double-royalty clause). The production companies even had to pay royalties to ERPI for copyrighted music, by an arrangement negotiated between the American Society of Composers and Publishers (ASCAP) and the sound company.

Competition from RCA

ERPI's preeminent position did not go unchallenged for long. Undaunted by the long-term exclusive contracts tying up the major studios, AT&T's arch rival, the Radio Corporation of America, simply created a full-blown film company of its own to exploit the Photophone sound system which it had developed with the help of the General Electric and Westinghouse laboratories. The new Radio-Keith-Orpheum Corporation was the brainchild of RCA's chief, David Sarnoff, and the resources of the Rockefeller banking interests. Founded in October, 1928, as a holding company, RKO merged Joseph P. Kennedy's Film Booking Office, the Keith-Albee-Orpheum circuit of vaudeville houses, and RCA Photophone into a vertically integrated giant containing three hundred theaters, four studios, $80 million of working capital, and a half-dozen subsidiaries.

By no means content merely to wire RKO theaters for Photophone, RCA pressed to compete with ERPI on equal terms for the business of the 13,000 theaters owned by independent nonaffiliated circuits. However, the Recording License Agreement which obligated the majors to distribute only to theaters wired by ERPI proved to be an insurmountable obstacle. RCA, as a result, prepared to sue AT&T under the terms of the Sherman Act. This threat, plus the pressure licensees brought to bear, forced ERPI in December, 1928, to modify its agreements to open the domestic exhibition market to both sound systems.

Abroad, ERPI and RCA joined forces to fight a common menace threatening to close off the international market. In 1929, a combine of German electric companies, the Klangfilm, Tobis, Tri-Ergon group, brought patent infringement suits against the two American firms in Germany, Holland, and, most important, England. ERPI and RCA retaliated by filing suits of their own in Switzerland, Austria, and Hungary, and countersuits in Holland and Germany. As this legal battle showed signs of dragging on for years with disastrous financial consequences, both sides sat down at the conference table in July, 1930, and drafted what is now known as the Paris Agreement.

ERPI, RCA, and the German companies formed a cartel to divide the world among them. To the Germans went the exclusive sound rights to Central Europe and Scandinavia. The United States, Canada, Australia, India, and Russia were awarded to the Americans. The royalties from the rich English market had to be split 75 per cent for ERPI and RCA, and 25 per cent for the German companies. The remainder of the world was considered open territory. Also signing this agreement were United Artists and the other major American film companies who were now free to sell their talkies throughout the world. Thereafter, ERPI and RCA cross-licensed their sound patents in the U.S. as they had with the German companies abroad, standardizing all sound reproducing and playback equipment. When ERPI agreed to revamp its royalty schedule in 1931 to drop the "double royalty" clause, amicable relations among members of the industry were restored.

UA's Shift to Talkies

United Artists converted to sound just three months after signing the Recording License Agreement, with the release of Art Cinema's *Tempest* on July 21, 1928. This picture contained a synchronized musical accompaniment and sound effects. UA's equivalent to *The Jazz Singer* was *Lady of the Pavements,* which contained singing and talking sequences in addition to synchronized sound. On March 30, 1929, UA released its first all-talking picture, Mary Pickford's *Coquette.* UA distributed a silent version of this picture, but by the end of 1929, the company released talkies exclusively.

THE FORTUNES OF THE ARTISTS

For the most part, producers had no difficulty coping with the complexities of sound. Mary Pickford won an Academy Award for *Coquette,* in 1929; Gloria Swanson was nominated the following year for hers, *The Trespasser;* and Griffith, with *Abraham Lincoln,* made one of the ten best pictures of 1930, according to *Film Daily.* Goldwyn lost Vilma Banky in the transition, but Ronald Colman, who had a rich and distinctive voice, made it in *Bulldog Drummond.* Goldwyn secured his

Ronald Colman and Lilyan Tashman in Goldwyn's *Bulldog Drummond* (1929)

position by bringing in nearly $1.5 million with *Whoopee,* a musical starring Eddie Cantor. Cantor made five more musicals for Goldwyn in about as many years and each was just as successful. Using the earnings from these hits, Goldwyn bankrolled more distinguished efforts, such as John Ford's *Arrowsmith,* starring Colman, and King Vidor's *Street Scene* and *Cynara.* But it remained for Chaplin in his inimitable way to top them all. Three years into the sound period, he astonished his partners by making a silent picture. *City Lights* premiered on February 6, 1931, and was acclaimed the apex of Chaplin's art. In the United States alone, it grossed $2 million; in its lifetime, it earned for Chaplin a profit of $5 million.

Retirement of Talmadge

The only production unit that faltered directly as a result of the talkies was Norma Talmadge's. It is fair to say, however, that when she came to United Artists in 1928, her career was already waning. *The Dove* and *The Woman Disputed* were Miss Talmadge's first UA releases. Both were

Noah Beery and Norma Talmadge in Schenck's *The Dove* (1928)

made as silents in 1928 and did moderately well at the box office despite tepid reviews. Her debut in the talkies had to be postponed for over a year while Miss Talmadge took daily lessons to train her voice. But her efforts proved futile; the picture, *New York Nights,* flopped, as did her next production in 1930, *Du Barry, Woman of Passion.* Although these two failures were caused just as much by stilted directing and weak scripts as by her voice (which still retained hints of a Brooklyn accent), Miss Talmadge decided to retire. She could well afford to, for her personal fortune was estimated in the millions.

The Swanson Disasters

Less fortunate were Gloria Swanson and D. W. Griffith, whose careers also came to a close in this period. Miss Swanson joined United Artists a wealthy woman at the height of her fame; when she left it in 1933, she was broke. This reversal resulted from her decision to become an independent producer.

Her start was auspicious. *The Love of Sunya* premiered on March 11,

Swanson's *Sadie Thompson* (1928) with Raoul Walsh

1927, the occasion of the opening of the new Roxy theater, the world's largest and most opulent movie palace, built at the cost of $10 million. The theater received more favorable reviews than the picture, however. *Sunya* barely broke even. *Sadie Thompson,* her next production, did better. It grossed over $850,000 and was acknowledged to be the best picture of Miss Swanson's career.

But the Swanson Producing Company had a problem: the returns on *Sunya* and *Sadie* were coming in regularly but with too little volume to make much of a dent in the production loans. The company could not raise the capital to begin a third picture. A new loan would have to be subordinated to the monies due on the first two, a condition guaranteed to turn away most bankers.

Miss Swanson wisely paused to reorganize her finances. Joseph Kennedy, who headed the Film Booking Office at the time, lent assistance. After conferring with Schenck and O'Brien, Kennedy concluded that Miss Swanson should close the books on her production venture and begin anew under his tutelage. United Artists, which had yet to receive payment for her capital stock, did not object. Art Cinema agreed to take over her first two pictures and, in so doing, cleared her books of $30,000 in debts, paid off the production loans, and gambled on the pictures' chances of turning a profit to finance Miss Swanson's subsequent work. In 1928 Kennedy organized a new company called Gloria Productions, Inc. Under this arrangement Miss Swanson would no longer be an independent producer but a Kennedy employee.

Kennedy thereupon entered into one of the costlier misadventures of the twenties by engaging Erich von Stroheim to direct Miss Swanson in a story of his own making, *Queen Kelly.* According to Richard Griffith, "It was Mr. von Stroheim's pleasure to play a sort of cat-and-mouse game with producers. He would sell them stories which they liked and approved, but after he finished directing the film, the story would prove to be quite different from the one they had originally bought. So with *Queen Kelly.*"[4] Four months into production, with the picture two-thirds finished, Miss Swanson found herself playing the madam of an East African brothel. Kennedy sent one of his men to investigate. The inevitable quarrel ensued and von Stroheim was fired. When Kennedy discovered that *Queen Kelly* would be too salacious for the tastes of local censorship boards, he shelved the picture, wrote off a $800,000 loss, and, like the gambler he was, gave the go-ahead on the next picture.

Although *The Trespasser,* in 1930, won for Miss Swanson an Academy Award nomination, her hopes for a comeback were short-lived as a result of the lukewarm reception of *What A Widow.* These two talkies did little to recoup the dead loss of *Queen Kelly,* and Kennedy, for reasons of his own, went his separate way, although not before assigning to Miss Swanson the rights to these pictures.

Next, Joe Schenck came to Miss Swanson's aid with a two-picture deal from Art Cinema. She would be paid a straight salary and would not have to put up any money for production costs. *Indiscreet* and *Tonight or Never* were delivered in 1931. The first picture did well enough to earn a unit of common stock, which was given to her at Schenck's recommendation. The following year, United Artists relieved her of the obligation to invest in the company when it redeemed all of the preferred stock.

There remained one additional picture to be delivered before Miss Swanson could become a full partner in United Artists. To make it, she decided to resume independent production in England. UA supported the move because costs could be kept at a minimum there and her picture, as a British-made product, would be easier to distribute in England, where legislation had created barriers for imported films. To help get her started UA advanced her $75,000, and Gloria Swanson British Productions, Ltd., started work on *Perfect Understanding.*

Perfect Understanding brought only grief. The production floundered at the outset, the result of a weak script. One writer after another had to be called in before the malady was cured. These delays, in turn, created the inevitable budget crisis. United Artists had to either lose its investment or provide additional financing. It chose to supply funds by purchasing Miss Swanson's stock in the company. She was paid $200,000, more than the stock was worth, according to Schenck, who did not want it said that Gloria Swanson had been forced to the wall by her partners in United Artists.

The money from the stock, unfortunately, did not cover production costs. To bring in the picture, Miss Swanson had to spend an additional $100,000, all of which was borrowed from English sources. Her creditors lost confidence in the picture even before its release and demanded payment. But an embarrassing situation was averted when her solicitor informed them that if they sued, Miss Swanson was sure to go into bankruptcy. If they would be patient, on the other hand, Miss Swanson would pay them in full, which she eventually did, but not from the profits of *Perfect Understanding.* The picture opened in New York in February, 1933, during the financial crisis that prompted Roosevelt to declare a bank holiday. No matter, the reviews were uniformly poor. *Perfect Understanding* grossed $170,000; Miss Swanson's share did not even approach her investment in the picture. This fiasco ended Miss Swanson's career as a producer and, for all practical purposes, her career as a screen actress as well.

The Griffith Failures

When D. W. Griffith returned to United Artists in 1927, he came not as an independent producer but as an employee of Art Cinema. Griffith and Zukor had parted ways after the disappointing results of Griffith's third production, *The Sorrows of Satan*. Paramount had hoped that this picture would be an outstanding roadshow success, but after a fourteen-day run at the George M. Cohan theater in New York, it was obvious that the picture would not live up to expectations. It brought in at the box office a little under $12,000, according to *Variety*. [5]

Joe Schenck ascribed the poor results to the fact that Griffith had "gone back tremendously or rather he stood still and the procession passed him by." [6] Iris Barry was more sympathetic. From the time he joined Famous Players-Lasky, she said, Griffith worked "under conditions ill-suited to his temperament and experience, while business and financial problems of increasing complexity beset him. At the age of fifty, when he had already directed hundreds of films which include the most profoundly original films ever made, he was placed in competition with much younger men who inherited ready-made the technique he had perfected through arduous years. Obviously they were far better able than he to adopt new methods, to adapt themselves to changing tastes and to represent the postwar age." [7]

Schenck's decision to produce for Griffith may have been an act of generosity on his part, because he was certainly not anxious for Griffith to return to the company. He confided to Dennis O'Brien, "I am glad you are in possession of the D. W. Griffith stock certificates. I sincerely hope he decides to remain with Paramount." [8] This statement was made before the release of *The Sorrows of Satan*.

Schenck had Griffith firmly in hand when he signed the Art Cinema contract on April 19, 1927. Griffith was hired to direct a series of five pictures that would cost no more than $400,000 each. In this regard, the contract read, "Griffith shall keep Cinema fully informed as to his plans and progress in or relative to the production of each such photoplay." It also specified that Griffith "report to Cinema at its offices in the United Artists Studios . . . or such other place as Cinema shall hereafter direct in writing" and that Griffith "shall have no connection whatsoever with the production or direction of any motion pictures produced by the Griffith Corporation."

Griffith was originally offered a salary of $4,000 a week, with a maximum of $80,000 a picture plus a percentage of the profits. But when he pointed out that the Griffith Corporation needed $1,000 a week to keep going, Schenck agreed to raise his salary. To justify this bonus, Griffith had to act as a consultant, "supervising and assisting in the production of such pictures as Cinema may require."

Griffith directed four pictures for Art Cinema, *Drums of Love* (1928), *The Battle of the Sexes* (1928), *Lady of the Pavements* (1929), and *Abraham Lincoln* (1930). An option in his contract allowed him to produce a fifth picture independently should he find outside financing. Accordingly, in 1932 he made *The Struggle,* the final production of his career.

Griffith's last pictures were failures in almost every respect. As Joe Schenck put it, "All he did was lose money for the Art Cinema Company."[9] Only *Abraham Lincoln* came close to measuring up to Griffith's former achievement. The others have been described as sensational, cheap, and hackneyed. To give Griffith his due, though, it should be pointed out that these pictures, which grossed on the average of $625,000, did better than Keaton's, as well as some of Goldwyn's, and better than many Art Cinema productions, including those of the highly touted stars Jack Barrymore and Dolores Del Rio.

Griffith sought to produce his fifth picture independently, not only because of personal differences with Schenck, but also because he stood to make more money. Griffith had to gamble all if his company was to survive. If there was animosity between the two men, Schenck, at least,

Walter Huston in Art Cinema's *Abraham Lincoln* (1930) directed by D. W. Griffith

did not bear a grudge when Griffith went to United Artists for a $45,000 production loan to complete *The Struggle*. Schenck agreed to help even though the Bank of America and the Irving Trust had already turned Griffith down.

The Struggle, released on February 6, 1932, cost $300,000 to make but grossed a little over $100,000. Griffith took a loss of over $200,000 and ascribed these results to luck. *The Struggle* was "superlatively bad," he said, but "the picture as it should be was never made. It was only put out to get the best we could out of it. Luck dropped in—I will not blame luck entirely, but the fact remains that one of the principals held up the picture for a week and another member, a leading member, had to go to Europe to fulfill a contract, and also, during the course of the picture, the bank that was supplying the money just happened to fail."[10]

The failure of *The Struggle* put Griffith in a desperate financial situation. His personal assets, including the United Artists stock, had been put up as collateral for a production loan from the Federation Bank and Trust Company. Unless he could find money to liquidate the loan, he would be in default and lose all. To guide him through these trying times, Griffith turned to his cousin, the Honorable Woodson R. Oglesby. Introducing Oglesby to his UA partners, Griffith said that he "showed more sense than yours truly and saved his 'jack.' He has retired to one of those little million dollar cottages at Lenox, Mass. To walk through it twice supplies all the exercise you could possibly need. Mr. Oglesby has consented to give up his time, his golf and other demure entertainment to try and straighten out my tangled affairs, merely through friendship."[11]

Griffith was further motivated to seek professional advice when he heard of Schenck's plan for UA to finance its producers. The Depression had hit the movie industry in 1932; box-office receipts were falling off drastically and banks were cutting back on production loans, about which more will be said in the next chapter. Schenck warned that unless UA made provisions to provide financing on a regular basis, it would face another product drought.

Because Griffith's UA stock was his most valuable asset, he saw Schenck's plan as a threat to his welfare. "To embark on the treacherous sea of financing," he said, "is far too hazardous, especially for those of us whose stake in the United Artists means a lot at the present time."[12] He had already warned the stockholders that

the great number of distributing companies already in the business who are put-ting out great sums for the maintenance of distributing offices with the incum-brance of salaries, office rent and overhead, is very unbusinesslike. It would appear to be certain that the banking interests will eventually start to consolidate the distributing companies so as to save this amount of wastage. It is sufficiently evident that when this time comes, the distributing companies that are the strongest of all of them are going to benefit, and when this consolidation happens it is most vital that United Artists . . . maintains its strong position, particularly in cash.[13]

With the company divided over future policies, Griffith thought it best to sell out. To do so he proposed that the company be dissolved and its surplus divided among the stockholders. This would net each partner about $325,000, he figured. United Artists could thereupon be reorganized by those who wanted to continue.

Schenck, astonished by Griffith's naivete, explained:

You understand that a corporation cannot be dissolved merely because one stockholder wishes to withdraw therefrom, and particularly a corporation such as ours that has many contracts for the distribution of photoplays which have yet many years to run. It is the duty of the directors and the stockholders to protect the finances of the corporation so that that corporation is able to carry out its anticipated obligations and also the business for which it was organized.

The matter of the Swanson stock purchase was irrelevant, continued Schenck:

As you well remember, a certain loan was made to Miss Swanson to finance the production of her photoplay, as a certain loan was made to you for the production of the last photoplay you produced. Miss Swanson was unable to finish the production of that photoplay without additional financial assistance, and if she failed to produce it, the loan was in jeopardy, subject to whatever might be realized upon the sale of her stock which was pledged as collateral, in which event the most United Artists could realize out of it would be a recapture of her stock. It seemed to the stockholders . . . to be more advisable to purchase her stock and thus afford her sufficient money to complete the photoplay which would then be delivered to United Artists Corporation for distribution, and thus aid the corporation through these difficult times. Her position was quite different from yours.[14]

Rather than mollifying Griffith these explanations served only to heat up the debate. He accused the company of

being conducted on the basis of a general log rolling by a majority bloc, each member of which is in the scramble to get the most possible for himself with entire disregard of the rights of stockholders who are not the recipients of special benefits. . . . This bloc control has resulted in the payment of what in my opinion are grossly excessive salaries to officers, in-laws, and proteges of certain stockholders, and the recipients of these salaries have become entrenched in comfortable jobs, immune against orderly processes of adjustment. This system also permits excessive charges . . . for the use of studios, etc., controlled by individual stockholders; the maintenance of large cash balances of the corporation's funds (without interest) in banks in order to aid certain members to obtain credit; and has in other ways so conducted the business as to favor individual stockholders at the expense of the corporation, and even at the expense of another stockholder. In fact, I have been informed on what I regard as reliable authority that pictures produced by me were sold to exhibitors along with pictures (of other stockholders) admittedly of less market value, and perhaps not desired at all by the exhibitors, and the prices obtained for the joint sales divided equally, to my great disadvantage.[15]

After meeting with Griffith to answer these accusations, Dennis O'Brien reported to Schenck:

I told . . . Mr. Griffith . . . that practically everything which had been done and which he now complained of was done with Mr. Griffith's acquiescence; that Mr. Griffith attended personally the annual meeting of the stockholders, took part in that meeting and voted affirmatively regarding your compensation . . . and also regarding the dividend paid at that time, which was determined primarily upon Mr. Griffith's urgent request because he, personally, needed $10,000. That the history of the corporation will show practically unanimity on the part of all stockholders in all business matters of importance of that corporation; that as far as I knew there were no relatives of the stockholders employed by the corporation . . . and that his letter contained many misstatements.[16]

Since it seemed that no amount of arguing was going to change his partners' minds, Griffith, or more accurately Oglesby, changed tactics. He threatened that a stockholder's action against the company would be initiated unless executive salaries were reduced, surplus employees dispensed with, and economies inaugurated. In Griffith's opinion, reported Oglesby,

Most of the salaries paid are at least twice as much as is necessary for equally as efficient service. A complete survey should be made, not by the present beneficiaries, but under the direction of the stockholders to determine what economies could be effected. . . . In this connection it may not be inappropriate to suggest that judging from inquiries I have already made, I believe arrangements with other distributing corporations may be made for handling the physical and clerical work of distribution through agencies jointly maintained and that it is possible in this way to effect additional large savings.[17]

On the other hand, UA could forestall such a suit by reaching a settlement. Griffith would be willing to accept $300 a share, said Oglesby. "In my humble opinion," retorted Schenck, "Mr. Oglesby is a bluff and is just writing letters trying to force the corporation to buy the Griffith stock."[18] As for Griffith, Schenck said he was "just an ungrateful fool being led by Oglesby."[19]

United Artists was finally prompted to resolve the controversy when it learned that Goldwyn had approached Griffith with an offer to personally buy out his stock. Faced with this possibility, Schenck and the others decided to settle. United Artists offered $200,000, the same amount it paid for Swanson's stock. Griffith accepted on the condition that UA add to the price an amount equal to the interest that was waived on the Swanson loan when her stock was purchased. This came to an additional $2,000.

The deal was consummated on April 19, 1933. Griffith was paid not out of surplus but from ready cash, in the following manner: a lump sum payment of $104,580; thirteen promissory notes totalling $97,000; and $419.44 in cash. The check was endorsed by Griffith and turned over immediately to a representative of the Federation Bank and Trust Company to pay off the production loan for *The Struggle*. The notes went for other debts Griffith had incurred. The cash he pocketed. This transaction marked the end of Griffith's association with United Artists. A short time later, D. W. Griffith, Inc., went into receivership and his career in the movies came to a close.

Chaplin's Continued Popularity

What were the contributions of the other UA producers during the dynamic years from 1928 to 1932? Chaplin produced two smash hits, *The Circus* and *City Lights*. His popularity survived the sensational Lita Grey

Chaplin's *City Lights* (1931) with Harry Myers

divorce trial, the Depression, and the new production styles brought about by the talkies. His audiences complained only that they had to wait three years between pictures.

Even UA's sales force misjudged Chaplin's appeal. The company hesitated to accept *City Lights.* Chaplin conceded that it could not be released completely as a silent and spent three months and $40,000 to add a musical accompaniment. But he would not compromise on terms. To his demand that UA charge 50 per cent of the gross in all first-run theaters, UA protested that none of the circuits would buy the picture for such an unprecedented price. Provoked by the company's attitude, Chaplin decided to handle the New York engagement himself. He rented the George M. Cohan theater on a four-wall basis and ran an expensive publicity campaign. UA's publicity for the picture had been pretty stale, he recalls. "They were running tiny ads which referred to me as 'our old friend.' Never mind telling them about 'our old friend,' I said. You're not selling chewing gum. Talk about the picture. We've got to let them know we're in town."[20]

City Lights set records at the Cohan. It ran for twelve weeks with as many as nine showings daily. The total gross exceeded $500,000, or an average of more than $40,000 per week. Chaplin's net after all charges, including the advertising, came to over $300,000. Theater circuits were eager to play the picture after the spectacular opening run, and United Artists had no difficulty getting top money for rentals.

City Lights and *The Circus* before it were magnificent personal achievements for Chaplin, both artistically and financially. It must be noted, however, that Chaplin's contribution to UA's coffers was modest. United Artists as well as Chaplin's public would have been happier if he had delivered pictures at a faster rate than one every three years.

Pickford's Decline

The contributions of Mary Pickford and Douglas Fairbanks were equally disappointing. Their careers, unlike Chaplin's, were going into an eclipse. Miss Pickford produced three pictures in this period: *Coquette* (1929), *Taming of the Shrew* (1929), and *Kiki* (1931). All can be considered experiments to establish a more mature screen character. Miss Pickford had long been dissatisfied with her popular image and in two previous releases, *Rosita* (1923) and *Dorothy Vernon of Haddon Hall* (1924), tried to introduce "the New Mary Pickford" by playing older girls. But her public preferred her as Little Mary, so, despite the respectable box-office returns of the two pictures (each grossed about $900,000), Miss Pickford resumed playing her former self in subsequent productions: *Little Annie Rooney* (1925), *Sparrows* (1926), and *My Best Girl* (1927). But grow up she must; Miss Pickford was now in her mid-thirties. For *Coquette,* her first talkie, she cut off her curls and shingled her hair in the fashion of the day. A more sophisticated Mary Pickford emerged in her portrayal of a southern small-town flirt. The picture was a great personal triumph and earned nearly $1.5 million. Her portrayal of Katherine in *Taming of the Shrew* was a setback, however, for, as Edward Wagenknecht has said, she "lacked the physical stamina traditionally associated with the role."[21]

Fairbanks and Pickford in *Taming of the Shrew* (1929)

Taming of the Shrew was the downward turning point of Miss Pickford's career. Her faith in her ability to make pictures was permanently destroyed during its production, she said, the result of Fairbanks' erratic behavior. There followed a false start on a remake of *Secrets,* the Norma Talmadge hit of 1924. "Everything went wrong," reports Jack Spears. "She was upset by her disintegrating marriage with Douglas Fairbanks, the script was poor and confused, her leading man (Kenneth MacKenna) photographed much too young, and [Marshall] Neilan [the director] was no longer so creative and imaginative. Miss Pickford abruptly shut down production with less than a third of the film completed, wrote off a $300,000 loss and burned the negative."[22]

She thereupon decided, probably at the urging of Joe Schenck, to do a re-make of *Kiki,* another former Talmadge vehicle. Miss Pickford seemed curiously out of place playing the part of a mischievous hoyden in a musical comedy chorus. At one point she wore a costume with a loud polka-dot blouse, a tight skirt, and an enormous feather which jutted over her head like "a restless question mark."[23] *Kiki* was the "misadventure" that Miss Pickford called it, for it brought in a little over $400,000. Produced by Art Cinema, *Kiki* was the first Mary Pickford film to lose money since the formation of United Artists.

Miss Pickford starred in one further production. In 1933, she had a second go at *Secrets.* By many accounts, she gave a fine performance. But because the story was maudlin and the picture was released during the worst days of the Depression, audiences largely ignored it. Miss Pickford formally announced her retirement from the screen on February 13, 1935, about a month after she divorced Fairbanks.

Fairbanks Fades Away

The Fairbanks persona remained constant to the end; in his pictures only the locales changed. He made two silents in this period, *The Gaucho* (1928) and *The Iron Mask* (1929). Both followed the formula of his previous costume spectaculars and were just as popular, grossing $1.4 million and $1.5 million respectively. In making his talking debut in *Taming of the Shrew,* he played Petruchio much in the same offhand manner as d'Artagnan and Robin Hood, which pleased his fans but not the critics. Although there was some doubt as to whether this picture was authentic Shakespeare, the teaming up of Doug and Mary proved an irresistible lure that enabled it to do passably well at the box office.

After *Taming of the Shrew,* Doug's career declined, not because his audience rejected him, but because he stopped making films of consequence. Marital problems and the ensuing affair with Lady Sylvia

Ashley were contributing factors no doubt. But for reasons best explored by a biographer, Doug entered into a state of restlessness and dejection that caused him to spend most of his time travelling.

His final picture of any note was *Reaching for the Moon,* released in February, 1931. For the first time in ten years, Fairbanks appeared on the screen in contemporary clothes, playing the part of a woman-shy millionaire aboard an ultramodern French liner. One reviewer described the picture as "buffoonery de luxe, a soupçon of musical comedy plot, a hybrid conception of French farce."[24] In 1931 he made *Around the World in Eighty Minutes with Douglas Fairbanks,* which was little more than a travelogue based on his global tour. He insisted on a UA release despite Schenck's objections. It grossed a mere $200,000. A trip to Tahiti in 1932 became the excuse for making *Mr. Robinson Crusoe,* Fairbanks' last production for the company. Audiences were indifferent to this picture as well.

His acting career came to a close in 1934 with the title role in the Alexander Korda production of *The Private Life of Don Juan.* Here one finds an instance in Doug's career where art mirrored life. Shortly before the picture was released, Lord Ashley filed suit for divorce naming Fairbanks as corespondent. The action was uncontested and Fairbanks was assessed $10,000 in costs. This unsavory business precipitated Mary Pickford's divorce proceedings. After the aggrieved parties had ordered their affairs in court and Doug and Sylvia became man and wife in 1936, "the kingdom of Hollywood had to be divided in two parts," said Anita Loos. "Mary continued to receive the homage of the film colony at the royal estate of Pickfair, and obeisance was given to the new queen, who was formally addressed as Mr. Fairbanks' wife, Lady Ashley."[25]

The Flourishing Schenck and Goldwyn Productions

With the company's big stars waning in popularity, it was primarily the production efforts of Joe Schenck and Sam Goldwyn that sustained United Artists from 1928 to 1932. Schenck, either individually or through Art Cinema, produced over thirty pictures. Goldwyn delivered twelve, the most successful of which were the Eddie Cantor musicals, *Whoopee* and *Palmy Days.* The total distribution gross for the Schenck output added up to $16 million; for Goldwyn, $10 million. But on the average the Goldwyn pictures earned more, about $850,000, compared to $600,000 for those of Schenck. Chaplin's pictures, by comparison, earned a little over $4 million, Fairbanks' about the same, and Miss Pickford's about $2 million.

<table>
<tr><td>

5

</td><td>

Depression and
Monopoly
[1932-1934]

</td></tr>
</table>

The dwindling output of United Artists' stockholders coincided with the worst part of the Depression. From a 1929 high of seventeen releases, its roster by 1932 dropped to thirteen pictures, one of which was the German-made *Congress Dances,* acquired out of desperation from UFA to get through the summer months. Not only did quantity decline, so did quality. This was the year of Griffith's *The Struggle,* Fairbanks' *Mr. Robinson Crusoe,* the Art Cinema flop, *The Greeks Had a Word for Them,* and a pair of Howard Hughes disasters, *Cock of the Air* and *Sky Devils.* Sales dropped to $10.8 million—off more than $9 million from the previous year—the lowest since 1925. And so did earnings; UA's world operations showed a $270,000 loss despite a scaling down of salaries and overhead expenses by $1.7 million. And the prospects for 1933 looked even bleaker. That United Artists managed to survive the Depression was not a consequence of farsighted thinking or cooperative planning; much less did it result from the U.S. government's intervention in the movie business through the New Deal's National Recovery Administration.

STRUCTURE OF THE INDUSTRY

By 1930, the motion picture industry had become, in economic terminology, a mature oligopoly.[1] The merger movement had run its course with the result that five companies dominated the screen in the United States. The largest was Warner Brothers with its one hundred subsidiaries; the wealthiest was Loew's, the theater chain that owned Hollywood's Babylon, Metro-Goldwyn-Mayer; and the most complex and far-flung was Paramount. These and two other giants with equally formidable holdings, RKO and Fox Film Corporation along with its allied theater enterprises, became known as the Big Five. All were fully integrated: they owned their own production facilities, possessed worldwide distribution outlets, and controlled chains of theaters where their pictures were guaranteed a showing.

With stables of stars, writers, directors, producers, cameramen, and the rest, each of these companies churned out from forty to sixty pictures a year. Although in total their productions represented at most 50 per cent of the industry's annual output, about three-fourths of the class-A features, the ones that played in the best theaters and received top billing, were made and distributed by the Big Five. The Big Five's greatest strength, however, was in the exhibition field. Of the 23,000 theaters operating in the United States in 1930, the five majors either owned or controlled only 3,000, but this number represented the best first-run houses in the metropolitan areas and accounted for nearly 50 per cent of domestic distribution revenues.

Operating in a sort of symbiotic relationship to the Big Five were the Little Three: Universal, Columbia, and United Artists. Universal and Columbia had their own studios and distribution facilities and were useful to the majors during the thirties and forties in supplying low-cost pictures to facilitate frequent program changes and double features. United Artists, the smallest of the eight, was unique in that it was solely a distribution company. It had no studio, no actors under contract, or theaters.

EFFECTS OF THE DEPRESSION

Sound staved off the Depression in the motion-picture industry for well over a year.[2] But when the novelty of the talkies wore off in 1931, box-office receipts plummeted, as Hollywood felt the effects of a disabled economy. Warner Brothers, after realizing profits of $17 million in 1929 and $7 million in 1930, lost nearly $8 million; Fox suffered a loss of $3 million after a $9 million profit the year before; and RKO's $3 million surplus from 1930 turned into a $5.6 million deficit. Paramount remained in the black that year, but Zukor saw his company's profits fall from $18 million to $6 million and by 1932 he had a deficit of $21 million. By 1933, Paramount, with its 501 subsidiaries, went into bankruptcy; Fox underwent reorganization; and RKO was thrown into receivership. Warner Brothers, battered by losses of $14 million in 1932 and $6 million in 1933, was fighting to stay afloat. Of the majors, only Loew's had not yet shown a deficit; however, its earnings dropped precipitously from $10 million in 1930 to $1.3 million in 1933. As for the minors, Universal had gone into receivership; Columbia and United Artists were wounded, but not down.

Admission prices were slashed, audiences shrank—average weekly attendance dropped from an estimated 80 million in 1930 to 50 million in 1932 and 1933—production costs as a result of sound more than doubled, and revenues from foreign markets dwindled, but these factors in themselves did not cause the collapse. It resulted from the companies having overextended themselves; first in the wild and ferocious battle of the majors for control of the country's theaters in the 1920s and then in the tremendous capital investment in studios and theater equipment required for the conversion to sound. The outlay for theaters in 1928 alone came to over $160 million. When this era of expansion ended in 1931, Paramount had 1,400 houses, Fox and Warner had 500 apiece, Loew's and RKO more than 150 each, and Universal, 66. These companies could no longer meet their fixed-cost obligations, which means, simply, they did not have the hard cash to pay their overhead and mortgage commitments.

Correspondingly, the common stock value of these majors was reduced from a 1930 high of $960 million to $140 million in 1934.[3] Theater after theater went dark. Paramount found it cheaper to close many of its unprofitable later-run houses than to pay the overhead. The company also shut down its Long Island studio and laid off almost 5,000 employees who had been earning between $35 and $50 a week.[4] The number of unemployed and underpaid extras in Hollywood became a national scandal. Wages for those lucky enough to find work dropped from $3 a day to $1.25.

When President Roosevelt declared a nationwide bank moratorium in March, 1933, Hollywood reeled from the shock. Universal immediately suspended all contracts by invoking the "national emergency" clause. Fox notified its employees that salaries would not be paid until bank funds became available, and studio heads met in emergency conferences to contemplate the temporary suspension of production activities.[5]

CODE OF FAIR COMPETITION FOR THE MOTION-PICTURE INDUSTRY

Such was the state of the motion-picture industry at the brink of the New Deal. In a comprehensive attempt to revive industry, President Roosevelt drafted the National Industrial Recovery Act, which became law in June, 1933. Its general aim was "to promote the organization of industry for the purpose of cooperative action among trade groups."[6] The Act assumed that collective action was superior to cutthroat competition and that members of the business community would be willing to put aside selfish interests for the good of the nation. It stipulated that industries were to draw up codes of fair competition enforceable by law. Business could ignore antitrust laws but, in return, had to make concessions such as

United Artists doing its part for the NRA

guaranteeing labor the right of collective bargaining and establishing minimum wages and maximum hours. To supervise and enforce the Act, the National Recovery Administration was set up with General Hugh S. Johnson as director.

The Code of Fair Competition for the Motion Picture Industry was signed into law on November 27, 1933. Reflecting the vertically integrated structure of the industry, it regulated trade practices among producers, distributors, and exhibitors.[7] In conformity with NIRA guidelines, the Code banned company unions, set minimum rates of pay, and allowed labor to organize and bargain collectively. Working conditions and pay scales for professional extras improved as a result; studio craftsmen enjoyed a reduction in hours, increased wage rates, and greater job security. One hundred and forty different labor unions in the industry approved and signed the Code without controversy.

However, Hollywood's chief industrial imbalance was not the underpayment of labor, but the overpayment of professionals and executives. Louis B. Mayer had quelled public indignation somewhat by taking a temporary cut in pay from $10,000 to $750 a week. Other high-priced executives followed suit, so that during the turbulent months while the Code was being prepared, the production chiefs felt free to blame the financial difficulties of their studios on the star system. They succeeded in writing in provisions barring star raiding, curbing the activities of agents, and limiting the high salaries of creative talent. How these provisions affected United Artists will be explained later. The reaction in Hollywood was frenzied. Actors and writers bombarded Washington with telegrams, held mass meetings, and launched publicity campaigns opposing the control of salaries on any basis other than free competition among producers. As the deadline approached for the signing of the Code, they threatened to strike. Eddie Cantor, representing the newly formed Screen Actors Guild, spent Thanksgiving with President Roosevelt discussing the situation. When the Code appeared, it contained the protested provisions, but they were all suspended by executive order. Seven months later, after NRA deputy administrator Sol A. Rosenblatt personally investigated the alleged problem of excessive salaries, he recommended the permanent suspension of the provisions.

The bitterness engendered by this fight turned Hollywood into a union-minded town, to the chagrin of the studios. However, in the larger and more significant battle over the marketplace, the majors were victorious. They succeeded in receiving government sanction for the trade practices that they had spent ten years developing through informal collusion and that had enabled them to make the highest possible profits. In short, the Motion Picture Code legalized the monopolistic structure of the industry.

Negotiations to formulate the marketing provisions for the Code began in August, 1933. On one side of the battle line stood the formidable Motion Picture Producers and Distributors of America, known as the Hays Office because its president was Will H. Hays. It was the dominant trade association for the industry composed of the Big Five, Little Three, and several lesser production companies. Created in 1922 primarily to combat the widespread indignation over scandals in Hollywood and agitation for movie censorship, the Hays Office by this time had armed itself to resist interference of any kind—most particularly from the courts through antitrust actions. Standing next to it was the Motion Picture Theater Owners Association (MPTOA), the powerful organization of exhibitors controlled by the theater chains affiliated with the majors, and the Theater Owners Chamber of Commerce, an organization of independents that usually went along with the Hays Office. On the other side was the Allied States Association of Motion Picture Exhibitors (Allied), a rebel group of small independent exhibitors and an outspoken critic of the industry.

The battle was really no contest. Allied dropped out early in the negotiations, charging that the interests of the independent exhibitor were not being safeguarded. Without Allied's presence, the others proceeded to draw up the Code, which they ratified for the industry on October 18, 1933, and sent to the President for his approval.

In protest, Allied staged a rally in Chicago to dramatize its cause.

Criticism was directed mainly at the administration of the Code. A Code Authority, vested with broad quasi-judicial powers to interpret and enforce the Code, was to act as the Supreme Court of the industry. Despite the appearance of having an unbiased composition—five voting members representing the majors and five representing the unaffiliated groups—all but two were connected in some way with the affiliated producers, distributors, and exhibitors and could not be classified as independent.[8] To insure sympathetic administration of the Code, the members of the Code Authority were named in the Code itself—an unusual expedient adopted in only three of the over five hundred codes of fair competition. The majors also succeeded in controlling the composition of the grievance boards and zoning and clearance boards to be set up in each of the industry's thirty-one sales districts to adjudicate local disputes.

Responding to the outcry, President Roosevelt, in his Executive Order approving the Code, gave NRA Administrator Johnson the power to review the acts of the Code Authority. The Hays Office, in turn, mobilized to fight what it considered government interference. The result was that Johnson issued a statement interpreting the Executive Order as giving him not the right of review but merely the responsibility of inquiring "into the general course of conduct of the mechanism of the Code." "The Administrator will exercise his discretion in accordance with the recommendation of at least a majority of the voting members of the entire Code Authority," he said.[9]

Allied's cause was later taken up by the National Recovery Review Board, headed by Clarence Darrow, an agency charged with investigating alleged monopolistic tendencies in codes of fair competition. The Darrow report on the Motion Picture Code, issued in May, 1934, stated that independents had little to say in its creation, that it was written by the Hays Office to serve the majors, and that it fostered a greater degree of monopoly power within the industry. General Johnson attacked the document as superficial, intemperate, and inaccurate.[10] Sol Rosenblatt called it "solely the vicious mouthings and conjecture of a few disgruntled enemies of NRA."[11] The report indeed contained inaccuracies and was poorly prepared, but its indictment of the Motion Picture Code was essentially accurate. It had little impact on the NRA however, because it vilified NRA policies.

THE TRADE PRACTICES SANCTIONED BY THE CODE

The controversial trade practices sanctioned by the Code may be divided into two classes: the first contained the components of the block-booking system, which had been used by the majors to maximize profits at the expense of the independent exhibitor; the second included clearance and zoning, setting of admission prices, and overbuying. These practices, which I shall discuss in detail, had either driven independents out of business or kept them in a subordinate position.[12]

Block Booking

Block booking was without doubt the most contested trade practice in the business. All the important companies except UA sold their pictures in blocks of varying size usually consisting of an entire season's output. These were offered to exhibitors on an all-or-none basis before the pictures had actually been produced. Typically, each spring, salesmen showered exhibitors with glittering prospectuses describing in glowing terms their company's hits that season and promising even greater achievements to follow. On the rental contracts, however, a complete list of picture titles and credits was nowhere to be found. Some pictures were described as containing such and such star, or to be made from any of several stories; others were designated merely by production number and approximate rental fee. In contracting for these blocks, exhibitors were required to take short subjects as well. This practice, the forcing of shorts, together with block booking, was known as full-line forcing. As a congressional investigating committee remarked, "This is the only industry in which the buyer, having no idea of what he is buying, underwrites blindly all the product offered him."[13]

The independent theater owner was not against block booking as such, since he needed a large number of pictures to fill the playing time of a theater that frequently showed double bills and changed programs two or three times a week. But he did vigorously object to having all of the pictures of a company foisted on him regardless of their quality or desirability. Compulsory block booking did not exist for the circuits affiliated with the majors, it should be noted. The majors negotiated selective contracts allowing them to play only the best of each other's pictures.

Block booking guaranteed that the majors could wrest the greatest possible profits from the marketplace. By shifting business uncertainties to the independent exhibitor, studios could function at capacity, churning out from forty to sixty productions a year with the assurance that even the poorest picture would be bought. This, in turn, helped them secure a steady flow of production financing. As a long-term policy, block booking in preempting exhibitor playing time stifled competition by foreclosing the market to independent producers and distributors.

Before it was endorsed by the NRA, block booking had been attacked by consumer groups, Congress, and the Federal Trade Commission in addition to the independents. In 1931, the FTC, in its cease and desist order against Famous Players-Lasky, declared block booking an unfair and improper practice. The following year, however, the appeals court reversed the ruling.[14] But this did not close the matter by any means, so, in drafting the Motion Picture Code, the majors made a few concessions in the hope of quelling the controversy. Exhibitors were granted the privilege of cancelling 10 per cent of all features bought in blocks (the 10 per cent elimination clause) and the right to contract for shorts in equal proportion to the percentage of features contracted from each distributor. However, exercise of the first privilege was hemmed in by numerous restrictions, one of which stated that a picture could be cancelled only after payment was received for nine others. While the second prevented individual distributors from forcing their complete line of short subjects, it still completely filled an exhibitor's playing time for shorts.

Clearance and Zoning

By controlling the clearance and zoning boards, the majors protected the favored status of their theaters. These boards took over the function of the local film boards of trade, established before NRA and dominated by the Big Five, to arrange theaters in a particular territory into a marketing pattern consisting of run, clearance, and zoning. Theaters first showing newly released pictures were designated first-run. Located in the large metropolitan areas and owned mainly by the affiliated circuits, these theaters accounted for nearly 50 per cent of all admissions. Neighborhood houses and those in surrounding towns had the subsequent right to show pictures and were designated second-run, third-run, and so on. Clearance referred to the number of days that had to elapse before a picture having closed in one theater could open in another. Zoning referred to the geographical area over which clearance restrictions applied. Since the value of a motion picture to an exhibitor depended on its novelty, the granting of excessive clearance to prior-run theaters had the effect of increasing their drawing power and keeping patronage in subsequent-run houses at low levels. The majors did just this, according to independent exhibitors.

Practically every legal action they or the government filed against affiliated circuits contained charges of inequitable clearance and zoning. In three important suits, filed in California, Illinois, and Nebraska, the courts had gone against the majors by ruling that they had monopolized first-run and instituted patterns of clearance to their advantage.[15] With the creation of the clearance and zoning boards, the majors now had the power to adjudicate these matters for themselves.

Price Discrimination and Overbuying

The same held true for complaints of admission price discrimination and overbuying heard by the grievance boards. In licensing their pictures, distributors stipulated minimum admission prices for each exhibitor. This eliminated price rivalry among theaters and captured optimum revenue from rentals. The affiliated circuits, which operated first- and second-run theaters primarily, had a vested interest in seeing later-run independents subjected to strict admission-price control since if these houses cut prices, the affiliates would stand to lose business. At the outset of the Depression, independents, to attract patrons, offered prizes, coupons, two-for-one admissions, and the like, which indirectly reduced prices of admission. To prevent these practices, grievance boards were vested with extraordinary power. They could punish exhibitors found violating admission price Code provisions by ordering a boycott by the distributors.

To the further dismay of exhibitors, these same grievance boards had the power to hear complaints relating to overbuying. Overbuying was the practice whereby one exhibitor contracted for more pictures than he would normally need to deprive a competitor of desirable product. It often occurred in smaller communities where independents competed with affiliated opponents. The independent theater owner no doubt wondered how these boards could deal fairly with abuses the affiliated circuits regularly engaged in.

INVALIDATION OF THE CODE

On May 27, 1935, the Supreme Court in a unanimous decision invalidated the NIRA on the grounds that Congress could not enact laws regulating the business practices of firms in intrastate trade and that the National Industrial Recovery Act represented an attempt on the part of Congress to delegate its legislative functions to the President. The immediate effect on the motion-picture industry was slight. It had come through the Depression virtually intact. Business improved steadily after 1933 and within two years, all the companies were once again earning profits, with Loew's the undisputed leader. By 1935, Paramount and Fox had undergone reorganization. In 1936, Universal, after selling off its theaters, came out of receivership. RKO was not stabilized until 1940. Just as important, the industry's monopolistic trade practices remained in force without significant alteration. But, the debate over them continued in the halls of Congress, the Department of Justice, and in the courts, culminating in the antitrust case in 1938, *United States* v. *Paramount, et al.* The case reached the Supreme Court ten years later after thousands of pages of testimony and exhibits, two consent decrees, two lower-court decisions, and appeals. In a landmark decision, the Court held that the Big Five were parties to a combination that had monopoly in exhibition as a goal. One result was that the five integrated companies were directed to divorce their theater holdings from the production-distribution ends of their businesses. This decision, together with television, brought an era of the movies to a close.

EFFECTS OF THE CODE ON UA

United Artists summed up the Code, initially, in one word, "innocuous." This was the term used by company counsel Edward Raftery in his report to Joe Schenck describing the extent of the government's intervention in the industry as a result of the Code.[16] The company was represented in the early negotiations on the eleven-man producers' committee, one of three committees of industry figures charged with drafting the Code, but was not named to the Code Authority itself. Schenck protested this omission, stating to the Hays Office that United Artists and "its producers occupy a position in the industry which entitles them to . . . representation."[17] The Little Three had been left out of the Code Authority completely when its membership was first announced. Only at the last moment, in fact just days before the Code was to be ratified by the industry, Robert H. Cochrane, Universal vice president, was chosen to represent the unaffiliated producers and distributors. Being forced to the sidelines allowed UA to dissociate itself from the controversy over the Code. It also caused the company to be ignored. To Harold Baresford, Administration representative on the Code Authority and its chairman, an outraged United Artists cried:

> Since its inception the Code Authority has passed resolutions and made rulings on problems of extreme and vital importance to many of our clients. Such rulings . . . have been made without notice to those affected, or without an opportunity for those concerned to be heard. Further . . . there has been no way for us to secure reports, official in character, of the exact resolutions which were adopted, or of the wording of the rulings rendered by the Authority.
>
> We communicated with Mr. Flinn's secretary on Saturday, [Flinn was Executive Secretary of the Code Authority] asking for a copy of the proceedings of the Code Authority and we were advised by her the sole information that was available to us was the cursory report of the proceedings that appear in narrative form in the trade journals. Such reports are certainly not satisfactory and not sufficiently complete for our purposes. . . .
>
> To have rulings costing our clients tremendous sums of money and some rulings destroying entire businesses kept behind closeted doors so that our request to see the exact wordings of these rulings is met with an announcement

that all information concerning the Code Authority's activities is disseminated through the trade journal, and there only can we find information concerning their proceedings, it seems to us a strange situation.[18]

Later, from a trade journal, UA discovered that its share of the assessment covering the administrative expenses of the Code Authority came to $20,000—the same that each of the majors had to pay—while Columbia and Universal were charged $15,000 apiece. UA said it was unfair and arbitrary and proposed, instead, a reassessment based on the comparative revenue figures of the eight companies.

As for the Code itself, UA quarreled with only two provisions—prohibiting the payment of excessive salaries to stars and the 10 per cent elimination clause. As stated earlier, the majors attempted to pin the blame for the economic plight of the studios on the high salaries demanded by the star system. As proof, they alleged that the studios paid out more than $16 million annually to fewer than 230 actors.[19] Without opening their books to substantiate this figure, the producers empowered the Code Authority to investigate cases of so-called unreasonably excessive salaries and to fine offending producers up to $10,000. United Artists interpreted this as an attempt to prevent independent producers from competing for big-name stars, thus curtailing competition in the area of production.

At the outset of the negotiations, this section of the Code contained an even more onerous provision, which, according to UA's counsel in a telegram to Joe Schenck, would have this effect:

> If star completes contract with employing producer and employing producer offers a salary to extend contract which in opinion of Arbitration Board is reasonable and the star is not interested in returning to employing producer but has no specific reason for leaving then any producer is barred from engaging star for period not less than one year and further the star cannot produce his own pictures with his own money as all distributors will be forbidden to distribute and all exhibitors forbidden to exhibit under proposed provision. Entire provision aimed at action similar to action taken by United Artists stars in Nineteen Nineteen when they formed their own producing company. Provision likewise extends to executives and any and all persons earning over two hundred fifty dollars per week. We feel that a provision of this character is dangerous and feel that any limitation such as suggested will eventually destroy the entire code.[20]

Schenck wired back, "I am unalterably opposed to control of salaries and peonage in the Code and have so informed Will Hays."[21] United Artists thereupon joined Columbia and Universal in an attempt to at least modify the measure, if they could not defeat it. In a lengthy memorandum sent to General Johnson in Washington, they argued that the measure would(1) tend to reduce employment contrary to the spirit of the NIRA; (2) inhibit producers from negotiating with talent; (3) reduce artists to a state of peonage; and (4) prevent actors from going into independent production. Further, they said that the measure was illegal and would not reduce excessive salaries.

Challenging the assumption that star salaries and high production costs were adverse economic factors in the industry, the memorandum pointed out that Columbia Pictures

> owns no theaters, music publishing houses, radio stations, nor has it invested any of its funds in any other side enterprise. It has devoted its entire time, effort and resources to production and distribution, and even without first-class representation in many of the important exhibition key centers, Columbia has made money every year during the depression. Its earnings have been over a million dollars in some of the years, and Columbia has had to face every situation with every artist, writer, technician and laborer that everyone of the other producers has faced.[22]

Paramount-Publix, on the other hand, which had acquired expensive deluxe theaters all over the country and purchased interests in the Columbia Broadcasting System as well as other companies in the U.S. and abroad, was in bankruptcy. The Paramount production and distribution companies, though, were solvent. As proof for the assertion that even expensive pictures could make money for producers and distributors, they cited Sam Goldwyn's *Whoopee*. The picture utilized the talents of Flo Ziegfeld and starred Eddie Cantor, one of the highest-paid actors of the day, and was shot in Technicolor. Its production cost was "terrific," said the memorandum (actual cost: $1.3 million), yet the picture made money.

United Artists, Columbia, and Universal would have liked the Motion Picture Code to free talent from the shackles of the option contract, but they realized that any attempt to do so would have been foolhardy. This type of contract typically ran for seven years, during which a producer exercised annual options to continue the employment of the employee. In picking up the option, the employer usually paid a specified increase in salary. However, the contract was designed to favor the producer since it bound him for one year at a time and bound the employee for seven. Studios used the option contract not only to maintain large stables of stars, feature players, writers, and directors, but also to freeze talent, which often meant letting artists sit idle to keep them from competitors. The majors would loan out personnel to one another occasionally, if it was to their mutual advantage, but rarely and at exorbitant fees to the minors or independent producers.

As a counterproposal, the Little Three fought to limit the Code to the curbing of star raiding, a practice particularly odious to the studios. Their recommendation stipulated that producers could not negotiate with or make an offer to an employee under contract to another producer prior to the last thirty days of the contract. It was designed to insure that actors would devote their entire energies to their employers undisturbed by such unsettling influences as lucrative job offers and to provide a designated period when producers could contend with offers from competitors.

A majority on the producers' committee went along with the proposal, persuaded less by its fairness than by the threats of strike emanating from their studios. This did not mollify the stars however. They opposed any restriction on their right to negotiate by arguing that an actor who could be thrown out of work at the whim of a producer under the option contract system had the right to protect his future. After personally investigating conditions in Hollywood, Rosenblatt saw merit in the actors' case. However, his decision to suspend the contested provisions was not a victory for either the stars or independent producers, since beneficial or corrective measures were not placed in the Code on their behalf.

United Artists did not anticipate trouble with the 10 per cent elimination clause because the company signed the Code only after receiving assurances from Rosenblatt that the clause would not apply to UA. This clause was placed in the Code as a concession to exhibitors who objected to block booking and blind selling. UA sold each of its pictures

"The greatest selling organization in pictures"

individually and on a separate contract; an exhibitor could not reject 10 per cent of one picture, so obviously the clause did not pertain to the company.

Shortly after the Code went into effect, Peter Harrison, publisher of *Harrison's Reports,* a partisan trade magazine for theater owners, wrote Rosenblatt a letter posing this query: "Suppose an exhibitor bought from United Artists eighteen pictures on one worksheet and on one deal. Does this entitle the exhibitor to a ten per cent cancellation?" To UA's astonishment, the answer was yes and was duly published. Harrison's question implied that UA engaged in block booking just as the other distributors did, and if Rosenblatt's ruling stood, UA's ability to attract independent producers would be seriously impaired, to say nothing of its effect on relations with Goldwyn and other UA producers. So, the company had an unexpected fight on its hands.

UA filed a brief with the Code Authority arguing that Rosenblatt's ruling was in error, impolitic, and, moreover, not binding on the tribunal because only the Code Authority itself could rule on the interpretation of the Code. It further contended that as a matter of equity UA should be exempted from the clause:

> Often the producers for the United Artists Corporation make only one or two pictures a year. The investment in any one of these pictures is from $300,000 to $1,000,000. The pictures are sold separately and treated separately by the United Artists. If the elimination is permitted it may be that the producer who has only made one picture a year would lose his entire revenue. United Artists, as you know, is the only distributor which sells in this fashion, and whose producers produce such good pictures. Economically the 10% elimination clause means nothing to the other companies. They sell 50 pictures and invariably an exhibitor has unplayed about 10 of them at the end of the season and these are written off upon the sale to the exhibitor of next year's product. Since the producing is all done by one producer it does not matter which picture makes money.[23]

The brief was filed in June, 1934. By April the following year, the Code Authority had yet to hand down a decision. Meanwhile, exhibitors were refusing to take on UA's product unless the company consented to respect the 10 per cent elimination clause, which it was not about to do. Also, three complaints relating to this clause had been lodged against the company in grievance boards and, in every case, the boards ruled against United Artists. "We see nothing left for us at this time," threatened Raftery in a letter to Rosenblatt, "but to begin an action against the Code Authority to compel them to read the Code as it was written, or, in the alternative, those portions of the Code which seek to set up Grievance Boards to hear and determine disputes, should be declared illegal on the ground that there has been an unlawful delegation of judicial power."[24]

Rosenblatt responded immediately with the promise to review the three grievance-board decisions and to clarify the relation of the cancellation clause to UA as expeditiously as possible. This became unnecessary when the Supreme Court struck down the NIRA in May. The Code was no longer binding. The other distributors, however, retained the 10 per cent elimination clause to mollify the exhibitors.

UA's treatment at the hands of the Code Authority and the Hays Office epitomized its status in the industry. The prestige of the United Artists name enabled the company to enjoy a sense of power that belied its size. Under Joe Schenck's leadership, UA secured access to the marketplace for independent producers. Affiliated theaters profited from a successful UA release just as much as they did from one of their own. Moreover, should cries of monopoly be heard, the majors could always point to United Artists as proof that independents were not shut out of the business. UA could play the game, but it could not make the rules. The companies with the longest purse strings managed the industry to suit themselves, and would in the future as long as the monopolistic structure of the industry existed.

Schenck's Last Years
[1932-1935]

Despite Joseph Schenck's enormous capabilities in managing United Artists, despite the fact that his innovations were responsible, time and again, for extricating the company from product crises and financial crises, he could not salvage the careers of the individual producers, nor could he, in the end, resolve the split between the producing and nonproducing stockholders, a split which eventually forced him to resign.

UA FACES THE DEPRESSION

The Hughes Failures

Howard Hughes, UA's only outside producer and from whom the company expected so much, decided to go out of the motion-picture business—for good reason. The Caddo Company, his production unit, was losing a fortune, which did not mean that Hughes was going broke. As his biographer John Keats has said, the Hughes Tool Company, of which Howard Hughes was the sole owner, "hovered in the background like a fairy godmother waiting to be called on at need."[1] Hughes did not have the "Midas touch" the trade press so often attributed to him. *Variety,* for example, reported that *Hell's Angels* cost $3.2 million to make and that by July, 1931, eight months after its release, the production cost had nearly been paid off. Keats claimed the picture cost $4 million to make and that it earned twice that much within twenty years.[2] The production cost estimate is probably correct. Hughes worked on the picture for over two years, shooting it first as a silent then as a talkie. Lewis Milestone said that in between Hughes experimented with shooting it in color as well.[3] But *Variety*'s earnings report must be the fabrication of a delirious publicity agent, and Keats' the working of a myth maker. During the seven years it was in United Artists distribution, *Hell's Angels* grossed $1.6 million in the domestic market, of which Hughes' share was $1.2 million. Whatever the foreign gross was, it seems unlikely that it was great enough to earn a profit for the picture.

Hell's Angels was the second Caddo production. Five additional pictures were delivered in 1931 and 1932: *The Front Page, The Age for Love, Cock of the Air, Sky Devils,* and *Scarface, Shame of the Nation.* It is conceivable that *The Front Page* and *Scarface* broke even, for they grossed $700,000 and $600,000 respectively. There is no doubt as to how the other three pictures fared; they grossed an average of $250,000 each and were

Paul Muni and Ann Dvorak in Hughes' *Scarface* (1932)

considered by all, with the exception of Hughes perhaps, as mistakes of a sublime order.

During this time, Hughes was also taking a beating on his other movie-related investments, a 125-house theater chain in Texas and Multi-Color, Inc., a laboratory experimenting with high-quality color film. By 1931 he had so extended himself that UA had to advance him $350,000 to complete the financing for *Cock of the Air* and *Sky Devils*. After *Scarface,* Hughes was forced to take Noah Dietrich's advice and call it quits.

Still, he was puzzled by the poor returns on his pictures. He thought perhaps that he was disliked by the executives at the home office, to which Arthur Kelly responded, "On the contrary, every member of this firm has been doing their utmost to get as much money to Mr. Hughes as quickly as we [sic] can, knowing very well that certain of his pictures have not been very successful and knowing also that he is desirous of collecting as quickly as possible."[4] Hughes waited two years for results to change. They didn't, so he asked UA to release him from his distribution contract. He wanted to turn over his pictures to another distributor, Robert M. Savini, who specialized in working with small independent theaters in the U.S. and abroad. The UA board turned down Hughes' request because it would "establish a dangerous precedent" and "lead to complications in the future."[5]

When his distribution contract ran its course, Hughes asked to examine the books. After the audit, Hughes accused United Artists of making unauthorized reductions, rebates, and adjustments on contracts with theaters amounting to $200,000. Hughes not only wanted this money refunded, he also put in a claim for $1 million, the amount he alleged he had lost because UA did not use its best efforts to sell his pictures and because they were sold in blocks with other UA releases.

There was "no conscience" at all in Hughes' allegations, said Schenck. He distinctly remembered that Hughes "authorized him to act as his representative in approving or refusing adjustments on all exhibition contracts. . . . United Artists got for him the finest returns possible . . . and that he personally devoted special effort and attention to see that Hughes' pictures received fine treatment."[6] Hughes' lawyer, Neil McCarthy, agreed with Schenck and persuaded his client not to bring suit against the company. There must have been a grain of truth to Hughes' allegations, because UA recognized his claims to the tune of $75,000.

Art Cinema and Theatre Circuit Fight with Fox Theaters

More serious than the disappointing results of the Hughes pictures was the curtailment of Art Cinema's production activities, which during the previous three years had been the mainstay of UA's releases. Schenck had to devote the better part of 1931 to Theatre Circuit business because UA had become involved in an imbroglio with Fox-West Coast theaters, which controlled four hundred of the strongest theaters in the Rocky Mountain states and on the West Coast. UA accused Fox theaters of being an "arrogant monopoly" that tried to dictate unfavorable terms to the company. To drum up support for its cause, UA issued a "Declaration of Independence" signed by the owners and such stars as Eddie Cantor, Al Jolson, and Ronald Colman. It denounced Fox and proudly proclaimed that "we must fight for our principles as the people of this nation have always fought. And because we hold to that belief, we announce that hereafter none of the motion pictures made by us as, United Artists, shall be shown in the Fox theatres as long as that monopoly maintains its present greedy and short-sighted policy."[7]

Fox theaters did not take the criticism lightly. It retaliated by barring UA's pictures from its screens, an action that intensified the battle. Schenck turned over Art Cinema's production reins to Goldwyn and drew up plans for the Theatre Circuit to build a couple of dozen theaters in key cities along the coast. About ten were under construction before the battle ended. The country was already overloaded with theaters and both sides thought it prudent to compromise. A deal was concluded in August, 1931, whereby Fox-West Coast agreed to buy all of UA's product and the Theatre Circuit turned over to Fox the operation of its new houses.[8]

Being shut out of the large market of Fox theaters for nearly a year meant for Art Cinema that the returns on its product for 1930 and 1931 would be slow coming in. The company had invested heavily in a record number of nine productions in 1930 and until these had paid off their costs, its ability to finance future productions would be impaired. In 1931, Art Cinema cut back to five productions, but these, as did the previous year's product, failed to live up to expectations. In fact, with each passing season, Art Cinema's program became less impressive.

By 1932, Art Cinema's banking credit had been fully extended. Only two pictures were planned for production that year and the likelihood of getting financing for additional product was nil. Goldwyn had two Colman pictures but no Eddie Cantor musicals in the works. A disastrous product crisis appeared imminent.

Walt Disney—a Bright Spot

The only thing United Artists could cheer about during that gloomy year was the cartoons it began distributing for Walt Disney. Disney had been with Columbia Pictures since 1929—shortly after the time he introduced Mickey Mouse in *Steamboat Willie* to delighted audiences— but after three years, he found the low production advances too constraining. He decided that his production company would have to be under his own financial control. Moreover, Disney resented Columbia's block-booking method of distribution, which lumped his products with inferior cartoons. As *Fortune* said, Mickey Mouse had become "a personality so notable and so powerful that his independence had become inevitable."[9] In 1931, therefore, Disney broke with Columbia and signed with United Artists.

Walt Disney (© Walt Disney Productions)

UA poster for *Mickey's Good Deed* (1932) (© Walt Disney Productions)

The Big Bad Wolf in *The Three Little Pigs* (1933) (© Walt Disney Productions)

Disney's contract called for the delivery of eighteen Mickey Mouse cartoons and thirteen Silly Symphonies for the 1932-1933 season. The terms for the Mickeys were based on a sliding scale, beginning with a split of 70 per cent to Disney and 30 per cent to UA for the first $50,000 gross on each cartoon to a 30-70 split on everything over $75,000. Disney received slightly better terms for the Sillies because of their greater production costs. Disney had the exclusive right to Technicolor's three-color process for cartoon production until the spring of 1935. Using color for the Sillies increased their production costs by about $1,500 each but it also gave Disney the edge on his competitors, who had to make do with the inferior two-color or Cinecolor processes.

The United Artists-Disney deal was highly profitable for both parties. UA's share of the gross from the Disney product in the 1932-1933 season was $1 million. Disney received an average of $44,000 for each Mickey and $50,000 for each Silly. Production costs averaged $10,000 and $20,000, respectively.

The hit of the season was the phenomenally successful *The Three Little Pigs*, which cost $22,000 and grossed a quarter of a million. This picture won for Disney his second Oscar in a row and made him preeminent in his field. The most popular animated cartoons of the day were Max Fleischer's Popeye (Paramount), Van Beuren's Esop's Fables (RKO), and Leon Schlesinger's Looney Tunes and Merrie Melodies (Warner Bros.), but none of these producers matched Disney's critical, popular, and financial achievement.

Schenck's Attempt To Finance Future Production

The splendid results of the Disney product in 1933 convinced Schenck that United Artists should begin financing independent producers to insure a constant flow of product. In the past, UA had loaned monies to producers in the form of advances, which were secured by the rental fees of pictures in distribution. But Schenck now wanted to invest money to spur future production. This could be done, he suggested, by amending the Certificate of Incorporation to give the officers of the company discretionary powers to borrow from banks, to make loans, and give credit—powers which only the stockholders held at the time.

We have already heard from Griffith on this subject. Mary Pickford said that she appreciated the necessity for the company to loan money, but not at the 6 per cent interest Schenck was suggesting. More than mere interest would be required from producers; a share of the profits, for example, would be more in order to compensate the company for the risks involved.

Nathan Burkan, speaking for Chaplin, objected to the proposal on legal grounds. Loaning money to stockholders, said Burkan, was too hazardous for the officers and directors concerned, especially if a picture did not earn the amount of the loan and the corporation sought to recover the balance. A producer might then claim the picture was not properly distributed and then set up a counterclaim against the balance of the loan and refuse to pay it. Any one of these actions would place the matter in litigation and delay repayment of the loan.

O'Brien saw in Schenck's proposal the seeds of discontent. "Each producer," he said, "will seek aid from the corporation, claiming he has as much right as the other producers to such aid, and the amount of money available will not be sufficient to provide the results that United Artists is seeking."[10]

These and other arguments were raised at a special meeting of the stockholders. When the vote came, Schenck's motion passed, but not unanimously, so he decided that it should not be put into effect. At the same time, though, he warned that the company was committing a serious mistake and imperiling its future. The surplus they so jealously guarded could have been dissipated within a year or two had Goldwyn decided to distribute elsewhere or had Schenck not taken decisive action on his own to supply the company with product.

Liquidation of Art Cinema

In the early part of 1933, Art Cinema decided to liquidate and go out of business. The immediate cause was the failure of the two pictures it financed that season, Mary Pickford's *Secrets* and the Al Jolson musical *Hallelujah, I'm a Bum.* But the main cause was that the company had been sustaining severe losses since about 1930. Motion-picture business was still at a low ebb, and Art Cinema's stockholders did not want to risk its remaining funds on any more pictures.

Before this decision, Schenck had offered to provide Art Cinema financing to the production team of Edward Small and Harry Goetz. Now, when Schenck presented the deal to Art Cinema's board, it was turned down. Schenck was in an embarrassing position. On the basis of his verbal commitment, Small and Goetz had gone ahead to form their production company, Reliance Pictures, Inc. Although they could not have held Schenck to his word, he was not the kind of man to renege on an agreement, so he personally put up 50 per cent of the production costs for three pictures; Small and Goetz put up the other 50 per cent.

Reliance delivered *I Cover the Waterfront* in 1933 and *Palooka* and *The Count of Monte Cristo* in 1934. William Philips then stepped in to provide financing in Schenck's place, and Reliance produced five more pictures in the next two years: *Trans-Atlantic Merry-Go-Round, Let 'em Have It,*

Red Salute, The Melody Lingers On, and *The Last of the Mohicans.*
Schenck withdrew from Reliance early in 1933 because he had lost heavily
on his investments in Art Cinema and the Theatre Circuit, and he doubted
whether UA could find enough product to survive. He even contemplated
retiring from the motion-picture business altogether.

TWENTIETH CENTURY

Darryl Zanuck's History

Then a fortuitous event occurred which was destined to change the
fortunes not only of Schenck but of United Artists as well. Darryl Zanuck,
the audacious production chief at Warner, had quit his job after a violent
argument with Harry Warner. The fight was over studio salaries. When
President Roosevelt declared the nationwide bank moratorium, workers
from all the studios voluntarily agreed to a 50 per cent salary reduction to
prevent the shutdown of operations. Zanuck agreed to the cut for himself
and for his people. The Academy of Motion Picture Arts and Sciences and
Price, Waterhouse, a firm of accountants, were to decide when each
company was to bring pay back to scale. But Harry Warner refused to
accept their ruling, preferring to wait a little longer. Zanuck, who had
promised to restore salaries on the date specified by the Academy, now
had to go back on his word. This he refused to do, and as a matter of
principle walked out on his $5,000-a-week job.

Zanuck had joined Warner in 1924 at the age of twenty-two to become
one of the most prolific scriptwriters in Hollywood. He made his name
creating the incredibly successful Rin Tin Tin series, after which he
became studio manager, helping to guide the studio through the transition
from silent to talking pictures. In 1930, he was made head of production
and developed the formula for action-filled, fast-paced, and topical
pictures that characterized the Warner output during the thirties. His
production of *Little Caesar* began the gangster cycle in 1930 and made
Edward G. Robinson a great star. *Public Enemy* did the same for James
Cagney the following year. *Five Star Final* (1931) and *I Am a Fugitive
from a Chain Gang* (1932) exploited the topical themes of yellow
journalism and prison reform. In 1932, he made *42nd Street,* launching a
new trend in mammoth musical extravaganzas when everyone said that
musicals had had their day.

Now, virtually the hottest young talent around, Zanuck was showered
with offers from all over Hollywood. Seeking out his old friend for help in
plotting his future, Zanuck was surprised by Schenck's proposal that they
team up to produce pictures for United Artists. "I didn't know you were
still interested in production," said Zanuck. "I wasn't," Schenck replied,

Darryl Zanuck

"but with you, I would be." On that day in April, 1933, Schenck summoned his secretary to his apartment in Hollywood and dictated a short letter of agreement to form Twentieth Century Pictures, Inc.[11] Schenck became president; Zanuck, first vice president in charge of production; and William E. Goetz, son-in-law of Louis B. Mayer and formally a producer at RKO, second vice president.

Twentieth Century's Deal with UA

Twentieth Century signed with United Artists on July 13, 1933. The event was heralded as "equivalent to the infusion of new hope into the national lifestream that came with the inauguration of President Roosevelt" by Al Lichtman, UA's vice president in charge of sales. As for Zanuck, Lichtman called him "a modern of moderns, with a unique knowledge of the trends of entertainment. He personifies youth, brilliance, smartness and timeliness. The pictures he will make for Twentieth Century will be the last word in box office values."[12]

To finance the Twentieth Century product, Schenck and Goetz put up $1.2 million. Consolidated Film Industries, a film-developing company, advanced $750,000. And the Bank of America came through with a $3 million loan.

The distribution deal with United Artists was for one year and called for the delivery of from three to twelve pictures. The one-year contract was Schenck's idea:

> At the time I organized the company, Darryl asked me whether we could get a share of stock of the United Artists Company as he knew that all producers in the United Artists received a share of stock for the delivery of pictures. I told him it wouldn't be fair at that time to approach the stockholders and ask for a share of stock as they didn't know what value we would contribute to the United Artists . . . and advised him to wait until we had delivered our first year's product, as I felt sure that on the delivery of that product, the stockholders would be happy and proud to give Twentieth Century a share of stock in the company.[13]

Twentieth Century delivered its full complement of twelve pictures for the 1933-1934 season. "Out of the twelve," said Schenck, "nine are big pictures and successes. Three are mediocre pictures."[14] Among the money-makers were *The Bowery,* starring Wallace Beery, George Raft, and Jackie Cooper; *The House of Rothschild,* featuring George Arliss; and *Bulldog Drummond Strikes Back,* with Ronald Colman. Twentieth Century was able to maintain this heavy production schedule for three reasons: first, it had access to MGM's stars in addition to those Zanuck had under contract from Warner; second, it was able to buy a controlling interest in the United Artists Studio on easy terms; and, third, United Artists advanced production financing for its pictures.

The Dispute over Stock

Although Twentieth Century saved the year for UA, the owners would not give it stock in the company. Outraged by this behavior, Zanuck prepared to distribute elsewhere. Earlier that year he had written to Schenck, saying,

I believe we have now whipped our organization into where we have one of the best producing machines in our industry. It has not been an easy task—starting with nothing but a bare office—but yet, today, we are unquestionably producing a type of quality production that cannot be denied and we have a growing business with real box-office personalities and everything in the way of a production organization to continue us to real success; therefore, I believe the time has come now when we should think about our releases for next year. It is certainly not fair that we, the biggest contributors to United Artists, should not participate as a partner in the profits. . . . Other producers participate in the profits of United Artists and there is no reason in the world why we should not. As a matter of fact, if you recall, it was your promise that we would.[15]

It took all of Schenck's considerable powers of persuasion to convince Zanuck to sign another one-year contract. Schenck and Dennis O'Brien had devised a plan they thought could bring in Twentieth Century as a partner while mollifying the owners. The plan called for Twentieth Century to sign a ten-year distribution contract with UA and for a reorganization of UA capital structure so as to vest operating control in the hands of active producers, namely, Twentieth Century and Goldwyn.

To do this, they proposed issuing two classes of stock: (1) preferred, having a par value of $2.4 million and carrying a 7 per cent dividend; and (2) common, no par value, to be divided 40 per cent among the so-called inactive producer group, and 60 per cent between Twentieth Century and Goldwyn. All six United Artists partners would then be asked to exchange their old common stock for $400,000 units of the preferred and one-sixth interests in the 40 per cent of the common. Upon signing the new distribution contract, Twentieth Century would guarantee the payment of dividends on both the common and preferred and would agree to purchase each $400,000 unit of the preferred on demand.

Goldwyn "heartily agreed" to the plan as did Robert Fairbanks, Doug's brother and business manager. Schenck reported that:

Mary was not in town at the time so we went over to see Charlie. . . . Charlie's first objection was on the ground that "where would he get off—he was a producing member and a contributor." I told him I had no objection to his participating in proportion. There never was any intention and there never was any thought in my mind that Mary Pickford and Douglas Fairbanks were not entitled to all benefits accruing from the prosperity of United Artists just because they were not producing pictures. In fact on many occasions I argued with Sam Goldwyn that very point when Sam constantly demanded that we reduce the cost of distributing . . . even during the time when we were losing $25,000 a week . . . always maintaining that we have a surplus and why not dissipate the surplus for the benefit of the producers. I maintained that the interests of all owners must be protected and constantly opposed Sam on the reduction of the cost of distribution.[16]

When Schenck took a straw vote on the issue, he discovered that Mary was adamant in her opposition and that Goldwyn and Fairbanks had inexplicably reversed themselves. Counting Chaplin's, the vote would have gone four to two against the plan. The other affirmative vote would have been Art Cinema's, whose trustees had informed Schenck in his words, "that they would stick by me as they felt that I was the man who was responsible for the success of the company and they naturally were interested in the company being a success and not being run just to please certain individuals for their own best interests."[17]

Continuing, Schenck said, "I then made up my mind to resign but some friends of mine talked me out of it and pleaded with me to try and settle the controversy in some amicable manner. My decision to do so was also brought about through a conference I had with Charlie Chaplin at which he expressed himself as being in favor of giving Twentieth Century a share of stock and making my stock non-voting stock. I knew that through giving a share of stock to the Twentieth Century Company, I could persuade Darryl Zanuck to go along and to sign a contract for distribution."[18]

Schenck's Resignation

But the deal did not go through. At the last moment, Goldwyn suggested a change in the contract, which not only broke off the negotiations with Twentieth Century but also led to Schenck's resignation from UA. Schenck describes what happened:

It was clearly understood that the stock was to be issued to the Twentieth Century Company on signing of the contract. Instead of that, Sam Goldwyn, in behalf of his triumvirate, instructed that the stock be issued . . . in five installments spread over five years. Both Darryl Zanuck and I consider that an insult and resent it very strongly and we have decided that we don't want the stock that is offered to us so grudgingly.

It is clear to me that Sam Goldwyn, Mary Pickford and Charlie Chaplin are determined to dominate and run the United Artists Distribution Corporation. Why they should at this time decide to do so is inexplicable to me as the company has been run by me very successfully and very fairly and they should be very happy with the results achieved. They never showed any desire to manage and run the company when the company was $1,200,000 in the red nor a couple of years ago when we were confronted with the prospect of not having any pictures to distribute and were gradually losing the surplus that we had accumulated. . . . I cannot contribute to the success of the United Artists . . . by being its president without the power to make decisions or take action and confronted in the future with having a hostile and an unreasonable and destructive board of directors and there is only one thing for me to do and that is to resign.[19]

Schenck was referring to more than the stock controversy. During the negotiations, the triumvirate demanded a number of changes in the way he conducted the company. It wanted the directors' meeting to be held in Los Angeles and closer control over the operations of the company. How the home office could be efficiently managed when the directors were three thousand miles away was not explained. Schenck was particularly incensed by this power grab and by another matter involving Reliance.

Before leaving for New York to draw up the Twentieth Century contract, Schenck told his partner that he had given Reliance a new contract with the same terms as those enjoyed by the stockholders—25 per cent in the United States, 30 per cent elsewhere. "They were sympathetic," he said, "and told me not to worry about it as they would see that my moral obligation to the Reliance Company was discharged."[20]

They did not, however. The terms authorized by the stockholders were 30 per cent for distribution in the U.S. and 35 per cent in England. Schenck charged, "There was no justification for raising the percentage in England, as we make terrific profits in the distribution of our pictures in England. This proposition was entirely in violation of their commitment to me at our meeting."[21]

Schenck's Accomplishments

Schenck's prowess in management is demonstrated by UA's earnings for 1934. The company showed a profit of $1.1 million based on a gross business of $23 million, up $10 million from the previous year. Twentieth Century delivered nine of the twenty pictures and accounted for well over half the business. Reliance delivered three and Goldwyn three. The remaining UA stockholders contributed nothing, but they did suggest declaring a $560,000 dividend, the largest ever.

When Schenck assumed the position of chairman of the board in 1924, he had provided the fledgling company with the leadership and savvy that not only stabilized its operations but also enabled it to survive intact the upheavals in the industry brought about by the battle for the theaters, then the sound revolution, and finally the maneuvering for control over the marketplace during the days of NRA. He formed the United Artists Theatre Circuit to guarantee access to first-run theaters and fought the company's perennial product crisis by organizing Art Finance Corporation in 1925 and then Art Cinema the following year, meanwhile bringing in Gloria Swanson and Sam Goldwyn as partners. Later, he signed up Howard Hughes, Disney, Reliance, and, of course, Zanuck. Gross business during these past ten years increased by over $16 million. UA retired its preferred stock and paid out more than $1 million in dividends

Fredric March in 20th Century's *Les Miserables* (1935)

to its owners. Had it merged with MGM in 1925 or with its associated companies and Warner Brothers in 1929 as Schenck suggested, the profit record would no doubt have been greater. But UA could have lost its distinctive character as a company that fostered independent filmmaking by adopting the mass-production techniques of the Hollywood studio system. Schenck deferred to the whims of his partners regarding the proposed mergers and worked to strengthen United Artists along its original lines by organizing Twentieth Century Pictures and proposing a reorganization of the company to adequately compensate Goldwyn and the Zanuck unit for their contributions. Pickford and Fairbanks were inactive by 1933 and Chaplin had settled down to a routine of producing one picture every four or five years. Yet Schenck was thwarted once again by his mercurial UA partners; he had good reason to resign.

Apparently, only Chaplin regretted Schenck's decision. But Schenck would not reconsider. He wrote to Chaplin saying,

> If you select a capable man for president and vest in him the necessary power to run the business without interference from the stockholders, I am absolutely certain that the company can and will be a success. . . . When I say "interference from the stockholders," I do not mean eliminating their right to recommend or discuss with the president the policy of the company, but you cannot hog-tie a man at the head of a concern and put him in a position where he cannot make

important decisions without the consent of people who know very little about the affairs of the distributing company and the necessities for the success of a company like ours.[22]

The UA board accepted Schenck's resignation on May 21, 1935. A month later he severed all connections with the company by selling back his stock for $550,000. Art Cinema's stock was also acquired by UA in the transaction for $650,000. Schenck held on to his interests in the Theatre Circuit, but sold Twentieth Century's stock in the United Artists Studio to Sam Goldwyn for $250,000. Goldwyn thereby became the sole owner of the stages, equipment, and other physical property at the studio. Title to the real estate was still retained by Pickford and Fairbanks.

The Merger of Twentieth Century and Fox

The Twentieth Century—Fox Film Corporation merger took place immediately. Zanuck and Schenck had correctly predicted the outcome of controversy over giving UA stock to Twentieth Century and had protected themselves. F. M. Guedalla, UA's legal counsel in England, told this story about the merger after meeting with William Philips:

Philips admitted to me that perhaps last December or January Darryl Zanuck had been approached by . . . the Fox Company, with rather tentative talks of a merger . . . but that nothing had come of it at the time. He did not think that Mr. Schenck knew . . . of these conversations. However, Philips was delightfully vague and seemed rather astonished that I knew anything.

I said, (which is a fact) that my information had come from Douglas and that I understood that Douglas in turn had learned it from Mary, and that it was common knowledge amongst all kinds of people in Los Angeles.

Philips again and again went out of his way to put the responsibility for these discussions on to Darryl Zanuck. He said it was the kind of thing that had to happen if Darryl Zanuck was not to be as big a noise in United Artists as he had been in Warner Brothers. He was going to be a big noise somewhere, and it did not hurt whether it was Paramount, Fox or M.G.M. or whoever it was.

He said that when last April or May the question again cropped up very incisively that Board Meetings were to be held in Los Angeles, Goldwyn and Schenck did not see eye to eye as to the treatment of their films by any means. It was then suggested, quite untruly, that preference was given in different territories to Twentieth Century films over those of any other producers, and this was so because all the staff were dependent on Mr. Schenck's nod as to increase in salary or even as to dismissals.

United Artists were all of one mind that they would not have Darryl Zanuck as voting on stock or still less as being a director. Darryl Zanuck then completed, very quickly, various arrangements with Mr. [Sidney] Kent, and Philips said that when Mr. Schenck heard of them he approved, because he had a standby in his further talks with his colleagues in United Artists, but they were obdurate, so Mr. Schenck decided to go over, lock stock and barrel to the Fox Company taking

Darryl Zanuck with him and making him the great Productions Manager for the Fox Company. Philips also remarked that Mr. Schenck also had a lift up in the film industry.

Philips again and again said that through this combination Fox was predestined to be the biggest film company in the world, much bigger than the M.G.M. Company.[23]

The motion-picture empire that William Fox had built with some 1,500 theaters in the United States and Britain and a big, rambling studio in Beverly Hills had toppled during the stock-market crash of 1929 and had not yet revived. Control of the company had passed from Fox to General Theatres Equipment headed by Harley L. Clarke and, then in 1933 following reorganization, to Chase National Bank. The persistent problem had been the company's inability to produce a sufficient number of moneymakers to fill the playing time of its heavily indebted theaters. Fox needed Twentieth Century to rectify this situation.

Schenck was named chairman of the board of Twentieth Century-Fox at a salary of $2,500 a week. Goetz and Zanuck became vice presidents. As head of production, Zanuck received a weekly salary of $5,000. The details of the merger need not be described here. Suffice it to say, however, that the net worth of the former United Artists production unit was placed at $5 million. Its earning capacity surpassed the huge Fox Film Corporation with its assets of over $50 million. Because of this, the name of Twentieth Century appeared first in the merged names.

<table>
<tr><td>

7

</td><td>

Without a Leader
[1934-1936]

</td></tr>
</table>

UA'S DISPUTE WITH SCHENCK

Zanuck's brashness may have nettled the stockholders, but it was the suspicion of a power grab on Schenck's part that caused the Twentieth Century stock controversy. F. M. Guedalla summed up conditions after a long conversation with Douglas Fairbanks:

> [Miss Pickford] had become more active in complaining that she knew so little about the conduct of the business. That Schenck, although spending a lot of time in Los Angeles, never told her anything about United Artists. That she had a very big investment in it and wanted to know more about matters of great personal interest to her. . . . Chaplin and Goldwyn had also taken up this attitude and that it was that proposition which had led to the demand to have Board Meetings in Los Angeles and for Stockholder Producers to be on the Board of United Artists, but that Schenck had steadily refused to entertain that proposition or even to discuss it. Schenck had stated that United Artists must always be guided under his Directorship and by the Executive chosen by himself. If this was not the case, United Artists was foredoomed to a very sad position, but he was not going to have his Executive bossed by temperamental people like Mary or Charles Chaplin or Douglas.[1]

Al Lichtman—a Weakened President, a Strengthened Board

So when the time came to choose Schenck's successor, the stockholders made certain that they would keep abreast of company affairs. During a hectic ten-day stockholders meeting in July, 1935, they reconstituted the board of directors to include the owners, elected Mary Pickford first vice president to work beside the new president, Al Lichtman, and amended the bylaws so that management could not make unilateral decisions.

An executive committee, consisting of Lichtman, Dennis O'Brien, Nathan Burkan, James Mulvey, and Edward Raftery, was formed to conduct the regular and routine business of the company in New York.

Under no circumstances could it alter company policy, for a new bylaw read: "Said Executive Committee shall have no power to inaugurate radical reversals of, or departures from, fundamental policies and methods of conducting the business." Only the board could do these things at its monthly meeting in Los Angeles.

The Tangle of UAC, Ltd., the UA Theatre Circuit, and Crescent Theatres, Ltd.

First on the stockholders' agenda was an investigation of how the UA Theatre Circuit became entangled with company operations in England. This led to the discovery that Schenck, even though he had dissociated himself from UA, could still materially affect its welfare as president of the Theatre Circuit. The stockholders were so alarmed that they charged Schenck with breach of duty.

The British market accounted for nearly 80 per cent of the company's profits. UA barely broke even in the United States, the result of high overhead costs. Its earnings came from abroad and the largest overseas market for United Artists, as well as the other American film companies, was Great Britain.

There, as in the United States, profitability depended directly on access to the best theaters. For years, the subsidiary in England, United Artists Corporation, Ltd., had searched for a first-run theater in London's West End to serve as a showcase for its British and American producers. Finally in 1934, a suitable house, the old London Pavilion, was found in that popular theater district. However, it came at a stiff price: UAC, Ltd., had to pay £25,000 towards the renovation costs and guarantee a minimum annual rental of £28,600. Schenck decided that the operation of the theater should be turned over to the Theatre Circuit. To do so he formed a holding company, Crescent Theatres, Ltd., for the purpose of taking over the lease from UAC, Ltd., and assuming beneficial control of the theater. The newly renovated London Pavilion opened on September 5, 1934, with the Alexander Korda production of *The Private Life of Don Juan.*

The British company could not adequately protect its position with only a showcase theater. As Guedalla had reported, "We also should have the possibility of using several hundred theatres in the Provinces not only for obtaining fair terms on which to show United Artists pictures therein, but also as means of counteracting terms which might be very arbitrary on the part of the big Gaumont-British Circuit and also the B.I.P. Circuit and any other big Circuits, particularly if as constantly contemplated, such Circuits should amalgamate."[2] So Guedalla and Murray Silverstone, the managing director of UAC, Ltd., began to acquire theaters. They bought into the Donada Circuit and the rapidly expanding Odeon Theatres. Both acquisitions were made in Crescent's name in February, 1935. The latter was a coup of sorts. Odeon, the fourth-largest circuit, with nearly 150 houses and an authorized capital of £200,000, was owned outright by the industrialist Oscar Deutsch. By shrewdly analyzing its market position, Guedalla and Silverstone purchased a half interest in this circuit for the nominal sum of £50. The bigger circuits, by reason of their greater purchasing strength and prior claims as owners of first-run theaters, had been receiving the pick of the new pictures. Odeon, to put it simply, desperately needed a source of quality pictures to survive, let alone expand. Deutsch, as a result, welcomed the deal. Crescent did not come in as an equal partner, however. A special clause in Odeon's Articles of Association gave Deutsch and his partners the right to elect the chairman and one-half of the directors; Deutsch, therefore, had the so-called casting vote and control.

Nonetheless, United Artists assumed it had secured a stronghold in the British exhibition market, that is, until it realized that the Theatre Circuit owned the Crescent holdings. Particularly galling as well was the knowledge that Crescent in taking over the Pavilion lease did not indemnify UAC, Ltd. This meant that the Theatre Circuit would be the beneficiary of the profits, leaving UAC, Ltd., liable for losses, maintenance fees, and so on. The stockholders wanted to know why. Guedalla told them:

> It was beyond the realms of my fancy that Mr. Schenck *could or would* ever sever himself and his own concerns from his United Artists Corporation connection. At the same time let it be plainly stated, that Mr. Silverstone and I were and are aware that technically the United Artists Theatre Circuit was and is an independent and different organization. We understood and still understand that it was and is tied by close "franchises" and in other ways with United Artists Corporation. We understood and still understand that its chief holders of Common Stock were the Stockholders of United Artists Corporation, with the exception of Mr. Chaplin, and that the majority of the Directors and Executives were common to both Companies and that the same offices were used by the two companies.[3]

Guedalla's main concern at the time was that the Theatre Circuit might some day pass to a third party and for that reason he suggested to Schenck that UAC, Ltd., should have the right to purchase Crescent's shares from the Theatre Circuit at par.

But the stock transfer was never made. Schenck was now firmly ensconced at Fox, in control of the Theater Circuit, and more disturbing, silent on the Crescent shares. The fear, of course, was that

Crescent would come under the control of the Twentieth Century-Fox, which by the way owned a substantial share of the Gaumont-British Circuit. "It would be an appalling thing, so far as United Artists is concerned," said Guedalla, "if through creating the Crescent Theatres Limited it had added an instrument which would be useful to Gaumont-British interests and adverse to those of United Artists."[4]

It was Nathan Burkan who pushed for litigation and it was he who had issued in the High Court of Justice Chancery in London a writ asserting that United Artists and UAC, Ltd., were beneficially entitled to the Crescent stock. Schenck and Philips, as officers of the Theatre Circuit, were joined as defendants and accused of misfeasance. United Artists charged that Schenck in negotiating with Deutsch and Donada failed to make clear the fact that the distributing company and the Theatre Circuit were discrete corporate entities. Later, in writing to Mary Pickford about the charge, Schenck said,

> Murray [Silverstone] did a very unethical thing to me. When I left the company, he was called upon to make a statement that it was Deutsch's intention to sell a one-half interest in the Odeon Circuit, not to the United Artists Theatre company but to the United Artists Distributing Company. This was not true, and Murray (if he had the strength of character) would have so testified, but knowing Murray as I do and knowing that he is lacking in backbone, I was not surprised that when he was called upon by Burkan or whatever attorney it was to maintain that Deutsch gave me stock in the Odeon Circuit thinking that he was giving it to the United Artists Distributing Company, Murray agreed. . . . Well, Murray is not the only man that would step away from the path of real truth under pressure. There are many other men who are good men, and honest men, but who cannot withstand pressure.[5]

The Theatre Circuit responded to UA's charges by issuing a writ of its own. But the case was never brought up for trial, perhaps because as Guedalla said, "whatever the verdict and whoever the victor there would be a lot of dirty linen washed in public." He went on to say, however, that "all the aces and kings in the pack were with Mr. Schenck and the Circuit group, and probably they would have won if they had fought this case to a finish."[6] The out-of-court settlement in September, 1935, awarded United Artists through its British subsidiary the right to purchase at nominal cost 51 per cent of the Crescent stock. The following year, the Theatre Circuit sold off its remaining shares and UAC, Ltd., assumed total control of the holding company. UA severed its relations with the Theatre Circuit after the lawsuit: the franchise agreement was allowed to lapse; the sharing of administrative personnel ceased; and the Theatre Circuit moved its headquarters from the United Artists building.

THE CONTINUING SEARCH FOR PRODUCT

United Artists looked to Britain for more than box-office revenue; it needed its product as well. With Twentieth Century gone, the company had a big gap to fill. Goldwyn, UA's second line of defense, stepped up production to deliver four pictures in 1935. Mary Pickford came out of retirement as a producer, to team up with Jesse Lasky. Together, they formed Pickford-Lasky Productions and were preparing for 1936 release two Nino Martini vehicles, *One Rainy Afternoon* and *The Gay Desperado.* Chaplin was at work putting the finishing touches on *Modern Times,* his first UA release in five years. Like *City Lights,* its precursor, *Modern Times* was being made as a silent picture with musical accompaniment. Chaplin's voice was heard only in a song at the end. Unhappily, this picture would be received with mixed reviews, not because it was a silent, but because it lacked form, pacing, and sustained comic touches. *Modern Times* grossed $1.4 million domestically, which meant that after the distribution fee was deducted, it did not cover the $1.5 million production cost. Its foreign distribution eventually put the picture in the black. Nonetheless, United Artists in 1935 needed additional product from more producers to sustain its operations.

Chaplin's *Modern Times* (1936)

The Quota Act, British-Made Films

UA had two British producers under contract, Herbert Wilcox and Alexander Korda. To understand the role they had been playing for the company, one has to go back to 1927, when Britain passed the Cinematograph Films Act (the Quota Act). Parliament had passed the measure in reaction to the growing encroachment of the American film industry on the British market. Less than 5 per cent of the films shown in 1926 were made in Britain (34 of the 749 offered to the trade). The leading distributors—Famous Players, Universal, Fox, Gaumont, First National, and Wardour—released a total of 306 pictures; all but 8 were made in America.

In an attempt to resuscitate a dying industry, the Quota Act sought to guarantee an outlet for British pictures. Exhibitors were required to devote 5 per cent of their screen time to British films; the quota for distributors was set at 7½ per cent. Although in retrospect the Quota Act can be credited with reviving the British film industry, the initial results were far from satisfactory. The purpose of the distributors' quota was to force American distributors to finance domestic production. But because the Act did not contain a quality clause, distributors financed "quota quickies," films churned out on miniscule budgets, to fulfill their obligations. Exhibitors, to comply with their legal obligations, would often show these in the morning or early afternoon, long before peak business hours. These pictures gave British films a bad name which took years to overcome.

United Artists distributed about twenty-five quickies from 1928 to 1933, although it was obvious that the company's survival, in the long run, depended on quality pictures. As an interim measure, UAC, Ltd., contracted with Herbert Wilcox's British and Dominions Film Corporation, Ltd., in 1932, for that company to fill UA's quota requirements from 1933 to 1936. Thirty-six pictures were to be produced of good quality and at an average cost of £30,000 each. To take up the slack after Art Cinema discontinued production in 1933, B & D's status changed. Thereafter, it was looked upon as a potential source of product for the American market. UA released two B & D pictures in the U.S. that year and, in 1934, two more.

Alexander Korda in Britain

United Artists signed up Alexander Korda and his production company, London Film Productions, Ltd., on May 17, 1933. Herbert Wilcox in his autobiography, *Twenty-Five Thousand Sunsets*, claimed that he was responsible for Korda joining UA by releasing the company from the exclusivity clause in his contract. Here is the story Wilcox tells:

Korda 'phoned. He wanted to see me urgently. Because of my embargo, he told me, he could not get airborne—financially or otherwise. He had an important script completed. He had raised £58,000 and the distributors interested were United Artists. Would I lift my ban for this one film, which he described. I demurred.

"I'm on by beam ends just now, Herbert," said Korda, "but I've always believed that one good film can make a company—a dozen good ones an industry. This is the film to spark everything off for me."

I was impressed. After all, I thought, one good British film would not hurt me. My object was keeping out the bad ones. I gave my consent. Korda went ahead and made the film which turned out an outstanding success. It was *The Private Life of Henry VIII.*[7]

There is more to the story than Wilcox discloses. No doubt Schenck also applied some pressure because the British company needed product for 1933 even worse than the parent company. Columbia Pictures, which in the previous year had distributed its pictures through UAC, Ltd., decided to open exchanges of its own. Korda had just completed a Paramount contract for three quota pictures. The final one, *Service for Ladies,* starring Leslie Howard, was superior to the dreadful quickies and recommended Korda as a suitable producer for United Artists.

Korda received a contract for two pictures, not one, as Wilcox implies. However, he was correct about *The Private Life of Henry VIII.* The

Charles Laughton in Korda's *The Private Life of Henry VIII* (1933)

picture had its world premiere at the Radio City Music Hall on October 12, 1933, and did very well indeed—for a British picture. In the United States, it grossed about $500,000; in Britain and elsewhere, much more. Charles Laughton won an Academy Award for his portrayal of Henry and Korda proved to the world that a British film could match the best that America could produce in spectacle and lavishness. The second picture Korda delivered on this contract was *Catherine the Great.*

The reception of both pictures had made Schenck ecstatic. When he was in England to inspect UA's overseas operations in 1934, Schenck wrote to the home office,

> I have arrived here at the right time. We have as you know a wonderful business here in Great Britain and will have a far greater year in 1934 than in 1933. I am confident we will do no less than £1,800,000. . . . Am enclosing long-term contract with London Films. *The Private Life of Henry VIII* is a terrific hit. *Catherine the Great,* is Korda's second picture, is great entertainment, lavishly produced, with two great performances by Elizabeth Bergner and Douglas Fairbanks, Jr., and no doubt will be a hit here and should do as well in the States as *Henry VIII* and may do better. . . . Korda will produce at least 6 pictures a year. You cannot conceive what these pictures are doing for us here. Where other American producers are compelled to sell quota pictures—and mind you the exhibitor has to play up to the audiences—in the high class theatres they hiss these pictures off and in the rough theatres they throw bottles at the screen. We sell them pictures that are great box-office pictures, with the result that these pictures we distribute help sell our pictures.[8]

Schenck signed Korda to a sixteen-picture contract. The new distribution terms were much better, a U.S. domestic rate of 25 per cent as compared to 50 per cent in the first contract.

Korda was heralded as the man who singlehandedly put the British film industry on its feet. Production companies mushroomed after 1934, lured into existence by the prospect of making another *Henry VIII,* whose grosses were then being inflated by the attendant ballyhoo. Financing flowed and the prestige picture became the standard. An economic study of the industry has reported that in England "during this period the marine market became slack and the underwriters turned their attention to film production, which seemed to have proved itself to be a 'good risk.' The total amount of these loans was prodigious . . . in the first ten months of 1936 alone production companies borrowed 'in excess of £4,050,000'."[9]

Now in the spotlight, Korda was showered with fabulous offers from American film companies. Had he jumped to another company upon the conclusion of his UA commitments, UA's future in Great Britain would have been bleak indeed. Korda stayed put, but not as an ordinary producer. United Artists had to recognize his asset value by bringing him

Alexander Korda

in as a partner in September, 1935. Korda tied himself to the company for ten years, in return for a thousand shares of stock at the purchase price of $650,000. The stock was practically a goodwill gift because payments were to extend over a long period and dividends were to apply to the purchase price. In other words, Korda became a partner without having to put up one cent of his own money.

David O. Selznick in the U.S.

United Artists had eased the product crisis somewhat by adding Korda to its ranks abroad, and in July, 1935, by signing David O. Selznick to an eight-picture contract at home. At thirty-two, Selznick, like Darryl

Zanuck, was a boy wonder. He had been head of production at RKO from 1932 to 1933. He had pulled that company out of its slump by producing such pictures as *What Price Hollywood?*, *A Bill of Divorcement*, and *King Kong*. During the following two years, as an MGM vice president, he produced a remarkable string of pictures that included *Viva Villa!*, *Manhattan Melodrama*, *David Copperfield*, and *A Tale of Two Cities*. Selznick then made the decision to go independent, a decision which was not reached lightly despite his dissatisfaction with the studio system and Louis B. Mayer, his domineering, egotistical father-in-law. Al Lichtman negotiated full time for two weeks in his suite at the Ambassador Hotel in Los Angeles to bring Selznick around. Selznick got no special concessions; he received the standard distribution contract with regular terms.

Selznick International Pictures, Inc., was formed shortly thereafter, with Selznick as president and John Hay Whitney chairman of the board. The other directors were Cornelius V. Whitney, chairman of the board of Pan American Airways; Robert Lehman of the Lehman Brothers banking firm; Dr. A. H. Giannini of the Bank of America; Myron Selznick, David's brother and a highly successful Hollywood agent; and Loyd Wright, prominent Los Angeles attorney. Financing came mainly from the Whitney family, which invested $2.4 million. Myron supplied $400,000, Robert and Arthur Lehman and John Hertz $300,000, and Irving Thalberg, through his wife Norma Shearer, $100,000. Selznick's contribution to the company was his talent. After setting up headquarters at the RKO Pathé Studio in Culver City, Selznick International began its first UA production, a remake of an early Mary Pickford hit, *Little Lord Fauntleroy*.

MARY PICKFORD'S MANAGEMENT OF THE COMPANY

Negotiating the Selznick contract became the one-and-only feat of the Lichtman regency. After only three months in office, Al Lichtman quit. It seemed that Sam Goldwyn had his own ideas as to how his pictures should be sold. Lichtman was not going to be harassed and took a job at MGM, from which he had just stolen David O. Selznick. Thereupon, Mary Pickford, as first vice president, took control. What Goldwyn thought about this is not recorded! United Artists more than ever needed a strong leader.

Loss of Walt Disney

Finally at the helm of the company, Mary Pickford could now display her executive talents. Her first task, negotiating the renewal of the Disney contract, tested her mettle straight off. UA lost Disney to RKO, the result of a foolish quibble over a minor detail. How this blunder happened is hard to fathom, but it did. As expected, Disney came in asking for better terms. For example, he wanted the distribution rate in the U.S. lowered from 30 to 27½ per cent. Although Goldwyn protested that the company might lose money on the deal, the board acceded to this request. But when Disney said that he might want to retain the television rights during the distribution period for his pictures, the board, Goldwyn and Pickford particularly, balked. The year was 1936, remember.

Negotiations came to a standstill, which provided RKO the opportunity to propose a deal of its own: a $40,000 production-cost guarantee for each negative; a $12,000 advance for prints and advertising; and a fifty-fifty split of the profits. Such a deal was too good to turn down, as Disney's attorney, Gunther Lessing, explained:

> It was with great reluctance and considerable regret that we decided to leave United Artists. The deal offered us, however, was one which we felt should be accepted. We believe that the serious problems which have been worrying us for some time will be solved through our new arrangement. . . . The deal as it stood would have been entirely acceptable to us had not the insistence of your directors on television delayed and impeded execution. . . . We could not understand why United Artists was so adamant in its demand for representation as fiscal agents covering a subject matter about which none of us had much information. I could not find it consistent to advise my clients to grant an agency without knowing what power the agent would exercise. When Arthur [Kelly] finally telephoned Roy [Disney] that your directors were willing to abandon their position with reference to television, it was too late. Perhaps this is another evidence of the fact that Walt seems to possess a "guardian angel" who intervenes periodically. It was in the interim of our disagreement that a much better proposition was offered us than any theretofore made.[10]

That United Artists committed the error of taking Disney for granted, there can be no doubt. Only after he signed with RKO, it seemed, did the board fully appeciate his value. Disney offered to buy out the remainder of his UA contract, fearing that with the change of distributorships, the company would not be able to get top prices for the eighteen cartoons scheduled for delivery during the 1935-1936 season. The offer was $180,000, an amount equivalent to the revenue UA would earn by distributing the pictures. Miss Pickford's reply was that "the company would not consider it, not even for three times that sum as it would prove a serious loss of prestige to the United Artists which at this time we could ill afford."[11] Although this appraisal came belatedly, Miss Pickford referred in part to Disney's Academy Award recognition. *Flowers and Trees, The Tortoise and the Hare, Three Orphan Kittens,* and *The Country Cousin* had won him an Oscar each year he was at UA.

Shortly after his departure, Disney produced his first feature-length cartoon, *Snow White and the Seven Dwarfs*. This picture became one of Hollywood's greatest hits, grossing $9 million on its first worldwide release, producing seven top tunes, and winning eight Academy Awards ("one for each dwarf and one for the picture," *Time* said). Disney recalled that in persuading him to join United Artists, Chaplin said, "Come over, study United Artists' figures, and learn how to make money." After *Snow White* opened at the Radio City Music Hall in December, 1937, Disney quipped, "Charlie came over and studied our books."

So, despite the addition of Korda and Selznick to its ranks, UA's condition was still precarious. UA had to face once again the specter of production financing. United Artists dared not supply financing to its producer-owners because of the potential of such a scheme for creating more strife in the company. But it would consider investing in an autonomous production unit that could supply the additional three to five pictures it needed annually. With this objective in mind, the company opened negotiations with Walter Wanger.

The Walter Wanger Deal

Wanger possessed many qualities that made him an attractive figure to UA. He was a gentleman of breeding, college educated, and given to making lofty statements about the social responsibilities of the filmmaker and his educational role in a democracy. He would certainly add class to the company and for that matter, make a cultured and well-mannered guest at Pickfair. As a producer, Wanger had the reputation for setting trends, for being daring yet tasteful, politically provocative yet having mass appeal. Just as important, most of his pictures had been made on modest budgets and earned money. Also, Wanger was widely regarded as a star maker, and many of these stars he now had under contract.

Wanger entered the movie business after flirting with a career in the theater, first on Broadway, when during his college days at Dartmouth he had once been an assistant to Granville-Barker, and later, after the war, in London, where he had produced several plays. In 1923, upon returning to New York, he went to work for Jesse Lasky as general manager in charge of production at Famous Players-Lasky. Wanger's job, in his own words, was to "lift the public taste a little bit" by bringing in top designers from Paris to improve sets and costumes and by instilling "good taste" in Cecil B. De Mille's productions.[12] Wanger personally produced only a few pictures during his eight-year stint at Paramount, but he was credited with discovering Claudette Colbert, Kay Francis, Miriam Hopkins, Walter Huston, the Marx Brothers, Maurice Chevalier, and Ginger Rogers, among others.

After he was fired by Adolph Zukor in 1931, over "policy differences," Wanger became vice president under Harry Cohn at Columbia. According to Cohn's biographer, Bob Thomas, Cohn liked Wanger because he was not a yes-man. Also, he looked good at a studio trying to shed its poverty-row image. Here, Wanger began to produce his so-called films of social consciousness. *Washington Merry-Go-Round,* for example, dealt with contemporary politics, and *The Bitter Tea of General Yen,* which Frank Capra directed, was a story about miscegenation between an American girl and a Chinese general. In his next job at MGM, Irving Thalberg put him to work producing *Gabriel over the White House,* a film about a President indifferent to his responsibilities who is visited by the Archangel Gabriel and told of the millions who depended on him. These three pictures became "major" films made on small budgets and spotlighted Wanger as a comer. And after his next two pictures, vehicles for Greta Garbo and Marion Davies, *Queen Christina* and *Going Hollywood,* respectively, he found himself in the top producer ranks.

He returned to Paramount at the end of 1934, as an independent producer with a ten-picture contract. Still in the hands of receivers, Paramount desperately needed new talent to put the company on its feet. Wanger continued to live up to his reputation. His *The Trail of the Lonesome Pine,* for example, the first outdoor Technicolor picture, was brought in for $625,000, well below the budgeted figure of $1 million. But

Mary Pickford and Walter Wanger

working on a shoestring, so to speak, by now proved burdensome, so that when his Paramount contract was about to expire, he had more than a passing interest in UA's offer.

It was an attractive one. United Artists offered to set up a production company to bear his name, Walter Wanger Productions, Inc., which would operate out of the United Artists Studio, and guarantee financing so that he could "expand all of his theories on the screen unencumbered by restricted negative costs." UA, in addition, would give Wanger a five-year contract at a salary of $2,000 a week and complete control of all production matters, and with it the management of his stock company, which now included Sylvia Sidney, Charles Boyer, Madeleine Carroll, Henry Fonda, Joan Bennett, and Warner Baxter. Wanger, in return, was asked to assign certain literary properties and employment contracts to the production company and to keep costs below $750,000 for each picture, unless he received permission from his board to spend more. However, as the owner of half the common stock, Wanger would be entitled to choose two of the five board members.

The deal originally called for the five UA stockholders to supply the capitalization by subscribing to $1 million of preferred stock. But on second thought, the stockholders agreed that they as individuals should be dissociated from the venture. So that it fell to United Artists to put up the capital, which money had to be borrowed from the Bank of America. Walter Wanger Productions was incorporated on July 24, 1936. A week later, after signing a UA distribution contract, it went into production.

A. H. GIANNINI, UA PRESIDENT

Not coincidentally, United Artists elected Dr. Attilio Henry Giannini president and chairman of the board before consummating the deal. Giannini, as chairman of the Bank of America's general executive committee, was the man primarily responsible for approving loans to the motion-picture industry. To suggest that the bank insisted on the Giannini appointment as a condition of its financing the Wanger deal would be going too far. On the other hand, it certainly wanted UA to have a strong and stable management, which Miss Pickford for all of her charm and resourcefulness could not provide. In any case, as one of the most influential men in the business, Giannini appeared to provide the perfect tonic to cure the ailing company. Moreover, he knew UA's affairs and problems intimately: he was a member of the board of Selznick-International; financial adviser to Goldwyn; and long-time associate of Joe Schenck.

A. H. Giannini was the younger brother of Amadeo Peter Giannini, the founder of the Bank of America. He trained as a physician, earning an M.D. from the University of California, but found banking more to his liking. After an apprenticeship working for his brother on the Coast, "Doc" Giannini went to New York and founded the East River National Bank in 1919. To build his business, he gambled on the film industry by offering loans to money-hungry producers.

In 1931, Giannini's bank was absorbed by Manhattan's National City Bank and he returned to brother Amadeo's Bank of America. His faith in the industry never wavered. "In the three weeks before I left the bank to head UA," he remarked, "I loaned approximately $10,000,000 to the motion picture industry."[13]

Giannini was more than a money man; as a counselor, he was credited with settling more cinema wrangles than the law courts of California. After joining UA, he said in this regard, "[The] only difference in my new position is that I am getting paid for what I used to do for nothing."[14]

8

The Goldwyn Battles
[1936-1941]

In one of his first public statements Giannini said,

> The greatest need of the motion picture industry at the present time is peace with itself—a peace which will wipe out personal enmities and personal animosities and permit cooperation which will enable the industry to progress as a whole. . . . It is unfortunate to see that personal differences should cause the trouble they do in this industry. There are many deals held up and never completed because one individual may not like another individual, no matter what the result may be. In the United Artists Corp. we shall never permit personal differences, either inside or outside the organization, to interfere with our work.[1]

Giannini was either deluding himself about UA or engaging in wishful thinking. The company was about to come apart at the seams and he knew it, or at least he should have if he understood the significance of the stockholders' actions when they elected him president. The bylaws were amended to reflect a new balance of power in the company. With Schenck gone, Fairbanks in retirement, Pickford once again inactive after a brief team-up with Lasky, and Chaplin as unreliable as ever, Goldwyn became a force to be reckoned with. His distribution contract had expired as had all the contracts with the owners. When the time came to draw up new ones, Goldwyn seized the opportunity to announce that he would discontinue releasing through UA unless the company granted him certain concessions. In essence, he demanded veto power. Since his pictures generated most of the revenue, he wanted the assurance that his partners could not radically alter the course of the company without his consent. This could be avoided, he suggested, simply by formalizing the concept of the unanimous vote.

It was now placed in writing that the unanimous approval of the stockholders would be required to elect officers, to engage all personnel, and to acquire product. Goldwyn also demanded unanimous consent for stock transactions either among the owners or involving the sale of treasury

Douglas Fairbanks, Alexander Korda, Mary Pickford, Murray Silverstone,
Charles Chaplin, A. H. Giannini, and Samuel Goldwyn

stock to bring in a new partner. On these matters, his partners acquiesced as well.

These amendments had the effect of divesting management of most of its power. But still Goldwyn was not content. As he had little faith in Giannini's sales ability, a provision had to be placed in the bylaws stipulating that "no person, other than Dr. A. H. Giannini or M. Silverstone, shall at any time be elected President or Chairman of the Board . . . unless such election of such person be first approved by the unanimous vote of all the shareholders." Silverstone, who had been setting sales records in Great Britain, was Goldwyn's choice for the presidency. The others preferred Giannini, so as a compromise they agreed to make Silverstone the prime candidate for the job should Giannini resign or, for that matter, be eased out. These were the concessions that Goldwyn wrung from his partners. He would have preferred to take over the company completely, of course, but the time was not yet ripe for such a move.

GOLDWYN'S ATTEMPTS TO BUY UA

Giannini was able to keep peace for nearly a year, something of an achievement considering the volatile temperaments of the owners. But inevitably they reached the flash point. At an unusually heated directors' meeting in May, 1937, Goldwyn cried out that Pickford, Fairbanks, and Chaplin were contributing nothing to the company and should have the decency to sell out. His offer to buy each of their interests for $500,000 was met with a flat rejection. The idea was intriguing, though. Miss Pickford, Fairbanks, and Chaplin excused themselves from the room and, after a short conference, returned to tell Goldwyn that they would sell out, but the price would be $2 million apiece. Turning to Korda, Goldwyn asked if he wanted to participate. Korda nodded and the two were granted an option giving them until December 21 to come up with the money.

Korda's Dissatisfaction with UA

By now, UA's relations with Alexander Korda had deteriorated. Of the ten pictures Korda delivered to the company after *Henry VIII*, only one, René Clair's *The Ghost Goes West*, could be considered a success. In his first year as a UA partner he lost $200,000 on the distribution of his films. The home office had promised better results and even chided its sales force by saying, "We in the Domestic Department have not made the contribution we should. There is a *tremendously wide difference between the contracts taken* and the play-off on London Films as against the pictures of our American producers. From now on I must inform you that this condition has got to be remedied. All alibis of salesmen that the exhibitor will not contract in advance for a London Films production but will book them as and when they come along, will not be tolerated."[2]

But the condition was not remedied. Returns on his 1936-1937 product were even more disappointing. For example, his two H. G. Wells fantasies, *Things to Come* and *The Man Who Could Work Miracles,* which cost £350,000, failed completely. Korda blamed United Artists and asked to be released from his distribution contract. In a cable sent from England he said:

> Recent happenings convinced me that it is contrary to vital interests of my company to be distributed in future by United Artists. When our basic agreement was made, I was led to believe by other partners . . . that my company's and my own position in British market would be recognised and that United Artists would regard us as mainstay of their British interests. . . . Also basis of our agreement was equal duties and rights for every stockholder which obviously is not case in practice, as production burden is absolutely unequally divided. Other stockholders not even giving a fair hearing to our demands as regards British market.[3]

In the response, the board stated that United Artists "has not in any particular breached the terms of intent of its contract with Mr. Korda and London Film Productions Limited, and that this corporation expects Mr. Korda and London Film Productions Limited to fulfill and perform their contract with this corporation in every particular."[4]

In truth, United Artists found it difficult to market British pictures. Two Elizabeth Bergner productions, *Dreaming Lips* and *Love from a Stranger*, for example, were refused by exhibitors, who claimed that they were unfit to be shown. Charging poor distribution of his four pictures, Victor Saville walked out on his contract with the company. United Artists gave him a release because he threatened to sue for damages. But Korda was too important to lose so easily.

London Films by 1937 had become the leading motion-picture company in Great Britain. It had the backing of the mighty Prudential Assurance Co. and two of the strongest banks in the country, Midlands and Lloyds. To meet its UA commitment, London Films went public in 1934, its goal being to raise the cost of financing an expanded production program, a new studio, and the development of a new color process. The company had an authorized capital of £428,799 in 6 per cent preferred stock and nearly two million shares of one-shilling common. Prudential became the largest shareholder with 250,000 shares of the preferred and 25,000 of the common.

In 1935, construction of Denham Studios began. Prudential provided additional support in the form of a £700,000 mortgage. When Denham was completed in May, 1936, London Films had the most up-to-date and best-equipped studio in Europe. Spread out on 165 acres were seven stages, two theaters, dressing rooms, machine shops, a large property building, eighteen cutting rooms, and luxurious administrative offices. In the following year, Denham Laboratories Ltd. was registered with an authorized capital of £100,000, with most of the money again coming from Prudential.

After scrutinizing the financial condition of Korda's burgeoning film empire in 1937, F. M. Guedalla filed this lengthy report at the home office:

> The losses are shewn at £330,842. Murray Silverstone believes that the figure today would be the best part of £1,000,000. That may be an exaggeration but the Prudential people say they have advanced about £2,000,000 and that they are advancing on payroll about £20,000 a week. Everybody who presses gets his money; people who behave in a gentle fashion fail to get their money.
>
> Korda keeps on grumbling about his having to work against such dead losses, but whose fault is it, if it is not his own? He gets a substantial salary which, I suppose, is paid to him week by week, but I know nothing about his own arrangements. . . .

He enters into huge commitments which his colleagues only learn gradually months afterwards and there is no choice but to implement them. If he breaks a contract he does not let them know about it until long afterwards, and the company has to wriggle out of these obligations as best it can. . . .

I have often said to him he signs anybody up on any kind of terms, and then so often absolutely disregards the written contract and, in most cases, he pulls it off because artistes are easy going souls and not only that, they are so desirous of playing the part in the film that has been suggested, they become of the most forgiving character. . . .

However, reverting to the Balance Sheets I should think Korda and L. F. P. must be in a terrible way, but inasmuch as the Prudential are owed mortgages for £1,100,000 and are stated to have another £900,000 invested in the business . . . I have thought and still think that the Prudential are bound to see Korda through his troubles.

On the other hand, they are getting very sick of paying out month after month. . . . If they decide to stop financing L. F. P., then the whole show blows up immediately. . . .

Korda day after day is closeted with the Prudential people. Silverstone says if only he would devote himself to producing and directing pictures, not only would he make a fortune for himself, but would make a fortune for the company. His mind is mixed up with various promoting and financial problems such as studios, printing, laboratories. Any ordinary person would be worried to death over that but I do not think it is his nature to worry unduly about the company's indebtedness.

He talks grandiloquently about his being a stockholder, as well as a director, of United Artists. . . . I think he really does look upon himself as having paid for his stock and delivered those twenty pictures. . . .

It is his own folly and the way he occupies his time that causes all his films to be so expensive. In the end they are made with undue rush. Also, I am sorry to say, owing to the way the whole studio is run, they are not made with that snappy perfection which characterizes the great Hollywood films. Many of Korda's great films are just a string of sequences. . . .

In his heart of hearts I think he curses everybody in connection with United Artists. Now and then if he has a favour to seek he seeks that favour with a particular person and blames everyone else. The one person who is never at fault is Korda himself!!![5]

Attempts by Goldwyn and Korda to Raise the Money

Irrespective of who was at fault, Korda and Goldwyn now had the opportunity to run things their own way. The others hoped that they could. Concerning Fairbanks in particular, Clarence Ericksen, his business manager, said, "Now all they have to do is raise the money and pay it to us, and let's all *hold the thought* that they will be able to do so. If the deal can be concluded, I feel it is the greatest break Douglas has had in years. . . . Under the present income tax laws, Douglas can realize a net of about $1,450,000.00 after paying income taxes."[6]

To raise the $6 million, Goldwyn and Korda reportedly approached Lehman Brothers and Kuhn, Loeb & Co. in this country and the Rothschilds and Prudential in England. Rumor had it that they also talked to Paramount and RKO about the possibility of merger. At most they could raise $4 million, so they had to propose that Chaplin take $2 million and Miss Pickford and Fairbanks each $1 million in cash and $1 million in preferred stock of the reorganized company. Ericksen hoped that, instead, Chaplin would take his proportionate share of preferred stock, so that each of the three would receive $1.3 million in cash and $700,000 in preferred stock. "I was unable to personally contact Mr. Chaplin," he told Dennis O'Brien, "but did contact Mr. Reeves and explained the situation to him and requested that he make an appointment for me with Mr. Chaplin. He came back with the reply that Mr. Chaplin would not accept anything other than two million in cash, and furthermore that he would not discuss the matter with anyone."[7] Pickford and Fairbanks did not want stock either, but they were willing to accept $250,000 less in cash.

This concession was not good enough. Goldwyn and Korda would have to try again. They met the deadline by coming up with a rather grandiose proposal: A Delaware holding company would be formed to which Goldwyn and Korda would transfer their UA stock. Then a group of British bankers headed by Cazenove, Ackroyds, and Greenwood would lend UAC, Ltd., $6 million with the understanding that this money would be loaned in turn to the holding company for the stock purchase.

Preposterous, said Guedalla; Goldwyn and Korda were not planning to contribute or risk a single cent of their own money. Neil McCarthy claimed that, should the deal go through, UA would be subject to attack by creditors upon the grounds that the company was attempting to liquidate. To Miss Pickford and Fairbanks he said, "The jeopardy to your personal reputations would be the possible charge that the transaction was illegal and fraudulent and the charge against you that you had participated in the fraud. The danger to your financial situation is that if the court should hold that the transaction was illegal, you would not have the money which you received to pay the judgment it would render against you."[8]

Goldwyn Outvoted by the Board

So much for this scheme. Goldwyn and Korda wanted the option extended, but their partners absolutely refused to consider the matter. Fairbanks said, "We should never have given lengthy option and exposed

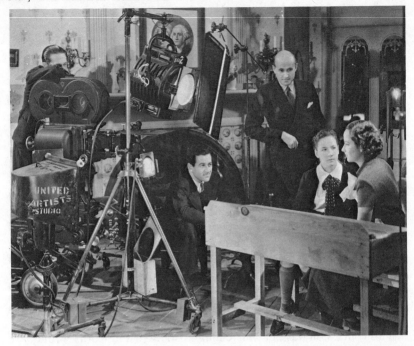

William Wyler, Samuel Goldwyn, Bonita Granville, and Merle Oberon
on the set of Goldwyn's *These Three* (1936)

ourselves and United to this publicity."[9] Nonetheless, the status quo could
not continue. London Films was in desperate straits, said Korda. If he
could not get a release from his distribution contract, UA should at least
permit him to make quota pictures for other producers. Ervin Lever of
Prudential described the situation this way:

> The problem of London Films is a relatively simple one, namely, that in view
> of the depressed conditions of film production in England the Company, as an
> owner of studios, has much more space available than it can possibly fill with its
> own productions. . . . The only immediate practical solution, therefore, is for the
> company to be allowed to collaborate with other production companies. . . . If
> there is an unwillingness on the part of the other share-holders of United Artists
> to deal with the matter on these common sense lines, the only alternative to the
> Prudential, as principal creditor of London Films, is to put the company into
> liquidation and to make arrangements for the occupation of the studios with
> some entirely fresh group.[10]

The Pickford-Fairbanks-Chaplin faction gave its approval, but Goldwyn
thundered no.

Goldwyn thereupon proposed that management be placed in the hands
of a committee consisting of himself, Giannini, and Silverstone. This

measure too was voted down. Neil McCarthy, who represented Mary Pickford at the meeting, led the opposition, insisting that he "would not be a party to any agreement predicated upon such a committee or upon any plan that had as part of it that Sam should have any authority over the distribution of pictures other than his rights as a director of the corporation. . . . If Sam is a part of the management . . . it will deter outside producers from distributing through United Artists."[11]

The Jock Whitney-Goldwyn Offer

Before anything was done about reorganizing, Pickford, Fairbanks, and Chaplin stopped to entertain another offer to purchase their stock. This one came from Jock Whitney who, at the instigation of Sam Goldwyn, offered each of them $750,000 in cash and $750,000 in preferred stock. McCarthy thought it unwise to accept preferred stock because the new management would be more interested in selling pictures at the lowest possible distribution rate than in earning profits for the company. In his opinion, "Sam is trying to muddle the situation as much as possible in an endeavor to worry Mary, Douglas, and Charlie and try to make them believe the company is in distress. If they are not stampeded, I believe they will be able to get more production, and the company go on with or without Sam, although, of course, as a producer he is a valuable asset."[12]

Chaplin's reaction to the proposition was that he did not want to talk about it. He had gone to Carmel for rest, and his doctor informed Whitney that he could not be bothered with business affairs. From this it was surmised that Chaplin wanted $2 million in cash or nothing. As for Pickford and Fairbanks, they countered by suggesting $1 million in cash and $750,000 in stock.

As in the previous deal, Whitney and Goldwyn were not planning to put up any of their own money to purchase the stock. It would come from England, where Oscar Deutsch assured them underwriting was available. Korda was not made a party to this deal. Whether he planned to leave the company or whether Goldwyn and Whitney were contemplating forcing him out is not known. But when Deutsch made the rounds at the banks, he discovered that "Prudential is seemingly so powerful that no group would furnish money if Prudential was not in accord, and evidently Prudential will not be in accord unless Korda is taken care of."[13]

Even with Korda in, the bankers were not interested in financing the takeover. According to Goldwyn, they were dissatisfied with UA's management, its meager source of product, and the divided purposes of the owners. Money would be forthcoming only if UA was to be rehabilitated and put on a sound operating basis, which Goldwyn claimed could be accomplished only by getting rid of Giannini and putting Silverstone in his place.

At this point, Whitney decided to pull out of the deal. Discord had developed between his family and Selznick and his relatives wanted to liquidate their investment in Selznick International.

GOLDWYN'S MANEUVERS FOR CONTROL

Replacement of Giannini with Murray Silverstone

Since Goldwyn could not find the means to buy out his partners, he pushed for a management shakeup. At a special meeting of the stockholders in March, 1938, he insisted that Silverstone be placed in charge of distribution. Among other things, Goldwyn said that he expected Silverstone to clean out all the dead wood in the sales force. It was pointed out that in so doing, UA would be breaching George Schaefer's contract in which he was described as general manager in charge of domestic distribution, to say nothing of the violation to Giannini's. He was also reminded that in 1937, United Artists, as a result of a magnificent sales job, racked up the largest gross in its history. But arguments of this nature would not sway Goldwyn. So rather than acting on the issue, his partners appointed a committee consisting of Goldwyn, Korda, and Fairbanks to investigate matters. In closing the meeting, Giannini remarked that he would probably want to resign if Silverstone were brought over, and he had a hunch that Schaefer would want to do the same.

There were at least two explanations of why Goldwyn was pushing Silverstone. One was given by Joe Schenck in a letter to Mary Pickford:

You may be somewhat surprised and I hope not suspicious why I am taking an interest in straightening out the situation in United Artists. I will try to give you the true reason for it.

It seems to me quite impossible for any man to have been connected with a company for ten years . . . and then entirely lose interest in it—and that is just the way I feel. I have always maintained that United Artists has a distinct position in the picture business and a distinct reason for existence and success. If United Artists ever becomes a failure, it can only be due to mismanagement brought about by lack of cooperation.

Sam came to see me the same as you did, and the same as Douglas did, and told me about the conditions existing. I could readily see his position. A producer who spends between eight and nine million dollars a year has a perfect right and good reason to be apprehensive if he thinks the company, through which he distributes, is not properly managed. . . . Please do not for one minute think that I am in any way alluding to Dr. Giannini not being a capable head of the company. That is not the case, but Dr. Giannini does not concern himself intimately enough with the distributing end of the business as it cannot be done from Hollywood.

In my opinion, knowing United Artists as well as I do and knowing Sam as I do, I am convinced that he has no ulterior motive in what he wants to bring about. . . .

I think you, Sam and Douglas . . . should pull together. The reason I don't mention Charlie is not because I disregard him but simply because I know Charlie and I know how little interest he takes in the management of the company. Furthermore, I know how bitter Charlie can get to be and he wouldn't hesitate to destroy the company rather than do something constructive that may be of benefit to Sam, whom at the present time he despises—but I am sure you will not prove yourself faithless to Charlie if you do something that will redound in a distinct benefit to him. It is not a difficult matter to destroy a good business and unless you get together and pull together, that is what you are going to accomplish.[14]

Another point of view was presented by Neil McCarthy, who told Fairbanks:

The result of putting Silverstone in New York . . . would indicate that Sam is in charge of the distribution of the company's pictures, whether or not he says that is true; and whether or not Sam states he would not want any man to favor his pictures over those of another, the men themselves are human beings and would insist upon so doing, and other pictures distributed through the company would be affected adversely.

The greatest strength of United Artists has always been that it had no pictures of its own and that no one whose pictures were being distributed through the company was in a position to so influence the selling organization that [that] person's pictures would be given preference over those of any others. . . .

All of this reasoning is predicated upon the assumption that Silverstone will be subservient to Sam and I am confident that this will be the fact. . . . If Sam gets control of this company, he will use it for his own personal selfish interests, regardless of the returns to the company. . . . He resents the fact that you and Mary and Charlie receive earnings from the distribution of his pictures and you will find, if you permit him to get in charge of the company, that he will work unceasingly to reduce the amount United Artists shall retain and increase the amount he gets from his product.[15]

Although Goldwyn's partners did not disagree in substance with this evaluation, they acceded to his plans for the company reorganization. The committee brought in the following recommendations, all of which were put into effect: (1) that the United Artists offices in Los Angeles were to be closed and all activities transferred to the home office; (2) that Giannini's contract be cancelled; (3) that Murray Silverstone be engaged as general manager of the entire company; (4) that the distribution fee in England and Canada be reduced from 30 per cent to

25 per cent; (5) that the "most favored nation" clause be eliminated from all distribution contracts to allow the company to distribute local product in England, France, Argentina, and elsewhere, at much lower rates than those given to UA producers; and (6) that a fund be established to allow producers to share in company profits.

Giannini was removed in an awkward manner. After the stockholders decided on Silverstone's responsibilities, they asked Giannini to negotiate the employment contract, which posed a problem. As he wrote to Dennis O'Brien, "Dear Captain, Have just read minutes of Board meeting of April 28th. In view of provisions of my contract assume as Chief Executive I am to negotiate with Silverstone along general lines set forth in minutes. Please advise me however as counsel for corporation how I can negotiate a contract with Silverstone in accordance with resolutions passed without violating the provisions of my contract?"[16] Actually, there was no way for him to do so and Giannini resigned, but not until he exacted a $168,000 settlement from the company. "The doctor was very much up-set, and justly so, over the way the entire matter was handled, and he has made it difficult," reported Clarence Ericksen. "While he is getting a very large settlement and perhaps more than he is entitled to, we have to keep in mind the necessity of making a settlement that would make him happy, and not do anything that would interfere with the present relations with the Bank of America. While the Doctor is not actively engaged at the bank, he is the brother of the head of the bank and a member of the advisory board, and if he desired could naturally make it very difficult in obtaining loans for United producers, of which, you know, there are many."[17]

Although Schaefer was offered a new three-year contract to work under Silverstone as head of domestic distribution, he too resigned. In October, he became the new president of RKO.

The Silverstone Plan

Silverstone, who came in on a five-year contract, had the task of working out the details of the profit-sharing plan for the producers. He proposed that at the end of each year, beginning in 1938, the company would pay the first $250,000 of profits in dividends; the next $250,000 would go into a fund to be allocated to the producers as bonuses; anything over that amount would be split fifty-fifty between the stockholders and the producers' fund.

Money from the producers' fund was to be allocated on a sliding-scale basis in the form of rebates to producers whose pictures grossed over $750,000 in the domestic market. If a picture grossed between $750,000 and $1 million, the company would give the producer 2 per cent of everything over $750,000; if the gross was between $1 million and $1.25 million, the rebate would be 3 per cent of everything over $1 million, and so on up to 10 per cent of everything over $1.75 million. The plan also applied to England, where the rebate percentages were to be the same but the scale would start at $300,000 and end at anything over $700,000. As an inducement to producers whose output was large but whose pictures did only moderately well, United Artists would also pay bonuses on the total grosses of a producer's annual output in both the domestic and foreign markets.

This plan, which came to be called the Silverstone Plan, was intended to benefit not only Goldwyn and Korda but also UA's non-stockholder producers as well, such as Selznick, Small, Wanger, and Roach. At the same time, Silverstone hoped that this system of rebates would attract other independents to the company.

To make this profit-sharing scheme palatable to the so-called inactive stockholders, the committee recommended that the board declare a $500,000 dividend for 1938. The motion for the dividend carried unanimously, but that did not insure acceptance of the plan. Chaplin opposed it and threatened to take legal action if it were put into effect. Ericksen described for Dennis O'Brien the attempts to get Chaplin to change his position:

> Many efforts were made to get in communication with Chaplin or to arrange for a conference with him. Al Reeves informed me that Chaplin was living at the Montiegle residence at Carmel, and gave me the telephone number which was "Carmel 1436." I endeavored to get in touch with Chaplin to make an appointment for Douglas to go up there and discuss all these matters with him; however, I only got as far as having a Japanese servant answer the 'phone, with the statement that Chaplin had gone away—he didn't know where—and didn't know when he would return. This information was given after telling the servant that I was talking for Mr. Fairbanks and he asked me to hold the 'phone presumably while he talked to Chaplin.
>
> I also know that Miss Pickford as also Mr. Goldwyn made many efforts to get in communication with him. . . .
>
> I also understand that Miss Pickford wrote Chaplin a letter, either from here, London or New York.
>
> Murray Silverstone tried to make an appointment to see Chaplin through Al Reeves, but was unsuccessful. . . .
>
> I further understand that Loyd [Wright, Chaplin's attorney] endeavored to arrange for a conference . . . but was unsuccessful, but that later he did finally talk to Chaplin on the 'phone with the result that Chaplin said that he was in favor of doing something along these lines but that "we had gone about the whole matter in the wrong way."[18]

It took many more letters, telephone calls, and a lot of explaining before Chaplin felt that he could live with the Silverstone Plan. He acquiesced finally in time for the stockholders' meeting in January, 1939, and the plan was formally approved.

The Korda Crisis

One would think that by now the company was well on its way to solving Korda's problems and assuaging Goldwyn's grievances. Not true. The UA reorganization came too late to rescue Korda. At the end of 1938, Prudential decided to take Denham out from Korda's control, judging that he could not do justice to both his production activities and the studio. Paul Tabori, sympathizing with Korda, described what happened:

> The crisis did not rise to any violent climax; yet Korda came to another parting of the ways. The liabilities of London Films had reached about £1,000,000. The Prudential was both chief shareholder and chief creditor. Korda carried on his gallant battle and managed again and again to extract new support from his backers. But in the end he was beaten. He had to give up the great Denham studios he had built himself—which, in three brief years, had created a tradition of great names and films. To the Prudential it seemed that the studios were the only tangible assets of London Films worth taking. A highly complicated deal was arranged between J. Arthur Rank, Richard Norton, C. M. Woolf, Korda and the insurance company, and a new company, D. & P. Studios Ltd., was created which took both Pinewood and Denham into its possession.[19]

Actually, Korda had to relinquish control in London Films as well, but Prudential by no means abandoned him. Korda was given $1.8 million to form a new production company called Alexander Korda Film Productions, Ltd. In addition, Prudential turned over to him half of its interest in the United Artists stock along with voting rights to the full unit. However, there remained on the stock an unpaid balance of $550,000, which Korda was personally liable for.

Goldwyn too should have been pleased with the reorganization. Giannini was out, his man Silverstone in, and he was about to receive what amounted to a gift of $170,000 in rebates from the producers' fund. But Goldwyn's relations with the company were not destined to be tranquil. An apparent misunderstanding shattered forever all hopes of accommodation. At the stockholders' meeting in June, 1938, Korda requested the distribution fee for his British quota pictures be set at 17½ per cent. Goldwyn replied that UA could not offer him anything less than 20 per cent, because if Korda received the lower rate, he could afford to sign up the best stars and directors in England and make it impossible for UA to negotiate with other successful British producers. The other members of the board took Goldwyn's position. Later on, however, Goldwyn got the idea that Miss Pickford was working secretly to get Korda the favored terms. His reaction was explosive. Clarence Ericksen, the first to feel the shock waves, described what happened:

> Sam telephoned me at my home about 8:30 or 9 o'clock after the night of the meeting. . . . He was like a maniac and said he would never trust Miss Pickford again and that you had "double crossed" him, and in short, that he was now through trying to reorganize United and get it running in a harmonious manner and was going to turn the entire situation over to his attorneys and get what was coming to him by way of rebates because of the favored nation clause in his distribution contract, because Korda had been given a 17½% distribution charge on certain of his pictures in England. I told him that I felt when he was acquainted with all of the facts that he would find that there was no intent not to go ahead with the producers' rebate plan and also the reorganization, and that if he would just set steady and wait until you returned that everything would be adjusted on a fair basis.[20]

GOLDWYN'S ACRIMONIOUS BREAK WITH UA

Matters evidently were not adjusted to Goldwyn's satisfaction, because at the opening of the stockholders' meeting in January, 1939, Goldwyn insisted that Pickford, Fairbanks, Chaplin, and Korda execute a voting-trust agreement transferring to Goldwyn the voting rights in the company and authorizing him to elect all of the directors on the board. Otherwise, he intended to vote against everything proposed by the other stockholders. The ultimatum was ridiculous and Goldwyn was told so in no uncertain terms. Thereupon Goldwyn did what he promised to do. When it came time to formally adopt the Silverstone Plan, which he helped write, his was the lone dissenting vote. Nonetheless the motion passed. Goldwyn refused to execute the agreement qualifying him to accept rebates. He also voted against an arrangement to allow Korda to substitute pictures to be made by his new company for those still due from London Films and voted against Korda and Fairbanks' participating in the benefits of the Silverstone Plan. Like Korda, Fairbanks was planning to start a new production company. Goldwyn thought that their pictures would not be good enough to give them the privilege of sharing in the profits. On these motions too, Goldwyn was overridden.

His next move was to go to court seeking a declaratory judgment regarding his right to end his distribution contract with United Artists. The case began on March 1, 1939, in the New York Supreme Court. For technical reasons, it was transferred to the U.S. District Court for the Southern District of New York on March 16. But since the court's calendar was over a year behind schedule, it thus ended up in the Federal

Laurence Olivier and Merle Oberon in Goldwyn's *Wuthering Heights* (1939)

Court, District of Delaware, on April 11. Goldwyn claimed that UA breached his contract, which stated that the contracts of the other owners could not be amended without his consent, by (1) authorizing Korda and Fairbanks to form new production corporations; (2) permitting the new companies to participate in the Silverstone Plan; (3) accepting pictures from Alexander Korda Film Productions, Ltd., and (4) allowing Korda to distribute pictures in Nationalist Spain.

To the press, Charles Schwartz, the counsel for UA, likened Goldwyn to a sulking "schoolboy who had been chastised and who avenges himself by making faces."[21] Max Steuer said on Goldwyn's behalf that he wanted out because UA "departed 'from the high plane on which it was organized,' that is, to distribute pictures made by companies of the first magnitude, or by artists of the first rank."[22] This settlement brought a rebuttal from Schwartz, of course, who said that Goldwyn "is in error and that unequivocally, pictures which David O. Selznick, Charles Chaplin, Alexander Korda and others will produce will be of a quality and standard second to none, 'not even second to Goldwyn.'"[23] In this battle of mutual harassment, Goldwyn emerged the victor, as this incident testifies:

> When the telephone operators at the United Artists studios arrived for work the other morning they were under instructions to answer their boards with "Samuel Goldwyn Studios" instead of "United Artists," as they had done for thirteen years. . . . An hour later workmen appeared outside the main entrance, where they took down the worn brass plate that bore the name of United Artists and replaced it with one bearing the name of the man who made "Cowboy and the Lady." These two physical acts were a part of the Goldwyn campaign to lick his partners . . . in his bitter fight for control of the concern.[24]

In the courts, however, that battle had yet to be fought, so Goldwyn took it upon himself to unilaterally terminate the distribution contract. But the District Court took exception to Goldwyn's decision by dismissing the suit on the grounds that he failed to name Alexander Korda and Douglas Fairbanks as co-defendants. Involving Fairbanks in the case would now be impossible, however, because he had died in his sleep in December, 1939.

Undaunted by the court decision, Goldwyn boldly announced that he was going to distribute his newest picture, *The Westerner,* through Warner Brothers. UA had yet to take Goldwyn's behavior seriously. Its lawyers merely used an array of tactics and maneuvers to delay the case and postpone the arguing of issues. But now that Goldwyn decided to take business away from the company, the game changed. UA took the offensive by informing Warner to prepare for a lawsuit if it accepted *The Westerner.* Schwartz declared that he "could not comprehend how

Warners would be a party to the breaking of a contract as that corporation always has insisted on sacredness of contracts, as in the instance of Bette Davis and James Cagney who endeavored to walk out on them."[25]

Warner backed off after reexamining Goldwyn's UA distribution contract. Goldwyn then approached Paramount, which also rejected the picture, stating that it did not see why "the company should be used as an 'experimental guinea pig' for Goldwyn to try to bring to an issue a contemplated walkout from UA obligations."[26]

Goldwyn therefore had no choice but to give *The Westerner* to UA. It had a price tag of $1 million, and because the delay in its distribution was proving costly, Goldwyn sued the company for damages. His list of grievances submitted to the New York federal court in February, 1940, had grown to thirty-seven printed pages plus exhibits. Among them were:

1. The defendants maliciously attempted to drive him out of business.
2. The defendants failed to secure as large a gross as possible on the distribution of Goldwyn's pictures.
3. The defendants used Goldwyn's pictures to influence the selling of other producers' pictures.
4. The defendants offered inducements to exhibitors not to take Goldwyn's pictures.
5. At the convention in 1939 the defendants prevented Goldwyn from securing the good will of UA's salesmen.
6. The defendants enticed members of Goldwyn's staff to leave his employ.
7. The defendants withheld moneys due to Goldwyn.
8. The defendants released misleading statements to the press intimating that Goldwyn was a contract-breaker.[27]

In addition to the claim for damages, Goldwyn demanded $54,559 in rebates, which he said was due him for 1938 from the Silverstone Plan. UA had earlier sent him a check for this amount even though Goldwyn did not waive the "most favored nation" clause, required of him to qualify for benefits. But Goldwyn refused to accept the check because UA had failed to include interest!

Once again, UA used tactics to prolong the case. For example, it moved that Goldwyn submit a bill of particulars and requested a separate statement of causes. Korda moved to dismiss the complaint against him on the ground that no cause was alleged against him and that no relief was demanded from him. All the while, UA's lawyers were relishing the opportunity to bring Goldwyn up for examination. As Ed Raftery wrote to Charles Schwartz,

> We could plead the action to show the entrance of Samuel Goldwyn into United Artists, his condition at the time of the entrance into the company, his purchase

of stock without ever paying a nickel therefor, the terrific distribution that he has received, his fight with Joe Schenck and the elimination of Mr. Schenck from the company, which meant the elimination of Darryl Zanuck and the amalgamation of Twentieth Century and Fox Films, his efforts to buy the stock of Miss Pickford, Mr. Fairbanks and Mr. Chaplin, the collapse of the deal, the trip to England, and how he secured reduced distribution, the Producers' Fund, which in reality meant the giving up of over 50% of the company by the so-called non-producing stockholders, the various moves made last Fall to eliminate Schwartz and O'Brien, et al., the meetings in January and the demands for the voting trust, his failure to secure a voting trust, followed by the retention of Mr. Steuer and this series of actions, notices, publicity, etc., all with a view to harass the company.[28]

On August 6, 1940, the court dismissed the complaint against Korda and granted UA's motion for a bill of particulars. In the meantime, Goldwyn had appealed the decision of the Delaware action. The appellate court reversed the lower court's decision on July 3, 1940, and ordered the suit reinstated. In the retrial, UA's lawyers argued that a declaratory judgment was no longer required because Goldwyn had unilaterally terminated his contract on December 18. The defendants, as a result, asked for a dismissal of the Delaware action, which was granted on July 29, 1940.

Shortly thereafter, Max Steuer died. The new attorney on the New York case filed an amended complaint, which gave the defense an opportunity to ask for an extension, which was duly granted. On the last day of the extension, UA moved to dismiss the amended complaint, which motion was not granted.

The question now became which side had the most staying power because it was evident that the case could be prolonged indefinitely. But Mary Pickford, for one, had had enough. The two years of harassment, threats, and name calling had proven wearisome. A settlement was reached on March 11, 1941. Goldwyn sold his stock to the company for $300,000 and his distribution contract was cancelled. An additional $200,000 was paid him from monies due under the Silverstone Plan. All claims of both parties were thereupon dropped.

GOLDWYN'S CONTRIBUTION

Goldwyn delivered fifty motion pictures in his fourteen-year association with United Artists. This tally approached the total for the various Schenck production ventures and was thirteen more than the combined Pickford-Fairbanks-Chaplin output. The potentially disastrous product gap created by Schenck's departure from the company was filled by the prodigious efforts of Sam Goldwyn, who came through with twenty-one pictures from 1935 to 1940. Among them were *Dodsworth, These Three, Dead End, Woman Chases Man,* and *Wuthering Heights.* Despite his enormous contribution, his UA partners refused to give him influence commensurate with his productivity.

After he left, and with business declining as a result of the war in Europe, United Artists would face another product shortage, one that was not to be overcome without sacrificing the quality of films UA distributed and, as a result, the reputation of the company.

9 | *Facing the War*
[1941]

Although the fight with Sam Goldwyn rivaled, in entertainment value, any films that United Artists had in release, thoughtful observers of the industry were not amused. *Variety,* for example, devoted an editorial to the subject:

> UA for more than 20 years has occupied a unique and highly important place in the film business.
>
> The principles on which it was formed to provide expert and showmanly handling of individual pictures, in contrast to program selling by its major competitors, have been repeatedly justified by the encouragement it has given to independent production. . . .
>
> United Artists provides an efficient and one of the few channels for film distribution to meet the requirements of the showman-entrepreneur—the producer, actor or director who is willing (and able) to match his wits and purse against the strongly entrenched major companies with their almost unlimited studio resources, their domestic and foreign exchanges, and their affiliated theatre circuits.
>
> At first glance the odds for success would appear against the individual and in favor of the integrated operations. It is a David versus Goliath struggle, and the UA producers have been tossing the pebbles with marked success for a score of years. . . .
>
> United Artists long ago justified its place in the film industry as a dominant influence for the production of better pictures. The organization always has had to do things the hard way—usually in direct challenge to routine. It has functioned best when the resistance has been strongest.
>
> There is no reason to believe that there will not be found the right solution to the current internal difficulties. [1]

During the name-calling, the bickering, and the lawsuits of the post-Schenck period, UA sustained its reputation with such hits as Chaplin's *Modern Times* (1936) and *The Great Dictator* (1941); Goldwyn's *Dodsworth* (1936), *Dead End* (1937), *Wuthering Heights* (1939), and *The Westerner* (1940); Selznick's *A Star Is Born* (1937) and

[161]

Rebecca (1940); Wanger's *Stagecoach* (1939) and *The Long Voyage Home* (1940); Hal Roach's *Of Mice and Men* (1940); and Korda's *The Thief of Bagdad* (1940).

Hal Roach became a UA producer in 1938. Then at the peak of his productivity, he delivered in quick succession a series of twelve features, with "a new slickness and high glossy polish," in the words of William K. Everson.[2] In addition to the Steinbeck movie, these included *Captain Fury, A Chump at Oxford, One Million B.C.,* and *Road Show.* Edward Small returned to UA the same year. In the next three seasons he contributed seven pictures, among them *The Man in the Iron Mask, My Son, My Son,* and *The Son of Monte Cristo.* Veterans Sol Lesser and Richard Rowland also signed contracts with UA, as did newcomer David Loew, among others.

Burgess Meredith and Lon Chaney, Jr., in Roach's *Of Mice and Men* (1940)

With this lineup, UA should have been able to maintain its enviable status as the Tiffany's of the industry. After 1941, however, it began to decline in both prestige and viability. An important factor, to be sure, was World War II, its effects on foreign markets and on the company's production units at home, which is the subject of the first section of this chapter; another, equally significant, factor was the bizarre behavior of the owners, which not only demeaned the principles on which the company was based but also prevented it from attracting a steady flow of quality product on a par with Goldwyn's. The concluding section describes the entry of David O. Selznick into United Artists as a partner to replace Goldwyn. The unhappy consequences of this action are discussed later.

CHAPLIN'S *THE GREAT DICTATOR*

As a prelude to the consideration of the war, it is only fitting to pay homage to Chaplin's brilliant antifascist film, *The Great Dictator*. Lewis Jacobs had characterized its achievement as "a trenchant and grandiloquent satire—daring to lampoon dictatorship, tyranny and

Chaplin's *The Great Dictator* (1941)

oppression, and to strike a blow at Hitler's image at the very height of his seeming invincibility. At the same time, it was also a tragicomic fantasy of man's inhumanity to man, with a passionate plea for the return of world sanity and an end to the barriers to universal peace."[3] Chaplin spoke on the screen for the first time in this picture and in two voices—as the little barber, in meek monosyllables, and as the dictator, "in fake Teutonic gutturals and double talk, in perfect mimicry of Hitler's mannerisms, poses, gestures, and choleric rantings."[4]

Chaplin began the picture early in January, 1939. Halfway through production, Britain declared war, and work on the film was halted. As Chaplin said in his autobiography, "I began receiving alarming messages from United Artists. They had been advised by the Hays Office that I would run into censorship trouble. . . . But I was determined to go ahead, for Hitler must be laughed at."[5] He went on to remark that had he known of the actual horrors of the German concentration camps, he could not have made the picture.

After pouring over $2 million of his own money into the project, and shooting a half million feet of film, he released *The Great Dictator* on October 15, 1940. Reflecting Chaplin's confidence in this picture, UA booked it to open in two New York theaters, the Astor and the Capitol. Critics and first-nighters at the opening found too much grim reality in the picture and objected to the last speech as out of place and propagandistic. But the public as a whole loved *The Great Dictator.* It had a fifteen-week run in New York and grossed nearly $5 million worldwide. This was Chaplin's greatest success, earning him not only acclaim but also a $1.5 million profit.

EFFECTS OF WORLD WAR II

As hostilities spread in Europe and the Orient during the thirties, United Artists together with other American film companies saw its foreign markets dwindle. UA closed its Spanish subsidiary in 1936, following the outbreak of the Civil War. In 1938, the company wrote down to one dollar the investment in its subsidiary in Japan. By then Japan had occupied parts of China, Manchukuo, and the Kwantung Peninsula. Nearly half of the Far Eastern market soon came under Japanese control.

In the wake of the German *Anschluss,* UA retreated from Austria, Czechoslovakia, Norway, and Occupied France. Europe, where United Artists had done one-fifth of its worldwide business in 1936, practically vanished as a market by 1941. Of its ten continental subsidiaries, only those in neutral Sweden and Switzerland remained in operation during the war.

Of greater consequence to the company was Great Britain, which accounted for over 60 per cent of its total foreign business. Revenues fell off alarmingly after war was declared in September, 1939. The Nazis began to bomb London and other English cities, which necessitated the evacuation of over three million people. Until the threat of air attack subsided, theaters remained closed. By 1940, however, all but about 10 per cent of the country's 4,800 movie theaters were open once more, providing, for the British as for Americans, escape and relaxation after long hours of work and danger. Average weekly attendance in Great Britain increased from nineteen million in 1939 to over thirty million in 1945, and gross box-office receipts nearly trebled. [6]

UA's business in Great Britain, as a result, did not suffer. In fact, its revenues in 1942 reached $7.5 million, up $3 million from 1939. However, because of currency restrictions, UA's producers could not share in the bonanza. Immediately following the declaration of war, Britain reduced the amount of sterling that American distributors could remove from the country; half of their former revenues or $17.5 million could be taken out in 1940 and only $12.9 million in 1941. Although restrictions were relaxed somewhat in 1942, UA had $3.6 million tied up in England; no producer had less than £50,000 frozen.

In a letter to the Chancellor of the Exchequer (July 24, 1942), UA vice president Arthur Kelly complained that these currency restrictions were seriously harming the company. Money from foreign markets had flowed in regularly before the war enabling independent producers to finance their pictures with actual income or anticipated income. Now, he said, producers had lost 16 per cent of the world gross from occupied territories and 50 per cent of earned revenue in other countries because of currency restrictions. "Big quality producers will be unable or unwilling to take the risk of making productions for the next year until they have realized part of their investment from the foreign markets on the product . . . already delivered . . . for distribution. This leaves United Artists seriously in danger of being destitute of product." Pressure from the American film industry forced the British Treasury to release all profits accumulated by American companies in Britain in 1943. Thereafter during the remaining war years, profits were withdrawn freely. But irreparable damage to United Artists producers had been done nonetheless.

EUROPEAN RESTRICTIVE PRACTICES

Currency restrictions such as those imposed by Great Britain were nothing new to United Artists and other American companies. They had long been subjected to quotas, taxes, contingents, and tariffs of all varieties. The rise of nationalism in Europe was one cause; another was protectionism for national film industries. The war merely put the finishing touch to a declining foreign film market as UA's experiences in Germany, Italy, and France exemplify.

The first nation to put up barriers to protect its film industry from American encroachment was Germany in 1925. The country was slowly recovering from the devastation of World War I, thanks mainly to America's Dawes Plan, which reduced German reparations and stabilized the monetary system. Its film industry, led by the great Universum Film A. G. (UFA), was vigorous, producing more films than any country except the United States. Formed in 1917 with government capital to combat Allied propaganda, UFA's filmmakers such as Fritz Lang, Ernst Lubitsch, Erich Pommer, F. W. Murnau, Paul Czinner, and G. W. Pabst created a great era of cinema. This did not deter American film moguls, to whom Germany, with a population of 65 million and over 3,600 theaters, appeared ripe for exploitation. To prevent a deluge of American films from strangling local production, Germany passed a contingent act in January, 1925. This law provided that for every film produced in Germany, a contingent or permit would be issued to its distributor to import and release a foreign film of equal length.

United Artists moved into Germany in 1926, five years after it began its continental operations. To secure its contingents, UA contracted with IFA Film Verleih, a distributing company connected with Phoebus Films, to grind out German films at the cost of $7,500 apiece. Then, UA formed a subsidiary called United Artists Film Verleih to distribute American-made UA films. During the first year it lost $65,000 on business of $150,000. The following year its deficit mounted to $91,000. Problems included inefficient exhibition practices, inadequate advertising on the part of theater owners, defaults on rental terms, and an unresponsive audience.

Rather than protect the home film industry, the contingent act, like the English quota, merely encouraged the production of cheap, low-quality pictures. And, like the English quota act, it failed to prevent American companies from establishing a firm foothold in the country. In 1925, for example, of the nearly 600 features exhibited, 218 or over a third were U.S. made.[7] As a result, the German government modified the law in 1929 to cut imports. It also put a stop to the trading of contingents. Accordingly, UA Film Verleih was notified that because it had purchased its contingents from Phoebus and had not actually distributed German pictures, it would not be allowed to import American Films. UA protested through the Hays Office, the State Department, the American ambassador to Germany, and the American commercial attaché in Berlin, but to no avail.

UA had no choice but to close its German subsidiary in 1929 and absorb a $179,000 loss. Thereafter, it released pictures through a local distributor, Terra Film Verleih. This arrangement lasted for three years and called for UA, on behalf of its producers, to split the gross fifty-fifty with Terra. In 1929, UA grossed $450,000, but 1930 was a very bad year, partly because of an American boycott in protest over the payment of sound royalties to Tobis-Klangfilm, but, more importantly, because of the Depression. Terra went into receivership in 1931. The next year, after the contract expired, UA was left with a $241,000 deficit.

The Depression, in devastating the German economy, brought Hitler to power. Joseph Goebbels, the Minister of Propaganda and Public Enlightenment, took over all forms of mass communication, including the cinema. The German film industry was nationalized. American film imports, which had been dropping steadily, from 229 in 1929 to 54 in 1932, became a trickle thereafter.

By 1936, Germany virtually ceased to exist as a market for American films. The Reich Film Law of 1934 instituted rigid censorship. The German Mark was frozen, and, with the passing of the Enabling Act in July, 1936, all imported films had to be "German" in character, which meant they had to be produced, directed, and acted by persons of Aryan descent. American distributors had no choice but to leave the country.

UA had encountered many of the same forms of protectionism in Italy, but with a few special twists. One was that Mussolini's government prohibited American companies from operating local subsidiaries. UA had to distribute its pictures through an Italian company, Artisti Associati, founded and headed by Mario Luporini in 1922 for the express purpose of handling UA's product. Another twist was that the government placed the distribution of all films under a government monopoly called the Ente Nazionale Industria Cinemotografica. This was something new in the way of restrictions. For the first time a national government went into the business of distributing foreign and domestic pictures for profit.

Although the monopoly was established in 1938, Italy laid the groundwork for it ten years earlier by instituting quota laws, dubbing restrictions, and currency restrictions to bleed, antagonize, and alienate American film companies. United Artists had never done more than $300,000 worth of business annually in Italy; after 1938, it did only a token amount until the United States declared war and severed all relations with the country.

As for UA's man in Italy, Luporini was denounced by his partner as an anti-Fascist. He received an official call at 3:00 in the morning from a Sr. Paolucci, head of the state monopoly, "suggesting" that Luporini "not take his contract with United Artists too seriously with respect to further payments."[8] Luporini wanted UA to advance him the money to buy control of the company, but he was refused. His partner, as a result, bought him out, placing Artisti Associati in Fascist hands.

UA fared no better on French soil. Les Artistes Associés, the French subsidiary, was originally established as the continental headquarters of the company, to supervise distribution in exchange-operated countries (France, Belgium, Denmark, Czechoslovakia, Switzerland, and Spain); to supply licensees in Norway, Holland, Italy, Portugal, and Turkey; and to sell outright to the Balkans, Baltic States, and the Near East. But proliferating French taxes and restrictions forced UA in 1934 to transfer these operations to London, where it formed United Artists Export, Ltd. Les Artistes Associés had a $314,000 deficit at this time. The French subsidiary continued to function until the Vichy government was established in July, 1940, but in the meantime, because of intensified protective measures, revenues dropped from $725,000 in 1935 to $249,000 the last year.

THE LATIN-AMERICAN MARKET IN WARTIME

To offset conditions in the war-torn European countries, Hollywood turned to Latin America. There, although the industry had a near monopoly, the market had never been fully exploited. Before the war, Brazil, Venezuela, and Argentina represented the greatest sources of revenue; of all the films exhibited, 86, 70, and 66 per cent in the respective countries were American-made.[9] Brazil and Argentina each had over a thousand theaters, which represented more than two-thirds of the total number in Latin America. Moreover, national film production, such as there was in Mexico and Argentina, was minimal.

The Department of State aided Hollywood's cause by creating the Office of the Coordinator of Inter-American Affairs (CIAA) in October, 1940. Its objective was to promote the Good Neighbor Policy and to initiate programs that would combat pro-Axis sentiment in South America. CIAA opened its Motion Picture Division almost immediately. Under the directorship of John Hay Whitney, it tried to convince the industry to abolish the stereotyped bloodthirsty Latin villain from its movies—such as was seen in MGM's *Viva Villa* made by Whitney's former partner, David Selznick—and to produce films having Latin-American themes and locales.

The immediate goal, however, was to neutralize propaganda flowing into Argentina, Brazil, and Chile from Axis wire services, features, newsreels, and documentaries. Whitney created the Newsreel Section for this purpose and by 1943 CIAA had shipped to South America over two hundred newsreels produced in cooperation with Paramount, Pathé,

Universal, Fox, and Hearst's News of the Day. These pictures reached an audience of over eighteen million by 1944, according to CIAA estimates.[10]

Although the industry responded with alacrity to the appeal to produce films with Latin themes, such features as *That Night in Rio, Carnival in Rio,* and *Down Argentine Way,* which typified Hollywood's efforts, could hardly be considered serious and careful treatments of timely subjects. "Too much Latin American Way," complained Whitney.[11] With the help of Walt Disney, CIAA approached Pan-Americanism in a new way. At Whitney's urging, Disney toured South America in 1941 to learn what Latins would like to see in films about their own countries. The visit was the source of two gems, *Saludos Amigos* and *Los Tres Caballeros.* Both were produced by RKO and contained live action and animation. Both were also substantial commercial hits, but *Los Tres Caballeros,* starring Carmen Miranda, was especially popular, topping even *The Song of Bernadette,* which had broken box-office records in Catholic Latin America.

Business in Latin America improved steadily during the war, but not as much as was expected. For UA, as an example, the market represented 16 per cent of its total foreign gross in 1946, up only 6 per cent since 1940. Several factors help explain this: First, shipping between the two continents operated erratically and less frequently than before; second, the films on war subjects, which Hollywood churned out in increasing numbers, had little mass appeal; and third, national film companies stepped up their own production. In 1941, Mexican and Argentinian features began to enjoy longer runs and gross more in their respective local markets. In 1942, they succeeded in gaining access to first-run houses. In the following year, Mexican films invaded South America.

As a form of political retribution against Argentina, which remained quietly pro-Axis despite its official neutral stance, CIAA rationed and then withheld raw film stock from Argentinian producers. At the same time, it poured technical assistance, equipment, and stock into the Mexican film industry, enabling it to overtake Argentina as the major producer in Latin America. Local productions could not supplant American pictures in the urban areas, but in the interiors where illiteracy was high and where English pictures with Spanish subtitles could not be understood, they prevailed. For example, *Variety* reported that in the six hundred theaters of Buenos Aires and major cities of Argentina 65 per cent of the films exhibited were made in Hollywood, 34 per cent were locally made, and Germany, Italy, and Japan supplied 1 per cent. In the five hundred theaters of the interior, the ratio was reversed: National productions together with Mexican made up 70 per cent; Hollywood, 29 per cent; the remainder, 1 per cent.[12]

Hollywood fought its competitors mainly by taking on the added expense of dubbing—it cost UA about $25,000 to dub a picture into Spanish. Dubbing did not make films more popular; in fact, educated filmgoers found the Spanish versions disagreeable. Often as not, these pictures were dubbed in a neutral Castilian dialect, which sounded foreign to Latin ears.

THE DOMESTIC MARKET IN WARTIME

By the time America entered the war, it was apparent to the industry that it would have to rely on the domestic market. Fortunately, conditions at home created a boom in business. Dollars were plentiful, while commodities were not. Movies were the most readily available entertainment. Although gasoline restrictions hurt attendance in some rural areas, the integrated companies, whose theaters were more favorably situated, flourished. Domestic film rentals for the Big Eight jumped from $193 million in 1939 to $332 million in 1946.[13] Weekly attendance by the end of the war reached 85 million, its highest since the boom days of the twenties.[14]

As business improved, pictures ran longer and longer to capacity houses, with a significant result. The Big Eight released 388 pictures in 1939, but only 252 in 1946.[15] In other words, studios were receiving more and more dollars for fewer and fewer pictures. Production costs rose during this period, to be sure, but not as fast as profit margins.

Two obstacles having the potential to cut revenues were thrown before the industry during the war years, but these were easily overcome. One was the shortage of raw film stock. When the government reduced basic allotments by 25 per cent on January 1, 1943, the industry, having anticipated this move, had already adopted conservation measures and hoarded films. Producers had on their shelves over one hundred unreleased pictures. The cut did not affect United Artists, which had the responsibility of allocating raw stock to its producers, because there was enough to go around; UA's problem was to get producers to use it.

The Paramount Case

Of greater consequence to the industry was the *Paramount* case. Agitation over block booking and monopolistic trade practices had reached its peak by 1938, prompting the Justice Department to bring suit against the Big Eight. In the amended and supplemental complaint filed on November 14, 1940, the government charged Paramount, Loew's,

RKO, Warner Brothers, and Twentieth Century-Fox with combining and conspiring to restrain trade unreasonably and to monopolize the production, distribution, and exhibition of motion pictures.[16] Columbia, Universal, and United Artists, the three minor defendants, were charged with combining with the majors to restrain trade and monopolize commerce in motion pictures. The specific charges against the defendants were nearly identical to those heard during the days of NRA. So were the suggested remedies; the government's petition asked for the divorcement of production from exhibition, the elimination of block booking, the abolition of unfair clearance, and the quashing of many other producer-distributor trade practices.

The case was originally scheduled for trial in the Southern District Court of New York in June, 1940, but after a period of negotiation, the government entered the amended complaint providing for the entry of a consent decree. Since the three minor defendants did not own any theaters, the suit against them was adjourned. On November 20, 1940, the government and the five majors became parties to a consent decree that was to run for three years. During this period the government agreed not to press for divorcement of the affiliated theaters from their production-distribution companies. Certain trade practices specified in the complaint were either modified or eliminated: Blind selling was prevented by requiring trade shows of films; block booking was limited to five pictures; the forced purchase of shorts was abolished; and the use of unreasonable clearance was proscribed. The significant and unique feature of the decree was its mode of enforcement through independent arbitration tribunals administered by the American Arbitration Association. Power to seek remedy was vested only in the exhibitors, not in the defendant distributors. The novel aspect of the arbitration scheme was that it applied not only to contract disputes, the traditional function of commercial arbitration, but also to complaints about run and clearance.

But there was a catch. The decree allowed tribunals to hear requests for earlier runs only from theaters that had filed for adjustments before the decree. Independent exhibitors were displeased with this provision, and with some others. They complained that they did not have time to attend trade showings and that the five-picture blocks inevitably contained one or two B-pictures for each top production, so they were no improvement over the old block-booking system. The majors, therefore, succeeded once again in warding off an attack on their market structure. The Justice Department reactivated the *Paramount* case in 1944. Four years later it reached the Supreme Court, where it had disastrous consequences for the industry.

UA'S WARTIME PRODUCTION

Korda's Difficulties

The first UA producer to feel the effects of war was Alexander Korda. When hostilities started, he was in England shooting *The Thief of Bagdad.* To complete this picture and to fulfill his obligations to UA, Korda was forced to transplant his entire organization to Hollywood. But before the British government allowed him to make the move, it required that he place directive control of his financial activities in the hands of the Bank of England, through the Foreign Exchange Control Board. The British government assumed that because Korda would have to secure American financing to complete the picture, they could compel him to transfer the principal and profits, if any, to England, thus creating a certain amount of dollar exchange.

Upon his arrival in the U.S., Korda formed a new production company called Alexander Korda Films, Inc. He obtained the money for *The Thief* and for three additional pictures at the Bankers Trust of New York and the Security First National Bank of Los Angeles. General Service Studios, where the pictures were to be made, put up additional money to complete the financing for the package.

The Thief of Bagdad opened on Christmas day, 1940. It grossed over $1 million, the most any Korda picture had earned in the United States. His second picture, *That Hamilton Woman,* was equally successful. *Lydia* did only moderately well, but *Rudyard Kipling's Jungle Book,* as it went into production, promised to be the biggest money-maker of them all.

However, Korda's production costs exceeded his budget, and the Bank of England decided to step in. The bank agreed to guarantee another loan, but required that all moneys earned by the original investment in *The Thief of Bagdad* and subsequent profits on the four pictures would have to be transferred to England to pay off Korda's indebtedness there. As a consequence, Korda lost the collateral to secure financing for additional production work in the United States.

This created a problem for UA above and beyond losing a valued producer. Korda had completed preproduction work on the picture *To Be Or Not To Be,* which was to be co-produced and directed by Ernst Lubitsch. Originally, this was to have been a Walter Wanger production, but when his board balked at the $1 million budget, Wanger arranged for Korda to take over the picture. But now that it was impossible for Korda to obtain financing, he was in an embarrassing situation. He had already invested considerable money of his own in the project. Moreover, Lubitsch had been guaranteed a UA release.

So, to salvage the picture as well as Korda's reputation—he was, after

Ernst Lubitsch and Jack Benny on the set of *To Be Or Not To Be* (1942)

all, an owner of the company—UA decided to take the extraordinary step of producing the picture itself. It had to act fast. The story was an anti-Nazi burlesque about a company of Polish actors in Warsaw who outwit an inept Gestapo and escape to England. It was now the summer of 1941; little time remained before such a picture would become an anachronism. A separate company was formed for the sole purpose of producing it. For financing, UA procured a $1.2 million production loan from Guaranty Trust Company in return for which it had to pledge its distribution fee in addition to the normal producer's share of the gross. Out of this, Korda was paid $75,000 to reimburse him for expenses incurred in the picture and a fee of $25,000 as executive producer. Lubitsch then assumed the function of producer under the supervision of George Bagnall, UA's nominee to the production company. Jack Benny and Carole Lombard were signed to play the leads, and the picture went into production.

To Be Or Not To Be was released on March 6, 1942. Many events conspired against it. Midway through production, Pearl Harbor had been attacked and Germany was sweeping across Europe into Africa. Whatever Americans may have thought about Germany before our entry into the war, they could no longer view this enemy as inept. Critics lambasted the movie as callous and tasteless. The picture was ill-timed in yet another way. Shortly before its release Miss Lombard was killed in a plane crash while on a war-bond selling tour. Few could laugh at the comic antics of the star who had died trying to defeat the very enemy she outwitted in the movie. *To Be Or Not To Be* eventually recovered its production cost, but the experience served to remind United Artists of the hazards of production financing.

Shortage of Product

UA's other sources of product were meanwhile beginning to dry up. Eddie Small decided to suspend his operations in 1941 and Hal Roach returned to making featurettes. As Everson said, "Roach was still loyal to his belief that featurettes would one day replace most of the second-feature 'B' product, and he tried to prove his point with several groups of light comedies which generally ran into four-and-one-half-reel lengths."[17] These became known in the business as "streamliners," and in the next two years he delivered nearly twenty to the company.

The Dispute with Wanger

Then the Wanger unit closed down. UA had invested $2 million in the company by the end of the 1938 season; seven pictures had been released, yet none had returned a profit. As UA saw the problem, Wanger had little regard for his budgets. *Walter Wanger's Vogues of 1938,* in particular, cost $1.4 million, $600,000 more than anticipated. The upshot was that UA's board decided to supervise more closely Wanger's mode of operations. Wanger would have none of this, so UA shut off any further financing. However, by subrogating its loans, UA made it possible for Wanger to seek support from the banks.

With financing primarily from the Bank of America, Wanger produced three hits, *Algiers, Trade Winds,* and *Stagecoach,* in 1938-1939. These did so well that their profits about equalled the losses of the first seven. But Wanger could not keep up the momentum. His next series of pictures, which included *Winter Carnival, Foreign Correspondent, The House Across the Bay,* and *The Long Voyage Home,* played off slowly. By 1941 his production unit was in the red by $300,000. More important, though, $1 million in revenue was frozen abroad as a result of wartime currency restrictions. This meant that Wanger could not use residual profits to repay the $800,000 production loan from the Bank of America and to finance additional product.

Wanger now had to face the choice of either bending to the will of his directors or getting out. He chose to leave. In an interview a few years ago he explained why:

Andy Devine, George Bancroft, and John Wayne in Wanger's *Stagecoach* (1939)

When the war broke out, I wanted to do an aviation picture called *Eagle Squadron*. I've always started cycles and trends in pictures. I like to do new things. *Eagle Squadron* starred Diana Barrymore and Bob Stack. My board of directors didn't believe in aviation pictures. I was infuriated and walked out on my contract even though it was brilliant tax-wise and they had just taken up the option for another five years. In my rush, I went over to Universal, which was considered to be the "other side of the tracks." Nevertheless, this picture was about the first of about 600 aviation pictures and was very successful.[18]

The records describe Wanger's departure less dramatically. He did not walk out on his contract; on the contrary, UA, on November 24, 1941 purchased his interest in the production unit for $100,000 and gave him the story rights to *Arabian Nights* and *Cheyenne* and the partially finished negative of *Eagle Squadron*. Universal took over the financing of *Eagle Squadron* and released it as one of its own productions.

The name of the Wanger Company was changed to United Artists Productions, Inc., which retained the copyrights and negatives to his seventeen productions, including the completed but still to be released *Sundown*. UA by far got the better of the deal. Within a year, the pictures paid off the Bank of America loans and the purchase price of Wanger's stock. Moreover, they returned a profit of $200,000 at home and

£100,000 in frozen funds in England. Most of this revenue came from *Sundown,* which grossed $1.1 million. Still to be enjoyed were the reissue rights to these pictures.

Dealings with Capra

With Wanger out, UA turned to David Selznick to rescue the company. Actually, UA tried to convince both Selznick and Frank Capra to come in as partners, but succeeded only in luring Selznick. Capra had once before been approached about a partnership. In 1939, Capra ended his long association with Columbia, after almost singlehandedly upgrading its image by directing such acclaimed productions as *It Happened One Night* (1934), *Mr. Deeds Goes to Town* (1936), *Lost Horizon* (1937), *You Can't Take It With You* (1938), and *Mr. Smith Goes to Washington* (1939). With Robert Riskin, who wrote the scripts for most of Capra's movies during the thirties, he had formed an independent production unit and was then looking for a distribution deal. This was just the time that Goldwyn was suing to break his distribution contract. Here was a fortuitous opportunity for United Artists to secure his replacement. So alluring was this prospect that Pickford, Fairbanks, Chaplin, and Korda as individuals offered to arrange financing and to turn over one-fifth of their dividends until the company could legally bring him in as a partner. Mary Pickford tells why the deal collapsed in a letter to Dennis O'Brien:

> It was a source of great disappointment to Douglas, Murray and me that we could not clinch the Capra contract. There is no question about it, the acquiring of a six year's contract with him would be a turning point in the life of United Artists. We are sorely in need of leaders with Goldwyn out, the possibility of our losing Selznick in the near future and Korda's affairs so uncertain. Capra is highly rated in Hollywood and undoubtedly he would have attracted to the company many of the leaders—both stars and producers.
>
> It was all very confusing with Schwartz claiming that the individual stock holders could not give one fifth of their dividends to Capra, and Loyd Wright claiming that they could. Korda and Douglas at Pickfair told Riskin and Capra they were all for giving them a unit. I was apprehensive about this promise knowing full well it would take an unanimous vote. I did not want to make an issue of it before Capra and Riskin, but I told both Douglas and Korda after they left that I doubted if it could be done until Goldwyn was out of the picture. Murray was given authority by the four of us; namely Douglas, Chaplin, Korda and myself to negotiate with Capra. He returned after much negotiation two days later with an agreement. . . . Chaplin was reluctant at first to agree but, after two hours, said he was willing to give Capra the unit by giving him one fifth of our dividends until we could give them a unit which would be just as soon as we were legally free to do so and to this we all agreed. Then Schwartz spoke to Murray on long distance the following day stating he thought it a very poor deal and that in

his opinion if we gave Capra one fifth of the dividends of the four of us we would legally complicate our suit with Goldwyn. It seems to me, Cap, it was a little late for Schwartz to give this advice and that it was inadmissable for him to upset the apple cart with Korda who, as you know, is a congenital barterer and trader. After Korda had talked to Schwartz he immediately called Chaplin up and got him on the rampage too. It places Murray and United Artists in a very embarrassing position; in fact, I go on record in saying we are morally obligated to go through with our proposition with Capra providing it is legally possible. . . .

So summed up, Cap, the behaviour of both the lawyers and the members of the company is utterly incomprehensible and, to say the least, deplorable. I left California with a heavy heart. Murray was still struggling trying to please both sides and no one knows what the outcome will be. In the event that Chaplin and Korda repudiate our agreement with Capra and Riskin and Murray's authority to deal with them, it will have a very devastating effect . . . upon the integrity of our company.[19]

Chaplin and Korda did not repudiate the Capra deal as Mary Pickford feared they would; nonetheless, negotiations had to wait until UA's internal affairs were stabilized. In the interim, though, both Capra's and Selznick's value to the company had gone up and the two producers were in an excellent bargaining position.

DAVID O. SELZNICK AND REORGANIZATION OF UA

Under the terms of the 1935 distribution agreement, Selznick had delivered seven pictures: *Little Lord Fauntleroy* (1936), *The Garden of Allah* (1936), *A Star Is Born* (1937), *The Prisoner of Zenda* (1937), *The Adventures of Tom Sawyer* (1938), *The Young in Heart* (1938), and *Made for Each Other* (1939).

That *Gone With the Wind* was not the eighth came as a surprise to United Artists. Murray Silverstone sent this telegram to Selznick on June 27, 1938:

Newspaper here carries story you will produce *Gone With the Wind* with Shearer-Gable but no distributor mentioned. Our English and continental sales convention at which entire organization present commences Friday and I do hope things will materialize such an extent that it will be my pleasure to then announce your continued and permanent association with us which we so highly value. Would like again mention that finance arranged by me as result our discussion at Sam's house is still available. Again reiterate my feelings towards you so often expressed.

Selznick replied:

Gone With Wind deal is set with Metro although not actually signed. However, hope to be able to get together with UA on future product. . . . It is vital to my

Fredric March and Janet Gaynor in Selznick's *A Star Is Born* (1937)

production plans that we know promptly whether we are continuing with UA and this is dependent upon official action on reduction plan England and Canada as well as upon some form of rebate plan being decided upon and made official. My anxiety to continue with you and your organisation has caused us to be patient but sometime within next two weeks I will have to know exactly where we are going in order to make my plans. . . . If we don't get together it will not be our fault nor will it be through any lack of desire on my part but simply because of delays in action which apparently so unfortunately characterise negotiations with your company. *Gone With Wind* would have long since been on UA program if it had not been for this inability to get action the delay being such as to make your offer of help come too late for it to seem as desirable as it might have had it been presented before Metro offer. There is no reason whatsoever why we cannot and should not promptly get together on rest of product and if there is a slip it will again be because of the dilatory tactics of your board in making official matters which have already been promised you must know.[20]

Selznick may have been bluffing to get better terms on his next UA distribution contract because he does not mention his major reason for approaching MGM—to secure Clark Gable on a loanout to play the role of Rhett Butler. It was common knowledge in the industry that his father-in-law, Louis B. Mayer, insisted that in return for Gable and a $1.5 million loan, Selznick had to give MGM the distribution rights to the picture and half the profits. These were harsh terms, and the fact that Selznick acceded to them testified to his need of Gable.

Selznick signed a second contract with UA in 1939, committing him to four additional pictures. As an inducement, UA cut him in on the Silverstone Plan and agreed to advance $150,000 per picture to aid in the financing. *Intermezzo* and *Rebecca* were the first two pictures delivered on this contract. Selznick hoped that *Rebecca,* which won for him in 1940 his second Academy Award for best picture, would sell as well as *Gone With the Wind.* But this is an example of what he found:

I was shocked the other day to discover that a West Coast theatre in San Bernardino was advertising *Rebecca* on the lower half of a bill with *Johnny Apollo.* It is true that the pictures were given equal or almost equal space, with *Johnny Apollo* having a shade the best of the space and having first position—but *Rebecca* was in the lower half of the ad and treated as the 'plus' picture, with the use of that very word.

I called at the Exchange, where MacLean, with his usual familiarity (!) with what's going on in his territory, looked up a lot of things and finally came through with the information that this was the second run in San Bernardino, and that *Johnny Apollo* was the second picture. I assured him that *Rebecca* was the second picture, whereupon he told me his information came from West Coast! He went on to say that we got $200.00 as a flat rental for the second run—and while I'm thoroughly aware of the fact that *Johnny Apollo* is a Fox picture

Joan Fontaine and Judith Anderson in Selznick's *Rebecca* (1940)

and that this is a Fox circuit, this is beside the point. I would be willing to bet that the terms for *Johnny Apollo* were either on a percentage or on a flat rental in excess of ours; and bear in mind just what a lousy, unimportant picture *Johnny Apollo* is, by comparison with *Rebecca*.

I suppose that I will again be told this is the exception. The exception always happens in things that I run into. . . .

I look back with no little bitterness to the days when you told me there was going to be a spirited competition between United Artists and MGM on the terms of *Rebecca* and *Gone With the Wind,* respectively.

If this is an indication of just how United Artists is watching *Rebecca* and just how it's improving the contracts, I suppose I might as well throw up [sic] the sponge.[21]

Rebecca came nowhere close to *Gone With the Wind*'s $20 million gross, but nonetheless it earned a tidy $700,000 profit and helped put Selznick in a confiscatory tax bracket. The result was he had to reduce his tax liability by dissolving Selznick International. His partner, John Hay Whitney, subscribed to this move because it provided an easy way out of the movie business. As *Variety* reported:

Company has been in business for five years. First four of those saw nothing better than an even break on investments, and in some cases a dead loss. There were successful pictures, but overhead was so high it ate into the profit. Fifth year, however, was the big coin producer, putting Whitney and the others ahead of the game. Whitney's idea now, it is believed, is that he's had enough and he'll quit while he is in the lead. In addition, Selznick is now in a soft position to obtain other financing, no longer having any need of Whitney.[22]

Negotiations with Selznick and Capra

The dissolution papers were filed in August, 1940. In liquidating SIP's assets, Selznick received these United Artists releases: *The Prisoner of Zenda, The Garden of Allah, The Adventures of Tom Sawyer, Intermezzo,* and *Rebecca;* Whitney took over *Little Lord Fauntleroy, The Young in Heart,* and *Made for Each Other.* The odds were that after delivering the two remaining pictures on his UA contract, Selznick would return to MGM or RKO. But not if UA could help it. Too much was at stake to lose either Selznick or Capra. UA presented them with a proposition whereby each would be given a unit of stock in return for three pictures from Selznick and two from Capra; the productions were to cost $1 million on the average and to be delivered within two years; and United Artists would help in the financing by providing revolving funds in the amount of $600,000 for Selznick and $400,000 for Capra. In recompense, UA was to receive 10 per cent of the profits. New distribution terms based on a sliding scale would guarantee top returns.

As the spokesman for the two, Selznick told Korda, the UA negotiator, that he was most sympathetic to the idea of saving United Artists, "both selfishly and altruistically from an industry standpoint," but for the moment he could not increase his commitment to UA beyond the two pictures he currently owed them. "What shall it benefit United Artists to be saved, if in the process its saviors go down! There has been no improvement in the United Artists situation, or in the national or international situation, or in theatre conditions, that would warrant a change in this viewpoint." In short, what Selznick wanted before anything else was a release from his present distribution contract.

Of the proposed financing plan, he said it was "trivial in terms of financial discussions that both Frank and I have had with other companies, where the financial obligations run into millions."

Selznick's opinion of the distribution terms was no better:

United Artists is asking for higher distribution terms than other distributors are asking, despite the fact that it has been very clearly demonstrated that United Artists is not even in the same class as these other distributors from a standpoint of ability to secure the proper gross for the producer. This statement is no longer conjecture, or opinion. Frank and myself have in our possession the comparative terms on *Meet John Doe,* released through Warners, and *Rebecca,* released through United Artists. The difference in these terms is shocking; and only today I have received word that even in those situations where *Meet John Doe* is not doing the box office gross that was achieved by *Rebecca,* the net film rental is greater because of the better terms, better playing time, and better selection of theatres, secured by the Warner Brothers sales force.

To Korda's possible rejoinder that they would be receiving valuable stock in the company, Selznick had this to say:

Let us examine the facts. In the first place we are not getting an interest until and unless we contract for several years, unquestionably the most productive years of Frank's and my own respective careers. According to present market . . . a fifth interest is presently worth Three Hundred Sixty Thousand Dollars. To secure an *option* on this interest, we have to contract for pictures, the distribution fee from which will in itself be probably at least double the value of both interests, and to *secure* this stock, we have to contract for pictures, the distribution fees from which will be several times the worth of the entire company! And in the process, we must face the certainty that we will do less business on our pictures, than we would elsewhere, unless through *our* efforts we revitalize the company, unless through *our* prestige we attract better pictures and better selling terms and better man power to the company, unless through *our* association with the company we turn the tide, and send United Artists on the way up by contrast with its present inevitable decline towards oblivion.

Yet Selznick clearly did not want to break with UA. In closing, he said:

If I didn't think that someday we might be owners, and if I didn't have the future well-being of United Artists at heart, I can assure you that I wouldn't have wasted the time that has been spent on all our long-winded meetings, that I wouldn't put up with the nonsensical or affected independence of some of your present owners, that I wouldn't be now wasting the time dictating this memo. I have kicked over a lot more attractive deals for a great deal less reason. And if we don't get together with United Artists, I have no intention of spending the equivalent amount of time on such other deal as Frank and myself may make.[23]

Capra, who had less patience in these matters than Selznick, pulled out of the deal after two more months of negotiations. The overlong discussions with the UA owners had led nowhere and he had been "unable to meet the people that were supposed to be my future partners. . . . I am in the business of making pictures," he said to the press, and "can't afford to deal forever."[24] As it turned out, Capra could not have contributed to UA in any event. After putting the finishing touches on his latest picture, *Arsenic and Old Lace,* produced for Warner Brothers, he became Major Frank Capra of the Special Services Branch of the U.S. Army.

The negotiations with Selznick boiled down to an argument over who was going to direct the reorganization of the company. Murray

Silverstone, the managing director, had resigned in May, unable to cope further with a company left in shambles after the Goldwyn battle. Korda, it seemed, fancied himself as the new UA leader now that he was out of production, but Selznick convinced him otherwise after two more months of haggling. So Korda stepped aside. On October 4, 1941, David O. Selznick became a partner in United Artists, and it took eight separate contracts, which were signed on the lawns of Pickfair, to make it official.

Selznick bought into the company for $300,000, to be paid after five

David O. Selznick

years. His stock was placed in escrow, giving him full rights to vote and receive dividends. To help him resume production, UA advanced him $300,000 to purchase the rights to A. J. Cronin's *The Keys of the Kingdom,* Rose Franken's Broadway play *Claudia,* and *Jane Eyre.*

Selznick agreed to deliver a minimum of ten pictures. These were divided into two groups for financing purposes. At Selznick's discretion, each could contain either five pictures which he personally produced, or six, if two of them did not bear his name. United Artists agreed to advance $125,000 per picture for the first four that he personally produced in each group. If picture number five was also a Selznick production, the advance for it would be increased to $200,000. This money was protected because the advances were to be recouped immediately from UA's share of the distribution receipts rather than subrogated to the production loans. Nonetheless the total commitment on the part of UA added up to $1 million. In addition, UA gave Selznick special distribution terms to maximize his returns on high-grossing pictures. These were based on a sliding scale, with UA getting 25 per cent of the gross up to $800,000 and 10 per cent of the gross over that amount.

Selznick felt that the most important part of the agreement was the change in the bylaws to give him special powers in the running of the company. Operational control was vested in a board of directors whose members came from management rather than from stockholders; and Selznick or his nominee was elected to the board. The reconstituted board was given authority to hire officers to run the domestic and foreign distribution business and to approve distribution contracts with producers. The need for these changes had been clearly spelled out by Arthur Kelly, UA vice president, in a letter to the stockholders:

> The lack of leadership in the sales organization is due entirely to the refusal of the directors of the company to clothe the operating head with the necessary authority to make his leadership real leadership. It is impossible from my point of view for a board to operate this company three thousand miles away. The decisions made in California without the operating officer's viewpoint and without the full knowledge of the effect of such decisions, particularly as to their bearing on the company's financial position for the future, cannot be constructive, while we are still servicing all possible information through Mr. Loyd Wright [secretary of the board], it is still an impractical thing to have so many informal and formal meetings at the Coast without proper consultation with the responsible officers on the operating end.[25]

UA's new board of directors was announced in November, 1941: Edward C. Raftery, of O'Brien, Driscoll, and Raftery, the law firm that represented the company from its inception, was named president; Gradwell L. Sears, former general sales manager of Warner, became vice president and general manager of domestic distribution; Laudy Lawrence, general European manager for MGM until October, 1941, when he joined the Selznick organization, became vice president and supervisor of foreign distribution; George Bagnall, former general manager of Alexander Korda Films, Inc., was chosen vice president in charge of United Artists Productions; and Arthur W. Kelly became vice president and chairman of the finance committee.

UA's policy was "to let this neutral management run the company rather than having it run by the owners," proclaimed a company release. It further meant "the elimination of any interference on the part of the owners or their representatives with the sales force or with any other phase of the company's distribution operations."[26]

Now identified as the leader of United Artists and the brain behind its reorganization, Selznick could say to an admirer:

> Thank you. I am of course happy if there is any feeling that I have contributed to this, or to the assembly of what I regard as the superb new management of the company. I am sure that the domestic distribution organization under Mr. Sears will very speedily put this branch of the company into tip-top shape.
>
> Now that the reorganization of United Artists is completed, I have stepped back into the role of a producer. I feel very strongly that the best contribution that the owners of United Artists can make to the company is to produce pictures. . . . United Artists is finished with the business of producers, even owner-producers, interfering in any way with the management of the company.[27]

With that, Selznick formed Vanguard Films, Inc., his new production company, and his partners in United Artists eagerly awaited his first film.

Worsening Strains Within

[1942-1944]

SETBACKS IN THE EARLY WAR YEARS

Loss of Korda

The vulnerability of United Artists during the Selznick negotiations gave Alexander Korda a wonderful opportunity for self-aggrandizement. When Selznick finally consented to come into the company, Korda went to his partners and said that if they wanted his vote for Selznick, United Artists would have to drop the $400,000 lien on his stock. Pickford and Chaplin countered by offering to extend the promissory note another five years, but Korda refused. So rather than lose Selznick, they had to acquiesce. Korda then scurried to England and purchased Prudential's half interest in the UA stock for £35,000, which concludes the story of how Korda became a full-fledged partner in the company.

Back in England, Korda offered his services to the British government as a contribution to the war effort. The exact nature of his work was not known to UA, but because it seemed likely that Korda would not be resuming production work for some time, the company thought it advisable to make a settlement clearing the books of Korda's indebtedness on the four pictures he made in the U.S. United Artists decided to cancel its loans, amounting to $600,000, by accepting the residual distribution receipts of *The Thief of Bagdad, That Hamilton Woman, Lydia,* and *Rudyard Kipling's Jungle Book* and the part ownership Korda had in Michael Powell's *One of Our Aircraft Is Missing* and Noel Coward's *In Which We Serve,* two British productions UA had in release at the time. This settlement was made on November 21, 1942 and, for a change, eventually turned out to be profitable, because when the play-off of these six pictures was completed, the company was ahead by $100,000. However, only a portion of the money came from distribution receipts. UA saved close to $500,000 by not having to pay Korda rebates under the terms of the Silverstone Plan and the special sliding-scale distribution charge that had been put into effect for the stockholders when Selznick joined the company. So, it would be accurate to say that in appearing to do a second favor for Korda, UA actually benefitted itself.

It came therefore as a shock to read in the *New York Times* a few months later MGM's announcement that the new head of its British production activities was none other than Alexander Korda. The story said,

> Sir Alexander Korda, producer and co-owner of United Artists, will leave here within two weeks to take charge of Metro-Goldwyn-Mayer's British production in a deal which Metro, in its official announcement today, describes as "the most important merger in the history of British-American film production."
>
> On his arrival in London a new Metro-Goldwyn-Mayer-British Company will be set up embodying the Korda interests and the M-G-M resources in England, all to be operated under the guidance of Sir Alexander. The new company thus will acquire Korda's interests in the contracts of Vivien Leigh, Ralph Richardson and certain writers and directors and part-ownership of the Denham studio from which the new unit will operate.
>
> The merger does not affect Sir Alexander's 25 per cent ownership of United Artists, which he shares with David O. Selznick, Charles Chaplin and Mary Pickford. [1]

Notwithstanding the fact that Korda relinquished his voting rights as a condition of the settlement, his alliance with a competitor was unholy. United Artists now had the task of trying to retire the Korda stock before the balance of power within the company was disturbed still another time. Alas, this did not happen. Selznick had the poor sense to tell the press that he stood ready to purchase Korda's interest any time he decided to sell out, which Chaplin correctly interpreted as a bald attempt to take control of the company.

Selznick's Failure to Produce

Another sore point for Chaplin was that Selznick, a year and a half after he became a partner, had yet to deliver a single picture. And, the properties Selznick bought with the UA advance—*The Keys of the Kingdom, Claudia,* and *Jane Eyre*—had been sold to Twentieth Century-Fox at a big profit. So incensed was Chaplin that at the May, 1943, stockholders' meeting he insisted that UA bring suit against Selznick for breach of contract. The motion lost for lack of a second. Chaplin was left to brood.

Inferior Product

Dan O'Shea, Selznick's head man at Vanguard, fanned the fires of discontent shortly thereafter by sending a letter to the board of directors excoriating it for failing to recapture Disney.

According to the trade papers, United Artists has again lost Disney to RKO. It is not surprising that United Artists has lost this distinguished producer whose product it desperately needed to take it out of the dumping-ground category, entirely regardless of the dollars and cents equation. We say it is not surprising, and we have reference to the management's preoccupation with securing the "product" of any promoter or entrepreneur, regardless of background or accomplishments. We are also mindful of the complete disintegration and destruction of the prestige of United Artists, a prestige to which the management seemingly is indifferent so long as it can build this year's gross, without regard to the future of the company, or to the effect upon the handling of producers who have with complete integrity tried to maintain a standard for United Artists.[2]

The product O'Shea had in mind was a twenty-one-picture package the company, through its subsidiary, United Artists Productions, purchased from Paramount. This package consisted of five features, Harry Sherman action specials, and two series of Hopalong Cassidy westerns. With the exception of René Clair's *I Married a Witch* and Elliott Nugent's *The Crystal Ball,* these pictures were definitely in the "B" category. The Hopalong Cassidy pictures were so cheaply produced, about $100,000 per picture, that UA sold them in blocks, counter to its standing sales policy.

Management was by no means unaware of the quality of this package, since most of the pictures had already been made at the time of the purchase. They were acquired for a single purpose—to forestall a product crisis. When Raftery's management team took office in December, 1941, it discovered that only one picture had been definitely committed to production and release for the 1942-1943 season. Wanger had departed to Universal, Korda had completed his commitments to the company, and Edward Small, who was scheduled to bring in seven pictures in 1941-1942, had announced that he intended to quit producing temporarily, after fulfilling his commitment. Moreover, now that the United States had entered the war, bank financing for independent production was uncertain. So, when UA vice president Grad Sears learned that Paramount had a product surplus, he was only too happy to open negotiations with the hope of acquiring product, any kind of product, to carry the company until such time as Selznick began production and other quality producers could be signed on.

The package came to UA as a result of deals in September, 1942 and June, 1943: total price, $4.8 million. Since the company's asset position had been weakened in 1941 by purchase of stock units from Goldwyn for $300,000 and from the estate of Douglas Fairbanks for $400,000, it had to go to the Guaranty Trust in New York for financing. The bank made the loan primarily because UA could pledge as collateral the Wanger pictures it now owned outright. The reissue rights for these films were valued at more than $1 million.

Excluding the René Clair and Elliott Nugent films, none of the Paramount pictures grossed more than $400,000; the Hopalong Cassidy movies averaged less than $200,000. They paid off the bank loan, however, and even earned a profit, but at a terrible cost in prestige to the company. Together with Hal Roach Streamliners, they made up a substantial portion of UA's program for all of 1943 and much of 1944, which meant that the company temporarily at least was supplying second features for double bills almost exclusively.

The few respectable pictures in release at the time were two Arnold Pressburger productions, *The Shanghai Gesture* directed by Josef von Sternberg and *Hangmen Also Die!* directed by Fritz Lang; Noel Coward's memorable film about a British destroyer, its captain and crew, and their families, *In Which We Serve;* the popular wartime morale-builder, Sol Lesser's *Stage Door Canteen,* which grossed an incredible $4.5 million; and *Lady of Burlesque* and *Johnny Come Lately,* produced by newcomers Hunt Stromberg and James Cagney, whom UA literally banked on to sustain its reputation.

RISE OF INDEPENDENT PRODUCTION

In its quest for product, UA had opened its doors to the growing number of independents who were entering the field. Before the war, there were only a handful, but by 1946 the number would reach forty. United Artists had sixteen under contract in 1943, among whom were Benedict Bogeaus,

Xavier Cugat and orchestra in Lesser's *Stage Door Canteen* (1943)

Samuel Bronston, Lester Cowan, Jules Levey, David Loew, Charles R. Rogers (not to be confused with Mary Pickford's husband, Charles "Buddy" Rogers), and Andrew Stone, in addition to the producers already mentioned. Most had fled the production ranks of Hollywood studios. By far the most distinguished of this group was Hunt Stromberg, the producer of more than one hundred MGM features, including *The Thin Man* series, *Naughty Marietta, Ah, Wilderness!, Night Must Fall,* and *Idiot's Delight. Fame* magazine in 1942 named him the ten-year "champion of champions" with the greatest number of box-office successes. MGM had allowed him to walk off the lot ending an eighteen-year association with the studio rather than meet his demands for more freedom of operation—which indicates what the majors thought of independent production. Bogeaus, an exception, had been a real-estate speculator in Chicago. He had earned enough to purchase General Service Studios in 1941, which became a production headquarters for independents. Another exception, of course, was Cagney, who terminated a brilliant twelve-year career at Warner in 1942 after winning the Academy Award for best actor portraying George M. Cohan in *Yankee Doodle Dandy.*

The attraction of artistic freedom by no means accounted for the sudden interest in independent production. A major factor was the marketplace: the drop in production output caused by the shortage of studio personnel, together with the increasing public demand for movies had the effect of making independent production a less speculative venture. Another had to do with the Treasury Department: the wartime income-tax rates had badly eroded the take-home pay of high-priced talent. By operating his own independent production company, a producer, director, or actor in the top income-tax bracket could reduce his effective tax rate from 90 to 60 per cent. Moreover, under certain conditions, an interest in a completed picture could be sold as a capital asset, making the profit from such sale subject to a 25 per cent capital-gains tax.[3]

Cagney's tax situation will serve to illustrate the benefits of independent production. During 1941, he had worked on three pictures. Each would typically gross about $1.5 million in the U.S. Since his take-home pay was based on profit participation, he earned over $350,000 that year. After taxes, however, the amount was reduced to a paltry $70,000.[4] If he were to independently produce just one successful picture a year, he would stand to make more money. Additional benefits would accrue as well: he could keep actors under contract; accumulate an asset position in completed pictures; and build a business for himself. More beguiling, he would not have to jeopardize his private financial resources.

Which brings up the matter of financing. Despite Cagney's box-office appeal and Stromberg's production record, the two men did not have the collateral in the form of properties or finished pictures to secure complete financing from the banks. UA, as a result, was forced to invest in the two production ventures.

Money to finance this new generation of independent producers fell into three categories: first money, second money, and completion money.[5] Each category was differentiated by the degree of risk attached to it and had to be obtained from separate sources. First money financed up to 70 per cent of a picture. Since its recoupment entailed the minimum possible risk, it could be secured from banks at current interest rates.

First money, however, was the last money to be raised by a producer. Second money in effect financed a picture. Second money is the remaining 30 to 40 per cent of the budget and is paid off after the first money is taken care of. It could be secured in cash and deferments in the form of producers' or actors' salaries, studio credits, and film laboratory costs. To compensate for the risk, a lender of second money—be he a financier, distributor, or family friend—often demanded a profit participation rather than interest.

The purpose of completion money was to guarantee that should a picture go over budget, money would be forthcoming to finish it. Since an uncompleted picture is totally worthless, the bank and risk-capital group, as a condition of their loans, demanded this of a producer. Completion money could be either a bond signed by a financially responsible person or cash up to 15 per cent of the production cost held in escrow.

UA IN PRODUCTION FINANCING

UA, it should be remembered, participated in production financing only twice before—in the Wanger company and in Lubitsch's *To Be Or Not To Be*. Occasionally it had loaned moneys to producers, most notably to Selznick, but because these were advances against distribution receipts, the company had minimized its risk. UA in such a case could recoup its money as soon as the picture was distributed rather than wait until the production loans had been paid off. Now, however, as a result of a dearth of quality product, UA had to put up risk capital to help Stromberg and Cagney establish their production units.

Hunt Stromberg signed with UA on May 29, 1942, agreeing to produce a minimum of five pictures at an average cost of $700,000 each. Security-First National Bank of Los Angeles and Bankers Trust of New York provided first money to the extent of 70 per cent of the production costs. UA, through its subsidiary United Artists Productions, put up as second money $150,000 for the first two pictures and $100,000 for the last three. The UA loans took last position in the financing package, meaning that repayment was subordinated to the bank loans, laboratory and studio credits, deferred salaries including Stromberg's, and the other sources of second money. As a special bonus, UA accorded to Stromberg the same sliding-scale distribution terms that Selznick enjoyed. In return, UA was to receive 10 per cent of the net profits of the five pictures in addition to 5 per cent interest on its loans.

Cagney joined UA on March 9, 1943. He had established a production

Cagney's *Johnny Come Lately* (1943)

company in partnership with his brother William, who had acted as Jimmy's associate producer during his last two years at Warner. The Cagney deal also called for the delivery of five pictures, with Security-First National and Bankers Trust financing 70 per cent of production costs. Cagney was to supply most of the second money by deferring his salary of $150,000. UA provided the remainder by putting up $90,000 per picture. Although it would not receive a share of the profit, UA nonetheless granted Cagney the favored distribution terms.

Improvement in UA's Position

In justification of management's record, Raftery responded to O'Shea's charges by stating,

We regret exceedingly the bickering that is going on at the present time and we want to point out that on December 1, 1941 when we stepped in the company's played and earned was running about $110,000 per week domestic. . . . We are now running approximately $400,000 per week domestic and will go up during the next several weeks. We expect the biggest year in the history of the company and we do not believe any action by any stockholder, either against the company or against another stockholder can result in anything but destruction of the company, or a serious impairment of its future activities.[6]

Raftery could have added that in 1942, UA's worldwide gross came to almost $23 million. His predictions for 1943 were correct; UA did $28 million in business, earning a profit of $1 million and increasing the company's asset position to nearly $2 million.

CHAPLIN'S BATTLE WITH SELZNICK

Charles Schwartz could not let O'Shea get away with sending what he called a "most presumptuous and offensive letter," and counseled Chaplin to start suit against Selznick, Vanguard Films, Twentieth Century-Fox, and of all things, United Artists Corporation. The complaint was served on July 20, 1943, and took the form of a derivative stockholder's action, which meant that Chaplin sought to recover not for himself but for United Artists. The complaint alleged (1) that with his $300,000 loan from UA, Selznick traded literary properties and talent, instead of producing pictures for the company; (2) that Twentieth Century-Fox's payments netted Selznick a profit of $1 million; (3) that Selznick had neither produced nor delivered to UA any motion pictures; (4) that UA failed to institute action against Selznick and Twentieth Century-Fox, counter to Chaplin's demand that it do so; (5) that the UA board was dominated by Selznick; and (6) that Selznick and his associates intimidated and coerced the UA board. In conclusion, the complaint prayed for an accounting of the profits Selznick and Vanguard derived from the transaction with Fox and that United Artists be declared trustees *ex maleficio* to the extent of $1 million and that a judgment be rendered against Fox for another $1 million.

Raftery's opinion was "that there does not now exist a cause of action either at law or at equity against the Selznick Company or David O. Selznick personally."[7] Loyd Wright concurred, stating that Selznick had the right to expend the $300,000 any way he chose, to abandon any story and sell it, to loan out his stars to a competitor, and to cast anyone he wished for his pictures.

Schwartz, who of course saw the matter differently, retorted,

> It is completely incomprehensible to me how anyone can justify Selznick's act legally, logically or ethically. For what was the $300,000 given to Selznick if it was not to complete the purchase of these three works and their scripting and to take care of other pre-negative costs in connection therewith so that Selznick in turn could sell them to some third party at an enormous profit to himself and give nothing to United in return? Frankly this doesn't sound logical or sensible to me.[8]

Beyond serving the complaint, the action was left in abeyance, the strategy apparently being to frighten Selznick into production. Instead, Schwartz and Chaplin succeeded merely in alienating Selznick. A deeply disturbed Mary Pickford tried to convince Chaplin to drop the case by pointing out the consequences of his behavior, both past and present:

> In three months United Artists will be twenty-five years old—a quarter of a century. Since its formation, Twentieth Century, Warners and M.G.M., to mention only a few, have come into being and reached unbelievable heights of profit and power. Even decrepit Universal has had a re-birth and is now a thriving, modern, motion picture organization. M.G.M.'s assets are today quoted at $167,000,000. And that company was formed by Louis B. Mayer on the strength of his contract with Anita Stewart and because he was able to secure the services of a then unknown young boy working at Universal by the name of Thalberg. Compare this to the United Artists' contracts with four of the greatest names the industry has ever known. I am listing the last year's profits, after taxes, of the above three companies as follows:

Twentieth Century	$10,609,784
M.G.M.	12,132,606
Warners	8,555,000

> Despite the fact that never before in history have motion pictures known such prosperity, United limps along with barely enough to meet its heavy obligations. Why? Because there has been nothing but dissension for the past fifteen years among the owners of the company which dissension spreads through the management and down to the salesmen in the field. Dissension which has paralyzed

the activities of the company. And now your lawsuit against David is not the least of these costly and public wrangles. I can name some of the specific deals which you, personally, turned down, Charlie.

Joe Schenck had a proposition whereby all M.G.M.'s pictures were to be released through United Artists at 30% and United Artists at 25%, the profits to be split fifty-fifty. I don't know what that would have meant in the intervening years but I do know that combined grosses of last year alone would exceed $75,000,000 which would have given [UA] . . . a profit of $15,000,000. There was another deal whereby you and Douglas were each to receive $8,000,000 apiece for your stock and I $7,000,000. There was the United Artists Theatre [Circuit] stock which Joe wanted to amalgamate with United Artists Corporation. You turned that down also. Douglas and I put up $100,000 apiece and signed a ten years' contract for our pictures. You did neither.

Although you were not financially or contractually interested in the theatre, you deprived the United Artists Corporation of this tremendous asset. You will recall after that circuit was built into a profitable business it was then turned over to the West Coast Theatres to be used as a stick against United Artists producers. . . .

It is said that you claim I have deserted you and am now in David Selznick's camp. Nothing could be more untrue or unfair. I am neither in his camp nor in yours, but am first and foremost for the company's best interests and for protecting my rights as a fourth owner of this potentially powerful organization, which attitude should redound to the benefit of all the stock holder members. . . .

I am perfectly willing to go on record in saying David was wrong morally and ethically in not producing and delivering pictures to us, but I believe legally under his contract he had that right as well as the right to part with the assets he sold to Twentieth Century.

Does it not strike you as being incongruous, Charlie, that you are suing David for not having produced a picture for three years and yet Douglas and I waited six years for the first Chaplin picture? And twenty odd years ago your picture was certainly as important, if not more so, than David's is to the organization today. Undoubtedly you, too, had reasons for not seeing fit to deliver the much needed product and I would think this fact would give you a more tolerant attitude toward David. True, you did not have $300,000 of the company's money, but, on the other hand, you were morally obligated to Griffith, Douglas and me to lend every possible assistance in starting the new and precarious organization. . . .

I am confident that you and David, without the interference of attorneys and those persons motivated by selfish interests, could get together and settle this lawsuit. The three of us could then formulate some plan whereby the partners vote as a unit thus forming a sound basis for our future policy. . . .

Surely you can take no pride in the truck that we are now forced to lend our name to and permit to pass through United Artists' channels. For myself, I am deeply embarrassed for there is neither profit nor pride in the United Artists of today.

You are the last person in the motion picture industry who should ever question my good faith and loyalty to you. But if after twenty-five years of such close partnership, you still don't know me, Charlie, it is useless for me to set forth the innumerable times I have stood loyally by you and have closed my eyes to the many hurts, rebuffs and humiliations I have endured at your hand.[9]

Miss Pickford waited nearly two weeks for Chaplin's response, but none came. Thoroughly out of patience now, she informed the board of her intention to likewise bring suit against United Artists. She had to do this to safeguard her holdings in the company, the holdings which she paid so dearly for, she said, "not alone in time and effort, but in agony of mind." Her goal was to have the unanimous vote provisions in the bylaws declared invalid because they threatened to destroy her 25 per cent interest in the company.

Chaplin's Rupture with Pickford

The next meeting of the stockholders in October, 1943, was a spirited one indeed in which the following exchange between Chaplin and Pickford took place:

Chaplin: The evil of the unanimous vote has only come up recently.
Miss Pickford: It has always existed.
C: It has always existed and we functioned.
P: And how we functioned.
C: That is a question of opinion, personal opinion. You are doing very well. So am I.
P: Thank you.
C: I think we have done very well in the past. I think your credit shows so.
P: My credit is nothing to the United Artists. If my credit was run like that of the United Artists I would be penniless today, and that is just why I am going to get relief from the courts. If we can't sit down and discuss our business like any other modern organization, then it is too bad.
C: I don't think this was ever intended to be a modern corporation. We never intended it.
P: It is not, if it was.
C: It was an ideal proposition in the beginning.
P: And I would like to go on record as to what I said.
C: We had it for the purpose of exploiting our own pictures without block booking from other sources.
P: And there is no reason why it cannot proceed.
C: And I think that you and Douglas and myself did very well under the organization under those conditions and we never had any trouble at all about the majority vote.
P: It was something we gave each other. It was never in the bylaws and Mr. Goldwyn had it put in, as you will recall. It was not in the original bylaws. There was an amendment and it cost us dearly.
C: I don't think it has cost very much, and I don't know about you, but frankly, I think I have done very well by this organization under its present set up. I

can say I believe I had gotten the maximum out of my pictures and I think you have, and I think—

P: Then I do not agree. I think that we ought to go into it—not at this time— but at a later date, and I can prove it to you conclusively that figures do not lie, that our company does not do as well as others.[10]

Mary Pickford and Charlie Chaplin were irreconcilable after this encounter. "In the future," she informed Raftery, "any business dealings I may be forced to have with him will be done as though with a total stranger."[11]

REPURCHASING KORDA'S STOCK

Galling Miss Pickford, in addition to the "stupid and costly wrangle" between Chaplin and Selznick, was that the asking price for the Korda stock had risen higher and higher, the result of her partners' procrastination. To her, this was another indication of "our ill advised, improvident manner of conducting business which I consider decidedly unreasonable and unfair to those partners who are desirous of handling the company from an impersonal and unemotional standpoint and who are willing to cooperate with management in seeing its affairs be run in a modern, efficient and intelligent manner."[12]

Earlier that August, Selznick came to the stockholders' meeting with the information that Korda would entertain an offer of $660,000 for his stock. Whereupon, he moved that the stockholders authorize management to complete the deal. Miss Pickford gave her assent, but Chaplin said no. Selznick, nonetheless, went to Korda personally to set a firm price. But in the meantime, Loew's had advised Korda that the stock was probably worth much more than he realized. So Korda decided to hold off for a while. That October, Korda informed the company that the price of the stock had been re-evaluated upwards to $1 million.

In the board's opinion, acquiring the Korda stock while the unanimous vote provisions remained in effect would merely deplete the company's surplus without providing adequate means of recoupment. Pickford and Selznick, however, advised the board to go ahead with the deal, hoping that they would get Chaplin's consent later. Teddie Carr, UA managing director in England, was instructed to wrap it up and on November 27, 1943, he wired the home office that Korda consented to take $950,000 in cash.

Confusion over Rank's Relations with UA

But a week later, Carr reported that the deal still had not been closed: "Korda professes to be very perturbed about reports that Rank buying his shares and despite my vehement denials still stupidly claims negotiations may be going on between New York and Rank."[13] Yet the previous day Carr wired Arthur Kelly about an informal conversation with Rank during which Rank expressed interest in purchasing a 50 per cent interest in the company and becoming chairman of the board of a merged Anglo-American distribution company.

As the two reports were in conflict, Ed Raftery sent the following cable to Carr demanding clarification:

> Find it utterly impossible to reconcile your cable of the second to Kelly with your cable of the third to me and must ask for an explanation and I have already determined from conversations with two of the stockholders that there is not the remotest possibility of the stockholders being interested in the Rank proposal, and I cannot conceive by what wild stretch of the imagination you would think there might be. Please immediately assure Korda there is no truth whatsoever to the Rank story and that on the contrary it should be apparent on its face that we would not buy out one stockholder who is 6000 miles away only to turn around and acquire another stockholder who has the same drawback.[14]

Nonplussed by Raftery's inability to grasp his seemingly contradictory reports, Carr replied,

> Cannot conceive why you find it impossible reconcile my cables. . . . As you know have been endeavoring for some considerable time interest Rank in distributing some or all of his pictures through United instead of setting up his own worldwide distribution organization. Believe you and everyone concerned will agree this would bring great benefits to United particularly view our Odeon relationship and Rank's intention acquire theatres throughout world. Rank has known for months that United negotiation purchase Korda's shares. The principal source of his information being Korda himself.[15]

On the same day, Carr sent a second cable informing UA that Korda called the deal off, not because of Rank but because Chaplin had not consented to the purchase! To which the exasperated Raftery answered, "The owners and the members of the management are inclined to agree . . . that you had a firm deal and that there has been a complete runout on the deal. In fact the opinion has been expressed that we doubt the sincerity of the entire negotiations."[16]

Alienating Rank

UA thereupon dispatched Arthur Kelly to England to make certain that Rank had not been offended by the company's unprofessional behavior. At stake was UA's very existence in Great Britain. A review of Rank's rise to power tells why. Rank entered the film business in 1935 as a co-founder of Pinewood Studio, Ltd. Sitting on the board with Rank were all the directors of British & Dominion Films and a representative of British National Films. These two companies formed the nucleus of the Rank production interests. In 1936, Rank formed the Cinema Finance Corporation, which in turn purchased control of General Film Distributors. That same year, General Film merged with Universal's British distribution company. His next goal was to acquire a theater circuit.

By 1937, Oscar Deutsch's Odeon Theatres had grown to become the third-largest circuit in Great Britain, on a par with Gaumont-British and Associated British Picture Corporation. It had reached this position by floating a public stock issue. In the process of reorganization this new company took the name Odeon Theatres, Ltd., while the old one was called Odeon Cinema Holdings, Ltd. (UA's 50 per cent interest was now held by Odeon Cinema Holdings.) In 1938, Odeon Theatres floated its second debenture issue, which was heavily subscribed to by Cinema Finance and enabled Rank to join the Odeon board. Upon the death of Deutsch in 1941, Rank took over as chairman of Odeon Cinema Holdings. Meanwhile, scoring another coup, Rank had become chairman of Gaumont-British with its three hundred theaters.

In a few short years, Rank had succeeded in creating a vertically integrated film empire with himself at the top. In exhibition, he controlled over six hundred theaters; in distribution, as a result, General Film Distributors was supreme; and in studio space, the Rank organization controlled over half of the available facilities. It will be recalled that Pinewood and Denham studios merged to form D & P Studios in 1939. Its reconstituted board now represented the combined interests of British & Dominions, General Cinema Finance, Pinewood, London Films, and Prudential.

No one knew better than Korda the necessity for UA to keep on the best of terms with Rank.

Rank's position today in British Cinemas you know perfectly well is second to none. UA are his partners in Odeon and our holdings became tremendously valuable during his management. United Artists' productions are played in his two circuits and if he did not play them in the future you would have here a very uphill fight as the only other existing circuit plays Warner and MGM pictures almost exclusively. These three circuits have virtual monopoly in Greater London area and without them films are simply nonexistent in Greater London district which gives a very substantial percentage of total British revenues. Rank also through the control of several studios and production units will have an important production [sic] and as his chief competitor here I have no doubt that his production will develop into a very successful and worthwhile enterprise. For these pictures he needs American distribution. United Artists need quota pictures plus added revenue in the British market through British pictures which for ten years I supplied but now nobody does . . . United Artists for a great many years were the foremost American company to give an even break to British films and fared very well with this policy.[17]

With this information as background, one can appreciate the significance of Kelly's meeting with Rank. Kelly apologized that United Artists had not invited Mr. Rank in as a partner, but explained that Miss Pickford and Selznick opposed him. Whereupon, Rank said he regretted the attitude of the stockholders and thought them rather ungrateful, especially in light of what he had done to increase the asset value of Odeon Theatres. Asked if he would supply UA with quota pictures, Rank was reported by Kelly to have said that

> Inasmuch as he apparently was not a desirable prospect as a partner he had no interest whatsoever in furnishing United Artists with pictures for distribution in Great Britain or anywhere else in the world and in spite of the pleas of Teddy and myself he simply told us he had no further interest in the United Artists. Regret to say United Artists have lost a staunch friend and an association which I think would have been the healthiest thing United Artists could have ever desired.[18]

Raftery wired back saying,

> Personally I am of the opinion that you and Carr have made a serious blunder and coming on top of the recent contradictory cables and final breakdown of the Korda negotiations it is unbelieveable and inexcusable that you and Carr in one session could so completely alienate so important a factor as Rank . . . you have succeeded in removing yourself from any supervision of the foreign department whatsoever . . . I advise you to return to the United States immediately.[19]

Kelly returned, but not as a UA employee. While in England, he had accepted a job from Rank to set up a distribution company in the United States patterned after UA to release British films. UA thus found itself in the anomalous position of having on its board the head of a competing organization now called Eagle-Lion Films, Inc. As for Teddie Carr, he too joined Rank to head Eagle-Lion in Britain.

Korda, evidently unaware of the problems UA was having, thought it madness for the company to reject Rank as a partner. In explanation, Raftery said,

> We have nothing but respect and admiration for Mister Rank but the owners have hesitated making a deal with anybody due to unsettled conditions existing internally in the corporation. As you know one stockholder is suing another in the New York courts. Another one of the owners has retained counsel to test its rights in the Delaware courts. With this situation how could anyone in conscience invite a man of Mister Rank's integrity and business ability to join as a partner. We do not want to make a mistake. On the contrary what we want is first, the elimination of internal differences between the present owners and then if advisable prudent expansion.[20]

UA's Purchase of Korda's Stock

The Korda stock problem was resolved not because the partners reconciled their differences but because the Department of Justice threatened to intervene in the matter. Observing that an employee of one of the giant film companies owned a quarter interest in the only independent distributor of consequence in the business, a Justice official told Korda, "The total effect of these arrangements appears to be inconsistent with the competitive distribution in this country of films released by United Artists and the films produced by you and released through Loew's, Inc."[21]

Korda therefore decided to graciously accept UA's offer of $950,000 for his stock. Chaplin, however, still refused to give his consent, saying,

> If this transaction is consummated I shall hold all directors responsible for depleting the asset value of the Company, and shall take such legal action as I am advised.
>
> The contemplated purchase of Sir Alexander Korda's shares is all part of a scheme and plan to enable one stockholder to become a third owner as against a fourth owner . . .
>
> The management and directors actions are dominated by Vanguard Films and its principal, David O. Selznick, in this transaction.
>
> I demand that the directors concern themselves with the conserving of the assets of the Company to build the Company to a formidable condition so that it can weather any storm.[22]

Chaplin could do little more than protest now, because the Delaware Court had handed down its decision on the Pickford suit, voiding the unanimous-vote provisions in the company's bylaws. United Artists bought out Korda on April 14, 1944.

11 | *Coming Apart at the Seams*
[1944-1948]

From World War II on, the fortunes of United Artists steadily declined. One by one all of the attributes that had made it synonymous with quality motion pictures fell away. At best, UA's movies in this period lacked distinction; too often they lacked merit altogether or were in questionable taste. The financial state of the company became more and more precarious. Producers decamped. Product became increasingly scarce. Tangled law suits occupied the time of the management, and among the owners, petty quarrels and vindictiveness replaced concern for independent production.

In such a climate, it was not surprising that UA was unable to cope with the many problems that beset the industry as a whole—increased competition, a dwindling audience, constricting foreign markets, television, and the consequences of the *Paramount* decision.

PROBLEMS AT THE WAR'S END

Whereas the rest of the movie industry enjoyed a tremendous boom during the war years, UA barely managed to eke out a profit. Paramount's earnings, for example, jumped from $4 million in 1939 to an all-time high of $44 million in 1946; Twentieth Century's profits rose from $4 million to $22 million; and Warner's from $1.7 million to $19 million. Among the Little Three, Columbia rebounded from a mere $2,000 to over $3 million. [1] By comparison, UA's net income was $445,000 in 1939; and $409,000 in 1946. In 1944, UA showed a deficit of $311,000, making it the only company to have an unprofitable year during the war. The cause was simply that UA did not release a single picture of note during the first four months of the season. It depended on the Paramount package to get through, hoping that the new roster of independents would soon deliver pictures worthy of the United Artists name. There were a few hits in this period, to be sure. Selznick finally resumed production and turned out three big pictures in 1944-1945, *Since You Went Away, I'll Be Seeing You,* and *Spellbound.* And in addition to those already mentioned in the previous chapter, there were Cagney's *Blood on the Sun* (1945) and Lester Cowan's *The Story of G. I. Joe* (1945). But product came in neither quantity nor quality.

UA's experience with Hunt Stromberg was particularly disappointing. His debut as an independent, *Lady of Burlesque,* was a great success, grossing over $2 million and earning a $650,000 profit. *Guest in the House* (1944) brought in $50,000 profit. But because the returns on these pictures had to help finance the remaining three in the group, the recovery of UA's loan was contingent upon total receipts. And with each succeeding production—*Young Widow* (1946), *The Strange Woman* (1946), and *Dishonored Lady* (1947)—Stromberg was less able to control costs. The first picture went over budget by $600,000; the second by $1 million; and the last, by $1.2 million. Although *The Strange Woman* was a moderate success, the others failed dismally at the box office. The final tally for the five Stromberg productions showed a $900,000 loss; UA, by 1946, had to write off the books its $250,000 loan to this former box-office champion of champions.

And then there was Howard Hughes' *The Outlaw.* UA gave Hughes a distribution contract in December, 1944, with the understanding that he would adhere to the production and advertising codes of the Motion Picture Association of America (formerly the MPPDA). The movie itself had received a seal of approval the previous year when Hughes opened it on his own in San Francisco, but his tasteless publicity campaign had antagonized the community. He had plastered the largest billboards in the Bay area with provocative and steamy likenesses of his star, Jane Russell. They created a furor. It was only when the chief of police issued warrants to seize the film and arrest the theater manager that Hughes had them removed. As a result of Hughes' efforts, *The Outlaw* was condemned by the Legion of Decency, the censorship board of the Catholic Church. After a short run, Hughes withdrew the picture from circulation and returned to his war-related projects.

For the UA release, *The Outlaw,* as well as its advertising material, had to be resubmitted to the MPA, because a movie had to receive seals of approval for both content and advertising to be exhibited in theaters belonging to MPA members. Hughes made the required cuts in the film, and UA, which by contract had charge of its exploitation, prepared acceptable advertising copy. After the picture was released in February, 1946, however, Hughes bypassed UA to let loose a lurid and vulgar campaign which he himself either prepared or directed. Hughes had the dubious distinction of dreaming up the slogan: "How Would You Like to Tussle with

Russell?" This invitation underscored pictures of Miss Russell that high-lighted her large and considerably exposed breasts. For other similar pictures there were such captions as "Who Wouldn't Fight for a Woman Like This?," "The Girl with the Summer-Hot Lips . . . and the Winter-Cold Heart," and "What Are the Two Great Reasons for Jane Russell's Rise to Stardom?"

The Hays Office responded by revoking its approval of the movie. Hughes in turn brought suit against the organization in federal court charging unlawful restraint of trade. He lost his fight on June 27, 1946, when Judge D. J. Bright held, "Experience has shown that the industry can suffer as much from indecent advertising as from indecent pictures.

Jane Russell in Hughes' *The Outlaw* (1946)

Once a picture has been approved the public may properly assume that the advertisement and promotional material is likewise approved. The blame for improper, salacious or false advertising is placed as much at the door of the association as of the producer."[2]

The court's decision gave impetus to state and local censorship boards, who held up distribution in Pennsylvania, Ohio, Maryland, Massachusetts, and elsewhere. The Catholic Church took a particularly strong stand. The Most Reverend George Lee Leech in Harrisburg, for example, warned parents to keep children away from *The Outlaw*, calling it "a destructive and corrupting picture which glamorizes crime and immorality."[3] The major circuits, as a result, refused to book the picture. But despite the censorship problems, unsavory advertising, and the court battles, or rather because of them, UA secured enough play dates in independent theaters to enable *The Outlaw* to earn over $3 million by 1948. Hughes had his way with the picture because *The Outlaw* was the only big grosser the company had in release. In addition to the advertising campaign, Hughes insisted on handling censorship fights and directing the marketing strategy. Considering the effect the picture had on the company's reputation, one has to wonder if it was worth the price.

ESTRANGEMENT OF THE PARTNERS

Edward Raftery in his 1946 report to the stockholders once again pointed out that for UA to attract producers of integrity and ability, the company would have to be refinanced so that it could participate in independent production. Paramount had been financing Cecil B. De Mille, Hal Wallis, and Buddy De Sylva, and receiving in return not only first-rate productions but also a share of the profits as well as hefty distribution receipts. Warner Brothers had recently set up production units for Mervyn LeRoy, Joseph Bernhard, and Milton Spirling; Universal for Jack Skirball; Columbia for Fred MacMurray; and RKO for Frank Capra, William Wyler, George Stevens, and others. The tax laws still favored independent production, and Raftery predicted that during the postwar years more and more stars, directors, and producers would go this route. If UA were to meet its competition, restore its image in the industry, and achieve stability, production financing on a large scale, up to $12 million, seemed to be the answer.

Pickford's Demands

Raftery's proposal, like the others before it, never really received serious consideration. This was partly because of the Stromberg experience, but chiefly because the bickering and backbiting among the stockholders paralyzed the company. In fact, after the unanimous-vote provisions of the bylaws were amended, the arguing became more petty, more vitriolic. For example, when Mary Pickford announced her intention to resume production work she asked the board for financing assistance, and threatened to distribute elsewhere if UA did not come through with money. Selznick's nominees were willing to help out only if the stockholders agreed not to sue the company should the loan become unrecoverable. Chaplin reported through his lawyer that he would go to court regardless of the outcome of the loan. After the cool response, Miss Pickford decided to drop the matter temporarily. Later, she wrote to Ed Raftery, "Since for twenty-six years my desire to help has seemingly been misunderstood, I honestly believe the less I have to do with the company from now on the better it will be, and this also applies to Mr. Chaplin and Mr. Selznick."[4]

Miss Pickford went ahead with her plans without any help from UA. In association with husband Buddy Rogers and former Columbia producer Ralph Cohn she formed Comet Productions to make a series of six streamliners for UA distribution. But Grad Sears, who in her words was "loud in his denunciation . . . and not at all backward in expressing his lack of enthusiasm in handling them," convinced the board not to grant Comet special distribution terms.[5] The regular rate of 30 per cent prevailed.

After delivering the fourth picture, Miss Pickford reported that the streamliners had gone considerably over budget; unless UA reduced the distribution terms, Comet might have to suspend operations. She also demanded special terms for two features planned as a second production venture with Cohn, Rogers, and Lester Cowan. She was furious because her distribution contract for these features did not contain the "most-favored nation" clause which would have given her the same sliding-scale rate that Selznick enjoyed. The board was eliminating this clause in contracts as they came up for renewal because the company simply could not afford to give producers such advantageous terms. In making her demands, Miss Pickford perhaps forgot her remark a few years earlier when the company contemplated bringing Goldwyn back as a producer: "I don't think St. Peter and St. Paul together should be given a Selznick contract," she said, "not unless we were plenty on the velvet and simply wanted Mr. Goldwyn as a trimming."[6] The shoe was on the other foot now. Instead of harping on dividends, Miss Pickford, like UA's regular producers, was out to get the best terms available. The board compromised by giving Miss Pickford the Selznick terms on any feature in preparation before the expiration of her old contract in September, 1946, and delivered by the same month the following year. Afterwards, she had to pay the same distribution rate for the features as for the streamliners.

The Ejection of Selznick

Miss Pickford was thus kept mollified for the time being, but the company's relationship with Selznick took a turn for the worse. Of the three pictures Selznick had delivered to the company—*Since You Went Away, I'll Be Seeing You,* and *Spellbound*—the first was the most successful, and was nominated for the 1944 Academy Award. But Selznick still aspired to produce a movie as profitable as *Gone With the Wind.* He thought his forthcoming picture, *Duel in the Sun,* would achieve this goal. "We have managed to convince all the readers of the Hollywood Reporter, including hundreds of newspaper correspondents, that *Duel in the Sun* is calculated to have the biggest gross in the history of motion pictures, the only question being whether it will or will not out-gross *Gone With the Wind,"* he said.[7] Selznick predicted that the picture would gross $30 million in the domestic market. But United Artists was destined not to handle it, because at a special stockholders' meeting in November, 1946, attorneys for Pickford and Chaplin, armed with proxies, voted to refuse to accept *Duel in the Sun;* to rescind Selznick's distribution contract; to

Jennifer Jones, Claudette Colbert, and Shirley Temple in Selznick's
Since You Went Away (1944)

force Selznick out of United Artists; and to compel Selznick through legal action to return his UA stock to the company.

Precipitating this confrontation was Selznick's act of turning over to RKO on a profit-sharing basis producers, directors, players, and completed scripts for *Notorious, The Spiral Staircase, Till the End of Time, Honeymoon, The Farmer's Daughter,* and *The Bachelor and the Bobby-Soxer.* An outside law firm hired by the board to investigate these transactions reported that Selznick "directly or indirectly" supervised the production of three of the RKO pictures with the result that he defaulted on his UA contract. The law firm recommended that UA seek a declaratory judgment regarding "material defaults in performance by Vanguard and Mr. Selznick, and . . . the discharge of United Artists obligations to Vanguard to accept delivery of any additional pictures and to make further loans or advances."[8] It did not advocate the extreme action taken by Pickford and Chaplin. In fact, one of Miss Pickford's directors, Isaac Pennypacker, whose law firm conducted the investigation, resigned from the board because the instructions for the meeting, he told her, went far beyond "the scope recommended in my firm's opinion and in my considered judgment would be damaging to your stockholder interest and to company's interest."[9]

The charge of breach of contract was only a smoke screen. Pickford and Chaplin wanted Selznick out because the special sliding-scale distribution rate they had given him was ruining the company. At an earlier stockholders' meeting in June, Charles Schwartz, the Chaplin representative, had complained that although the gross for 1946 would probably reach a record $23 million, the company would show a deficit in the domestic market. The reason was simply that a vast amount of business was being done at 10 per cent rather than at the break-even point of 22 per cent. "The Selznick contract not only results in a loss to the company," he said, "so that every dollar we take in on the Selznick contract is to the detriment of the company, but it also does something which is even more serious, it prevents us from getting quality product. We cannot afford to give such terms to others, and the result is the present condition of the company, where we do an enormous amount of business but we finally wind up in the red."[10]

When UA decided to go to court, Milton Kramer, the Selznick counsel, warned his fellow proxy holders:

> Before taking a vote, hippodrome as it may be, on whether this company should go into a sea of litigation and cease doing the business for which it is organized, let me point out that if litigation is to commence, it will, of course, commence on all fronts and against all persons. . . . Our client, Vanguard Films, is not unmindful of the fact that through Miss Pickford's own directors and by

their vote, she obtained a reduction in terms on her distribution agreement . . . without any business consideration. We are not unmindful of other rights in respect to our distribution and loan agreement, and we will persecute and prosecute all of those rights when and if Miss Pickford and Mr. Chaplin, in their own selfish interests, seek what they think is gain for themselves by litigation, irrespective of the interests of the company.[11]

Immediately thereafter, Selznick brought a countersuit against the company, and another suit against Pickford and Chaplin, charging them with inducing the breach of contract. He accused United Artists of repudiating its contract by failing to advance $200,000 for Selznick's fifth production, *The Paradine Case,* by mishandling the distribution of *Since You Went Away, I'll Be Seeing You,* and *Spellbound,* and by refusing to distribute *Duel in the Sun.* Selznick demanded $7.5 million in damages. The essence of the complaint against Pickford and Chaplin was that they "maliciously and oppressively" conspired to deprive Selznick's company of a distribution agreement "for the purpose of injury." Wherefore Selznick prayed for a $6 million judgment against the defendants, making a grand total of $13.5 million in damages.

Selznick took the position that he had the right to loan out contract personnel when they were between projects, as was the custom in the industry. He claimed, as well, the right to abandon stories. Chaplin and Pickford, on the other hand, maintained that Selznick went far beyond the standard practices in his arrangements with RKO. In the case of *Notorious,* he not only turned over a story for which he said he had no use, but also a completed script, the star, director, and producer. What more does any executive producer ever contribute to a picture, they asked, except some supervision, which Selznick also gave? Moreover, Selznick received 50 per cent of the profits, which was more than a reasonable return for an abandoned story.

This stockholders' battle was short-lived, lasting a mere two months, until February, 1947. In the settlement, Selznick was paid $2 million for his one-third interest in United Artists. UA purchased the stock by paying out $164,000 in cash, returning Selznick's $300,000 which had been placed in escrow for the stock, and by cancelling $1,536,000 in production loans. The three court actions were dismissed with prejudice, which is to say they could never be revived.

Both sides were elated over the settlement. Chaplin and Miss Pickford considered the purchase price a bargain. Besides, in making a quick settlement, they not only ousted Selznick, but also saved money by not releasing *Duel in the Sun* and five additional Selznick pictures that would have had to be distributed at the sliding-scale rates. The Selznick forces were joyful over averting a costly and drawn-out court battle, over having their debts cancelled, and, most importantly, over being freed of the UA affiliation. United Artists, though, was left in a precarious state; the stock purchase, which depleted the company's working capital, would have serious ramifications later on.

Selznick formed his own distribution company, the Selznick Releasing Organization, to market *Duel in the Sun.* "Instead of begging one of the majors for their distribution facilities, he hired one of the best distribution men in the country, Neil Agnew, and formed his own company," said Donald M. Nelson, in an article entitled "The Independent Producer." "Selznick displayed further daring in launching an experiment in mass exhibition by simultaneous showings of 'Duel in the Sun' in cities, throughout the United States. In six months box office receipts equaled $9 million, so that in the domestic market alone, Selznick, starting from scratch in distribution, not only made up the cost of 'The Duel' but actually exceeded it by $2 million."[12]

Chaplin's Politics, and HUAC

Immediately following the Selznick lawsuits was the *Monsieur Verdoux* debacle. More than six years had passed since Chaplin had delivered a picture to the company and his new work was eagerly anticipated. But the critical reception from the daily press after the opening on April 11, 1947, was hostile: "It has little entertainment weight, either as somber symbolism or sheer nonsense. . . . It is also something of an affront to the intelligence" (Howard Barnes in the *Herald Tribune*); "The film is staged like an early talkie with fairly immobile camera, self-conscious dialogue, acting that looks like the late twenties . . . an old-fashioned production, almost quaint in some of its moments" (Eileen Creelman in *The Sun*); "It is slow—tediously slow—in many stretches and thus monotonous" (Bosley Crowther in the *New York Times*).

Chaplin consented to a press interview the following day to drum up support for the movie. He confidently expected to answer questions on why he abandoned his famous tramp to play the role of a cynical middle-class bank clerk who happened also to be a modern Bluebeard. The UA publicity department warned him to expect questions on his sex life and his politics as well. Chaplin's popularity had sunk to its all-time low, as a result of the sensational lawsuits involving Joan Barry, the Mann Act, and the paternity of her child, and rising resentment over Chaplin's so-called pro-Communist stand during the war.

The conference took place in the Grand Ballroom of the Gotham Hotel. Radio producer George Wallach reported that "the Ballroom was filled literally to the rafters. Every seat on the floor was taken. People were standing in the doorways and on the seats encircling the balcony. They

Chaplin's *Monsieur Verdoux* (1947) with Martha Raye

represented every major newspaper and magazine, and also there were journalists from any and all minor papers able to squeeze in."[13] After his introduction by a UA spokesman, Chaplin told his audience to "proceed with the butchery." He was asked if he was a Communist, he was asked why he had not become an American citizen, and he was accused of being unpatriotic. Much was made of the fact that Chaplin advocated a second front against the Nazis early in the war. The press conference was an excruciating ordeal for the filmmaker, who intended in his characteriza- tion of Verdoux "to create a pity for all humanity under certain drastic circumstances—in times of stress."[14]

After it had run for a short time in New York, Chaplin decided to with- hold the picture from national release until October, to enable his new publicity man, Russell Birdwell, to revamp the promotion campaign. Birdwell's plan was to capitalize on the controversy surrounding both Chaplin and *Monsieur Verdoux* by adopting the slogan "Chaplin changes; can you?"

Chaplin received another dose of notoriety that summer when he learned from the newspapers that he was being called to testify before the House Committee on Un-American Activities, which was beginning a probe into the alleged Communist infiltration of the motion-picture in- dustry. In response, Chaplin sent the following telegram to HUAC's chair- man, J. Parnell Thomas:

> From your publicity I note that I am to be "quizzed" by the House Un-Ameri- can Activities Committee in Washington in September. I understood I am to be your "guest" at the expense of the taxpayers. Forgive me for this premature ac- ceptance of your headlined newspaper invitation. You have been quoted as saying you wish to ask me if I am a Communist. You sojourned for ten days in Hollywood not long ago and could have asked me the question at that time, ef- fecting something of an economy. Or you could telephone me now—collect. In order that you be completely up-to-date on my thinking I suggest that you view carefully my latest production "Monsieur Verdoux". It is against war and the futile slaughter of our youth. I trust you will find its humane message dis- tasteful. While you are preparing your engraved subpoena I will give you a hint on where I stand. I am not a Communist. I am a peace-monger.

The sojourn referred to by Chaplin in his telegram set the stage for HUAC's investigation of the industry. Behind closed doors in the Los Angeles Biltmore Hotel, Thomas and a subcommittee took testimony from producers, actors, and other industry personnel, most of whom were members of the Motion Picture Alliance for the Preservation of American Ideals. Founded in 1944, the Alliance was a militant anticommunist organization dedicated to combatting "the growing impression that this industry is made up of, and dominated by Communists, radicals and crackpots."[15] Using as evidence the testimony from such witnesses as Robert Taylor, Mrs. Lela Rogers (mother of Ginger), and Adolphe Menjou—who revealed that "Hollywood is one of the main centers of Communist activity in America"—the Committee drew up its indictment: "The N[ational] L[abor] R[elations] B[oard] was abetting the effort of Communist organizers to take control of the industry; scores of highly paid screen writers were injecting propaganda into movies; White House pressure had resulted in the production of 'some of the most flagrant Communist propaganda films'; subtle techniques were used for glorifying the Communist Party, while the Communists prevented the production of films which glorified loyal American citizens; the heads of the studios had done nothing to prevent all of this. Exposure was essential; public hearings were promised."[16] Although not one of the above charges would ever be substantiated, they typified the fervor of HUAC's inquisition.

Learning that HUAC planned to take up the case of movie composer Hanns Eisler, on September 25, as a prelude to its full-scale investigation of Hollywood, Chaplin instructed United Artists to open *Monsieur Verdoux* in Washington the following day. The Capitol theater was booked for the run, but its management at the last moment decided to "postpone" the engagement. UA's interpretation of the action was that "official Washington has been led to believe that a big, bad wolf is running around loose on the screen and that it should be caged before some damage is done."[17] The picture opened on schedule, nonetheless. UA managed to book five theaters in an attempt to blanket the city. To Thomas and the other members of the Committee, Chaplin sent the following telegraphed invitation: "I am opening my comedy, 'Monsieur Verdoux' on September 26th in five Washington, D.C. theaters and it would indeed be a pleasure to have you as my guest on opening day. Respectfully—Charles Chaplin."[18]

Birdwell's ballyhoo broke attendance records at the opening and elicited an avalanche of booking requests from across the country. UA confidently expected a five-hundred-theater release after the Washington run.

The HUAC hearings began on October 20, 1947, and lasted for two weeks. Chaplin was subpoenaed to testify, but his appearance was postponed three times. Then he received a courteous letter stating that his testimony would not be needed and that he could consider the matter closed. Forty-one witnesses were heard in all. During the first half of the session, Alliance members and other friendly witnesses held the floor; the second half was devoted to unfriendly witnesses who announced as a matter of principle they would refuse to answer the Committee's questions. Ten were called—they were dubbed the Hollywood Ten—and each indeed did refuse to answer questions by invoking the First Amendment to the Constitution. Each was cited for contempt of Congress and subsequently sent to the federal penitentiary.

Hollywood's response to the hearings was prompt. Fifty leading motion-picture executives emerged from a two-day secret session at the Waldorf on November 24, 1947, to announce that the members of the Hollywood Ten had by their actions "been a disservice to their employers," "impaired their usefulness to the industry," and were suspended without compensation. More ominously, though, the executives said, "We will invite the Hollywood talent guilds to work with us to eliminate any subversives in the industry."[19] So began the blacklist, which would hang like a pall over the industry for ten years.

This history need not describe the effects of the Red scare on Hollywood, except to say that the philosophy that motivated the committee was accepted as gospel by a frightened and morally enfeebled industry. This philosophy, in the words of HUAC chronicler Walter Goodman, "held not only that Communism was a subversive doctrine, not only that Communists in sensitive positions were threats to the nation, but that the presence in this land of every individual Communist and fellow traveler and former Communist who would not purge himself was intolerable; that the just fate of every such creature was to be exposed in his community, routed from his job, and driven into exile."[20]

Returning now to Chaplin's *Monsieur Verdoux,* American audiences apparently agreed with HUAC-member John E. Rankin, who that summer in Congress had called for Chaplin's deportation. Chaplin's character was "detrimental to the moral fabric of America"; by deporting him, said Rankin, "he can be kept off the American screen and his *loathsome pictures* can be kept from the eyes of American youth."[21]

There followed a hate campaign of frightening proportions led primarily by the Catholic War Veterans and the American Legion. These and other pressure groups succeeded in instituting boycotts against the picture. First the Independent Theater Owners Organization in Columbus, Ohio, representing 325 theaters, called on theater owners "to give serious thought to the matter of withholding screen time" from *Monsieur Verdoux.*[22] Then Loew's and certain of the Paramount affiliates refused to supply play dates. *Monsieur Verdoux* had played only 2,075 dates and had grossed a mere $325,000 when Chaplin ordered it withdrawn from distribution two years later. Even though the picture grossed more than $1.5 million abroad, Chaplin felt that the UA sales force was responsible for its poor domestic showing, with the result that he lost confidence in his company.

Attempted Sale of UA

Mary Pickford and Chaplin, sharing, for once, the same sentiment toward their company, announced in a rare moment of unanimity that United Artists was up for sale. An offer came almost immediately from a syndicate headed by Si Fabian, president of Fabian Theaters, and Serge Semenenko, an officer of the First National Bank of Boston. The offer was reputed to be for $12.5 million, with $5 million going to Chaplin in cash and $7.5 million to Pickford in deferred payments. All the contracts had been drawn when Chaplin through an unidentified spokesman "with a sense of humor and an eye for publicity," in *Variety*'s words, announced that he had never participated in any negotiations for the sale of his stock and never intended to.[23] Miss Pickford, who was in New York to complete the deal, was stunned. She offered to sell her half interest in the company, nonetheless, but negotiations had to be broken off because of the syndicate's all-or-nothing proposition.

REPERCUSSIONS OF THE OWNERS' QUARRELS

After releasing a statement to the press from the home office, Miss Pickford dashed to the Waldorf, where to a surprised UA sales convention she announced that the new president of the company, replacing Ed Raftery, would be George Bagnall. Since she had not consulted Chaplin on the matter, her announcement was a bit premature. Although Chaplin had nothing against the UA vice president, he would not be dictated to by Miss Pickford.

No longer able to exercise effective leadership in the company, Raftery resigned and returned to private practice. Choosing his successor was bound to be difficult, since the two owners were barely on speaking terms, so the board suggested that Joe Schenck be brought in as an arbitrator with the authority to name a new president and to reorganize management. Schenck, who now had the title of executive head of production at Twentieth Century-Fox, was happy to do this for the company as a gesture of good will. All he required from both the stockholders was their power of attorney. Miss Pickford gladly gave hers, but Chaplin, in typical fashion, refused. In her autobiography, *Sunshine and Shadow,* Miss Pickford describes her attempt to change his mind:

> I shall never forget the day I went to Charlie's home to urge him to do the same. I thought I had seen Charlie in a tantrum, but this beat everything.
> "I wouldn't give my power of attorney to my own brother," he shouted. "I'm perfectly capable of voting my own stock."

"But, Charlie, you know Schenck is a good businessman."

"I'm as good a businessman as anybody else!"

Of course poor Charlie was no businessman at all. I appealed to his sense of fair play and sportsmanship.

"Charlie," I said, "I'm not here as your partner today. I'm not even here as someone that's been your friend for so many years. I'm here as the voice of our thousands of employees the world over, of the producers and bankers— —"

At that word he cut me short.

"If you're here as the voice of the bankers the interview is terminated."

"Very well, Charlie," I said, and without another word from either of us I started for the door.[24]

The board therefore acted on its own to choose Gradwell Sears as president. Sears had been with the company since 1941 as vice president in charge of domestic sales. He took over supervision of foreign distribution as well, when Arthur Kelly joined Eagle-Lion in 1944. As president, Sears could no longer handle worldwide distribution, so UA rehired Kelly to resume his former position. George Bagnall, Mary Pickford's nominee, had no desire for the top position, by the way, and had taken himself out of consideration.

Such behavior on the part of the owners had serious repercussions. The banks now considered UA a poor risk. Alex Ardrey of Bankers Trust, for example, noting that the purchase of the Selznick stock had nearly depleted UA's reserves, warned that his bank would discontinue financing its producers until the owners either relinquished their control or pumped working capital into the company. George Yousling of Security-First National went so far as to demand that Pickford and Chaplin put up $1 million apiece, otherwise his bank and others would go on a "film financing holiday." Since the owners would do no such thing, Security, true to its word, made no production loans to anyone in 1948. The Bank of America, in that year, insisted on 100 per cent guarantees before loaning any moneys to independents. Commenting on the action of the banks, UA vice president George Bagnall informed the board, "When you dispose of the Bank of America and Security-First National, insofar as Hollywood is concerned, there is no other real source for bank money. Neither the Bank of Manhattan nor Irving Trust are making picture loans and Guaranty Trust is also eliminated. It is my understanding that Bankers Trust are still making loans of a very selective nature. . . . This presents a very serious problem from the standpoint of United Artists—that is, how will we get sufficient product to keep us in business."[25]

In response to this unsettled situation, UA's producers staged a revolt. The Cagneys, David Loew's Enterprise Productions, Benedict Bogeaus, and Howard Hawks all refused to complete their contracts. "United

Artists is completely solvent and is being operated at a substantial profit," claimed Sears, and threatened to haul them all to court unless they completed their obligations.[26]

The Cagneys had signed with Warner for the distribution of *The Time of Your Life*. UA said the film belonged to them under the terms of its 1942 contract calling for the delivery of up to fifteen pictures. So far, only two had been produced, *Johnny Come Lately* and *Blood on the Sun*. But the contract had stipulated that the Cagneys were required to turn over those pictures UA helped finance. And the Cagneys had not asked UA for money. The company, therefore, thought it wiser to reach a settlement than go to court. To secure the picture UA agreed to furnish the second money, $250,000. Unfortunately, *The Time of Your Life* turned out to be the least successful of the Cagney group. It grossed $1.5 million as compared to $2.4 million and $3.4 million respectively for the others. UA lost its entire investment.

To secure Enterprise's *Arch of Triumph*, UA was prepared to go to court. Completed at a cost of over $5 million, the picture was ready for release. If UA slapped an injunction on it, the picture would have to sit on the shelf until the case was settled, accumulating interest charges and losing the benefits of advance publicity. Loew and his partner, Charles Einfeld, had no choice but to deliver the picture, which in the words of Sears became "the most outstanding disappointment in the year 1948." Directed by Lewis Milestone and starring Ingrid Bergman and Charles Boyer, "It was anticipated throughout the entire motion picture industry that *Arch of Triumph* would be a box office sensation," Sears said. "Instead, it has proved to be the most disappointing picture and probably the greatest commercial failure in the history of motion pictures. . . . No satisfactory explanation has yet been offered by anybody in the motion picture trade for the unprecedented failure of this picture."[27]

Next to be dealt with was Benedict Bogeaus, who, on the advice of his lawyers, was searching for another company to distribute *Christmas Eve* and *On Our Merry Way*. Although UA demanded and received the two pictures, claiming that Bogeaus' contract was exclusive, the company allowed him to release *Lulu Belle*, his forthcoming production, through Columbia. The reason for this concession was that Bogeaus needed financing which UA did not want to provide. This turned out to be a lucky decision because *Lulu Belle* proved an utter failure.

Howard Hawks was withholding his picture *Red River* because he had gone $1 million over budget and was hoping to secure a guarantee of a minimum return from another distributor. UA had no intention of releasing him, since *Red River* promised to be the hit of the season. Whereupon the backers of Hawks' production company, Monterey Productions, threatened to foreclose on the picture, and place Monterey's assets in the hands of a trustee, who would then be free to release the picture elsewhere. UA forced this controversy to arbitration and won. Still, Hawks held back until Sears agreed to personally supervise *Red River*'s national sales campaign.

There was another producer's revolt, this one unrelated to the banks. When Howard Hughes purchased operating control of RKO in 1948, he decided that *The Outlaw* and his two latest productions, *Mad Wednesday*, starring Harold Lloyd, and *Vendetta*, a vehicle for Hughes' recent discovery, Faith Domergue, should be handled by his new company. The Lloyd picture had been previewed by UA and theater circuit chiefs, who unanimously agreed that it was a most inferior production. After an unenthusiastic opening in Miami, Hughes withdrew the picture for re-editing. *Vendetta* had yet to be seen, but reports from California were not favorable.

To retrieve the pictures, Hughes planned to charge UA with incompetence. UA did not fall for the ploy and demanded that Hughes pay for his release, which he did after threats of litigation and reprisals from both sides. Hughes agreed to establish a $600,000 fund to be used as second money to finance UA producers. This money could bankroll a minimum of three $1 million pictures. But because Hughes required so many guarantees as to script, cast, and director, the money was virtually unattain-

Montgomery Clift in Hawks' *Red River* (1948)

able. Only one UA producer met his qualifications and this was Sam Bischoff for his picture *Mrs. Mike.*

In its fight to hold onto its recalcitrant producers, UA won a Pyrrhic victory. Enterprise, the Cagneys, and the others fulfilled their contracts, but afterwards moved on. By 1948, for reasons to be discussed later, nearly all of the majors were beginning to accommodate independents by providing financing, studio space, and attractive distribution terms. UA now had nothing unique to offer producers, and discontent with the company was heightened by the continuous quarrels of the owners. UA failed to attract any producer of distinction in the postwar period. The bulk of its releases were made by producers signed on during the boom. A staple in the roster continued to be westerns—five Hopalong Cassidy films in 1947 and six in 1948. UA would have added more westerns if it could have gotten them.

Anticipating a product shortage for 1948, Sears worked out a deal with RKO president Peter Rathvon to purchase four westerns. RKO had a large inventory that year and was willing to sell these pictures at cost plus studio overhead. To come up with the $4.5 million asking price, Sears went to the banks. Surprisingly, the Irving Trust was willing to finance the package. But one of UA's directors, "unfortunately and without the knowledge of management," reported Sears, "made it his business to visit certain officials of the Irving Trust downtown office . . . and supplied them information of such detrimental character to United Artists interests that the Irving Trust Company were left with no alternative except to withdraw their offer to make the loan."[28]

THE VANISHING FOREIGN MARKET

UA sustained a $517,000 loss in 1948, its largest up to that time. In explanation, Arthur Kelly actually spouted to Pickford and Chaplin the old cliché that there was nothing wrong with the company a good picture could not cure. This was true of course, but there were others factors involved, as he well knew, since he headed the foreign department.

UA's foreign business had declined 45 per cent since 1946 and for the first time in ten years this realm of the company's operations lost money— $278,000. After World War II, the American film industry, with its tremendous backlog of pictures yet to be released abroad, flooded foreign markets. Protective barriers established during the 1920s and 1930s had disappeared, and national film industries, with the exception of Great Britain's, had been totally disrupted by the war. Hollywood, it seemed, was in an excellent position to dominate the international motion-picture business. Increasing this likelihood was the fact that the American film industry had organized a united front to exploit its interests. The MPA in April, 1946, formed the Motion Picture Export Association representing the major companies, United Artists among them, to pool distribution in thirteen countries closed to American films during the war. These included the Balkan countries, Austria, the Netherlands, Germany, Japan, and Russia. The MPEA acted as the sole sales agent for its members, set prices and terms of trade, and made arrangements for the distribution of American pictures in these markets. It had even more clout than other cartels, because Hollywood's economic interests coincided with Washington's foreign policy. Eric Johnston, the new MPA president, spelled this out in his 1946 annual report: "Our Government's policy of free exchange of media of expression is . . . a powerful asset in the highly competitive situation which confronts the American industry. We expect this policy to be vigorously prosecuted and also implemented in numerous treaties and trade agreements to be negotiated with foreign countries."[29] The Export Association then had a second objective; with the cooperation of the State Department, which saw the movies as a means to inculcate ideology, it would fight to create an open market for American films everywhere.

Foreign governments, however, pressed just as vigorously to protect their impoverished countries. As Thomas Guback pointed out in his book *The International Film Industry,* "European nations, in debt and with little or no dollar reserves, could not afford the questionable luxury of importing American pictures when their peoples and businesses demanded more essential commodities; these nations believed that dollars not spent on American films could be used to alleviate more pressing needs."[30] To stem the dollar outflow, foreign governments passed import quotas, currency restrictions, and confiscatory taxes, much as they had after World War I. Great Britain remained the most lucrative market for Hollywood and it was there that United Artists and the MPEA waged their crucial battles.

Rank as Empire Builder in Britain

Despite J. Arthur Rank's treatment at the hands of United Artists over the disposition of Korda's stock, the company had been able to remain on good terms with him—temporarily at least. In 1944, Rank had given UA the domestic distribution rights for a six-picture package consisting of *Mr. Emmanual, Colonel Blimp, Johnny in the Clouds, Blithe Spirit, Caesar and Cleopatra,* and *Henry V.* The last two established United Artists as the leading distributor of British-made films in America, a position MGM had held previously by handling *Pygmalion,* which grossed $1.4 million. But *In Which We Serve* topped that by $300,000 and *Caesar and Cleopatra* set a record of $2 million. *Henry V* matched this figure when United Artists abandoned orthodox sales techniques to distribute the picture slowly on a roadshow basis to selected markets.

Laurence Olivier in *Henry V*

After the war, however, relations with Rank deteriorated, not because UA alienated him further, but because it could no longer serve Mr. Rank's interests. Rank now wanted a regular outlet for his pictures in the American market. In an excellent bargaining position, he visited the United States and offered Paramount, RKO, and Twentieth Century-Fox playing time in his houses in exchange for circuit deals for the Rank output. It was a proposition the American companies could not afford to ignore, as MGM and Warner filled the ABC houses, Great Britain's only other big circuit. Universal already had access to Odeon and Gaumont houses, because Rank was a large stockholder in that company. As for

United Artists, Columbia, Republic, and Monogram, the companies not owning theaters, they were left out in the cold.

An international cartel was in the making, charged Raftery, who went on to tell the board that "it is time for a complete FBI investigation and a criminal prosecution."[31] United Artists thought it the better part of valor not to take legal action, although the feeling of impotence was humiliating. UA owned a 50 per cent interest in Odeon Cinema Holdings, valued at £2 million in 1948, and yet was powerless to get the playing time to meet its requirements. At best, it could send Rank cablegrams chiding him for destroying the UA subsidiary in Great Britain and threatening the demise of the company at home. Conditions in England became so acute in 1947 that UAC, Ltd., had to sell off its "free" shares of the Odeon Theatre Circuit (still retaining its shares in the Holding company) for $500,000, so that the subsidiary could meet its operating expenses and settle its accounts with UA's producers.

Rank had secured a foothold in the New World, but the dollar flow between the two countries had not been equalized by any means. The imbalance amounted to about $1 million a week. The new Labour government, as a result, took action on August 7, 1947, by imposing an ad valorem tax on all motion pictures imported to England after that date. Upon entering the country, every film would be subject to a customs duty of 75 per cent of its expected earnings. The reaction of the American motion-picture industry was to boycott the British market. Fortunately for UA, it had a few unreleased pictures in England which Rank reluctantly agreed to play in his theaters. The rentals from these pictures plus the proceeds from the Odeon stock sale enabled UAC, Ltd., to hobble through the 1947-1948 season.

Faced with a shortage of pictures to fill his six hundred theaters, Rank decided to step up production. In November, 1947, he announced plans to produce a program of forty-seven pictures to be made at a cost of £9 million. Retaliation of this sort was to be expected, but the question loomed, where was the money to come from? UA soon learned the answer: Odeon Theatres would purchase General Cinema Finance Corporation, the Rank holding company controlling Two Cities, Gainsborough, and other production companies. This meant "that Odeon shareholders, then reaping rich dividends from exhibition, were to have their money invested in the much more risky business of production. Again, Odeon Theatres was a public company, with a great deal of public money invested in it; G.C.F. was a private company, under no obligation to publish accounts. So Odeon shareholders would be paying Rank for the shares . . . in a concern of unknown financial prospects."[32]

Now, even UA's asset position in Odeon was being threatened! It protested bitterly, of course, but Rank took the position that United Artists had no rights, other than as a stockholder. As Arthur Kelly correctly pointed out, UA could only "make a formal protest or a noise which might be picked up by the minority stockholders, but unless one can make out a real case of fraud there is not much hope of preventing such a plan going through."[33]

The ad valorem tax was repealed in May, 1948, as a result of MPEA negotiations with the British Board of Trade and also of the boycott. In the nine-month interim, British film production had been fully protected, enabling it to get a hold on the home market for the first time, but exhibitors had suffered from the absence of American films. Britain, therefore, agreed to a compromise by concluding the Anglo-American Film Agreement with the MPEA that March. The 75 per cent duty was lifted, but for the next two years, American companies could withdraw only $17 million annually from the company—all other earnings were frozen and could not be taken out. The pact reduced the drain on dollars, but had the added feature of encouraging American companies to invest in British production.

If in negotiating the Anglo-American Film Agreement, the MPEA thought it was business as usual in Great Britain, Parliament had a surprise in store. Later that same year, it passed the Films Act of 1948 that revised the exhibitors' quota upwards, from 20 to 45 per cent. Rank strongly advocated this measure as a reprisal against the Big Five for not living up to a promise to promote British product. The Films Act would guarantee a market for Rank's pictures at home. Taking advantage of this situation, the J. Arthur Rank Organization announced that it would extend its production activities to supply the Odeon and Gaumont circuits with all their quota requirements. The new productions, together with the regular pictures on its production program and thirty British reissues, would just about fill the playing time of both circuits. Whatever dates remained would be allocated to the cream of the pictures from America and at terms that Mr. Rank would dictate. Paramount and RKO were offered two booking dates for 1949; Twentieth Century-Fox, four; and United Artists, one. As it turned out, Rank's plunge into heavy production eventually brought about the collapse of his empire, but in the meantime, his tactics were putting the squeeze on United Artists abroad.

THE SHRINKING DOMESTIC MARKET

Nor could the industry look to the domestic market for solace. Motion-picture attendance had begun to drop after 1946—precisely how much cannot be ascertained. The trade paper *Film Daily* put attendance at about 85 million a week in 1948, off about 5 per cent from its 90 million in 1946. The Audience Research Institute, a private polling organization, put weekly attendance at 69 million in 1948, off 14 per cent from a peak of 81 million in 1946. Other private estimates by heads of companies and by bankers placed the figure as much as 25 per cent off.[34] Although these estimates varied widely, the lush days of the mid-forties were over.

The war's aftermath had much to do with it. For one thing, when the servicemen returned, the birth rate increased sharply. Families with babies tended to listen to the radio at nights rather than attend movies. Veterans, moreover, swarmed into educational institutions, and studies cut into their leisure time. And now that the country was at peace, goods and services could be diverted to civilian purposes. Houses, automobiles, appliances, and other commodities were purchased in abundance, cutting in on disposable income.

These factors as well as conditions overseas had a devastating effect on the industry. UA's earnings declined from $409,000 in 1946 to a deficit of $517,000 in 1948; Warner's earnings dropped $8 million; Loew's dropped $13 million; and Paramount's, nearly $17 million. The losses were primarily in the areas of production and distribution.[35] After 1948, exhibition would suffer as well.

Television, rearing its antennae across the landscape, began its real commercial expansion in 1948. The number of sets in use jumped by more than 1,000 per cent, from 14,000 in 1947 to 172,000 that year. In the next, it would go up to 1,000,000; then to 4,000,000 in 1950; and to 10,000,000 in 1951. Simultaneously, the number of commercial television stations would increase from 6 to 107.[36] In less than a decade, the tube would come to dominate the leisure-time activities of the American people.

UA's Entry into the Television Market

All the signs portending television's growth were clearly evident in 1948, and while the motion-picture industry as a whole chose to ignore them, United Artists surprisingly had the foresight to establish a distribution department for television. It had no UA product to distribute, it should be noted, because the company had sold off the reissue rights to the old Walter Wanger pictures, *To Be Or Not To Be,* and the Paramount package. These pictures went as a group to financier Jacques Grinieff for $800,000, which money UA needed to offset an anticipated deficit in 1947. Since UA did not own a film library—pictures reverted to producers after the distribution period—it could only function within television as it had within the motion-picture industry, namely as a sales agent for producers.

Network programming in those early days was chiefly live. Films constituted only about one-fifth of program time. These, by the way, consisted of old westerns and shorts released to TV by minor studios. Local stations, however, possessing neither the facilities nor the financial resources for extensive live broadcasting, had greater needs. The major film studios, which regarded television as an arch rival, were not about to aid the enemy. Hollywood, as a result, saw the development of an entire subindustry, consisting of small, independent production companies devoted to turning out series of low-budget telefilms, usually a half-hour in length. This was the product UA sold. But the television department could not reverse the declining fortunes of the company. By the end of 1950, the department's annual gross was a mere $350,000, which was neither a significant share of the market nor enough to meet overhead expenses. The tally after its first two and a half years showed a $30,000 deficit.

THE IMPACT OF THE *PARAMOUNT* CASE

While TV nibbled away at the box office, an event of singular magnitude was about to shake the industry. And that event, of course, was the disposition of the *Paramount* case. The arbitration provisions of the 1940 Consent Decree had brought the many complaints of exhibitors out into the open with the result that the Department of Justice reactivated the case by pressing for the divorcement of the exhibition from the production-distribution branches of the five majors. The case went to trial in October, 1945, before a special three-judge statutory court in New York. Although the court held that the eight defendants—the Big Five and the Little Three—had engaged in a nationwide conspiracy in restraint of trade, and listed several infractions of the Sherman Act, divorcement was held to be irrelevant since ownership of only one-sixth of the theaters was not judged a potent weapon of monopoly. Instead, the court ordered a system of competitive bidding to end unreasonable discriminations against small independent theaters.

Both sides appealed the case to the Supreme Court; the Department of Justice because of the holding on divorcement, and the defendants because of the court's prohibitions of various trade practices. In May, 1948, the Supreme Court handed down its opinion. It had voted unanimously to uphold the general verdict of the District Court. Block booking, the fixing of admission prices, unfair runs and clearances, and discriminatory pricing and purchasing arrangements favoring theater circuits were declared illegal restraints of trade and their future use by the eight defendants was prohibited. The five majors were ordered to terminate all pooling arrangements and joint interests in theaters belonging to one another or to other exhibitors. The Supreme Court, however, rejected the competitive bidding mandate on the grounds that it would play into the hands of the buyer with "the longest purse." Concerning the charge of monopoly in exhibition, it suggested that the District Court make a fresh start on the issue of theater divorcement and divestiture.

RKO and Paramount, apparently tired of the ten-year battle with the government, began negotiations for consent decrees. The Department of Justice rejected compromise proposals calling for the divestiture of selected theaters and insisted on the complete divorcement of the affiliated circuits from their production and distribution branches. Both decrees were approved by the District Court in 1949 and contained these provisions: (1) the prohibition of unfair distributor trade practices so that each picture would be rented on a separate basis, theater by theater, without regard for other pictures or exhibitor affiliation; (2) the splitting of the existing companies into separate theater and producer-distributor companies with no interlocking directors or officers; (3) the divestiture of all theaters operated in pools with other companies or one or more theaters in closed towns, that is, where they had no competitors; and (4) the establishing of voting trusts to prevent shareholders in the former integrated companies from exercising common control of both successor companies.

The other three defendants—Loew's, Twentieth Century-Fox, and Warner—refused to go along with these decrees until the District Court and then the Supreme Court forced them into submission. Theater divestiture progressed slowly, into 1957 for the foot-dragging Loew's; nonetheless, the disintegration of the motion-picture monopoly progressed irreversibly.

Before discussing the impact of the *Paramount* case on United Artists, the question arises as to why the company was involved in the suit at all. Michael Conant, in his book *Antitrust in the Motion Picture Industry,* has argued that none of the three minor distributors—Columbia, Universal, and United Artists—should have been made defendants, because they owned no theaters. "True, they were members of the film boards of trade and released their pictures in the same run and clearance patterns as the majors. Was it not better for them to join the film boards of trade and try to have some little say in the governing of a cartelized industry than to stay on the outside?" Conant goes on to say: "They could not release films in any pattern other than that set by the majors and still remain solvent. For all first class pictures (A pictures), costs could be recovered only if the pictures were screened in a majority of the large downtown theaters. Most of these theaters were owned and controlled by the five majors. In order to obtain sufficient showings in the largest theaters and thereby recover costs on more costly films, the three minor defendants were forced to acquiesce in the entire regimented run and clearance pattern adopted by the five majors in the majority of American cities."[37]

The Paramount *Case As It Related to UA*

United Artists was the only minor that did not engage in block booking. The company was predicated on the idea of selling pictures singly and individually for independent producers. Each producer possessed the right by contract "to direct the distributor to license the exhibition of his own photoplay with each exhibitor, upon such terms and conditions as to the producer may seem fit." This meant in practice that every contract with every exhibitor had to be submitted to the home office where it was approved not by the sales department but by the producer's representative. Such a procedure precluded the selling of pictures in blocks.

Moreover, the fact that UA, alone of the eight defendants, was a distributor exclusively made its inclusion in the *Paramount* case even more tenuous. Having no control over the production schedules of its producers and without a production department of its own, the company could not guarantee a minimum supply of pictures to exhibitors. And when it did acquire product, the company had to find theaters whose playing time was not fully preempted by the majors or other distributors under block-booking agreements. In fact, UA had found it progressively more difficult to secure first-run access for its releases. The boom in attendance during the 1944-1947 period enabled the majors to extend the runs of their pictures in their own and each other's theaters. In San Francisco, as a result, UA in 1944 went into partnership with California circuit owner Joseph Blumenfeld to operate the United Artists theater in that city. In 1945, the partnership was extended to include the four Music Hall theaters in Los Angeles. Although these ventures proved to be profitable, Blumenfeld, by 1948, wanted out because, as Grad Sears remarked, he "feared the scarcity of product combined with its inferior quality would not be sufficient to continue profitably."[38] Blumenfeld, accordingly, disposed of his half interest to a theater syndicate called Principal Theaters, Inc. of America. Conditions in New York forced UA in 1947 to lease the Broadway theater for an eighteen-month period. UA's lackluster product coupled with a weekly overhead of $5,000 added up to a $164,000 loss the first year and a $195,000 loss the second. And as a final example, to break the grip Fox and Warner had on Milwaukee, UA was forced to purchase a third interest in the independently owned Towne theater and spent nearly $70,000 in remodeling costs to secure a first-run outlet in that area.

The government's case against United Artists, unjust though it might have been, went uncontested. For thirty years, UA had fought for the right to co-exist within the industry; now it had to face the consequences of guilt by association. With Columbia and Universal, it filed for a separate consent decree—the goal for UA being not to extricate itself from the proceedings, but merely to modify certain injunctions in special consideration

Gradwell Sears and Loew's, Inc., president Nicholas Schenck

for the Little Three. The District Court, however, subjected them to the same price-fixing and trade-practice prohibitions as it had the majors. As a consequence, UA became a party to the hundreds of treble-damage suits against the *Paramount* defendants instituted by independent exhibitors under the provisions of the Sherman Act. In 1949, the claims for damages amounted to $50 million.

RETRENCHMENT

UA, nonetheless, should have looked to the future with confidence because the *Paramount* decision, as Conant said, could be regarded as the charter of freedom for independent producers. The prohibitions against block booking and the court order forcing the majors and former theaters to treat each other at arm's length under penalty of contempt equalized access to the marketplace. Other factors were at work as well. Theater attendance, as mentioned earlier, had been declining as a result of the inroads made by television, the abundance of goods and services, and the growing disenchantment with the puerile Hollywood fare.

After 1947, the big studios underwent a period of retrenchment. Fewer pictures were put into production. The trend was toward quality, since this type of picture had the greatest potential for attracting audiences. Low-budget, class B pictures were phased out completely—they could no longer be forced on independent exhibitors. And lastly, actors, writers, producers, and directors were taken off long-term contracts or pared from the payrolls. Because of favorable tax laws, many of the best turned independent.

The ranks of independent producers swelled to over one hundred by the time of the Supreme Court decision, according to *Variety*.[39] The newcomers were Leo McCarey, Burt Lancaster, Frederick Brisson, Dudley Nichols, Bob Hope, Bette Davis, Elliott Nugent, Michael Curtiz, and Alfred Hitchcock, to name a few. But they did not join United Artists! Paradoxically, the very companies that had created the barriers to independent production in the prewar period were now vying to provide financing and studio space to independents and to distribute their films.

Surveying the situation at the beginning of 1949, Grad Sears, in a letter to Chaplin and Pickford, gave this prognosis of UA's prospects for survival:

> Your company is in a most perilous predicament. The company finds itself without credit, working capital or any guarantee of forthcoming production. Theatre receipts are declining and, in your President's opinion, will continue to do so due to inferior pictures and the competition offered by television. The foreign markets are rapidly depleting and will undoubtedly get worse before they get better. It is our opinion that your Odeon asset is a dead asset and saleable only through one source, namely, J. Arthur Rank. It is true the corporation has a sizeable backlog which, with the exception of one picture *Red River,* will be slow liquidation due to the inferior quality of the unliquidated pictures. Your forthcoming production, such as it is, is questionable at best.
>
> I assure you that it is with no pleasure or satisfaction that your management must forecast such a dismal outlook. Nevertheless, we are honest and realistic enough to present the facts in their true light and perspective. We have realized this condition was imminent for some time and have so advised your directors. . . . The United Artists Corporation has a great name, but it must have working capital in order to inspire confidence of banking institutions and worthwhile production. Without capital, credit or proper production, it cannot now long continue to meet its obligations.[40]

The End and the Beginning of UA
[1949-]

THE BRINK OF DISASTER

Something had to be done—and quickly—to solve the predicament of the United Artists Corporation. A four-member committee of the board was asked to bring in recommendations for the owners to consider. At a stockholders' meeting early in 1949, it set out these options: (1) that the stockholders appoint an underwriter to sell treasury stock in an amount sufficient to guarantee proper working capital; or (2) that United Artists merge with one of the existing motion picture companies; or (3) that a person be given full authority to replace the present management with people who have the confidence of the banks and/or producers; or (4) that the stockholders guarantee an adequate supply of working capital.

Rather than take steps to implement any of these recommendations, Chaplin and Pickford decided merely to exchange options to purchase one another's stock, which was, as everyone knew, a delaying action. After ninety days during which little of constructive value took place, the options lapsed, in June, 1949. So far that year the company had lost $400,000. Sears reported that "as of June 10, 1949, there are but four additional pictures completed and undelivered, and only two pictures in production. Beyond this our prospects for future production are highly dubious. The corporation's working capital is non-existent and its bank balances are perilously low."[1] Sears' closing advice was to dissolve United Artists if none of the committee's recommendations were implemented within sixty days.

By now, the trade papers were tossing out rumor after rumor of a sell-out, which demoralized management and thoroughly confused UA's remaining producers. Actually, one deal was nearly consummated when the Nasser brothers almost mustered $5.4 million to buy out the two partners. Selmer Chalif, Miss Pickford's nephew, who was employed by the company, told Sears that Miss Pickford was "very depressed about the situa-

Mary Pickford and husband Buddy Rogers (1949)

tion and from what she has told me about her meeting with Chaplin I think he was badly hit by the collapse of the deal."[2]

Other offers were made, studied, and ultimately rejected. In August, Chalif reported to the home office that "I've had several conversations with Madam and she seems to still be playing around with mysterious plans. She now says there are two situations that might mean something but she always winds up with a little touch of discouragement. This, of course, makes me feel that she is simply going through the various possibilities . . . which were deemed impractical. I don't know what her ultimate goal is . . . but I do have a distinct feeling that both she and Chaplin are waiting for a miracle."[3]

McNUTT'S ATTEMPT TO SALVAGE UA

United Artists' producers and the bankers were not willing to wait for divine intervention, however, which meant that the company had to look to its assets to satisfy the demands of its creditors. The first to go was the $1 million life insurance policy the company had taken out on Joe Schenck. The cash value for the policy was swallowed up by the $200,000 deficit in 1949. To raise additional working capital for the year ahead, the board out of desperation wanted to make an offer of the company's treasury stock. But to its surprise, the owners had negotiated a deal on their own. On July 11, 1950, they announced that a new management group headed by Paul V. McNutt would take over the management of the company. McNutt, former governor of Indiana, United States High Commissioner to the Philippines, and American Legion Commander, was named chairman of the board; Frank L. McNamee, Philadelphia lawyer, took Sears' job as president; Miss Pickford became vice president; and Max Kravetz, movie promoter, confidant to Miss Pickford, and the intermediary in the negotiations, came in as secretary. In essence, Pickford and Chaplin brought in the McNutt group to operate the company until July, 1952, during which time it could exercise an option to purchase 90 per cent of their stock for $5.4 million. The deal had been negotiated over a ten-month period, making it one of Hollywood's best-kept secrets.

McNutt inherited a deficit of $465,000. Neither instituting drastic economies nor thinning the managerial ranks could stem the outflow. By the end of the year the deficit dipped to $871,000. McNutt brought prestige to the company but not the expertise needed to gain the confidence of producers and bankers. During the first six months of his regency, virtually no new pictures were put into distribution.

What once looked like a bargain—a $5.4 million option for a company appraised at $12.5 million by the Fabian group three years earlier—now appeared to McNutt a bust. It was clear that the option had to be revised. He first proposed that his management group should be issued treasury stock to enable it to function with authority. Miss Pickford replied by saying that although she favored the idea, she was sure that Chaplin would never consent to making them partners. McNutt then asked Miss Pickford if she would consider buying out her partner. Here, Miss Pickford hesitated, explaining that she did not want to be burdened with the full responsibilities of the company. Besides, there were offers from such people as Sam Katz, Stanley Kramer, and, yes, Eva Peron, she added. McNutt could only agree with his colleagues that both principals were "not sufficiently realistic about the condition of this company to make whatever moves may be necessary for its preservation."[4]

KRIM AND BENJAMIN TAKE OVER

So to avoid being saddled with a bankruptcy, McNutt looked for a graceful way out. Ready to rescue him were Arthur B. Krim and Robert S. Benjamin.[5] The two men were partners in the firm of Phillips, Nizer, Benjamin & Krim, one of the ablest law firms in the film industry. Since that firm had represented many film companies and other clients active in the film industry during the 1930s and 1940s, Krim and Benjamin knew a great deal about movie law, personalities, theater operations, and antitrust laws. Moreover, they had what the McNutt group lacked, practical experience in the business. Benjamin, after the war, had become head of the J. Arthur Rank Organization in America, a director of Universal Pictures, and vice president of United World Pictures. Krim had been president of Eagle-Lion Films, Inc., when the company was owned by Robert R. Young, the railroad financier.

The two groups were brought together in September, 1950, by Matthew Fox, a close friend of Krim and Benjamin's, who discovered that McNutt was running into trouble. During those initial meetings, McNutt tried to convince them to join the company and share the managerial responsibilities. As an inducement, he offered to make them parties to his option. But after studying the situation, Krim and Benjamin decided that a partnership would be unworkable. They also rejected his suggestion that they take over the management by agreeing to pay Chaplin and Pickford $5.4 million from the proceeds of the business. In Krim and Benjamin's estimation, the stock was worthless.

However, Krim and Benjamin thought that United Artists could be saved. All that remained was getting Pickford and Chaplin to accept the notion that a new managerial team should be recompensed for reviving the company rather than paying for the privilege. McNutt agreed to step aside and allow Krim to press his case. Mustering all of the forensic skills he learned back in college as head of Columbia's debating team, Krim began the agonizing process of convincing Chaplin and Pickford to take a realistic look at their company. By the beginning of 1951, it was losing $100,000 a week. Moneys due to producers were being diverted to pay operating costs. Soon, a receiver would be at the company's door. Arthur Krim described these conversations:

> All the conversations I had with them were based on the supposition that the industry was in good shape, and I hoped that UA would not go bankrupt, which would give a bad name not only to the company but also to the industry. Whether or not we succeeded in coming in to manage it, I wanted to convince them that unless they agreed on a solution quickly, theirs would be a bankrupt company. I spent a lot of time persuading them that . . . the McNutt option was not worth anything to them because McNutt had no intention of paying them the $5.4 million. Their only chance of salvaging anything was to bring in a management that would build the confidence of financing sources and the producers and turn this company around. Every day made that a much more difficult task because money was going into deficit operations that should really be going into building up the company. This was the whole process of negotiation. We were never talking about how much we would pay them. We wanted to convince them that they had nothing of value to offer and finally they got the message. You see, all this talk with Eva Peron and Jacques Grinieff . . . kept allowing Mary to think she had something to sell. These people would talk of $10 million, $15 million, $4 million, $8 million and each time she had to be given a dash of cold water to realize that this was pie in the sky and while she was delaying in coming to grips with the reality of the situation because of these so-called proposals, the company was getting sicker and sicker. If she and Charlie hadn't made the deal with us the day they did, there would have been a receiver in within three or four days. And because there were producers whose money was being diverted to improper purposes and because this was an *in extremis* situation, Bob Benjamin and I did a lot of soul-searching as to whether we should take this on. We were ready to take it on in August or September, but by February, we were terribly pessimistic. But you know, once you get on into something, it's a challenge. We went through with it and I must say it was six or eight months later before I felt that maybe we had done the right thing, because as we got into it, it was even worse than we had anticipated.[6]

On February 7, 1951, Krim made a final offer, which was as follows: Krim and Benjamin were to be made trustees for 100 per cent of the United Artists' stock, which would give them operating control of the company for a period of ten years; 8,000 shares of unissued common stock were to be set aside in escrow for them so that if the company made a profit in any one of the next three years, they would be allowed to buy the 8,000 shares for a nominal $1 a share. These shares would give them half ownership in the company. Krim and Benjamin also asked for a ten-day option to see what kind of working capital they could raise. A unique proposition! Chaplin and Pickford accepted.

It should be pointed out here that for federal income tax purposes, United Artists had reorganized its capital structure in 1937 to increase its authorized common stock from 9,000 shares to 36,000 shares. The stockholders of record—Pickford, Fairbanks, Chaplin, Goldwyn, and Korda—received common stock dividends to increase each stock unit from 1,000 to 4,000 shares. In 1951, UA held 12,000 treasury shares (the Fairbanks, Goldwyn, and Korda units repurchased by the company—the Selznick stock unit had been held in escrow and hence never issued) and 16,000 unissued shares. The stock units of Pickford and Chaplin consisted of 8,000 shares issued and outstanding.

In a day, Krim and Benjamin succeeded in borrowing $500,000 from their good friend Spyros Skouras, the head of Twentieth Century-Fox. Although United Artists was his competitor, Skouras felt that a major bankruptcy would be bad for the industry as a whole. The money came with strings attached, however; UA had to agree to give De Luxe Laboratories, a Fox subsidiary, its film-processing work. Next another friend, Walter E. Heller, the brilliant Chicago financier who had made many large movie loans, came through with a $3 million loan at 12 per cent, his normal fee. With this money as a cushion, Krim and Benjamin exercised their option and took control of United Artists.

Now they had to find product. As a starter, the new managers were able to secure five pictures from UA's recalcitrant producers. A search through film vaults in Europe supplied a few others. But more were needed, obviously, so Krim went to his former employer, Robert R. Young, with an offer to buy the rights to Eagle-Lion's library of three hundred titles for $500,000. That company too was on the verge of going out of business and although its product lacked quality, the films could generate the needed revenue to keep United Artists afloat. Young accepted the offer in April, 1951, and soon the Eagle-Lion pictures were grossing $200,000 a week for United Artists.

Shortly thereafter, the company got hold of two big pictures. Stanley Kramer, who signed with UA in 1948, was now at Columbia and had still to deliver his final picture on his UA contract. Columbia looked over his properties and suggested that he give to UA "the western without action." This was *High Noon,* which grossed $12 million worldwide. The next one came when Heller learned that Sam Spiegal was making a film with British money and needed a loan to cover dollar costs. Heller put up the funds in return for the U.S. distribution rights to *African Queen,* which grossed $4.3 million domestically.

The worst was over. By the end of 1951, United Artists was out of the

Charles Chaplin and wife Oona O'Neill Chaplin (1950)

red, showing a profit of $313,000. In March, 1952, Krim and Benjamin received their 8,000 shares of stock when an independent audit confirmed their figures. They now owned half the company.

Buying Out Chaplin and Pickford

Intermittently over the next several years, there were separate discussions with Chaplin and Pickford about selling their stock in the company, but agreement seemed unattainable. Unexpectedly, in February, 1955, Krim received a telephone call from Chaplin asking for $1.1 million in cash within five days for his 25 per cent of the company. Krim called Heller in Chicago, got the response he hoped for, and closed the deal. Chaplin was now living permanently in Vevey, Switzerland, where he had taken refuge in 1953 from the incessant political harassment in this country. In 1952, Attorney General James McGranery had declared the intent of the U.S. government to bring action against Chaplin for "being a member of the Communist Party."[7] McGranery had made the announcement while Chaplin was at sea beginning a European vacation. Subsequently, the American Legion picketed his latest UA release, *Limelight,* and forced its withdrawal from the Fox theaters on the West Coast and the Loew's in New York. Chaplin chose not to return to answer the charges. He handed in his re-entry permit in April, 1953.

In 1956, Mary Pickford too agreed to sell. Her asking price was $3 million. UA borrowed $2 million, and gave Miss Pickford a debenture for the rest. Krim, Benjamin, and their partners now owned the company outright.

THE FORMULA FOR SUCCESS

UA's worldwide gross for that year came to $64 million, up $45 million from 1950. Its earnings record was just as spectacular, over $6 million as compared to the $871,000 deficit at the end of 1950. Krim and Benjamin had turned the company around. First of all, they hired some of the best men in the business to fill out the management team—men such as William J. Heineman, Max E. Youngstein, Arnold M. Picker, Seymour M. Peyser, Charles Smadja, and Robert F. Blumofe. Next they implemented a concept that UA from its inception dared not adopt, namely the financing of independent producers. As Krim explained it:

> The history of the company and its original purposes were really antithetical to the idea of getting financing for producers. This was not supposed to be a company for profit. This was supposed to be a company to service producers at actual cost of distribution allowing the producers to enjoy as production profit what otherwise would be a distributor's profit. The only reason a distributor

Press conference in Arthur Krim's office, October, 1951. Left to right: Al Bollengier (then treasurer of the company), Seward Benjamin (then and now secretary of the company), Bill Heineman, Seymour Peyser (then general counsel of the company), Bob Benjamin, Arthur Krim, Arnold Picker, Max Youngstein, and Matty Fox.

would want to finance pictures would be to make a profit and so the two never went together. Our approach to the company was to change it in just that way, and that is to alter the structure of the company so that we were no longer distributing for the benefit of producers but distributing as well for our own benefits with interests in the pictures that were being distributed by United Artists.[8]

On the basis of the company's profitable record in 1951 and 1952, Krim and Benjamin were able to initiate a broad financing program by gaining the confidence and support of an increasing number of banking institutions and thus were able to attract important producers, stars, and directors to the independent ranks. In 1957, its roster included fifty independents, among them such actor-producers as John Wayne, Frank Sinatra, Gregory Peck, Bob Hope, and Robert Mitchum; such director-producers as William Wyler, Joseph Mankiewicz, and Otto Preminger; and such production units as the Mirisch Corporation and the Hecht-Hill-Lancaster group. In that year, UA was able to procure financing for 85 per cent of all of its pictures. It released 55 pictures and financed 47 of them at a cost of $3.5 million from the company and $17.6 million from outside sources.

UA, in essence, went into partnership with its producers. Together, the company and producer would reach agreement as to story, cast, director, and budget; afterwards, the producer had complete autonomy in the making of the picture. Commenting on this setup, Otto Preminger said, "Only United Artists has a system of true independent production. They recognize that the independent has his own personality. After they agree on the basic property and are consulted on the cast, they leave everything to the producer's discrimination. Most of the time, when the others make an independent contract, they want to be able to approve the shooting script and the final cut."[9] Another facet of this relationship was to allow the producer to own a share of his picture and to participate in its profits. As a result, UA's producers often became co-venturers with the company by deferring salary considerations until all costs had been recouped. Further, many of UA's independents were allowed to appoint their own sales representatives to collaborate in the distribution process.

During the period 1953 to 1957, UA released nearly fifty pictures a year. Some of them, such as Preminger's *The Moon Is Blue* (1953) and *The Man With the Golden Arm* (1956), the Hecht-Lancaster production of *Marty* (1955), and Michael Todd's *Around the World in 80 Days* (1957), made motion-picture history. UA's output, controversial, offbeat, but eminently entertaining, demonstrated to a stagnating motion-picture industry how to tear audiences away from their TV sets. During the fifties, the majors began to emulate the UA idea. In fact, by 1958, 65 per cent of Hollywood's movies were made by independent producers.

After the purchase of Mary Pickford's stock unit, the Krim and Benjamin group held full ownership of United Artists for only twelve months. In early 1957, the company went public by placing on the market 350,000 shares of common stock at $20 a share and $10 million in 6 per cent convertible debentures. By the summer, the stock was listed on the New York Stock Exchange. The company issued two classes of common stock; Class A, which was sold to the public, and Class B, which was held by Krim and Benjamin (310,000 shares) and by four key vice presidents and partners (77,000 shares each).

In that same year, UA made a major acquisition. It purchased from a television distributor, Associated Artists Productions, Inc., the Warner Brothers library of over 800 pre-1950 feature films and over 1,500 short subjects and cartoons. The acquisition served to boost the company's already profitable television distribution operations which had acquired the rights to more than 250 motion pictures and had experienced a jump in revenues from $2 million in 1956 to $4.7 million in 1957.

UA continued on course during the sixties. In 1968, its income reached a new high for the company, an impressive $250 million which generated $20 million in profits after taxes. In the Academy Award sweepstakes, UA led the pack, capturing Oscars for best picture five times with *The Apart-ment* (1960), *West Side Story* (1961), *Tom Jones* (1963), *In the Heat of the Night* (1967), and *Midnight Cowboy* (1969).

UA's earnings record attracted the interest of Transamerica Corpora-tion, a diversified service organization, which purchased 98 per cent of UA's stock in 1967 and made it a subsidiary. Transamerica did little to interfere with the formula developed by Krim and Benjamin, who remained, respectively, as president and chairman of the board of directors. UA's most spectacular coup in recent years occurred in 1973. MGM, which had been going downhill ever since the divorcement proceedings of the fifties, decided to go out of the distribution business, curtail its production program, and spend its resources developing a hotel in Las Vegas called Grand Hotel. United Artists acquired the domestic theatrical and syndicated television distribution rights to all MGM pictures for ten years and purchased outright MGM's music-publishing companies: price, $15 million. A UA-MGM consolidation that Joe Schenck tried to effect back in the twenties finally took place.

UA—OLD AND NEW

So, the moribund United Artists that Mary Pickford and Charlie Chaplin relinquished in 1951 revived to become the pacesetter of the industry. This happened because the new managers had a singleness of purpose in running the company, earned the confidence and support of the banks, and offered stars, directors, and producers a chance to be masters of their own talent—circumstances all too often lacking in the old UA.

The comparison between the old and the new company is not meant to be invidious. The achievements of Mary Pickford and Charlie Chaplin's company were unique. UA's founders were pioneers in every sense of the term. Their enormous popularity as stars had stimulated the growth of an infant industry and helped establish film as an art form of consequence. They were strong-willed, temperamental, idiosyncratic, but eminently gifted artists who possessed the fortitude to buck a system that was beginning to pride itself more on efficiency and standardization than on individuality and craftsmanship. The formation of United Artists was not only an economic move on their part but also an idealistic one.

Their company succeeded against great odds, just barely in the beginning, but when a strong leader was found in the person of Joe Schenck, UA took root. Thereafter, in an oligopolistic market, UA was able to function exclusively for the benefit of the independent producer. UA's output as a whole will bear comparison to that of any other studio. Many of its releases, those of the founders, Goldwyn's, Schenck's,

Disney's, and Selznick's, in particular, are among the finest achievements of the industry.

Unfortunately, UA's output, both in terms of quality and quantity, could have been greater. Its flaw was that those traits of independence, flamboyance, and melodramatics that characterized the owners' work as artists could not be checked in the board room, severely handicapping the management of the company throughout much of its history. The founding stockholders were correct in resisting Schenck's schemes in the twenties to create a vertically integrated company out of UA or to merge it with another distributor. The pressure to adopt the mass-production system of the majors would have been enormous, to the detriment of the independent idea.

But they were wrong in not reorganizing the capital structure of the company in 1934 to give the active producer-owners operating control. The intent of the reorganization was to return the company to its original cooperative structure, while at the same time guaranteeing the founders substantial rewards in form of dividends. UA had served the founders well during their productive years. Now that Pickford and Fairbanks had become inactive and Chaplin nearly so, it was time to recognize the demands of those partners who were sustaining the company. Their negative decision led to Schenck's resignation and the loss of Twentieth Century. It also spurred Goldwyn's unsuccessful takeover attempts and departure to RKO. In the meantime, the owners demonstrated their managerial incompetence by losing Disney to a competitor.

Selznick was made a partner to fill the product gap left by Goldwyn. Relations between him and the owners and management deteriorated too soon, however. Much of the blame must rest with Selznick in not living up to at least the spirit of his UA contract, but Chaplin fanned the fires of discontent by threatening litigation. In the midst of all this, UA's confused management bungled the Korda stock purchase and alienated J. Arthur Rank in the process.

Relations among the stockholders continued to deteriorate after the war. By precipitating the fight to oust Selznick, UA not only lost its remaining "name" producer, but depleted its capital reserves as well. And because Pickford and Chaplin remained irreconcilable afterwards, the instability of the company became all too apparent. Banking institutions placed a freeze on independent production financing, UA's producers revolted, and others struck deals with the majors. The ensuing product crisis was insoluble. The company that Pickford and Chaplin held on to so tenaciously now passed to a new breed of showmen.

Reference Matter

United Artists Corporation Releases, 1919-1950

Picture	Release Date*	Producer
1919		
His Majesty, the American	Sept. 1	Fairbanks
Broken Blossoms	Oct. 20	Griffith
When the Clouds Roll By	Dec. 28	Fairbanks
1920		
Pollyanna	Jan. 18	Pickford
Down on the Farm	April 25	Sennett
Romance	May 30	Griffith
The Mollycoddle	June 13	Fairbanks
Suds	June 27	Pickford
The Love Flower	Sept. 5	Griffith
The Mark of Zorro	Dec. 5	Fairbanks
1921		
Love Light	Jan. 9	Pickford
The Nut	March 6	Fairbanks
Through the Back Door	May 15	Pickford
Dream Street	May 16	Griffith
Carnival (B)†	Aug. 7	Knowles
Way Down East	Aug. 21	Griffith
Disraeli	Aug. 28	Arliss
The Three Musketeers	Oct. 2	Fairbanks
I Accuse	Oct. 9	Gance
The Iron Trail	Oct. 30	Whitman Bennett
Little Lord Fauntleroy	Nov. 13	Pickford
1922		
A Doll's House	Feb. 12	Nazimova

*The date a picture went into general release after the roadshow and/or preview.
†Denotes a British production.

Picture	Release Date	Producer
1922 (cont'd)		
The Ruling Passion	Feb. 19	Arliss
Fair Lady	March 19	Whitman Bennett
Orphans of the Storm	April 30	Griffith
Glorious Adventure	Aug. 27	Blackton
The Three Must-Get-Theres	Aug. 27	Linder
A Woman's Woman	Sept. 24	Giblyn
The Man Who Played God	Oct. 1	Arliss
A Tailor-Made Man	Oct. 15	Ray
Tess of the Storm Country	Nov. 12	Pickford
One Exciting Night	Dec. 24	Griffith
1923		
Garrison's Finish	Jan. 1	Jack Pickford
Robin Hood	Jan. 28	Fairbanks
The Birth of a Nation (reissue)	Feb. 15	Griffith
Salome	Feb. 15	Nazimova
The Girl I Loved	Feb. 15	Ray
Suzanna	Feb. 18	Sennett
The Shriek of Araby	March 4	Sennett
Paddy the Next-Best-Thing (B)	June 2	Wilcox
The White Rose	Aug. 19	Griffith
Richard the Lion-Hearted	Oct. 21	Associated Authors
Rosita	Oct. 28	Pickford
A Woman of Paris	Nov. 4	Chaplin
1924		
Loving Lies	Feb. 15	Associated Authors
No More Women	Feb. 15	Associated Authors
A Woman's Secret (B)	Feb. 15	Wilcox
The Hillbilly	March 15	Jack Pickford
Dorothy Vernon of Haddon Hall	Aug. 3	Pickford
America	Aug. 17	Griffith
Isn't Life Wonderful	Nov. 23	Griffith
The Thief of Bagdad	Dec. 25	Fairbanks
1925		
The Salvation Hunters	Feb. 1	Von Sternberg
Waking Up the Town	March 29	Jack Pickford
Wild Justice	July 6	Schenck
Sally of the Sawdust	Aug. 2	Griffith
The Gold Rush	Aug. 16	Chaplin
Don Q, Son of Zorro	Aug. 30	Fairbanks
Little Annie Rooney	Oct. 18	Pickford

Picture	Release Date	Producer
1925 (cont'd)		
The Eagle	Nov. 8	Schenck
Tumbleweeds	Dec. 20	Hart
1926		
Partners Again	Feb. 14	Goldwyn
The Only Way (B)	March 1	Wilcox
The Bat	April 5	Schenck
Stella Dallas	Aug. 29	Goldwyn
The Son of the Sheik	Sept. 5	Schenck
The Black Pirate	Sept. 12	Fairbanks
Sparrows	Sept. 19	Pickford
The Winning of Barbara Worth	Sept. 26	Goldwyn
1927		
The Night of Love	Jan. 22	Goldwyn
The General	Feb. 5	Keaton
The Beloved Rogue	March 5	Art Cinema
The Love of Sunya	March 12	Swanson
Resurrection	March 19	Inspiration-Carewe
Topsy and Eva	July 24	Art Cinema
College	July 29	Keaton
The Magic Flame	Aug. 14	Goldwyn
Two Arabian Knights	Sept. 23	Hughes
My Best Girl	Oct. 31	Pickford
The Devil Dancer	Nov. 19	Goldwyn
Sorrell and Son	Dec. 2	Art Cinema
1928		
The Gaucho	Jan. 1	Fairbanks
The Circus	Jan. 7	Chaplin
The Dove	Jan. 7	Schenck
Sadie Thompson	Jan. 7	Swanson
The Garden of Eden	Feb. 4	Art Cinema
Ramona	Feb. 11	Inspiration-Carewe
Drums of Love	March 31	Art Cinema
Steamboat Bill, Jr.	July 15	Keaton
Tempest	July 21	Art Cinema
Two Lovers	Aug. 12	Goldwyn
The Battle of the Sexes	Oct. 13	Art Cinema
The Woman Disputed	Oct. 21	Schenck
Revenge	Nov. 3	Art Cinema
The Awakening	Nov. 17	Goldwyn

Picture	Release Date	Producer
1929		
The Rescue	Jan. 12	Goldwyn
Lady of the Pavements	Feb. 16	Art Cinema
The Iron Mask	March 9	Fairbanks
Coquette	March 30	Pickford
Alibi	April 20	Art Cinema
Eternal Love	May 11	Art Cinema
The Three Passions (B)	June 1	St. George's
This Is Heaven	June 22	Goldwyn
She Goes to War	July 13	Inspiration
Bulldog Drummond	Aug. 3	Goldwyn
Evangeline	Aug. 24	Art Cinema
Three Live Ghosts	Sept. 15	Art Cinema
The Trespasser	Oct. 5	Swanson
Venus	Oct. 12	Mercanton
Taming of the Shrew	Oct. 26	Pickford-Fairbanks
The Locked Door	Nov. 16	Art Cinema
Condemned	Dec. 7	Goldwyn
New York Nights	Dec. 28	Schenck
1930		
Lummox	Jan. 18	Art Cinema
Be Yourself	Feb. 8	Art Cinema
Puttin' on the Ritz	March 1	Art Cinema
Hell Harbor	March 22	Inspiration
One Romantic Night	April 12	Art Cinema
The Bad One	May 3	Art Cinema
Raffles	July 26	Goldwyn
The Eyes of the World	Aug. 30	Inspiration
What a Widow	Sept. 13	Swanson
Whoopee	Sept. 27	Goldwyn
DuBarry, Woman of Passion	Oct. 11	Art Cinema
The Lottery Bride	Oct. 25	Art Cinema
Abraham Lincoln	Nov. 8	Art Cinema
Hell's Angels	Nov. 15	Hughes
The Bat Whispers	Nov. 29	Art Cinema
1931		
One Heavenly Night	Jan. 10	Goldwyn
The Devil to Pay	Jan. 31	Goldwyn
Reaching for the Moon	Feb. 21	Art Cinema
City Lights	March 1	Chaplin
Kiki	March 14	Art Cinema
The Front Page	April 4	Hughes

Picture	Release Date	Producer
1931 (cont'd)		
Indiscreet	April 25	Art Cinema
Street Scene	Sept. 5	Art Cinema-Goldwyn
Palmy Days	Oct. 3	Goldwyn
The Unholy Garden	Oct. 10	Goldwyn
The Age for Love	Oct. 17	Hughes
Corsair	Nov. 28	Art Cinema
Around the World in Eighty Minutes with Douglas Fairbanks	Dec. 12	Fairbanks
Tonight or Never	Dec. 26	Art Cinema-Goldwyn
1932		
Cock of the Air	Jan. 16	Hughes
The Struggle	Feb. 6	Griffith
The Greeks Had a Word for Them	Feb. 13	Goldwyn
Arrowsmith	Feb. 27	Goldwyn
Sky Devils	March 12	Hughes
Scarface, Shame of the Nation	April 9	Hughes
The Silver Lining	April 16	Patrician
Congress Dances	April 25	UFA
White Zombie	Aug. 4	Halperin
Mr. Robinson Crusoe	Sept. 17	Fairbanks
Rain	Oct. 22	Art Cinema
Magic Night (B)	Nov. 5	British & Dominions
Cynara	Dec. 23	Goldwyn
1933		
The Kid from Spain	Jan. 27	Goldwyn
Hallelujah, I'm a Bum	Feb. 8	Art Cinema
Perfect Understanding	March 11	Swanson
Secrets	April 16	Pickford
I Cover the Waterfront	May 12	Reliance
Yes, Mr. Brown (B)	May 16	British & Dominions
Samarang	June 23	Zeidman
The Masquerader	Sept. 1	Goldwyn
Bitter Sweet (B)	Sept. 22	British & Dominions
The Emperor Jones	Sept. 29	Krimsky-Cochran
The Bowery	Oct. 13	20th Century
Broadway Thru a Keyhole	Oct. 27	20th Century
The Private Life of Henry VIII (B)	Nov. 3	London Films
Blood Money	Nov. 24	20th Century
Advice to the Lovelorn	Dec. 1	20th Century
Roman Scandals	Dec. 29	Goldwyn

Picture	Release Date	Producer
1934		
Gallant Lady	Jan. 5	20th Century
Moulin Rouge	Jan. 19	20th Century
Palooka	Feb. 16	Reliance
Nana	March 2	Goldwyn
Looking for Trouble	March 9	20th Century
Catherine the Great (B)	April 13	London Films
Sorrell and Son (B)	April 20	British & Dominions
The House of Rothschild	April 27	20th Century
Born To Be Bad	May 18	20th Century
Bulldog Drummond Strikes Back	July 20	20th Century
The Affairs of Cellini	Aug. 24	20th Century
The Count of Monte Cristo	Sept. 7	Reliance
The Last Gentleman	Sept. 21	20th Century
Our Daily Bread	Sept. 28	Vidor
Trans-Atlantic Merry-Go-Round	Nov. 2	Reliance
We Live Again	Nov. 16	Goldwyn
The Private Life of Don Juan (B)	Nov. 30	London Films
The Runaway Queen (B)	Dec. 21	British & Dominions
The Mighty Barnum	Dec. 25	20th Century
Kid Millions	Dec. 28	Goldwyn
1935		
Clive of India	Jan. 25	20th Century
The Scarlet Pimpernel (B)	Feb. 15	London Films
Folies Bergere	Feb. 22	20th Century
The Wedding Night	March 8	Goldwyn
Cardinal Richelieu	April 28	20th Century
Les Miserables	May 10	20th Century
Thunder in the East (B)	May 13	Lianofilm
Let 'em Have It	May 17	Reliance
Brewster's Millions (B)	May 20	British & Dominions
Nell Gwyn (B)	June 14	British & Dominions
Escape Me Never (B)	June 21	British & Dominions
Sanders of the River (B)	July 4	London Films
The Call of the Wild	Aug. 9	20th Century
The Dark Angel	Sept. 6	Goldwyn
Red Salute	Sept. 13	Reliance
Barbary Coast	Sept. 27	Goldwyn
The Melody Lingers On	Nov. 9	Reliance
Splendor	Nov. 23	Goldwyn
1936		
Strike Me Pink	Jan. 24	Goldwyn
The Ghost Goes West (B)	Feb. 7	London Films

Picture	Release Date	Producer
1936 (cont'd)		
Modern Times	Feb. 21	Chaplin
Little Lord Fauntleroy	March 6	Selznick
These Three	April 10	Goldwyn
The Amateur Gentleman (B)	April 17	Criterion
Things to Come (B)	April 24	London Films
One Rainy Afternoon	May 8	Pickford-Lasky
I Stand Condemned (B)	June 19	London Films
The Last of the Mohicans	Sept. 4	Reliance
Dodsworth	Sept. 18	Goldwyn
The Gay Desperado	Oct. 2	Pickford-Lasky
Come and Get It!	Nov. 13	Goldwyn
The Garden of Allah	Nov. 20	Selznick
Rembrandt (B)	Nov. 27	London Films
Beloved Enemy	Dec. 25	Goldwyn
1937		
Accused (B)	Jan. 8	Criterion
Men Are Not Gods (B)	Jan. 22	London Films
You Only Live Once	Jan. 29	Wanger
The Man Who Could Work Miracles (B)	Feb. 19	London Films
Fire Over England (B)	March 5	Pendennis
History Is Made At Night	April 2	Wanger
Elephant Boy (B)	April 23	London Films
A Star Is Born	April 30	Selznick
Woman Chases Man	May 7	Goldwyn
Love from a Stranger (B)	May 14	Trafalgar
Dreaming Lips (B)	May 28	Trafalgar
When Thief Meets Thief (B)	June 4	Criterion
Walt Disney's Revue	June 18	Disney
Dark Journey (B)	July 2	Saville
Knight Without Armor (B)	July 23	London Films
Stella Dallas	Aug. 6	Goldwyn
Dead End	Aug. 27	Goldwyn
The Prisoner of Zenda	Sept. 3	Selznick
Walter Wanger's Vogues of 1938	Sept. 17	Wanger
Troop Ship (B)	Oct. 8	Pendennis
Stand-In	Oct. 29	Wanger
52nd Street	Nov. 19	Wanger
Nothing Sacred	Nov. 26	Selznick
Murder on Diamond Row (B)	Dec. 10	London Films
The Hurricane	Dec. 24	Goldwyn

Picture	Release Date	Producer
1938		
Action for Slander (B)	Jan. 14	London Films
I Met My Love Again	Jan. 28	Wanger
The Goldwyn Follies	Feb. 4	Goldwyn
The Adventures of Tom Sawyer	Feb. 11	Selznick
Storm in a Teacup (B)	Feb. 25	Saville
The Adventures of Marco Polo	March 4	Goldwyn
The Gaiety Girls (B)	March 18	London Films
Divorce of Lady X (B)	April 15	London Films
The Return of the Scarlet Pimpernel (B)	April 29	London Films
Blockade	June 17	Wanger
South Riding (B)	July 1	London Films
Algiers	Aug. 5	Wanger
Drums (B)	Sept. 30	London Films
There Goes My Heart	Oct. 14	Roach
The Young in Heart	Nov. 3	Selznick
The Cowboy and the Lady	Nov. 17	Goldwyn
Trade Winds	Dec. 22	Wanger
The Duke of West Point	Dec. 29	Small
1939		
Topper Takes a Trip	Jan. 12	Roach
Made for Each Other	Feb. 10	Selznick
King of the Turf	Feb. 17	Small
Stagecoach	March 3	Wanger
Prison Without Bars (B)	March 10	London Films
Wuthering Heights	April 7	Goldwyn
Zenobia	April 21	Roach
Captain Fury	May 26	Roach
Winter Carnival	July 28	Wanger
The Four Feathers (B)	Aug. 4	London Films
The Man in the Iron Mask	Aug. 11	Small
They Shall Have Music	Aug. 18	Goldwyn
Intermezzo	Sept. 22	Selznick
The Real Glory	Sept. 29	Goldwyn
Eternally Yours	Oct. 12	Wanger
The Housekeeper's Daughter	Oct. 26	Roach
Slightly Honorable	Dec. 22	Wanger
Raffles	Dec. 29	Goldwyn
1940		
Of Mice and Men	Jan. 12	Roach
The Lion Has Wings (B)	Jan. 19	London Films
A Chump at Oxford	Feb. 16	Roach

Picture	Release Date	Producer
1940 (cont'd)		
The House Across the Bay	March 1	Wanger
My Son, My Son	March 22	Small
Over the Moon (B)	March 29	London Films
One Million B.C.	April 5	Roach
Rebecca	April 12	Selznick
Saps At Sea	May 3	Roach
Turnabout	May 17	Roach
Our Town	May 24	Lesser
South of Pago-Pago	July 19	Small
Captain Caution	Aug. 9	Roach
Foreign Correspondent	Aug. 16	Wanger
Kit Carson	Aug. 30	Small
Pastor Hall	Sept. 13	Roosevelt
The Westerner	Sept. 20	Goldwyn
The Long Voyage Home	Nov. 22	Wanger
Blackout (B)	Nov. 29	British National
The Thief of Bagdad (B)	Dec. 25	Korda
1941		
The Son of Monte Cristo	Jan. 10	Small
Road Show	Jan. 24	Roach
So Ends Our Night	Feb. 14	Loew-Lewin
Cheers for Miss Bishop	Feb. 21	Rowland
The Great Dictator	March 7	Chaplin
Topper Returns	March 21	Roach
Pot O' Gold	March 28	Roosevelt
That Uncertain Feeling	April 20	Lesser-Lubitsch
That Hamilton Woman (B)	April 30	Korda
Broadway Limited	June 13	Roach
Three Cockeyed Sailors (B)	July 4	Ealing
Major Barbara (B)	Sept. 12	Pascal
Tanks a Million	Sept. 12	Roach
International Lady	Sept. 19	Small
Lydia (B)	Sept. 26	Korda
New Wine	Oct. 10	Sekely
Niagara Falls	Oct. 17	Roach
All-American Co-Ed	Oct. 31	Roach
Sundown	Oct. 31	Wanger
Miss Polly	Nov. 14	Roach
Fiesta	Nov. 28	Roach
The Corsican Brothers	Dec. 20	Small

Picture	Release Date	Producer
1942		
Hayfoot	Jan. 2	Roach
The Shanghai Gesture	Jan. 6	Pressburger
Brooklyn Orchid	Feb. 20	Roach
A Gentleman After Dark	Feb. 27	Small
To Be Or Not To Be	March 6	Korda-Lubitsch
Dudes Are Pretty People	March 13	Roach
Mister V (B)	March 20	British National
Rudyard Kipling's Jungle Book (B)	April 3	Korda
About Face	April 17	Roach
The Gold Rush (reissue)	April 17	Chaplin
Twin Beds	April 24	Small
Ships with Wings (B)	May 15	Ealing
Flying with Music	May 22	Roach
Miss Annie Rooney	May 29	Small
Friendly Enemies	June 26	Small
Kukan, The Battle Cry of China	Aug. 7	Edwards
The Moon and Sixpence	Oct. 2	Loew-Lewin
One of Our Aircraft Is Missing (B)	Oct. 16	British National
Undercover Man	Oct. 23	Paramount
I Married A Witch	Oct. 30	Paramount
Silver Queen	Nov. 13	Paramount
The Devil with Hitler	Nov. 20	Roach
Jacaré	Nov. 27	Levey
American Empire	Dec. 11	Paramount
Lost Canyon	Dec. 18	Paramount
McGuerins from Brooklyn	Dec. 31	Roach
1943		
The Powers Girl	Jan. 15	Rogers
The Crystal Ball	Jan. 22	Paramount
Calaboose	Jan. 29	Roach
Young and Willing	Feb. 5	Paramount
In Which We Serve (B)	Feb. 12	Two Cities
Fall In	March 5	Roach
Hoppy Serves a Writ	March 12	Paramount
Hangmen Also Die!	March 26	Pressburger
Border Patrol	April 2	Paramount
Taxi, Mister	April 16	Roach
Lady of Burlesque	April 30	Stromberg
Stage Door Canteen	May 12	Lesser
Buckskin Frontier	May 14	Paramount
Prairie Chickens	May 21	Roach
Leather Burners	May 28	Paramount

Picture	Release Date	Producer
1943 (cont'd)		
Somewhere in France (B)	June 11	Ealing
Colt Comrades	June 18	Paramount
Yanks Ahoy	June 25	Roach
Nazty Nuisance	Aug. 8	Roach
Victory Through Air Power	Aug. 13	Disney
Hi, Diddle Diddle	Aug. 20	Stone
Johnny Come Lately	Sept. 3	Cagney
The Kansan	Sept. 10	Paramount
Bar 20	Oct. 1	Paramount
False Colors	Nov. 5	Paramount
Riders of the Deadline	Dec. 3	Paramount
Jack London	Dec. 24	Bronston
The Woman of the Town	Dec. 31	Paramount
1944		
Three Russian Girls	Jan. 14	Rabinovitch
The Bridge of San Luis Rey	Feb. 11	Bogeaus
Texas Masquerade	Feb. 18	Paramount
Knickerbocker Holiday	March 17	Brown
It Happened Tomorrow	April 7	Pressburger
Voice in the Wind	April 21	Ripley-Monter
Lumberjack	April 28	Paramount
Up in Mabel's Room	April 28	Small
Mystery Man	May 31	Paramount
Song of the Open Road	June 2	Rogers
The Hairy Ape	June 16	Levey
Forty Thieves	June 23	Paramount
Sensations of 1945	June 30	Stone
Summer Storm	July 14	Nebenzal
Since You Went Away	July 20	Selznick
Abroad with Two Yanks	Aug. 4	Small
Dark Waters	Nov. 10	Bogeaus
3 Is a Family	Nov. 23	Lesser
Guest in the House	Dec. 8	Stromberg
Tomorrow, the World	Dec. 29	Cowan
1945		
I'll Be Seeing You	Jan. 5	Selznick
Mr. Emmanuel (B)	Jan. 19	Rank
Delightfully Dangerous	March 31	Rogers
Brewster's Millions	April 7	Small
It's in the Bag	April 21	Skirball
Colonel Blimp (B)	June 1	Rank

Picture	Release Date	Producer
1945 (cont'd)		
Blood on the Sun	June 15	Cagney
Bedside Manner	June 22	Stone
The Great John L	June 24	Crosby
The Story of G.I. Joe	July 13	Cowan
Guest Wife	July 27	Skirball
The Southerner	Aug. 10	Loew-Hakim
Captain Kidd	Aug. 24	Bogeaus
Paris Underground	Sept. 14	Constance Bennett
Getting Gertie's Garter	Nov. 30	Small
Blithe Spirit (B)	Dec. 14	Rank
Spellbound	Dec. 28	Selznick
1946		
Abilene Town	Jan. 11	Levey
Whistle Stop	Jan. 25	Nebenzal
The Outlaw	Feb. 8	Hughes
The Diary of a Chambermaid	Feb. 15	Bogeaus-Meredith
Breakfast in Hollywood	Feb. 22	Golden
Young Widow	March 1	Stromberg
Johnny in the Clouds (B)	March 15	Rank
Henry V (B)	April 22	Rank
A Night in Casablanca	May 10	Loew-Lewin
Mr. Ace	Aug. 2	Bogeaus
Caesar and Cleopatra (B)	Aug. 16	Rank
The Bachelor's Daughters	Sept. 6	Stone
Angel on My Shoulder	Sept. 20	Rogers
Little Iodine	Oct. 11	Comet
The Strange Woman	Oct. 25	Stromberg
The Devil's Playground	Nov. 15	Hopalong Cassidy
The Chase	Nov. 22	Nebenzal
Susie Steps Out	Dec. 13	Comet
Abie's Irish Rose	Dec. 27	Crosby
1947		
Fool's Gold	Jan. 31	Hopalong Cassidy
The Red House	Feb. 7	Lesser
The Fabulous Dorseys	Feb. 21	Rogers
The Private Affairs of Bel Ami	March 7	Loew-Lewin
Fun on a Weekend	March 14	Stone
The Macomber Affair	March 21	Bogeaus-Robinson
Unexpected Guest	March 28	Hopalong Cassidy
New Orleans	April 18	Levey
Ramrod	May 2	Enterprise

Picture	*Release Date*	*Producer*
1947 (cont'd)		
The Adventures of Don Coyote	May 9	Comet
Dishonored Lady	May 16	Stromberg
Dangerous Venture	May 23	Hopalong Cassidy
Copacabana	May 30	Coslow
Stork Bites Man	June 21	Comet
The Other Love	July 11	Enterprise
Hoppy's Holiday	July 18	Hopalong Cassidy
Carnegie Hall	Aug. 8	Morros-Le Baron
Hal Roach Comedy Carnival	Aug. 29	Roach
Curley		
The Fabulous Joe		
Lured	Sept. 5	Stromberg
Heaven Only Knows	Sept. 12	Nebenzal
Monsieur Verdoux	Oct. 24	Chaplin
Christmas Eve	Oct. 31	Bogeaus
The Marauders	Nov. 6	Hopalong Cassidy
Body and Soul	Nov. 14	Enterprise
The Roosevelt Story	Nov. 21	Levine-Unger
Intrigue	Dec. 23	Bischoff
1948		
Man of Evil (B)	Jan. 30	Rank
On Our Merry Way	Feb. 13	Bogeaus
Sleep My Love	Feb. 20	Pickford-Rogers-Cohn
Silent Conflict	March 19	Hopalong Cassidy
Lafftime	April 9	Roach
Here Comes Trouble		
Who Killed Doc Robbin?		
Arch of Triumph	April 30	Enterprise
The Dead Don't Dream	April 30	Hopalong Cassidy
Kings of the Olympics	May 7	Westport
The Angry God	May 14	Peskay
Four Faces West	May 21	Enterprise
Olympic Cavalcade	June 11	Westport
Sinister Journey	June 11	Hopalong Cassidy
So This Is New York	June 25	Kramer
Texas, Brooklyn, and Heaven	July 16	Golden
Borrowed Trouble	July 23	Hopalong Cassidy
Pitfall	July 29	Bischoff
The Time of Your Life	Sept. 3	Cagney
The Vicious Circle	Sept. 3	Wilder
False Paradise	Sept. 10	Hopalong Cassidy

Picture	Release Date	Producer
1948 (cont'd)		
Red River	Sept. 17	Hawks
Urubu	Sept. 24	Krasne
The Girl From Manhattan	Oct. 1	Bogeaus
Strange Gamble	Oct. 8	Hopalong Cassidy
Don't Trust Your Husband	Oct. 15	Nasser
The Plot to Kill Roosevelt (B)	Oct. 22	Pendennis
My Dear Secretary	Nov. 5	Popkin
High Fury	Nov. 19	Comet
Just William's Luck (B)	Dec. 10	Diadem-Alliance
Siren of Atlantis	Dec. 17	Nebenzal
1949		
Valiant Hombre	Jan. 21	Krasne
The Lucky Stiff	Feb. 11	Benny
Cover-Up	Feb. 25	Nasser
Jigsaw	March 11	Danziger
Impact	April 1	Popkin
The Crooked Way	April 22	Bogeaus
Outpost in Morocco	May 6	Bischoff
The Gay Amigo	May 13	Krasne
Champion	May 20	Kramer
Africa Screams	May 27	Nassour
The Daring Caballero	June 24	Krasne
Too Late for Tears	July 8	Stromberg
Home of the Brave	July 15	Kramer
The Great Dan Patch	July 22	Frank
Black Magic	Aug. 19	Ratoff
Red Light	Sept. 16	Del Ruth
Satan's Cradle	Oct. 7	Krasne
Without Honor	Oct. 21	Hakim
The Big Wheel	Nov. 4	Steifel
A Kiss for Corliss	Nov. 25	Miller
Mrs. Mike	Dec. 23	Bischoff
1950		
Davy Crockett, Indian Scout	Jan. 6	Small
Deadly Is the Female	Jan. 20	King
Johnny Holiday	Feb. 17	Alcorn
The Girl from San Lorenzo	Feb. 24	Krasne
Love Happy	March 3	Pickford-Cowan
The Great Plane Robbery	March 10	Belsam
Quicksand	March 24	Steifel
Champagne for Caesar	April 7	Popkin

Picture	*Release Date*	Producer
1950 (cont'd)		
D.O.A.	April 21	Popkin
Johnny One-Eye	May 5	Bogeaus
So Young, So Bad	May 26	Danziger
The Iroquois Trail	June 16	Small
Once a Thief	July 7	Wilder
The Underworld Story	July 21	Chester
The Admiral Was a Lady	Aug. 4	Rogell
The Men	Aug. 25	Kramer
If This Be Sin	Sept. 8	Ratoff
Three Husbands	Nov. 3	Goldsmith

Appendix 2 — United Artists Corporation Producers

Roland W. Alcorn
    Johnny Holiday   1950

George Arliss
    Disraeli   1921
    The Ruling Passion   1922
    The Man Who Played God   1922

Art Cinema
    See Joseph M. Schenck

Associated Authors
    Richard the Lion-Hearted   1923
    Loving Lies   1924
    No More Women   1924

Michael Balcon
    See Ealing Studios

Martin Belsam
    The Great Plane Robbery   1950

Constance Bennett
    Paris Underground   1945

Whitman Bennett
    The Iron Trail   1921
    Fair Lady   1922

Jack Benny
    The Lucky Stiff   1949

Samuel Bischoff
    Intrigue   1947
    Pitfall   1948
    Outpost in Morocco   1949
    Mrs. Mike   1949

Edward Black
    See J. Arthur Rank

J. Stuart Blackton
    Glorious Adventure   1922

Benedict Bogeaus
    The Bridge of San Luis Rey   1944
    Dark Waters   1944
    Captain Kidd   1945
    The Diary of a Chambermaid (with Burgess Meredith)   1946
    Mr. Ace   1946
    The Macomber Affair (with Casey Robinson)   1947
    Christmas Eve   1947
    On Our Merry Way   1948
    The Girl From Manhattan   1948
    The Crooked Way   1949
    Johnny One-Eye   1950

William Boyd
    See Hopalong Cassidy Productions

British & Dominions
    See Herbert Wilcox

British National Films
    Blackout (produced by John Corfield)   1940
    Mister V (produced by Leslie Howard)   1942
    One of Our Aircraft Is Missing (produced by Michael Powell)   1942

Samuel Bronston
    Jack London   1943

Harry Joe Brown
    Knickerbocker Holiday   1944

Caddo Productions
    See Howard Hughes

James and William Cagney
    Johnny Come Lately   1943
    Blood on the Sun   1945
    The Time of Your Life   1948

Walter Camp

    Inspiration Pictures
    Resurrection (with Edwin Carewe)   1927
    Ramona (with Edwin Carewe)   1928
    She Goes to War   1929
    Hell Harbor   1930
    The Eyes of the World   1930

      Patrician Productions
    The Silver Lining   1932

Edwin Carewe
    See Walter Camp

James Carter
    See Diadem-Alliance

Hopalong Cassidy Productions (William Boyd)
    The Devil's Playground   1946
    Fool's Gold   1947
    Unexpected Guest   1947
    Dangerous Venture   1947
    Hoppy's Holiday   1947
    The Marauders   1947
    Silent Conflict   1948
    The Dead Don't Dream   1948
    Sinister Journey   1948
    Borrowed Trouble   1948
    False Paradise   1948
    Strange Gamble   1948

Charles Chaplin
    A Woman of Paris   1923
    The Gold Rush   1925
    The Circus   1928
    City Lights   1931
    Modern Times   1936
    The Great Dictator   1941
    The Gold Rush (reissue)   1942
    Monsieur Verdoux   1947

Hal E. Chester
    The Underworld Story   1950

Ralph Cohn
    See Comet, Mary Pickford

Comet (Buddy Rogers-Ralph Cohn)
    Little Iodine   1946
    Susie Steps Out   1946
    The Adventures of Don Coyote   1947
    Stork Bites Man   1947
    High Fury   1948

David Coplan
    See Diadem-Alliance

John Corfield
    See British National Films

Samuel Coslow
    Copacabana   1947

Lester Cowan
    Tomorrow, the World   1944
    The Story of G. I. Joe   1945
    Love Happy (with Mary Pickford)   1950

Noel Coward
    See J. Arthur Rank, Two Cities

Criterion Films (Douglas Fairbanks, Jr.)
    The Amateur Gentleman   1936
    Accused   1937
    When Thief Meets Thief   1937

Bing and Harry Crosby
    The Great John L   1945
    Abie's Irish Rose   1946

Paul Czinner
    See Trafalgar Films

Edward and Harry Danziger
    Jigsaw   1949
    So Young, So Bad   1950

Roy Del Ruth
    Red Light   1949

Diadem-Alliance (David Coplan-James Carter)
    Just William's Luck   1948

Walt Disney
    Walt Disney's Revue   1937
    Victory Through Air Power   1943

Ealing Studios (Michael Balcon)
    Three Cockeyed Sailors   1941
    Ships With Wings   1942
    Somewhere in France   1943

Herbert T. Edwards
    Kukan, The Battle Cry of China   1942

Charles Einfeld
    See David Loew

Enterprise Productions
    See David Loew

Douglas Fairbanks
    His Majesty, the American   1919
    When the Clouds Roll By   1919
    The Mollycoddle   1920
    The Mark of Zorro   1920
    The Nut   1921
    The Three Musketeers   1921
    Robin Hood   1923
    The Thief of Bagdad   1924
    Don Q, Son of Zorro   1925
    The Black Pirate   1926
    The Gaucho   1928
    The Iron Mask   1929
    Taming of the Shrew (with Mary Pickford)   1929
    Around the World in Eighty Minutes with Douglas Fairbanks   1931
    Mr. Robinson Crusoe   1932

Douglas Fairbanks, Jr.
    See Criterion Films

W. R. Frank
    The Great Dan Patch   1949

Abel Gance
    I Accuse   1921

Leon Garganoff
    See Lianofilm Productions

Charles Giblyn
    A Woman's Woman   1922

Harry M. Goetz
    See Edward Small

Robert S. Golden
    Breakfast in Hollywood   1946
    Texas, Brooklyn, and Heaven   1948

I. Goldsmith
    Three Husbands   1950

Samuel Goldwyn
    Partners Again   1926
    Stella Dallas   1926
    The Winning of Barbara Worth   1926
    The Night of Love   1927
    The Magic Flame   1927
    The Devil Dancer   1927
    Two Lovers   1928
    The Awakening   1928
    The Rescue   1929
    This Is Heaven   1929
    Bulldog Drummond   1929
    Condemned   1929
    Raffles   1930
    Whoopee   1930
    One Heavenly Night   1931
    The Devil to Pay   1931
    Street Scene (with Art Cinema)   1931
    Palmy Days   1931
    The Unholy Garden   1931
    Tonight or Never (with Art Cinema)   1931
    The Greeks Had a Word for Them   1932
    Arrowsmith   1932
    Cynara   1932
    The Kid from Spain   1933
    The Masquerader   1933
    Roman Scandals   1933

Nana	1934
We Live Again	1934
Kid Millions	1934
The Wedding Night	1935
The Dark Angel	1935
Barbary Coast	1935
Splendor	1935
Strike Me Pink	1936
These Three	1936
Dodsworth	1936
Come and Get It!	1936
Beloved Enemy	1936
Woman Chases Man	1937
Stella Dallas	1937
Dead End	1937
The Hurricane	1937
The Goldwyn Follies	1938
The Adventures of Marco Polo	1938
The Cowboy and the Lady	1938
Wuthering Heights	1939
They Shall Have Music	1939
The Real Glory	1939
Raffles	1939
The Westerner	1940

D. W. Griffith

Broken Blossoms	1919
Romance	1920
The Love Flower	1920
Dream Street	1921
Way Down East	1921
Orphans of the Storm	1922
One Exciting Night	1922
The Birth of a Nation (reissue)	1923
The White Rose	1923
America	1924
Isn't Life Wonderful	1924
Sally of the Sawdust	1925
The Struggle	1932

Anatole de Gruenwald
See J. Arthur Rank

Robert and Raymond Hakim

Without Honor	1949

See David Loew

Edward Halperin
    White Zombie   1932

William S. Hart
    Tumbleweeds   1925

Howard Hawks
    Red River   1948

Leslie Howard
    See British National Films

Howard Hughes
    Two Arabian Knights   1927
    Hell's Angels   1930
    The Front Page   1931
    The Age for Love   1931
    Cock of the Air   1932
    Sky Devils   1932
    Scarface, Shame of the Nation   1932
    The Outlaw   1946

Rex Ingram
    See St. George's Productions

Inspiration Pictures
    See Walter Camp

Buster Keaton
    See Joseph M. Schenck

Frank and Maurice King
    Deadly Is the Female   1950

Harley Knowles
    Carnival   1921

Alexander Korda

    London Film Productions
    The Private Life of Henry VIII   1933
    Catherine the Great   1934
    The Private Life of Don Juan   1934
    The Scarlet Pimpernel   1935
    Sanders of the River   1935
    The Ghost Goes West   1936

Things to Come	1936
I Stand Condemned	1936
Rembrandt	1936
Men Are Not Gods	1937
The Man Who Could Work Miracles	1937
Elephant Boy	1937
Dark Journey	1937
Knight Without Armor	1937
Murder on Diamond Row	1937
Action for Slander	1938
The Gaiety Girls	1938
Divorce of Lady X	1938
The Return of the Scarlet Pimpernel	1938
South Riding	1938
Drums	1938
Prison Without Bars	1939
The Four Feathers	1939
The Lion Has Wings	1940
Over the Moon	1940

Alexander Korda Films

The Thief of Bagdad	1940
That Hamilton Woman	1941
Lydia	1941
To Be Or Not To Be (with Ernst Lubitsch)	1942
Rudyard Kipling's Jungle Book	1942

Stanley Kramer

So This Is New York	1948
Champion	1949
Home of the Brave	1949
The Men	1950

Philip N. Krasne

Urubu	1948
Valiant Hombre	1949
The Gay Amigo	1949
The Daring Caballero	1949
Satan's Cradle	1949
The Girl from San Lorenzo	1950

John Krimsky and Gifford Cochran

The Emperor Jones	1933

Jesse Lasky
See Mary Pickford

William Le Baron
    See Borros Morros

Sol Lesser
    Our Town   1940
    That Uncertain Feeling (with Ernst Lubitsch)   1941
    Stage Door Canteen   1943
    3 Is a Family   1944
    The Red House   1947

Jules Levey
    Jacaré   1942
    The Hairy Ape   1944
    Abilene Town   1946
    New Orleans   1947

Martin Levine-Oliver Unger
    The Roosevelt Story   1947

Albert Lewin
    See David Loew

Max Linder
    The Three Must-Get-Theres   1922

Lianofilm Productions (Leon Garganoff)
    Thunder in the East   1935

David Loew
    So Ends Our Night (with Albert Lewin)   1941
    The Moon and Sixpence (with Albert Lewin)   1942
    The Southerner (with Robert Hakim)   1945
    A Night in Casablanca (with Albert Lewin)   1946
    The Private Affairs of Bel Ami (with Albert Lewin)   1947

      Enterprise Productions (with Charles Einfeld)
    Ramrod   1947
    The Other Love   1947
    Body and Soul   1947
    Arch of Triumph   1948
    Four Faces West   1948

London Films
    See Alexander Korda

Ernst Lubitsch
    See Alexander Korda, Sol Lesser

Louis Mercanton
  Venus   1929

Burgess Meredith
  See Benedict Bogeaus

Colin Miller
  A Kiss for Corliss   1949

Rudolph Monter
  See Arthur Ripley

Borros Morros-William Le Baron
  Carnegie Hall   1947

James and Ted Nasser
  Don't Trust Your Husband   1948
  Cover-Up   1949

Edward Nassour
  Africa Screams   1949

Alla Nazimova
  A Doll's House   1922
  Salome   1923

Seymour Nebenzal
  Summer Storm   1944
  Whistle Stop   1946
  The Chase   1946
  Heaven Only Knows   1947
  Siren of Atlantis   1948

Laurence Olivier
  See J. Arthur Rank

Steven Pallos
  See Pendennis Pictures

Paramount Productions

    Cinema Guild
    I Married a Witch   1942
    The Crystal Ball   1943
    Young and Willing   1943

Harry Sherman Action Specials

Silver Queen	1942
American Empire	1942
Buckskin Frontier	1943
The Kansan	1943
The Woman of the Town	1943

Hopalong Cassidy Westerns (produced by Harry Sherman)

Undercover Man	1942
Lost Canyon	1942
Hoppy Serves a Writ	1943
Border Patrol	1943
Leather Burners	1943
Colt Comrades	1943
Bar 20	1943
False Colors	1943
Riders of the Deadline	1943
Texas Masquerade	1944
Lumberjack	1944
Mystery Man	1944
Forty Thieves	1944

Gabriel Pascal

Major Barbara	1941
(See J. Arthur Rank)	

Patrician Productions
See Walter Camp

Pendennis Pictures

Fire Over England (produced by Erich Pommer)	1937
Troop Ship (produced by Erich Pommer)	1937
The Plot to Kill Roosevelt (produced by Steven Pallos and John Stafford)	1948

Edward Peskay

The Angry God	1948

Jack Pickford
See Mary Pickford

Mary Pickford

Pollyanna	1920
Suds	1920
Love Light	1921
Through the Back Door	1921
Little Lord Fauntleroy	1921

Tess of the Storm Country	1922
Rosita	1923
Dorothy Vernon of Haddon Hall	1924
Little Annie Rooney	1925
Sparrows	1926
My Best Girl	1927
Coquette	1929
Taming of the Shrew (with Fairbanks)	1929
Secrets	1933
One Rainy Afternoon (with Jesse Lasky)	1936
The Gay Desperado (with Jesse Lasky)	1936
Sleep My Love (with Buddy Rogers and Ralph Cohn)	1948
Love Happy (with Lester Cowan)	1950

Jack Pickford Productions

Garrison's Finish	1923
The Hillbilly	1924
Waking Up the Town	1925

Erich Pommer
See Pendennis Pictures, UFA

Harry Popkin

My Dear Secretary	1948
Impact	1949
Champagne for Caesar	1950
D.O.A.	1950

Michael Powell
See British National Films, J. Arthur Rank

Arnold Pressburger

The Shanghai Gesture	1942
Hangmen Also Die!	1943
It Happened Tomorrow	1944

Emeric Pressburger
See J. Arthur Rank

Gregor Rabinovitch

Three Russian Girls	1944

J. Arthur Rank-General Film Distributors

Mr. Emmanuel (produced by William Sistrom)	1945
Colonel Blimp (produced by Michael Powell and Emeric Pressburger)	1945

Blithe Spirit (produced by Noel Coward)	1945
Johnny in the Clouds (produced by Anatole de Gruenwald)	1946
Henry V (produced by Laurence Olivier)	1946
Caesar and Cleopatra (produced by Gabriel Pascal)	1946
Man of Evil (produced by Edward Black)	1948

Gregory Ratoff
Black Magic	1949
If This Be Sin	1950

Charles Ray
A Tailor-Made Man	1922
The Girl I Loved	1923

Reliance
See Edward Small

Arthur Ripley-Rudolph Monter
Voice in the Wind	1944

Hal Roach
There Goes My Heart	1938
Topper Takes a Trip	1939
Zenobia	1939
Captain Fury	1939
The Housekeeper's Daughter	1939
Of Mice and Men	1940
A Chump at Oxford	1940
One Million B.C.	1940
Saps at Sea	1940
Turnabout	1940
Captain Caution	1940
Road Show	1941
Topper Returns	1941
Broadway Limited	1941

Hal Roach Streamliners
Tanks a Million	1941
Niagara Falls	1941
All-American Co-Ed	1941
Miss Polly	1941
Fiesta	1941
Hayfoot	1942
Brooklyn Orchid	1942
Dudes Are Pretty People	1942
About Face	1942

Flying with Music   1942
The Devil with Hitler   1942
McGuerins from Brooklyn   1942
Calaboose   1943
Fall In   1943
Taxi, Mister   1943
Prairie Chickens   1943
Yanks Ahoy   1943
Nazty Nuisance   1943
Hal Roach Comedy Carnival   1947
    Curley
    The Fabulous Joe
Lafftime   1948
    Here Comes Trouble
    Who Killed Doc Robbin?

Casey Robinson
    See Benedict Bogeaus

Albert S. Rogell
    The Admiral Was a Lady   1950

Buddy Rogers
    See Comet, Mary Pickford

Charles R. Rogers
    The Powers Girl   1943
    Song of the Open Road   1944
    Delightfully Dangerous   1945
    Angel on My Shoulder   1946
    The Fabulous Dorseys   1947

James Roosevelt
    Pastor Hall   1940
    Pot O'Gold   1941

Richard A. Rowland
    Cheers for Miss Bishop   1941

St. George's Productions (Rex Ingram)
    The Three Passions   1929

Victor Saville Productions
    Dark Journey   1937
    Storm in a Teacup   1938

Max Schach
    See Trafalgar Films

Joseph M. Schenck

Joseph M. Schenck Productions	
Wild Justice	1925
The Eagle	1925
The Bat	1926
The Son of the Sheik	1926
The Dove	1928
The Woman Disputed	1928
New York Nights	1929

Art Cinema	
The Beloved Rogue	1927
Topsy and Eva	1927
Sorrell and Son	1927
The Garden of Eden	1928
Drums of Love	1928
Tempest	1928
The Battle of the Sexes	1928
Revenge	1928
Lady of the Pavements	1929
Alibi	1929
Eternal Love	1929
Evangeline	1929
Three Live Ghosts	1929
The Locked Door	1929
Lummox	1930
Be Yourself	1930
Puttin' on the Ritz	1930
One Romantic Night	1930
The Bad One	1930
DuBarry, Woman of Passion	1930
The Lottery Bride	1930
Abraham Lincoln	1930
The Bat Whispers	1930
Reaching for the Moon	1931
Kiki	1931
Indiscreet	1931
Street Scene (with Samuel Goldwyn)	1931
Corsair	1931
Tonight or Never (with Samuel Goldwyn)	1931
Rain	1932
Hallelujah, I'm a Bum	1933

Buster Keaton Productions
The General	1927
College	1927
Steamboat Bill, Jr.	1928

20th Century (with Darryl Zanuck)
The Bowery	1933
Broadway Thru a Keyhole	1933
Blood Money	1933
Advice to the Lovelorn	1933
Gallant Lady	1934
Moulin Rouge	1934
Looking for Trouble	1934
The House of Rothschild	1934
Born To Be Bad	1934
Bulldog Drummond Strikes Back	1934
The Affairs of Cellini	1934
The Last Gentleman	1934
The Mighty Barnum	1934
Clive of India	1935
Folies Bergere	1935
Cardinal Richelieu	1935
Les Miserables	1935
The Call of the Wild	1935

William Sekely
New Wine	1941

David O. Selznick

Selznick International Productions
Little Lord Fauntleroy	1936
The Garden of Allah	1936
A Star Is Born	1937
The Prisoner of Zenda	1937
Nothing Sacred	1937
The Adventures of Tom Sawyer	1938
The Young in Heart	1938
Made for Each Other	1939
Intermezzo	1939
Rebecca	1940

Vanguard Productions
Since You Went Away	1944
I'll Be Seeing You	1945
Spellbound	1945

Mack Sennett
    Down on the Farm   1920
    Suzanna   1923
    The Shriek of Araby   1923

Harry Sherman
    See Paramount Productions

William Sistrom
    See J. Arthur Rank

Jack Skirball
    Guest Wife   1945

Edward Small

    Reliance (with Harry M. Goetz)
    I Cover the Waterfront   1933
    Palooka   1934
    The Count of Monte Cristo   1934
    Trans-Atlantic Merry-Go-Round   1934
    Let'em Have It   1935
    Red Salute   1935
    The Melody Lingers On   1935
    The Last of the Mohicans   1936

    Edward Small Productions
    The Duke of West Point   1938
    King of the Turf   1939
    The Man in the Iron Mask   1939
    My Son, My Son   1940
    South of Pago-Pago   1940
    Kit Carson   1940
    The Son of Monte Cristo   1941
    International Lady   1941
    The Corsican Brothers   1941
    A Gentleman After Dark   1942
    Twin Beds   1942
    Miss Annie Rooney   1942
    Friendly Enemies   1942
    Up in Mabel's Room   1944
    Abroad with Two Yanks   1944
    Brewster's Millions   1945
    Getting Gertie's Garter   1945
    Davy Crockett, Indian Scout   1950
    The Iroquois Trail   1950

John Stafford
   See Pendennis Pictures

Samuel Steifel
   The Big Wheel   1949
   Quicksand   1950

Josef von Sternberg
   The Salvation Hunters   1925

Andrew Stone
   Hi, Diddle Diddle   1943
   Sensations of 1945   1944
   Bedside Manner   1945
   The Bachelor's Daughters   1946
   Fun on a Weekend   1947

Hunt Stromberg
   Lady of Burlesque   1943
   Guest in the House   1944
   Young Widow   1946
   The Strange Woman   1946
   Dishonored Lady   1947
   Lured   1947
   Too Late for Tears   1949

Gloria Swanson
   The Love of Sunya   1927
   Sadie Thompson   1928
   The Trespasser   1929
   What a Widow   1930
   Perfect Understanding   1933

Trafalgar Films (Max Schach)
   Love from a Stranger   1937
   Dreaming Lips (with Paul Czinner)   1937

20th Century
   See Joseph M. Schenck

Two Cities
   In Which We Serve (produced by Noel Coward)   1943

UFA
   Congress Dances (produced by Erich Pommer)   1932

King Vidor
   Our Daily Bread   1934

Walter Wanger
    You Only Live Once   1937
    History Is Made At Night   1937
    Walter Wanger's Vogues of 1938   1937
    Stand-In   1937
    52nd Street   1937
    I Met My Love Again   1938
    Blockade   1938
    Algiers   1938
    Trade Winds   1938
    Stagecoach   1939
    Winter Carnival   1939
    Eternally Yours   1939
    Slightly Honorable   1939
    The House Across the Bay   1940
    Foreign Correspondent   1940
    The Long Voyage Home   1940
    Sundown   1941

Westport International
    Kings of the Olympics   1948
    Olympic Cavalcade   1948

Herbert Wilcox
    Paddy the Next-Best-Thing   1923
    A Woman's Secret   1924
    The Only Way   1926

      British & Dominions
    Magic Night   1932
    Yes, Mr. Brown   1933
    Bitter Sweet   1933
    Sorrell and Son   1934
    The Runaway Queen   1934
    Brewster's Millions   1935
    Nell Gwyn   1935
    Escape Me Never   1935

W. Lee Wilder
    The Vicious Circle   1948
    Once a Thief   1950

Darryl Zanuck
    See Joseph M. Schenck

Bennie F. Zeidman
    Samarang   1933

United Artists Corporation
The Walt Disney Cartoons

Title	Date of First Release
MICKEY MOUSE CARTOONS	
1932	
Mickey's Nightmare	Aug. 13
Trader Mickey	Aug. 20
The Whoopee Party	Sept. 17
Touchdown Mickey	Oct. 15
The Wayward Canary	Nov. 12
The Klondike Kid	Nov. 12
Mickey's Good Deed	Dec. 17
1933	
Building a Building	Jan. 7
The Mad Doctor	Jan. 21
Mickey's Pal Pluto	Feb. 18
Mickey's Mellerdrammer	March 18
Ye Olden Days	April 8
The Mail Pilot	May 13
Mickey's Mechanical Man	June 17
Mickey's Gala Premiere	July 1
Puppy Love	Sept. 2
The Steeple-Chase	Sept. 30
The Pet Store	Oct. 28
Giantland	Nov. 23
1934	
Shanghaied	Jan. 13
Camping Out	Feb. 17
Playful Pluto	March 3
Gulliver Mickey	May 19
Mickey's Steam-Roller	June 16

Orphans' Benefit	Aug. 11
Mickey Plays Papa	Sept. 29
The Dognapper	Nov. 17
Two-Gun Mickey	Dec. 15

1935

Mickey's Man Friday	Jan. 19
The Band Concert	Feb. 23
Mickey's Service Station	March 16
Mickey's Kangaroo	April 13
Mickey's Garden	July 13
Mickey's Fire Brigade	Aug. 3
Pluto's Judgment Day	Aug. 31
On Ice	Sept. 28

1936

Mickey's Polo Team	Jan. 4
Orphans' Picnic	Feb. 15
Mickey's Grand Opera	March 7
Thru the Mirror	May 30
Mickey's Rival	June 20
Moving Day	June 20
Alpine Climbers	July 25
Mickey's Circus	Aug. 1
Donald and Pluto	Sept. 12
Mickey's Elephant	Oct. 10

1937

The Worm Turns	Jan. 2
Don Donald	Jan. 9
Magician Mickey	Feb. 6
Moose Hunters	Feb. 20
Mickey's Amateurs	April 17
Modern Inventions	May 29

SILLY SYMPHONY CARTOONS

1932

The Bears and Bees	July 9
Just Dogs	July 30
Flowers and Trees	July 30
King Neptune	Sept. 10
Bugs in Love	Oct. 1
Babes in the Woods	Nov. 19
Santa's Workshop	Dec. 10

1933
Birds in the Spring	March 11
Father Noah's Ark	April 8
Three Little Pigs	May 27
Old King Cole	July 29
Lullaby Land	Aug. 19
The Pied Piper	Sept. 16
The Night Before Christmas	Dec. 9

1934
The China Shop	Jan. 13
Grasshopper and the Ants	Feb. 10
Funny Little Bunnies	March 24
The Big Bad Wolf	April 14
The Wise Little Hen	June 9
The Flying Mouse	July 14
Peculiar Penguins	Sept. 1
The Goddess of Spring	Nov. 3

1935
The Tortoise and the Hare	Jan. 5
The Golden Touch	March 22
The Robber Kitten	April 35
Water Babies	May 11
The Cookie Carnival	May 25
Who Killed Cock Robin	June 29
Music Land	Oct. 5
Three Orphan Kittens	Oct. 26
Cock O' the Walk	Nov. 30
Broken Toys	Dec. 14

1936
Three Little Wolves	April 18
Elmer Elephant	March 28
Toby Tortoise Returns	Aug. 22
Three Blind Mouseketeers	Sept. 26
The Country Cousin	Oct. 31
Mother Pluto	Nov. 14
More Kittens	Dec. 19

1937
Woodland Cafe	March 13
Little Hiawatha	May 15

Appendix 4

United Artists Corporation Income History

(rounded to the nearest thousand)

FROM CONSOLIDATED INCOME STATEMENTS OF UA, 1919-1950

Year	Domestic Gross (Inc. Canada)	Foreign Gross	Total Gross	Profit or (Loss)
1919-20	$ 3,700,000*		$ 3,700,000*	$ (191,000)
1921	4,906,000		4,906,000	(16,000)
		1921-22		
1922	5,190,000	$ 2,122,000*	7,312,000*	(140,000)
1923	6,066,000	1,989,000	8,056,000	68,000
1924	4,215,000	2,383,000	6,599,000	(236,000)
1925	6,974,000	2,286,000	9,260,000	(136,000)
1926	8,697,000	5,044,000	13,741,000	86,000
1927	7,202,000	4,127,000	11,328,000	(465,000)
1928	12,939,000	7,641,000	20,580,000	1,598,000
1929	12,291,000	7,427,000	19,718,000	1,328,000
1930	10,507,000	6,547,000	17,053,000	363,000
1931	11,803,000	8,794,000	20,596,000	874,000
1932	5,745,000	5,058,000	10,803,000	(270,000)
1933	6,804,000	6,879,000	13,683,000	79,000
1934	11,154,000	11,952,000	23,106,000	1,085,000
1935	11,204,000	13,192,000	24,396,000	1,496,000
1936	10,258,000	13,554,000	23,812,000	858,000
1937	13,479,000	11,766,000	25,246,000	752,000
1938	12,476,000	12,653,000	25,128,000	254,000
1939	14,314,000	10,119,000	24,432,000	445,000
1940	13,818,000	8,652,000	22,469,000	242,000
1941	12,456,000	11,445,000	23,901,000	98,000
1942	12,293,000	10,493,000	22,786,000	145,000
1943	18,249,000	10,098,000	28,347,000	1,007,000
1944	15,100,000	9,045,000	24,145,000	(311,000)
1945	22,677,000	11,819,000	34,396,000	576,000
1946	24,523,000	12,459,000	36,982,000	409,000
1947	22,287,000	9,786,000	32,073,000	460,000
1948	17,726,000	7,020,000	24,746,000	(517,000)
1949	17,746,000	5,227,000	22,973,000	(209,000)
1950	13,122,000†	4,608,000†	19,586,000†	(871,000)†

*Approximate figures.

†For eleven months ending Dec. 2, 1950.

United Artists Corporation Record of Dividend Payments

1929
(on Preferred Stock)

Mary Pickford	$	33,179.55
Charles Chaplin		33,060.66
Douglas Fairbanks		33,216.21
D. W. Griffith and D. W. Griffith, Inc.		30,239.53
Joseph M. Schenck		22,496.23
Art Cinema		15,600.66
Samuel Goldwyn		11,506.23
	$	179,299.07

1930
(on Common Stock)

Pickford	$	20,000
Chaplin		20,000
Fairbanks		20,000
D. W. Griffith and D. W. Griffith, Inc.		20,000
Schenck		20,000
Art Cinema		20,000
Goldwyn		20,000
Gloria Swanson		20,000
	$	160,000

1931
(on Common Stock)

Pickford	$	10,000
Chaplin		10,000
Fairbanks		10,000
D. W. Griffith and D. W. Griffith, Inc.		10,000
Schenck		10,000
Art Cinema		10,000
Goldwyn		10,000
Swanson		10,000
	$	80,000

1932
(on Common Stock)

Pickford	$	10,000
Chaplin		10,000
Fairbanks		10,000
D. W. Griffith and D. W. Griffith, Inc.		10,000
Schenck		10,000
Art Cinema		10,000
Goldwyn		10,000
Swanson		10,000
	$	80,000

1934
(on Common Stock)

Pickford	$	93,330
Chaplin		93,330
Fairbanks		93,330
Schenck		93,330
Art Cinema		93,330
Goldwyn		93,330
	$	559,980

1935
(on Common Stock)

Pickford	$	50,000
Chaplin		50,000
Fairbanks		50,000
Goldwyn		50,000
Alexander Korda		50,000
	$	250,000

1936
(on Common Stock)

Pickford	$	100,000
Chaplin		100,000
Fairbanks		100,000
Goldwyn		100,000
Korda		100,000
	$	500,000

1937
(on Common Stock)

Pickford	$	50,000
Chaplin		50,000
Fairbanks		50,000
Goldwyn		50,000
Korda		50,000
	$	250,000

1938
(on Common Stock)

Pickford	$	100,000
Chaplin		100,000
Fairbanks		100,000
Goldwyn		100,000
Korda		100,000
	$	500,000

1939
(on Common Stock)

Pickford	$	50,000
Chaplin		50,000
Fairbanks		50,000
Goldwyn		50,000
Korda		50,000
	$	250,000

1940
(on Common Stock)

Pickford	$	25,000
Chaplin		25,000
Fairbanks		25,000
Goldwyn		25,000
Korda		25,000
	$	125,000

1941
(on Common Stock)

Pickford	$	50,000
Chaplin		50,000
Korda		50,000
	$	150,000

DIVIDENDS RECEIVED BY EACH STOCKHOLDER

Mary Pickford	$	591,509.55
Charles Chaplin		591,390.66
Douglas Fairbanks		541,546.21
D. W. Griffith and D. W. Griffith, Inc.		70,239.53
Joseph M. Schenck		155,826.23
Art Cinema		148,930.66
Samuel Goldwyn		519,836.23
Gloria Swanson		40,000.00
Alexander Korda		425,000.00
Total		$3,084,279.07

<table>
<tr><td colspan="3">

	United Artists Corporation
Appendix 6	Capital Stock Purchased
	by the Company

</td></tr>
</table>

Year	Purchased From	Price
1920	McAdoo	$ 25,000
1932	Swanson	200,000
1933	Griffith	202,000
1935	Schenck	550,000
1935	Art Cinema	650,000
1941	Goldwyn	300,000
1941	Fairbanks Estate	400,000
1944	Korda	950,000
1947	Selznick	2,000,000
Total		$5,277,000

A DESCRIPTIVE INVENTORY

The United Artists Collection of the Center for Film and Theater Research is housed in the manuscripts library of the State Historical Society of Wisconsin, Madison. The collection is divided into eight sections, each dealing with a major function or aspect of the corporation. The sections, in turn, are divided into record series, each containing the entire original working file obtained from United Artists (subdivided into boxes and folders).

Section A: *Legal Files*

Series 1A   United Artists Corporation Minutes (1919-1951)
Minutes, incorporation documents, stock certificates, miscellaneous.

Series 2A   O'Brien Legal File (1919-1951)
The files of the firm that acted as United Artists' legal counsel. Documents and correspondence dealing with the full range of UA's activities, including such matters as incorporation papers, stock transactions, and subsidiary corporations; correspondence with stockholders; files on the MPPDA; case files relating to stockholders' lawsuits, antitrust actions, plagiarism cases, and censorship proceedings; contracts and negotiations with producers; and myriad other matters. This is the largest and most comprehensive series in the collection. Indexed.

Series 3A   Producers Legal File (1933-1966)
Financial documents and related correspondence in regard to the financing of motion pictures. Includes distribution contracts, mortgages of chattels, bank and film laboratory assignments, authors' and composers' contracts, copyrights, etc. The files document the order in which distribution receipts paid off financiers and producers. Indexed. Emphasis on 1940-1953.

Series 4A   Muller Legal File (1919-1951)
Files of the treasurer/comptroller, similar in content to those of the above series, but dealing with motion pictures which United Artists assisted in financing.

Additional miscellaneous files in this section deal with general production financing, antitrust cases, and taxes.

Section B: *Executive Correspondence*

Series 1B   George Bagnall (1936-1950)
Vice president; corporate relations with producers before and during production and during exhibition, primarily concerned with financing.

Series 2B   Harry Buckley (1922-1951)
Vice president 1926-1938, personal representative for Fairbanks and Pickford 1924-1929, and assistant secretary after 1938; advertising, publicity, sales expenses, and home office administration.

Series 3B   Buckley and Bollengier (1941-1954)
Labor relations in conjunction with treasurer A. E. Bollengier.

Series 4B   Buckley and Muller (1922-1951)
Financial and legal matters in conjunction with comptroller H. J. Muller.

Series 5B   A. H. Giannini (1936-1938)
President; minor matters concerning producers and employees.

Series 6B   Arthur Kelly (1946-1950)
Vice president; foreign production and distribution.

Series 7B   Edward C. Raftery (1941-1947)
President and partner in the O'Brien firm, UA's legal counsel; corporate matters, domestic and foreign distribution, and advertising.

Series 8B   Gradwell Sears (1941-1951)
Vice president in charge of distribution 1941-1947 and president 1947-1950; rich material on distribution, particularly foreign, and correspondence with producers and UA executives.

Series 9B   Herbert Weimer (1933-1935)
Treasurer; financial information relating to the corporation, producers, and productions.

Section C: *Financial Materials*

Series 1C   Pre-Incorporation Ledger/Journal (1919-1920)
Receipts, disbursements, expenses, and sales of Joseph M. Schenck's Norma Talmadge productions.

Series 2C   Corporate Financial Journals (1919-1950)
Day-by-day account of receipts and disbursements.

Series 3C   Corporate Ledgers (1919-1950)
Individual accounts of parent corporation and major subsidiaries, as well as such related corporations as Hal Roach Studios, Selznick International Pictures, and Samuel Goldwyn, Inc. Entries within each volume are chronological, permitting the tracing of each transaction to the corporate journals (see series 2C).

Series 4C   Balance Sheets and Associated Papers (1919-1950)
Balance sheets, consolidated accounts, and income statements for each year, together with working papers and drafts. Includes annual Price, Waterhouse audit reports. Also included are similar materials for foreign operations, arranged by country of origin.

Additional miscellaneous files in this section include information on producers' payments and allocations; foreign exchange and circuit ledgers and journals; contract and played-and-earned registers; and other miscellaneous financial materials.

Section D: *Advertising and Publicity*

Newspaper campaigns, celebrity appearances, publicity on films and actors, and related expenses, 1935-1950.

Section E: *Domestic Sales*

Correspondence with independent theaters and theater circuits; producers representatives who approved exhibition contracts; exchange sales managers; and play dates, sales campaigns, circular letters, litigations, and roadshowings, 1930-1950.

Section F: *Foreign Sales*

Agreements with producers and distributors; legal aspects of foreign distribution; sales reports; financial and background information; and correspondence from individual countries, mainly from 1940-1950.

Section G: *Subsidiaries and Related Corporations*

Walter Wanger Productions, United Artists Productions, Eagle Lion, and Producers Releasing Corporation. Financing, litigation, foreign and domestic sales, financial reports, and miscellaneous material.

Section H: *Miscellaneous Materials*

Notes

In the notes that follow, citations to documents in the United Artists Collection are designated by series, box, and folder (the collection call number, US/Mss/99AN, is omitted). For example, 1A/24/5 refers to series 1A, box 24, folder 5.

Chapter 1: *Artists in Business*

1 *Moving Picture World,* February 1, 1919, p. 619.
2 Ibid., January 4, 1919, p. 53.
3 Benjamin B. Hampton, *A History of the Movies* (New York: Covici, Friede, 1931), p. 165.
4 For background information in this section, I have relied upon the following sources: Ralph Cassady, Jr., "Monopoly in Motion Picture Production and Distribution: 1908-1915," *Southern California Law Review,* 32 (Summer 1959), 325-90; Michael Conant, *Antitrust in the Motion Picture Industry* (Berkeley and Los Angeles: Univ. of California Press, 1960), pp. 18-27; Hampton, *A History of the Movies,* pp. 64-120; and Mae Huettig, *Economic Control of the Motion Picture Industry* (Philadelphia: Univ. of Pennsylvania Press, 1944), pp. 24-31.
5 Charles Chaplin, *My Autobiography* (New York: Simon & Schuster, 1964), p. 222.
6 *Moving Picture World,* February 1, 1919, pp. 607-8.
7 Ibid., p. 619.
8 *Variety,* January 31, 1919, p. 58.
9 Arthur Mayer, "The Origins of United Artists," *Films in Review,* 10 (1959), 390.
10 Hampton, *A History of the Movies,* p. 148.
11 Edward Wagenknecht, *The Movies in the Age of Innocence* (Norman: Univ. of Oklahoma Press, 1962), p. 190.
12 Hampton, *A History of the Movies,* p. 155.
13 *Variety,* November 1, 1918, p. 42.
14 Ibid., October 1, 1915, p. 18.

15 Alistair Cooke, *Douglas Fairbanks: The Making of a Screen Character* (New York: The Museum of Modern Art, 1940), p. 14.

16 Richard Griffith, *The Movie Stars* (Garden City, N.Y.: Doubleday, 1970), p. 145.

17 Cooke, *Fairbanks*, pp. 20, 21.

18 Iris Barry, *D. W. Griffith: American Film Master* (New York: Museum of Modern Art, 1965), p. 20.

19 Robert Henderson, *D. W. Griffith: His Life and Work* (New York: Oxford Univ. Press, 1972), p. 120.

20 *Moving Picture World,* February 15, 1919, p. 899.

21 See, for example, Will Irwin, *The House that Shadows Built* (Garden City, N.Y.: Doubleday, 1928); Hampton, *A History of the Movies;* Mayer, "The Origins of United Artists"; Gertrude Jobes, *Motion Picture Empire* (Hamden, Conn.; Archon, 1966).

22 *Benjamin P. Schulberg* v. *Hiram Abrams,* Supreme Court of New York, 1920.

23 Letter from Dennis O'Brien to Morris Greenhill, August 20, 1920. 1A/211/3.

24 *Moving Picture World,* February 1, 1919, p. 619.

25 *In re* Famous Players-Lasky Corp., 11 F.T.C. 187 (1927).

26 *Moving Picture World,* November 27, 1926, p. 205.

Chapter 2: *Starts and Fits*

1 Clipping from *Photoplay Magazine,* 1920 (date unknown).

2 Richard Griffith, *The Movie Stars* (Garden City, N.Y.: Doubleday, 1970), p. 151.

3 Letter from Dennis O'Brien to John Fairbanks, May 22, 1920. 1A/210/5.

4 Letter from Dennis O'Brien to Helen Walker, October 26, 1940. 1A/14/7.

5 Interview with Charles Chaplin, Vevey, Switzerland, January 10, 1971.

6 Marquis James and Bessie R. James, *Biography of a Bank: The Story of Bank of America NT & SA* (New York: Harper, 1954), p. 246.

7 *The Motion Picture Industry as a Basis for Bond Financing* (Halsey, Stuart & Co., Inc., May 27, 1927).

8 *Variety,* November 28, 1919, p. 62.

9 *Moving Picture World,* July 24, 1920, p. 473.

10 Ibid., July 3, 1920, p. 72.

11 Donald M. Nelson, "The Independent Producer," *The Annals of the American Academy of Political and Social Sciences,* 254 (November 1947), 52.

12 Letter from Dennis O'Brien to John Fairbanks, March 28, 1921. 1A/210/12.

13 Letter from Sam Berman to Dennis O'Brien, May 27, 1921. 1A/210/12.

14 Letter from Mary Pickford and Douglas Fairbanks to D. W. Griffith, June 24, 1922. 1A/209/14.

15 Letter from Bank of Italy to Associated Authors, Inc., October 15, 1923. 1A/212/9.

16 Letter from N. A. McKay to Dennis O'Brien, November 6, 1923. 1A/212/9.

17 Theodore Huff, *Charlie Chaplin* (New York: Schuman, 1951), pp. 170-71.

18 Letter from Hiram Abrams to Dennis O'Brien, April 3, 1923. 1A/209/11.
19 *Variety,* November 15, 1923, p. 19.
20 Letter from Dennis O'Brien to Mary Pickford, April 18, 1923. 1A/209/13.
21 Telegram from D. W. Griffith to Douglas Fairbanks, September 18, 1924. 1A/210/9.

Chapter 3: *Joe Schenck's Reorganization*

1 Letter from Joseph Schenck to Dennis O'Brien, November 11, 1920. 1A/201/11.
2 Richard Griffith, *The Movie Stars* (Garden City, N.Y.: Doubleday, 1970), p. 68.
3 Richard Griffith, *Samuel Goldwyn: The Producer and His Films* (New York: The Museum of Modern Art, 1956), p. 10.
4 *Variety,* December 2, 1925, p. 27.
5 *Moving Picture World,* December 12, 1925, p. 529.
6 Letter from Joseph Schenck to the Trustees in the Dissolution of Art Cinema, May 20, 1935. 1A/165/3.
7 Mae Huettig, *Economic Control of the Motion Picture Industry* (Philadelphia: Univ. of Pennsylvania Press, 1944), pp. 31-39.
8 Ibid., pp. 74-84.
9 Telegram from Dennis O'Brien to Robert Fairbanks, March 4, 1927. 1A/201/19.
10 Telegram from Mary Pickford and Douglas Fairbanks to Dennis O'Brien [n.d.]. 1A/201/19.
11 Letter from Dennis O'Brien to N. A. McKay, November 1, 1927. 1A/201/19.
12 *Variety,* April 17, 1929, p. 4.

Chapter 4: *Adjusting to the Talkies*

1 For the following analysis of the industry's accommodation to sound, I am indebted to N. R. Danielian, *AT&T: The Story of Industrial Conquest* (New York: Vanguard, 1939), pp. 138-72; and William I. Greenwald, "The Impact of Sound upon the Film Industry," *Explorations in Entrepreneurial History,* 4 (May 15, 1952), 178-92.
2 *New York Times,* October 8, 1926, p. 23.
3 Benjamin B. Hampton, *A History of the Movies* (New York: Covici, Friede, 1931), p. 387.
4 Richard Griffith, *The Movie Stars* (Garden City, N.Y.: Doubleday, 1970), p. 177.
5 *Variety,* October 27, 1926, p. 55.
6 Letter from Joseph Schenck to Dennis O'Brien, November 12, 1926. 1A/210/9.

7 Iris Barry, *D. W. Griffith: American Film Master* (New York: The Museum of Modern Art, 1965), p. 32.

8 Letter from Joseph Schenck to Dennis O'Brien, January 12, 1926. 1A/210/9.

9 Letter from Joseph Schenck to Dennis O'Brien, December 12, 1932. 1A/159/2.

10 Letter from D. W. Griffith to UA Stockholders, July 8, 1932. 1A/159/2.

11 Ibid.

12 Letter from D. W. Griffith to Mary Pickford, September 2, 1932. 1A/159/2.

13 Letter from D. W. Griffith to UA Stockholders, July 8, 1932. 1A/159/2.

14 Letter from Joseph Schenck to D. W. Griffith, November 25, 1932. 1A/159/2.

15 Letter from D. W. Griffith to UA Stockholders, November 26, 1932. 1A/159/2.

16 Letter from Dennis O'Brien to Joseph Schenck, December 5, 1932. 1A/159/2.

17 Letter from W. R. Oglesby to Dennis O'Brien, January 14, 1933. 1A/159/2.

18 Letter from Joseph Schenck to Dennis O'Brien, December 5, 1932. 1A/159/2.

19 Letter from Joseph Schenck to Dennis O'Brien, December 16, 1932. 1A/159/2.

20 Interview with Charles Chaplin, Vevey, Switzerland, January 10, 1971.

21 Edward Wagenknecht, *The Movies in the Age of Innocence* (Norman: Univ. of Oklahoma Press, 1962), p. 155.

22 Jack Spears, *Hollywood: The Golden Era* (New York: Barnes, 1971), pp. 196-97.

23 *New York Times,* March 6, 1931, p. 26.

24 Ibid., December 30, 1930, p. 24.

25 Anita Loos, *A Girl Like I* (New York: Viking, 1966), pp. 172-73.

Chapter 5: *Depression and Monopoly*

1 Mae Huettig, *Economic Control of the Motion Picture Industry* (Philadelphia: Univ. of Pennsylvania Press, 1944), pp. 54-95.

2 Michael Conant, *Antitrust in the Motion Picture Industry* (Berkeley and Los Angeles: Univ. of California Press, 1960), pp. 29-32.

3 Sol A. Rosenblatt, *Report Regarding Code of Fair Competition* (Washington, D.C.: Government Printing Office, 1934). 1A/143/1.

4 Gertrude Jobes, *Motion Picture Empire* (Hamden, Conn.: Archon, 1966), p. 298.

5 Murray Ross, *Stars and Strikes: Unionization of Hollywood* (New York: Columbia University Press, 1941), pp. 44-45.

6 Arthur M. Schlesinger, Jr., *The Age of Roosevelt: The Coming of the New Deal* (Boston: Houghton Mifflin, 1958), pp. 98-99.

7 For my analysis of the provisions of the Code, I am indebted to J. Douglas Gomery, "The N.R.A. and the American Film Industry," unpublished paper, The University of Wisconsin-Madison, 1972.

8 U.S. Temporary National Economic Committee, *The Motion Picture Industry: A Pattern of Control,* Monograph No. 43, (Washington, D.C.: Government

Printing Office, 1941), p. 8. Representing the majors on the Code Authority were Merlin H. Aylesworth, president of RKO; Sidney R. Kent, president of Fox; George J. Schaefer, vice president of Paramount; Nicholas M. Schenck, president of Loew's; and Harry M. Warner, president of Warner Brothers. Representing the unaffiliated groups were Robert H. Cochrane, vice president of Universal; W. Ray Johnston, president of Republic; Ed Kuykendall, president of MPTOA; Charles L. O'Reilly, president of TOCC; and Nathan Yamins, independent theater owner.

9 Quoted in the complaint, *Independent Theater Owners Association* v. *Aylesworth et al.,* Supreme Court of New York, 1934.

10 Ellis W. Hawley, *The New Deal and the Problem of Monopoly* (Princeton, N.J.: Princeton Univ. Press, 1966), p. 96.

11 Jobes, *Motion Picture Empire,* p. 330.

12 For this analysis, I rely heavily on TNEC Monograph No. 43.

13 Ibid., p. 31.

14 *In re* Famous Players-Lasky Corp., 11 F.T.C. 187 (1927); *Federal Trade Commission* v. *Paramount Famous Players-Lasky Corp.,* 57 F. (2d) 152 (C.C.A. 2d., 1932).

15 Conant, *Antitrust,* pp. 84, 180-81.

16 Letter from Edward C. Raftery to Joseph Schenck, October 14, 1933. 1A/142/11.

17 Telegram from Edward C. Raftery to Will H. Hays, October 17, 1933. 1A/142/11.

18 Letter from Paul O'Brien to Harold Baresford, April 9, 1934. 1A/142/11.

19 Rosenblatt, *Report.*

20 Telegram from Edward C. Raftery to Joseph Schenck, September 28, 1933. 1A/142/11.

21 Telegram from Joseph Schenck to Edward C. Raftery, September 28, 1933. 1A/142/11.

22 Memorandum from UA, Columbia and Universal to General Hugh S. Johnson [n.d.]. 1A/142/12.

23 Brief submitted to Code Authority from UA, June 8, 1934. 1A/143/1.

24 Letter from Edward C. Raftery to Sol A. Rosenblatt, April 15, 1935. 1A/142/1.

Chapter 6: *Schenck's Last Years*

1 John Keats, *Howard Hughes* (New York: Random House, 1966), p. 24.

2 Ibid., p. 44.

3 Interview with Lewis Milestone, Los Angeles, March 22, 1972.

4 Letter from Arthur Kelly to Edward C. Raftery, July 15, 1932. 1A/169/3.

5 Telegram from Dennis O'Brien to Neil S. McCarthy, November 15, 1934. 1A/168/5.

6 Memorandum from Edward C. Raftery to Dennis O'Brien, June 2, 1938. 1A/168/8.

7 *New York Times,* November 7, 1930, p. 32.

8 *Variety,* August 11, 1931, p. 4.

9 "The Big Bad Wolf," *Fortune,* 10 (November 1934), 146.

10 Letter from Dennis O'Brien to Joseph Schenck, June 3, 1932. 1A/172/4.

11 Memorandum by Dennis O'Brien, n.d. 1A/165/3.

12 *Hollywood Reporter,* July 18, 1933. Twentieth Century was incorporated on May 2, 1933.

13 Letter from Joseph Schenck to the Trustees in the Dissolution of Art Cinema, May 20, 1935. 1A/165/3.

14 Letter from Joseph Schenck to Dennis O'Brien, February 28, 1934. 1A/162/15.

15 Letter from Darryl Zanuck to Joseph Schenck, December 15, 1933. 1A/162/15.

16 Letter from Joseph Schenck to the Trustees in the Dissolution of Art Cinema, May 20, 1935. 1A/165/3.

17 Ibid.

18 Ibid.

19 Ibid.

20 Ibid.

21 Ibid.

22 Letter from Joseph Schenck to Charles Chaplin, May 24, 1935. 1A/165/3.

23 Letter from F. M. Guedalla to Nathan Burkan, September 24, 1935. 1A/27/18.

Chapter 7: *Without a Leader*

1 Letter from F. M. Guedalla to Nathan Burkan, September 24, 1935. 1A/27/18.

2 Letter from F. M. Guedalla to Nathan Burkan, August 20, 1935. 1A/27/18.

3 Letter from F. M. Guedalla to Nathan Burkan, September 24, 1935. 1A/27/18.

4 Ibid.

5 Letter from Joseph Schenck to Mary Pickford, March 16, 1938. 1A/136/5.

6 Letter from F. M. Guedalla to Nathan Burkan, September 24, 1935. 1A/27/18.

7 Herbert Wilcox, *Twenty-Five Thousand Sunsets* (London: Bodley Head, 1967), p. 158.

8 Letter from Joseph Schenck to Dennis O'Brien, January 11, 1934. 1A/165/3.

9 *The British Film Industry* (London: Political and Economic Planning, 1952), pp. 68-69.

10 Letter from Gunther R. Lessing to Edward C. Raftery, March 7, 1936. 1A/151/6.

11 Letter from Mary Pickford to UA Board of Directors, May 4, 1936. 1A/151/6.

12 Bernard Rosenberg and Harry Silverstein, eds., *The Real Tinsel* (New York: Macmillan, 1970), pp. 83-84.

13 *Variety,* August 26, 1936, p. 31.

14 Ibid., July 15, 1936, p. 79.

Chapter 8: *The Goldwyn Battles*

1 *Variety,* August 26, 1936, pp. 5, 31.
2 Letter from Arthur Kelly to UA Domestic Exchanges, January 8, 1936. 1A/137/6.
3 Cable from Alexander Korda to UA Stockholders, March 10, 1937. Microfilm 448/Reel 19.
4 Minutes of the UA Board of Directors, March 13, 1937. Microfilm 448/Reel 19.
5 Letter from F. M. Guedalla to Loyd Wright, February 9, 1937. 5B/2/6.
6 Letter from Clarence Ericksen to Dennis O'Brien, May 25, 1937. 1A/135/9.
7 Letter from Clarence Ericksen to Dennis O'Brien, September 22, 1937. 1A/135/9.
8 Letter from Neil S. McCarthy to Mary Pickford and Douglas Fairbanks, December 7, 1937. 1A/135/9.
9 Telegram from Douglas Fairbanks to Dennis O'Brien, November 21, 1937. 1A/135/9.
10 Letter from Ervin Lever to Mary Pickford [n.d.]. 1A/136/5.
11 Letter from Neil S. McCarthy to Clarence Ericksen [n.d.]. 1A/135/9.
12 Letter from Neil S. McCarthy to Dennis O'Brien, January 17, 1938. 1A/136/1.
13 Letter from N. A. McKay to Mary Pickford, February 26, 1938. 1A/136/1.
14 Letter from Joseph Schenck to Mary Pickford, March 16, 1938. 1A/136/5.
15 Letter from Neil S. McCarthy to Douglas Fairbanks, March 18, 1938. 1A/136/5.
16 Telegram from A. H. Giannini to Dennis O'Brien, May 5, 1938. 1A/136/6.
17 Letter from Clarence Ericksen to Edward C. Raftery, June 4, 1938. 1A/136/5.
18 Letter from Clarence Ericksen to Dennis O'Brien, June 16, 1938. 1A/207/5.
19 Paul Tabori, *Alexander Korda* (London: Oldbourne, 1959), p. 207.
20 Letter from Clarence Ericksen to Douglas Fairbanks, December 13, 1938. 1A/136/5.
21 *Variety,* April 5, 1939, p. 3.
22 Ibid., April 12, 1939, p. 3.
23 Ibid., April 19, 1939, p. 3.
24 *New York Times,* May 28, 1939, p. X 3.
25 *Daily Variety,* January 4, 1940, p. 4.
26 Ibid., January 5, 1940, p. 5.
27 *Samuel Goldwyn and Samuel Goldwyn, Inc.* v. *United Artists Corporation,* United States District Court for the Southern District of New York, 1940. 1A/204-206.
28 Letter from Edward C. Raftery to Charles Schwartz, December 27, 1939. 1A/204/8.

Chapter 9: *Facing the War*

1 *Variety,* December 25, 1940, p. 5.
2 William K. Everson, *The Films of Hal Roach* (New York: The Museum of Modern Art, 1971), p. 69.

3 Lewis Jacobs, "World War II and the American Film," in Arthur F. McClure, ed., *The Movies, An American Idiom* (Rutherford, N.J.: Fairleigh Dickenson Univ. Press, 1968), p. 160.

4 Theodore Huff, *Charlie Chaplin* (New York: Schuman, 1951), p. 263.

5 Charles Chaplin, *My Autobiography* (New York: Simon & Schuster, 1964), p. 392.

6 *The British Film Industry* (London: Political and Economic Planning, 1952), pp. 80-83.

7 C. J. North, "Our Foreign Trade in Motion Pictures," *Annals of the American Academy of Political and Social Sciences,* 127 (November 1926), 102.

8 Memorandum from Walter Gould to Gradwell Sears, December 19, 1944. 8B/"Gould."

9 *Film Daily Yearbook,* various years.

10 *Variety,* October 25, 1944, p. 13.

11 Ibid., October 29, 1941, p. 3.

12 Ibid., January 6, 1943, p. 149.

13 Michael Conant, *Antitrust in the Motion Picture Industry* (Berkeley and Los Angeles: Univ. of California Press, 1960), p. 46.

14 *Film Daily Yearbook,* 1948.

15 Conant, *Antitrust,* p. 46.

16 Ibid., p. 94. My analysis of the *Paramount* case relies heavily on Conant's book.

17 Everson, *Roach,* p. 78.

18 Bernard Rosenberg and Harry Silverstein, eds., *The Real Tinsel* (New York: Macmillan, 1970), p. 93.

19 Letter from Mary Pickford to Dennis O'Brien, December 13, 1939. 1A/10/3.

20 Telegram from Murray Silverstone to Edward C. Raftery, June 28, 1938. 1A/176/6.

21 Letter from David O. Selznick to Lowell V. Calvert, June 12, 1940. 1A/176/7.

22 *Variety,* August 7, 1940, p. 5.

23 Memorandum from David O. Selznick to Alexander Korda, June 5, 1941. 1A/11/2.

24 *Variety,* August 20, 1941, p. 5.

25 Letter from Arthur Kelly to UA Stockholders, October 27, 1941. Microfilm 448/Reel 19.

26 *Variety,* December 17, 1941, p. 5.

27 Letter from David O. Selznick to Charles Schlaifer, December 22, 1941. 8B/"Selznick."

Chapter 10: *Worsening Strains Within*

1 *New York Times,* March 10, 1943, p. 15.

2 Letter from Daniel O'Shea to UA Board of Directors, July 9, 1943. 1A/209/4.

3 Michael Conant, *Antitrust in the Motion Picture Industry* (Berkeley and Los Angeles: Univ. of California Press, 1960), p. 114.

4 Letter from Paul O'Brien to Newlin & Ashburn, Esq., June 10, 1942. 1A/65/14.

5 Terry B. Sanders, "The Financing of Independent Feature Films," *Quarterly of Film, Radio, and Television,* 9 (1955), 381-89.

6 Letter from Edward C. Raftery to Vanguard Films, Inc., July 14, 1943. 1A/209/4.
7 Letter from Edward C. Raftery to Charles Schwartz, July 17, 1943. 1A/209/4.
8 Letter from Charles Schwartz to Loyd Wright, July 26, 1943. 1A/209/4.
9 Letter from Mary Pickford to Charles Chaplin, October 18, 1943. 1A/209/6.
10 Transcript of the meeting of the UA Stockholders, October 28, 1943. Microfilm 448/Reel 19.
11 Letter from Mary Pickford to Edward C. Raftery, November 9, 1943. 1A/209/6.
12 Ibid.
13 Cable from Teddie Carr to Edward C. Raftery, December 3, 1943. 7B/"Korda negotiations."
14 Cable from Edward C. Raftery to Teddie Carr, December 4, 1943. 7B/"Korda negotiations."
15 Cable from Teddie Carr to Edward C. Raftery, December 7, 1943. 7B/"Korda negotiations."
16 Cable from Edward C. Raftery to Teddie Carr, December 9, 1943. 7B/"Korda negotiations."
17 Letter from Alexander Korda to Edward C. Raftery, January 12, 1944. 8B/"Foreign dept."
18 Letter from Arthur Kelly to Edward C. Raftery, January 5, 1944. 8B/"Foreign dept."
19 Cable from Edward C. Raftery to Arthur Kelly, January 11, 1944. 8B/"Foreign dept."
20 Letter from Edward C. Raftery to Alexander Korda, January 13, 1944. 8B/"Foreign dept."
21 Letter from Wendell Berge to Alexander Korda, February 14, 1944. 7B/"Korda negotiations."
22 Letter from Charles Chaplin to Edward C. Raftery, April 7, 1944. 7B/"Korda negotiations."

Chapter 11: *Coming Apart at the Seams*

1 "Movies Come Out of the Dog House," *Business Week,* No. 1158 (November 10, 1951), p. 140.
2 Quoted in Murray Schumach, *The Face on the Cutting Room Floor* (New York: Morrow, 1964), p. 59.
3 Ibid., p. 60.
4 Letter from Mary Pickford to Edward C. Raftery, February 10, 1945. 7B/11/7.
5 Letter from Mary Pickford to Edward C. Raftery, January 22, 1946. 7B/11/7.
6 Letter from Mary Pickford to Gradwell Sears, June 1, 1943. 8B/"Pickford."
7 Memorandum from David O. Selznick to Paul Lazarus, March 14, 1946. 8B/"Selznick."
8 Opinion of Pepper, Bodine & Stockes to UA, October 29, 1946. 1A/179/7.
9 Letter from Isaac Pennypacker to Mary Pickford, November 18, 1946. 7B/11/7.
10 Minutes of the Annual Meeting of the UA Stockholders, June 11, 1946. Microfilm 448/Reel 19.

11 Minutes of the Special Meeting of the UA Stockholders, November 11, 1946. Microfilm 448/Reel 19.

12 Donald M. Nelson, "The Independent Producer," *The Annals of the American Academy of Political and Social Sciences,* 254 (November 1947), 54-55.

13 George Wallach, "Charlie Chaplin's *Monsieur Verdoux* Press Conference," *Film Comment,* 5 (Winter 1969), 34.

14 Ibid., p. 36.

15 Quoted in John Cogley, *Report on Blacklisting, I: The Movies* (New York: The Fund for the Republic, 1956), p. 11.

16 Walter Goodman, *The Committee: The Extraordinary Career of the House Committee on Un-American Activities* (New York: Farrar, Straus and Giroux, 1968), p. 203.

17 UA News Release, September 18, 1947. 1A/67/4.

18 UA News Release, September 19, 1947. 1A/67/4.

19 Quoted in Cogley, *Blacklisting,* p. 22.

20 Goodman, *Committee,* p. 225.

21 Quoted in Theodore Huff, *Charlie Chaplin* (New York: Schuman, 1951), p. 285.

22 Quoted in Terry Hickey, "Accusations Against Charles Chaplin for Political and Moral Offenses," *Film Comment,* 5 (Winter 1969), 53.

23 *Variety,* July 9, 1947, p. 3.

24 Mary Pickford, *Sunshine and Shadow* (Garden City, N.Y.: Doubleday, 1955), p. 235.

25 Letter from George L. Bagnall to Gradwell Sears, December 16, 1948, quoted in President's Report to Stockholders of UA, August 5, 1947, to December 31, 1948, dated January 5, 1949. 8B/"Miscellaneous."

26 *New York Times,* December 10, 1947, p. 42.

27 President's Report to Stockholders of UA, August 5, 1947, to December 31, 1948. 8B/"Miscellaneous."

28 Ibid.

29 Quoted in *The 1946-47 Motion Picture Almanac,* p. 748.

30 Thomas Guback, *The International Film Industry: Western Europe and America Since 1945* (Bloomington: Indiana Univ. Press, 1966), p. 17.

31 Memorandum to Stockholders, Directors, and Management of UA from Edward C. Raftery, June 13, 1947. 1A/11/9.

32 Alan Wood, *Mr. Rank: A Study of J. Arthur Rank and British Films* (London: Hodder and Stoughton, 1952), p. 228.

33 Letter from Arthur Kelly to Gradwell Sears, December 12, 1947. 8B/"Kelly."

34 "Movies: End of An Era?" *Fortune,* 39 (April 1949), 102.

35 "Movies Come Out of the Dog House," *Business Week,* No. 1158 (November 10, 1951), 140.

36 These data are taken from Henry Williams, "Economic Changes in the Motion Picture Industry as Affected by Television and Other Factors," Ph.D. dissertation, Indiana University, 1968.

37 Michael Conant, *Antitrust in the Motion Picture Industry* (Berkeley and Los Angeles: Univ. of California Press, 1960), p. 204.

38 President's Report to Stockholders of UA, August 5, 1947, to December 31, 1948, dated January 5, 1949. 8B/"Miscellaneous."

39 *Variety,* January 7, 1948, p. 43.

40 Letter from Gradwell Sears to Charles Chaplin and Mary Pickford, quoted in President's Report to Stockholders of UA, August 5, 1947, to December 31, 1948, dated January 5, 1949. 8B/"Miscellaneous."

Chapter 12: *The End and the Beginning of UA*

1 Letter from Gradwell Sears to Charles Chaplin, June 10, 1949. 8B/"Miscellaneous."

2 Letter from Selmer Chalif to Gradwell Sears, May 9, 1949. 8B/"Chalif."

3 Letter from Selmer Chalif to Gradwell Sears, August 9, 1949. 8B/"Chalif."

4 Letter from Frank L. McNamee to Paul V. McNutt, December 21, 1950, quoted in President's Report, January 4, 1951. 1A/12/5.

5 The information in this section is based on my interview with Arthur B. Krim, New York, December 8, 1972.

6 Ibid.

7 *New York Times,* September 20, 1952, p. 1.

8 Interview with Arthur B. Krim, December 8, 1972.

9 Quoted in "The Derring-Doers of Movie Business," *Fortune,* 57 (May 1958), 141.

Index

Abrams, Hiram: sued by Schulberg, 25; reputation as salesman, 26-27; salary, 29, 47; release schedule, 30; relations with exhibitors, 37, 38, 47-48; sales policy, 39, 48-49; urges forming of Allied Producers, 43; relations with producers, 45, 47-49; death of, 68; mentioned, 51, 54

Academy Awards, 68, 134, 138, 179, 190, 207, 239-40

Academy of Motion Picture Arts and Sciences, 118

Admission price discrimination, 103

Ad valorem tax, 223

Agnew, Neil, 210

Aitken, Harry: signs Fairbanks, 18-19; operation of Triangle Film Corporation, 20-21, 23; finances Griffith, 23-24

Aitken, Roy, 24

Alexander Korda Film Productions, Ltd., 154, 157

Allied Artists Corporation, Ltd., 41

Allied Producers and Distributors, 43, 45

Allied States Association of Motion Picture Exhibitors, 99-100

American Arbitration Association, 171

American Legion, 214, 237

American Mutoscope and Biograph Company: Griffith's career at, 21-23; mentioned, 6, 8, 14

American Society of Composers and Publishers, 78

American Telephone and Telegraph Co., 75, 78

Anderson, Bronco Billy, 5

Anger, Louis, 65

Anglo-American Film Agreement, 223

Antitrust: government suit against MPPC, 7; FTC investigation of Famous Players-Lasky, 26, 101-102; Chaplin's opinion of UA-MGM merger, 62; RCA threatens suit against AT&T, 79; indictment of Code of Fair Competition, 100-103; *Paramount* case, 103-104, 170-71, 225-28; Fox-West Coast—UA imbroglio, 113; intervention in Korda stock negotiations, 201

Arbuckle, Fatty, 10, 52

Ardrey, Alex, 216

Arliss, George, 120

Art Cinema Corporation: formation of, 66-68; acquires Pickford-Fairbanks Studio, 67-68; becomes UA partner, 69; profits, 72; signs Griffith, 85-86; curtails production, 112, 113; liquidation of, 117-18; supports reorganization, 122; sells stock, 125; mentioned, 57, 71, 83, 84, 93, 118, 123, 132

Artcraft Pictures Corp., 16, 17, 21, 24

Art Finance Corporation, 56-57, 66, 67, 123

Artisti Associati, 167

Ashley, Lord, 94

Ashley, Sylvia: affair with Fairbanks, 93-94

Associated Artists Productions, Inc., 239

Associated Authors, Inc., 43-44

Associated British Cinemas, 220

Associated British Picture Corporation, Ltd., 199

Astor theater, 164

Atherton, Gertrude, 60

Attendance, 63, 96-97, 170, 223-24

Bagnall, George, 173, 185, 215, 216

Balaban and Katz Corp., 63

Ballin, Hugo, 59

Bankers Trust of New York, 172, 191, 216

Bank of America: pioneers in film industry, 36; as financier of UA producers, 87, 120, 140, 152, 174, 175; insists on 100 per cent guarantees, 216; mentioned, 136, 141. *See also* Bank of Italy

Bank of England, 172

Bank of Italy, 44, 52. *See also* Bank of America

Bank of Manhattan, 216

Banks: attitude toward independents, 35-39 *passim;* consider UA a poor risk, 216

Banky, Vilma, 60, 70, 80

Banzhaf, Albert, 27, 29, 50

Bara, Theda, 5

Baresford, Harold, 104

Barnes, Howard, 210

Barry, Joan, 210

Barrymore, Diana, 175

Barrymore, John, 9, 39, 68, 76, 86

Baxter, Warner, 140

Beach, Rex, 60

Beaverbrook, Lord, 41

Beery, Wallace, 44, 120

Belasco, David, 14

Bellamy, Madge, 44

Benjamin, Robert S.: pre-UA career, 233. *See also* Krim-Benjamin management

Bennett, Joan, 140

Benny, Jack, 173

Bergman, Ingrid, 217

Bergner, Elizabeth, 134, 145

Berman, Sam, 41

Bernhard, Joseph, 205

Bernhardt, Sarah, 9

Big Five, 95, 96, 99, 104

"Big Five" Agreement, 76

Biograph. *See* American Mutoscope and Biograph Company

"The Biograph Girl," 8

B.I.P. Circuit, 128

Birdwell, Russell, 212, 213

Bischoff, Samuel, 219

Blacklisting, 214

Blair & Co., 72

Blind selling: prevented by consent decree, 171. *See also* block booking

Block, Paul, 56, 66

Block booking: Zukor introduces at Paramount, 10-11; revamped by Pickford, 14-16; in relation to UA sales policy, 35, 107-109, 188, 227-28; as means of financing, 36; Chaplin's opinion of, 62; analyzed, 101; in relation to shorts, 101; agitation over, 101-102, 170; declared unfair practice, 102; modified by Code of Fair Competition, 102; Disney's resentment of, 114; limited by consent decree, 171; declared illegal, 225

Blue, Monte, 44

Blumenfeld, Joseph, 227

Blumofe, Robert F., 237

Bogeaus, Benedict, 189, 216, 217

Bosworth, Inc., 9

Boyer, Charles, 140, 217

Brennon, Herbert, 68

Bright, D. J., 204-205

Brisson, Frederick, 229

British & Dominions Film Corporation, Ltd., 132, 199

British Board of Trade, 223

British National Films, Ltd., 199

Broadway theater, 227

Bronston, Samuel, 190

Buchanan, Thompson, 43-44

Buckley, Harry, 65, 68

Bunny, John, 5

Burkan, Nathan: involvement in UA's formation, 27, 29; on production financing, 116-17; elected to executive committee, 127; institutes UA Theatre Circuit suit, 130; mentioned, 35, 44, 65

Burke, Billie, 20

Bushman, Francis X., 5

Bylaws: unanimous vote provisions in, 70, 196-97, 201, 206; amended during Selznick reorganization, 184

Caddo Company, 110

Cagney, James: career at Warner, 190; production financing of, 191, 192-93; distribution terms, 192-93; forms partnership, 193; refuses to complete contract, 216, 217; mentioned, 118, 158, 189, 203, 219

Cagney, William, 193

Cantor, Eddie, 81, 94, 99, 106, 113

Capitol theater, 30, 164, 213

Capra, Frank: career at Columbia, 176; partnership negotiations, 176, 181-82; mentioned, 139, 205
Carr, Teddie, 197-98, 200
Carroll, Madeleine, 140
Case, Frank, 18
Case Laboratory, 76
Catholic Church, 203, 205
Catholic War Veterans, 214
Cazenove Ackroyds and Greenwood, 147
Chaplin, Charles: pre-UA career, 11, 17-18, 26; investigates merger rumor, 12; on McAdoo's resignation, 35; attitude toward company, 41-42, 55, 151, 196, 201; on production financing, 44, 56, 116-17, 206; cumulative distribution grosses, 50, 94; dissatisfaction with distribution contract, 54; profits, 57, 72, 81, 131, 164; opinion of MGM, 61; opposition to MGM merger, 61-62; opposition to UA Theatre Circuit, 64; opposition to Warner merger, 73; popularity of, 90-91; Lita Grey divorce trial, 90-91; *City Lights,* 91; achievements of, 91, 240; opposition to capital structure reorganization, 121-22; production routine, 124; on Schenck's management, 124, 127; on Goldwyn-Korda stock option, 144, 147, 149; opposition to Silverstone Plan, 153-54; *The Great Dictator,* 163-64; institutes stockholder's suit against Selznick, 187, 193-94, 207-209; behavior reviewed by Pickford, 194-97; rupture with Pickford, 196-97; opposition to purchase of Korda stock, 197, 201; *Monsieur Verdoux,* 210-14; political harassment of, 210-14, 237; offers to sell company, 215, 230-32; brings in McNutt group, 232-33; sells stock, 237; mentioned, 5, 13, 24, 25, 29, 30, 40, 76, 129, 131, 138, 142, 155, 157, 159, 176, 187, 234, 235, 241
Chaplin, Sydney, 12, 76
Chase National Bank, 126
Chevalier, Maurice, 138
Chinese theater, 65
Cinecolor, 116
Cinema Finance Corporation, 199
Cinematograph Films Act. *See* Quota Act
Clair, René, 144, 188, 189
Clarke, Harley L., 126

Claudia, 184, 187
Clearance and zoning: grievance boards, 100; defined, 102; proscribed, 171; declared illegal, 225
Cleary, Maurice, 49
Clifton, George B., 29
Cochrane, Robert H., 104
Code of Fair Competition for the Motion Picture Industry: approved by labor unions, 98; salary provisions, 98-99; opposed by independent exhibitors, 99-103; administration of, 100; trade practices sanctioned, 100-103; invalidated, 103; effects on UA, 104-109; on excessive salaries, 105-107; star raiding provisions, 106-107
Cohan, George M., 190
Cohen, Sydney, 38
Cohn, Harry, 139
Cohn, Ralph, 206
Colbert, Claudette, 138
Colman, Ronald, 60, 70, 80, 81, 113, 120
Columbia Broadcasting System, 106
Columbia Pictures: position in industry, 96; effects of Depression on, 96; Disney contract, 113-14; distributes through UA in Great Britain, 133; defendant in *Paramount* case, 171; image upgraded by Capra, 176; wartime earnings, 202; finances independent production, 205; mentioned, 77, 105, 106, 139, 217, 222, 235
Comet Productions, 206
Competitive bidding: rejected by Supreme Court, 227-28
Compulsory block booking. *See* Block booking
Consolidated Film Industries, 120
Coolidge, Calvin, 77
Cooper, Jackie, 120
Coordinator of Inter-American Affairs: Motion picture operations during war, 168-69
Cowan, Lester, 190, 203, 206
Coward, Noel, 186, 189
Cowl, Jane, 59
Creelman, Eileen, 210
Crescent Theatres, Ltd., 128-30
Cronin, A. J., 184
Crowther, Bosley, 210

Currency restrictions: effects on producers, 165; in Great Britain, 165, 223; in Germany, 167; mentioned, 176, 220
Curtiz, Michael, 229
Czinner, Paul, 166

Darrow, Clarence, 100
D & P Studios, Ltd., 154, 199
Davies, Marion, 139
Davis, Bette, 158, 229
Dawes Plan, 166
Del Rio, Dolores, 86
De Luxe Laboratories, 235
De Mille, Cecil B., 10, 16, 59, 138, 205
De Navarro, Mary Anderson, 20
Department of Justice, 225-26
Department of State, 166, 168, 220
De Sylva, Buddy, 205
Deutsch, Oscar, 129, 130, 149, 199. *See also* Odeon Theatres, Ltd.
Disney, Roy, 137
Disney, Walt: Columbia contract, 113-14; terms of UA distribution contract, 116; use of Technicolor, 116; Mickey Mouse grosses, 116; Silly Symphony grosses, 116; preeminence in field, 116, 137; controversy with, 136-38; tours South America for CIAA, 169; turns down UA offer, 187-88; mentioned, 123, 241
Distribution: number of companies, 5, 7; of the MPPC, 6-7; "states rights" defined, 9; innovations of Paramount, 9, 10-11, 16; exchanges opened, 29; "roadshowing" defined, 46; of Fairbanks specials, 48; franchise agreements with circuits, 64, 65-66; as affected by sound, 78; strength of majors, 95-96; revenues from first-run houses, 96; effects of World War II on, 170; Warner's, 180-81; of telefilms, 225; divorcement of, 226; to television, 239
—trade practices: modified by Code of Fair Competition, 100-103; modified by 1940 consent decree, 171; effect of *Paramount* case on, 225-28
—sales policy: stipulated in distribution contracts, 28; effect on production financing, 35; exhibitors' complaints of, 38, 47-48; Abrams introduces percentage method, 39; producers' complaints of, 47-50; affected by Code of Fair Competition,

108-109; on Hopalong Cassidy westerns, 188; compared to majors, 227
—fees: Paramount's, 9; original, 28; "most-favored nation" clause, 28, 206; raised, 42, 54; roadshowing, 47; in MGM merger, 61; standard, 123; Silverstone Plan, 152-54; Selznick's opinion of, 179-80; sliding scale, 184, 206, 208, 209
—problems: with exhibitors, 37-38, 112-13; 179-80, 205, 237; bargaining, 47-49; overhead, 61, 87-88; during battle of theaters, 64-66; with *City Lights,* 91; during administration of Code of Fair Competition, 104-109; with British pictures, 144-45; because of Giannini, 150-51; because of oligopoly, 161, 227-28; during World War II, 170; in sales organization, 184
Dividends, 71, 123, 153, 176, 235
Divorcement. *See Paramount* case
Domergue, Faith, 218
Donada circuit, 129, 130
Dubbing, 167, 170
Duncan Sisters, 68
Dwan, Allan, 34
D. W. Griffith, Inc.: formation of, 36-37; financial condition of, 50-51; operating expenses of, 85; goes into receivership, 90; mentioned, 41

Eagle-Lion Films, Inc., 200, 216, 233, 235
Eastman Kodak Co., 6
East River National Bank, 36, 141
Edison Manufacturing Company, 6
Egyptian theater, 47, 65
Einfeld, Charles, 217
Einstein, Albert, 33
Eisler, Hanns, 213
Electrical Research Products, Inc., 77-80 *passim*
Elliot, Maxine, 59
Emerson, John, 20, 21
Eminent Authors, 60
Enabling Act, 167
Ente Nazionale Industria Cinemotografica, 167
Enterprise Productions, 216, 219
Ericksen, Clarence, 146-53 *passim*
Esop's Fables, 116
Essanay Film Manufacturing Company, 6, 18

Exhibition: MPPC royalty-collecting operation, 6; vertical integration of, 10, 51, 62-64, 71-73; role in production financing, 11, 35-36, 39, 63, 65; roadshowing, 20, 46-47, 51; trade organizations, 38, 99; earning power, 63; conversion to sound, 75-78; strength of majors, 96; investment in, 97; effect of World War II on, 170, 190; effect of 1940 consent decree on, 170-71; effect of television on, 223-24; effect of *Paramount* case on, 225-28
—theaters: number of, 5, 96; construction spurred by feature films, 9, 30; battle for control of, 13, 26, 37, 62-64, 79; importance of first-run, 64, 65-66; first-run defined, 102
—circuits: formation of, 11, 34-35, 36, 62-65, 75; buying power of, 37, 91, 101; location of, 63; holdings of, 97, 103. *See also* United Artists Theatre Circuit, Crescent Theatres, Ltd., Odeon Theatres, Ltd.
—independent theaters: attitude toward Code of Fair Competition, 99-103

Fabian, Si, 215, 232
Fabian Theaters, 215
Fairbanks, Douglas: investigates merger rumors, 12; pre-UA career, 18-21; produces first UA release, 30; weds Mary Pickford, 32-33; opinion of McAdoo, 35; production financing, 37; goodwill tours abroad, 40; helps form Associated Authors, 43-44; attitude toward outside product, 45; criticized by exhibitors, 48; criticizes Abrams' sales policy, 48; cumulative gross in 1924, 50; invests in Art Finance, 56; on proposed MGM merger, 61-62; invests in UA Theatre Circuit, 64; on Goldwyn as partner, 69-70; annual profits, 72; on proposed Warner merger, 73; divorced by Pickford, 93; declining career of, 93-94; distribution earnings, 94; marries Sylvia Ashley, 94; on reorganization, 121-22; becomes inactive, 124; on Goldwyn-Korda stock option, 144, 146-47, 149; death of, 157; stock from estate purchased, 188; mentioned, 5, 10, 13, 24, 25, 27, 40, 62, 91, 125, 142, 150, 153, 155, 159, 176, 235, 241
Fairbanks, Douglas, Jr., 32, 134

Fairbanks, John, 41
Fairbanks, Robert, 121
Famous Players Co., 8-9, 10
Famous Players-Lasky Corp.: position in industry, 5; formed by Zukor, 10; merges with *Paramount,* 10; proposed merger with First National, 11-12; investigation by FTC, 26; assets, 36; stock listed, 36; battle for theaters, 63; Griffith's association with, 85; mentioned, 24, 25, 28, 30, 35, 51, 56, 63, 138
Farnum, Dustin, 20
Farrar, Geraldine, 59
Feature films: rise of, 8; European imports, 8; policies of MPPC regarding, 8, 23; early distribution of, 9; early producers of, 9
Feature Productions, Inc., 56-57
Federal Trade Commission: investigation of Famous Players-Lasky, 26, 101-102
Federation Bank and Trust Company, 87, 90
Film Booking Office, 79, 83
First National Bank of Boston, 215
First National Exhibitors Circuit: 1919 convention, 3; formation of, 5, 11; method of operation, 11; signs Pickford, 11, 16-17; signs Chaplin, 11, 18, 36; proposed merger with Famous Players-Lasky, 11-12, 26; signs Griffith, 30; merges Associated Producers, 34; signs Talmadge, 52-54, 72; builds Burbank studio, 63; loses battle for theater control, 63; purchased by Warner, 72-73; signs "Big Five" Agreement, 76; wires for sound, 77; mentioned, 14, 28, 35, 40, 58, 60, 66, 132
Fitzmaurice, George, 43, 60
Fleischer, Max, 116
Fonda, Henry, 140
Ford, John, 81
Foreign distribution: arrangements with stockholders, 39, 40, 41-42, 55; establishing, 39-42; as a source of revenue, 40, 128, 164-65; Morris Greenhill deal, 40-41; fee, 42, 151-52; effects of Depression on, 97; protective barriers abroad, 132, 165-68, 222-23; effects of World War II on, 164-65, 168-70; continental, 168, 220; postwar conditions, 202, 219-23
—Argentina, 168, 169

Foreign distribution (*cont.*)
—Australia, 41
—Austria, 164, 220
—Balkan countries, 168, 220
—Baltic States, 168
—Belgium, 41, 168
—Brazil, 168
—Chile, 168
—Czechoslovakia, 164, 168
—Denmark, 41, 168
—France, 41, 164, 168
—Germany, 41, 166-67, 169, 220
—Great Britain: Pickford-Fairbanks good-
   will tour in, 40; American companies in,
   40, 132, 221-22; establishing a subsidiary
   in, 40-41; distribution fees, 123, 151-52;
   importance of, 128, 164-65; UAC, Ltd.,
   theater acquisition, 128-30; quota pic-
   tures, 132, 200; passes Quota Act, 132,
   223; effects of World War II on, 165; cur-
   rency restrictions in, 165, 222-23; prob-
   lems with Rank, 198-200, 221-23; con-
   cludes Anglo-American Film Agreement,
   223
—Holland, 168, 220
—Italy, 41, 167, 168, 169
—Japan, 164, 169, 220
—Latin America, 41, 168-70
—Mexico, 168
—Near East, 168
—Norway, 41, 164, 168
—Orient, 41
—Portugal, 168
—Russia, 220
—Spain, 4, 164, 168
—Sweden, 41, 164
—Switzerland, 41, 168
—Turkey, 168
—Venezuela, 168
Fox, Matthew, 233
Fox, William, 7, 9, 76-77
Fox Film Corporation: location of theaters,
   63; as innovator of sound, 76-77; profits
   during sound revolution, 78; place in in-
   dustry, 95; effects of Depression on, 96;
   theater holdings, 97; undergoes reorgani-
   zation, 103; merger with Twentieth Cen-
   tury, 125-26; controlled by Chase Na-
   tional Bank, 126; controlled by General

Theatres Equipment, 126; mentioned, 9,
   35, 40, 66, 132, 159, 169, 227
Fox-West Coast Theatres, Inc., 113, 179-80
Foy, Brian, 76
Franchise agreements, 9, 64, 65-66, 101,
   130, 225
Francis, Kay, 138
Franken, Rose, 184
Frederick, Pauline, 10
Frohman, Daniel, 9
Frozen funds. *See* Currency restrictions

Gable, Clark, 177, 179
Gainsborough, 222
Garbo, Greta, 139
Gaston Méliès, 6
Gaumont-British circuit, 128, 130, 199, 221,
   223
Gaumont-British Distributors, Ltd., 132
General Cinema Finance, 222-23
General Electric, 79
General Film Company, 7, 9
General Service Studios, 172, 190
General Theatres Equipment, 126
George M. Cohan theater, 85, 91
Giannini, Amedeo Peter, 36, 44, 52, 79, 140
Giannini, Attilio Henry: banking career, 36,
   140-41; elected president and chairman,
   140; as a counselor, 141, 142, 144; sales
   ability, 143; forced out of company, 150-
   52; mentioned, 136, 154
Gish, Lillian, 5, 24
Gloria Productions, Inc., 83
Gloria Swanson British Productions, Ltd.,
   84
Godowsky, Leopold, 18
Godsol, Joseph, 35
Goebbels, Joseph, 167
Goetz, Harry, 117-18
Goetz, William E., 119, 120, 126
Goldwyn, Samuel: given distribution contract, 57; Fairbankses' opinion of, 58, 69-
   70; pre-UA career, 58-60; invests in UA
   Theatre Circuit, 64; becomes partner, 69-
   70; annual profits, 72; loses Vilma Banky,
   80; offers to buy Griffith stock, 89; dis-
   tribution earnings, 94; heads Art Cinema's production, 113; opinion of capital
   structure reorganization, 121-22; pre-

Goldwyn, Samuel (*cont.*)
cipitates Schenck's resignation, 122; owner of UA Studio property, 125; criticisms of company, 125, 127, 150-51, 157; harasses Lichtman, 136; complicates Disney deal, 137; demands bylaw changes, 142-43, 196; forces out Giannini, 143, 150-52; stock option to purchase company, 144, 146-50; demands management reorganization, 148-49; "double crossed" by Pickford, 155; court battles to break distribution contract, 155-59; renames UA Studio, 157; settlement, 159; contributions, 159-60; lawsuits' effects on company, 176-77, 183, 188; mentioned, 66, 108, 117, 123, 124, 131, 140, 153, 163, 206, 235, 240, 241

Goldwyn Pictures Corporation: acquired by Loew's, 51; formation of, 59; ousts Goldwyn, 60; mentioned, 9, 12, 35, 40, 63

Grand Hotel, 240

Granville-Barker, Harley, 138

Grauman, Sidney, 65

Greater New York Film Rental Company, 7

Grey, Albert, 41, 49, 54

Griffith, D. W.: opinion of Fairbanks' acting, 20; pre-UA career, 21-24, 26; signs with First National, 30; produces *Romance*, 34; forms D. W. Griffith, Inc., 36-37; criticisms of company, 41-42, 49-51, 88-89; invests in Associated Authors, 44; introduces roadshowing, 46-47; signs with Paramount, 49-51; cumulative gross in 1924, 50; signs with Art Cinema, 85-86; opinion of Schenck's financing plan, 87-88; stock controversy, 87-90; mentioned, 10, 13, 25, 28, 29, 40, 54, 72, 80, 116

Grinieff, Jacques, 224, 234

Guaranty Trust Company, 173, 188

Guedalla, F. M., 125-30 *passim,* 145

Hackett, James K., 9

Harris, Elmer, 43-44

Harrison, Peter, 108

Hart, William S., 5, 10, 12, 13, 24, 57

Hawks, Howard, 216, 217-18

Hays, Will H. *See* Motion Picture Producers and Distributors of America, Inc.

Hays Office. *See* Motion Picture Producers

and Distributors of America, Inc.

Hearst, William Randolph, 41

Hecht-Hill-Lancaster production company, 238

Hecht-Lancaster, 239

Heineman, William J., 237

Heller, Walter E., 235, 237

Hertz, John, 136

Hitchcock, Alfred, 229

Hitler, Adolf, 164, 167

Hodkinson, W. W., 9, 10, 16

Hollywood Ten, 213-14

Hopalong Cassidy, 188, 189, 219

Hope, Bob, 229, 238

Hopkins, Miriam, 138

Hopper, De Wolf, 20

Hopwood, Avery, 57, 59

House Committee on Un-American Activities, 210-14

Howard, Leslie, 133

Hughes, Howard: wins Academy Award, 68; first distribution contract, 68, 110-12; financed by Hughes Tool Company, 110; Caddo Company, 110; investments, 112; seeks release from distribution contract, 112; receives settlement, 112; receives second distribution contract, 203; *The Outlaw* controversy, 203-205; loses suit against MPA, 204-205; takes over RKO, 218; revolts, 218-19; establishes producers fund, 218-19

Hughes, Robert, 60

Huston, Walter, 138

IFA Film Verleih, 166

"The Imp Girl," 8

Ince, Thomas, 20, 23

Independent Motion Picture Company, 7, 8, 14

Independent production: defies MPPC, 6; early innovations of, 8; advantages of, 58, 190, 205; in relation to UA, 96; handicapped by option contracts, 106; rise of, 189-90; stoppage, 216-19; accommodated by majors, 219; of telefilms, 225; effect of *Paramount* case on, 228-29; policy of Krim-Benjamin, 239; stimulated, 240. *See also* Production—financing, Star system

Independent Theater Owners Organization, 214

Irving Trust Company, 87, 216, 219

J. & W. Seligman & Co., 64, 65, 67
Jane Eyre, 184, 187
J. Arthur Rank Organization, 233
Jessel, George, 76
Jesse L. Lasky Feature Motion Picture Co., 9, 58
Johnson, Hugh S., 100, 105
Johnston, Eric, 220
Jolson, Al, 76, 77, 113, 117
Jones, Robert Edmund, 59

Kalem Company, 6
Karno, Fred, 17
Katz, Sam, 233
Keane, Doris, 34
Keaton, Buster, 52, 68, 86
Keith-Albee circuit, 63
Keith-Albee-Orpheum circuit, 79
Kelly, Arthur: named second vice president, 54; heads foreign department, 68; on distribution problems, 184; named chairman of finance committee, 185; joins Eagle-Lion, 200; rehired, 216; mentioned, 112, 137, 165, 219, 223
Kennedy, Jeremiah, 23
Kennedy, Joseph P., 79, 84
Kent, Sidney, 125
Kessel, Adam, 17
The Keys of the Kingdom, 184, 187
Keystone Film Company, 7, 17-18
Kind, Basil, 60
King, Henry, 60
Klangfilm, 79
Kleine Optical Company, 6
Knickerbocker theater, 20
Korda, Alexander: joins UA, 132-35; produces quota pictures, 133, 148, 154-55; achievement in Great Britain, 134; stock option to purchase company, 144, 146-50; dissatisfaction with UA, 144-46; management of London Films, 145-46; loses control of Denham Studio, 154; Prudential settlement, 154; forms Alexander Korda Film Productions, Ltd., 154, 157; amended contract, 157; as party to Goldwyn lawsuit, 158-59; forms Alexander

Korda Films, Inc., 172; wartime difficulties, 172-73; directs Selznick negotiations, 181-83; purchases Prudential's stock interest, 186; stock lien dropped, 186; awarded settlement, 186-87; heads MGM in Britain, 187; stock sale negotiations, 197-201; mentioned, 94, 128, 132, 138, 150, 153, 155, 157, 176, 188, 241
Kramer, Milton, 208
Kramer, Stanley, 233, 235
Kravetz, Max, 232
Krim, Arthur B., 233. *See also* Krim-Benjamin management
Krim-Benjamin management: stock-option terms, 234-35; acquires Eagle-Lion film library, 235; secures financing, 235; acquires ownership, 237; formula for success, 237-40
Kuhn, Loeb & Co., 63, 147

Labour government, British, 222
Laemmle, Carl, 8, 14
Lancaster, Burt, 229
Lang, Fritz, 166, 189
Langtry, Lillie, 9
Lasker, Albert D., 56
Lasky, Jesse, 131, 138, 142
Lauder, Harry, 18
Laughton, Charles, 134
Lawrence, Florence, 8
Lawrence, Laudy, 185
Leech, George Lee, 205
Legion of Decency, 203
Lehman, Arthur, 136
Lehman, Robert, 136
Lehman Brothers, 56, 136, 147
LeRoy, Mervyn, 205
Les Artistes Associés, 41, 168
Lesser, Sol, 162, 189
Lessing, Gunther, 137
Lever, Ervin, 148
Levey, Jules, 190
Liberty Loan drive, 24
Lichtman, Al: becomes vice president, 68; characterizes Zanuck, 120; elected president, 127; negotiates Selznick contract, 136; joins MGM, 136
Lindberg, Charles, 77
Linder, Max, 43
Lloyd, Harold, 218

Lloyds Bank, 145

Loew, David, 162, 190, 216, 217

Loew, Marcus, 51, 52, 63

Loew's, Inc.: stock listed, 36, 63; theater holdings, 63, 97; wires for sound, 77; status in industry, 95; effects of Depression on, 96, 103; defendant in *Paramount* case, 170-71, 226; advises Korda, 197; refuses playdates for *Verdoux,* 214; postwar earnings, 224; mentioned, 61, 65, 66, 201. *See also* Metro-Goldwyn-Mayer

Lombard, Carole, 173-74

London Film Productions, Ltd.: joins UA, 132-35; playoff of productions, 144; status in Britain, 145; financing of, 145; financial condition, 145-46, 148, 154; mentioned, 155, 199

London Pavilion, 128

Looney Tunes, 116

Loos, Anita, 20, 21

Lubin Manufacturing Company, 6

Lubitsch, Ernst, 166, 172-74, 191

Luporini, Mario, 167-68

McAdoo, William Gibbs: pre-UA career, 24; becomes UA counsel, 24, 29; issued stock, 27; invests in *Romance,* 34; resignation, 34-35

McCarey, Leo, 229

McCarthy, Neil, 112, 147, 149, 151

McGranery, James, 237

MacKenna, Kenneth, 93

MacMurray, Fred, 205

McNamee, Frank L., 232

McNutt, Paul V., 232-34

Majestic Film Company: hires Pickford, 14

Mankiewicz, Joseph, 238

Marcus Loew Theatrical Enterprises, 52

Marsh, Mae, 5, 24

Martini, Nino, 131

Marx Brothers, 138

Mary Pickford Corporation, 16

Mayer, Louis B., 63, 98, 119, 136, 179, 194

Mayo, Margaret, 59

Melba, Nellie, 18

Menjou, Adolphe, 213

Merrie Melodies, 116

Metro-Goldwyn-Mayer: proposed merger with, 61-62; signs "Big Five" Agreement, 76; profits during sound revolution, 78; hires Lichtman, 136; acquires *Gone With the Wind,* 177-78; hires Korda, 187; attitude toward independent production, 190; British distribution, 199, 221; as distributor of British films in U.S., 220; sells distribution rights, 240; mentioned, 68, 95, 120, 124, 125, 126, 139, 181, 185, 194. *See also* Loew's, Inc.

Metro Pictures, 12, 51, 63

Mickey Mouse, 113, 114, 116

Midlands Bank, 145

Milestone, Lewis, 110, 217

Miranda, Carmen, 169

Mirisch Corporation, 238

Mitchum, Robert, 238

Monogram Pictures, 222

Moore, Matt, 44

Moore, Owen, 32, 33

Morosco Photo Play Company, 9

Morris, Gouverneur, 60

Moscowitz, Joseph, 65

Motion Picture Alliance for the Preservation of American Ideals, 212-13

Motion Picture Export Association, 220, 223

Motion picture grosses:

—*Abraham Lincoln,* 86

—*African Queen,* 235

—*The Age for Love,* 111

—*Around the World in Eighty Minutes with Douglas Fairbanks,* 94

—*The Battle of the Sexes,* 86

—*The Birth of a Nation,* 21

—*Blood on the Sun,* 217

—*Broken Blossoms,* 31

—*Bulldog Drummond,* 71

—*Caesar and Cleopatra,* 220

—*The Circus,* 71

—*City Lights,* 81

—*Cock of the Air,* 111

—*Coquette,* 71, 92

—*Dorothy Vernon of Haddon Hall,* 91

—*Drums of Love,* 86

—*Duel in the Sun,* 210

—*Front Page,* 111

—*The Gaucho,* 71, 93

—*The Gold Rush,* 57

—*Gone With the Wind,* 180

—*The Great Dictator,* 164

—*Hell's Angels,* 110

—*Henry V,* 220

Motion picture grosses (*cont.*)
—*High Noon,* 235
—*In Which We Serve,* 220
—*The Iron Mask,* 71, 93
—*Johnny Come Lately,* 217
—*Kiki,* 93
—*Lady of Burlesque,* 203
—*Lady of the Pavements,* 86
—*Little Lord Fauntleroy* (Pickford), 42
—*Modern Times,* 131
—*Monsieur Verdoux,* 214
—*The Outlaw,* 205
—*Perfect Understanding,* 84
—*The Private Life of Henry VIII,* 134
—*Pygmalion,* 220
—*Robin Hood,* 45
—*Rosita,* 91
—*Sadie Thompson,* 83
—*Scarface, Shame of the Nation,* 111
—*Sky Devils,* 111
—*Snow White and the Seven Dwarfs,* 138
—*The Son of the Sheik,* 56
—*The Sorrows of Satan,* 85
—*Stage Door Canteen,* 189
—*The Struggle,* 87
—*Sundown,* 176
—*Taming of the Shrew,* 71
—*The Thief of Bagdad* (Korda), 172
—*The Three Little Pigs,* 116
—*The Three Musketeers,* 42
—*The Time of Your Life,* 217
—*The Trespasser,* 71
—*Way Down East,* 42
—*Whoopee,* 81
—*A Woman of Paris,* 45
Motion picture industry: structure in 1908, 5-6; patents monopoly, 5-7; early struggles for control, 5-11; merger movement, 10, 51, 61-64, 71-73, 79, 95, 125-26; structure in 1930, 63, 95-96; sound revolution, 75-79; effects of the Depression on, 87, 96-97; theater holdings of majors, 97; labor conditions, 97-99, 118; Code of Fair Competition, 97-109; controversial trade practices of, 100-103; monopolistic structure, 104; foreign markets, 132, 168-70, 219-23; effects of World War II on, 164-70, 174, 190, 194, 202; impact of *Paramount* case on, 170-71, 225-28; postwar conditions, 223-28

Motion Picture Patents Company: operations, 5-7, causes of dissolution, 7-9; policy regarding feature films, 8-9
Motion Picture Producers and Distributors of America, Inc.: as trade association of the industry, 99; mobilizes to fight antitrust actions, 100; changes name, 203; revokes seal for *The Outlaw,* 203-204; forms MPEA, 220; mentioned, 104, 164
Motion pictures mentioned in the text:
—*Abraham Lincoln,* 80, 86
—*The Adventures of Dollie,* 21-22
—*The Adventures of Tom Sawyer,* 177, 181
—*African Queen,* 235
—*The Age for Love,* 111
—*Ah, Wilderness!,* 190
—*Algiers,* 174
—*The Apartment,* 240
—*Arabian Nights,* 175
—*Arch of Triumph,* 217
—*Around the World in 80 Days,* 239
—*Around the World in Eighty Minutes with Douglas Fairbanks,* 94
—*Arrowsmith,* 81
—*Arsenic and Old Lace,* 182
—*Ashes of Vengeance,* 52
—*The Bachelor and the Bobby-Soxer,* 208
—*The Bat,* 57, 66
—*The Battle of the Sexes,* 86
—*The Beloved Rogue,* 68
—*The Better 'Ole,* 76
—*A Bill of Divorcement,* 136
—*The Birth of a Nation,* 21, 23, 24, 43
—*The Bitter Tea of General Yen,* 139
—*The Black Pirate,* 66
—*Blithe Spirit,* 220
—*Blood and Sand,* 56
—*Blood on the Sun,* 203, 217
—*The Bowery,* 120
—*Broken Blossoms,* 30, 31
—*Bulldog Drummond,* 71, 80
—*Bulldog Drummond Strikes Back,* 120
—*The Cabinet of Dr. Caligari,* 60
—*Caesar and Cleopatra,* 220
—*Camille,* 52
—*Captain Fury,* 162
—*Carmen,* 58
—*Carnival in Rio,* 169
—*Catherine the Great,* 134
—*Cheyenne,* 175

Motion pictures mentioned in text (*cont.*)
—*Christmas Eve,* 217
—*A Chump at Oxford,* 162
—*The Circus,* 71, 90
—*City Lights,* 71, 81, 90-91, 131
—*Cock of the Air,* 95, 111, 112
—*College,* 68
—*Colonel Blimp,* 220
—*Congress Dances,* 95
—*Coquette,* 71, 80, 91, 92
—*The Count,* 18
—*The Count of Monte Cristo,* 117
—*The Country Cousin,* 137
—*The Cowboy and the Lady,* 157
—*The Crystal Ball,* 188
—*Cynara,* 81
—*David Copperfield,* 136
—*Dead End,* 161
—*Dishonored Lady,* 203
—*Dodsworth,* 160, 161
—*Don Juan,* 76
—*Don Q, Son of Zorro,* 57
—*Dorothy Vernon of Haddon Hall,* 39, 91
—*The Dove,* 81
—*Down Argentine Way,* 169
—*Down on the Farm,* 34
—*Dreaming Lips,* 145
—*Dream Street,* 42
—*Drums of Love,* 86
—*DuBarry, Woman of Passion,* 82
—*Duel in the Sun,* 207, 209-10
—*The Eagle,* 56
—*Eagle Squadron,* 175
—*Easy Street,* 18
—*The Farmer's Daughter,* 208
—*Five Star Final,* 118
—*The Floorwalker,* 18
—*Flowers and Trees,* 137
—*Foreign Correspondent,* 174
—*42nd Street,* 118
—*The Four Horsemen of the Apocalypse,* 56
—*Front Page,* 111
—*Gabriel over the White House,* 139
—*The Garden of Allah,* 177, 181
—*Garrison's Finish,* 43
—*The Gaucho,* 71, 93
—*The Gay Desperado,* 131
—*The General,* 68
—*The Ghost Goes West,* 144
—*Going Hollywood,* 139

—*The Gold Rush,* 57
—*Gone With the Wind,* 177-80, 207
—*A Good Little Devil,* 14
—*The Great Dictator,* 161, 163-64
—*The Greeks Had a Word for Them,* 95
—*Guest in the House,* 203
—*Hallelujah, I'm a Bum,* 117
—*Hangmen Also Die!,* 189
—*Hell's Angels,* 71, 110, 111
—*Henry V,* 220
—*High Noon,* 235
—*His Majesty, the American,* 30, 39
—*His Picture in the Papers,* 20
—*Honeymoon,* 208
—*Hopalong Cassidy westerns,* 188
—*The House Across the Bay,* 174
—*The House of Rothschild,* 120
—*I Am a Fugitive from a Chain Gang,* 118
—*I Cover the Waterfront,* 117
—*Idiot's Delight,* 190
—*The Idle Class,* 42
—*I'll Be Seeing You,* 203, 207, 209
—*I Married a Witch,* 188
—*Indiscreet,* 84
—*Intermezzo,* 179, 181
—*In the Heat of the Night,* 240
—*In Which We Serve,* 189, 220
—*The Iron Mask,* 71, 93
—*Isn't Life Wonderful,* 50
—*It Happened One Night,* 176
—*The Jazz Singer,* 76, 77, 80
—*Johnny Apollo,* 179-80
—*Johnny Come Lately,* 189, 217
—*Johnny in the Clouds,* 220
—*The Kid,* 36, 42
—*Kiki,* 91, 93
—*King Kong,* 136
—*Lady of Burlesque,* 189, 203
—*Lady of the Pavements,* 80, 86
—*The Lamb,* 20, 33
—*The Last of the Mohicans,* 118
—*Let 'em Have It,* 117
—*Lights of New York,* 77
—*Limelight,* 237
—*The Little American,* 16
—*Little Annie Rooney,* 57, 91
—*Little Caesar,* 118
—*A Little Princess,* 16
—*Little Lord Fauntleroy* (Pickford), 42

Motion pictures mentioned in text (*cont.*)
—*Little Lord Fauntleroy* (Selznick), 136, 177, 181
—*The Long Voyage Home*, 162, 174
—*Lost Horizon*, 176
—*Los Tres Caballeros*, 169
—*The Love Flower*, 39, 50
—*Love from a Stranger*, 145
—*Love Light*, 35
—*The Love of Sunya*, 82-83
—*Loving Lies*, 44
—*Lulu Belle*, 217
—*Lydia*, 172, 186
—*Made for Each Other*, 177, 181
—*Mad Wednesday*, 218
—*Manhattan Melodrama*, 136
—*The Man in the Iron Mask*, 162
—*The Man Who Could Work Miracles*, 144
—*The Man With the Golden Arm*, 239
—*The Mark of Zorro*, 39-41
—*Marty*, 239
—*Meet John Doe*, 181-82
—*The Melody Lingers On*, 118
—*Mickey Mouse cartoons*, 116
—*Midnight Cowboy*, 240
—*Modern Times*, 131, 161
—*The Mollycoddle*, 35
—*Monsieur Beaucaire*, 56
—*Monsieur Verdoux*, 210-14
—*The Moon Is Blue*, 239
—*Mr. Deeds Goes to Town*, 176
—*Mr. Emmanual*, 220
—*Mr. Robinson Crusoe*, 94, 95
—*Mr. Smith Goes to Washington*, 176
—*Mrs. Mike*, 219
—*My Best Girl*, 91
—*My Son, My Son*, 162
—*Naughty Marietta*, 190
—*New York Nights*, 82
—*Night Must Fall*, 190
—*No More Women*, 44
—*Notorious*, 208, 209
—*Of Mice and Men*, 162
—*One Million B.C.*, 162
—*One of Our Aircraft Is Missing*, 186
—*One Rainy Afternoon*, 131
—*On Our Merry Way*, 217
—*Orphans of the Storm*, 42
—*The Outlaw*, 203-205, 218
—*Palmy Days*, 94

—*Palooka*, 117
—*The Paradine Case*, 209
—*Partners Again*, 66
—*Perfect Understanding*, 84
—*Pollyanna*, 32, 39, 41
—*The Poor Little Rich Girl*, 16
—*The Pride of the Clan*, 16
—*The Prisoner of Zenda* (Famous Players), 9
—*The Prisoner of Zenda* (Selznick), 177, 181
—*The Private Life of Don Juan*, 94, 128
—*The Private Life of Henry VIII*, 133-34, 144
—*Public Enemy*, 118
—*Pygmalion*, 220
—*Queen Christina*, 139
—*Queen Elizabeth*, 9
—*Queen Kelly*, 83
—*Reaching for the Moon*, 94
—*Rebecca*, 162, 179, 180, 181-82
—*Rebecca of Sunnybrook Farm*, 16
—*Red River*, 217-18, 229
—*Red Salute*, 118
—*Richard the Lion-Hearted*, 44
—*Road Show*, 162
—*Robin Hood*, 39, 44, 45, 47, 48
—*Romance*, 34
—*A Romance of the Redwoods*, 16
—*Rosita*, 39, 45, 47, 91
—*Rudyard Kipling's Jungle Book*, 172, 186
—*Sadie Thompson*, 83
—*Sally of the Sawdust*, 50
—*Saludos Amigos*, 169
—*The Salvation Hunters*, 57
—*Scarface, Shame of the Nation*, 111, 112
—*Secrets* (Pickford), 93, 117
—*Secrets* (Talmadge), 52
—*Service for Ladies*, 133
—*The Shanghai Gesture*, 189
—*The Sheik*, 56
—*Silly Symphony shorts*, 116
—*Since You Went Away*, 203, 207, 209
—*The Singing Fool*, 77
—*Sky Devils*, 95, 111, 112
—*Smiling Through*, 52
—*Snow White and the Seven Dwarfs*, 138
—*The Song of Bernadette*, 169
—*The Son of Monte Cristo*, 162
—*The Son of the Sheik*, 56, 66

Motion pictures mentioned in text (*cont.*)
—*Sorrell and Son,* 68
—*The Sorrows of Satan,* 85
—*Sparrows,* 66, 91
—*Spellbound,* 203, 207, 209
—*The Spiral Staircase,* 208
—*Stagecoach,* 162, 174
—*Stage Door Canteen,* 189
—*A Star Is Born,* 161, 177
—*Steamboat Bill, Jr.,* 68
—*Steamboat Willie,* 113
—*Stella Dallas,* 66
—*Stella Maris,* 16
—*The Strange Widow,* 203
—*Street Scene,* 81
—*The Struggle,* 86, 87, 95
—*Suds,* 50
—*Sundown,* 176
—*Suzanna,* 45
—*A Tale of Two Cities,* 136
—*Taming of the Shrew,* 71, 91, 92-93
—*Tempest,* 80
—*Tess of the Storm Country,* 14, 43
—*That Hamilton Woman,* 172, 186
—*That Night in Rio,* 169
—*These Three,* 160
—*The Thief of Bagdad* (Fairbanks), 45
—*The Thief of Bagdad* (Korda), 162, 172, 186
—*Things to Come,* 144
—*The Thin Man,* 190
—*The Three Little Pigs,* 116
—*The Three Musketeers,* 39, 42, 48
—*Three Orphan Kittens,* 137
—*Till the End of Time,* 208
—*The Time of Your Life,* 217
—*To Be Or Not To Be,* 172-74, 191, 224
—*Tom Jones,* 240
—*Tonight or Never,* 84
—*Topsy and Eva,* 68
—*The Tortoise and the Hare,* 137
—*Trade Winds,* 174
—*The Trail of the Lonesome Pine,* 139
—*Trans-Atlantic Merry-Go-Round,* 117
—*The Trespasser,* 71, 80
—*Tumbleweeds,* 57
—*Two Arabian Knights,* 68
—*Vendetta,* 218
—*Viva Villa!,* 136, 168
—*Walter Wanger's Vogues of 1938,* 174

—*Washington Merry-Go-Round,* 139
—*Way Down East,* 39, 41, 42, 46, 51
—*The Westerner,* 157, 158, 161
—*West Side Story,* 240
—*What a Widow,* 83
—*What Price Hollywood?,* 136
—*When a Man Loves,* 76
—*When the Clouds Roll By,* 32
—*Whoopee,* 71, 81, 94, 106
—*The Winning of Barbara Worth,* 66
—*Winter Carnival,* 174
—*Woman Chases Man,* 160
—*The Woman Disputed,* 81
—*A Woman of Paris,* 45, 47, 54
—*Wuthering Heights,* 160, 161
—*Yankee Doodle Dandy,* 190
—*Yes or No?,* 52
—*You Can't Take It With You,* 176
—*The Young in Heart,* 177, 181
—*Young Widow,* 203
    See also Motion Picture grosses; Production—costs
Motion Picture Theater Owners Association, 99
Motion Picture Theater Owners of America, 38
Mulvey, James, 127
Murnau, F. W., 166
Music Hall theaters, 227
Mussolini, Benito, 167
Mutual Bank, 39
Mutual Film Corporation, 7, 9, 18, 23

Nasser brothers, 230-32
National City Bank of New York, 141
National Industrial Recovery Act, 97-98, 103, 105, 109
National Labor Relations Board, 213
National Recovery Administration, 95, 98-109, 123, 171
National Recovery Review Board, 100-103
Nayfack, Bertram, 65
Nazimova, Alla, 10, 39
Neilan, Marshall, 16, 34, 93
Nepotism, 49
News of the Day, 169
New York Philharmonic Orchestra, 76
New York Stock Exchange, 36
Nichols, Dudley, 229
Nickelodeons, 5

"A Night in a Music Hall," 17
Norton, Richard, 154
Nugent, Elliott, 188, 189, 229

O'Brien, Dennis: opinion of Schulberg suit, 25-26; counsel for Pickford and Fairbanks, 27; draws up incorporation contracts, 27; named to board, 29; named vice president, 29; opinion of McAdoo, 34; law firm becomes counsel, 35; on McAdoo's resignation, 35; advises on financing, 43; named first vice president, 54; on Griffith's characterization of UA, 89; opinion of Schenck's financing plan, 117; proposes capital structure reorganization, 121; elected to executive committee, 127; mentioned, 41-54 *passim,* 83, 85, 147, 152, 153, 176
O'Brien, Driscoll, and Raftery, 184
Odeon Cinema Holdings, Ltd., 222-23, 229
Odeon Theatres, Ltd., 129, 199, 221, 222-23
Oglesby, Woodson R., 87-90
O'Neill, James, 9
Option contract, 106
Orpheum circuit, 63
O'Shea, Daniel, 187, 188, 193
Overbuying, 103

Pabst, G. W., 166
Paderewski, Ignace, 18
Palace theater, 41
Palisades Amusement Park, 52
Paramount case: instituted, 170-171; drawbacks of 1940 consent decree, 171; provisions of 1940 consent decree, 171; charges against majors, 171; suit against minors adjourned, 171; independent exhibitor reaction, 171; reactivated in 1944, 171; impact of, 202, 225-28; provisions of consent decrees, 226; Little Three as defendants, 226-28
Paramount Pictures: picture grosses, 9; formation, 9-10; block-booking arrangements, 10-11, 14-16; releases in 1919, 11; signs Griffith, 49-51; bids to retain Swanson, 58; forms Publix Theatres, 63; theatres, 63, 97; signs "Big Five" Agreement, 76; wires for sound, 77; profits during sound revolution, 78; status in industry, 95; effects of Depression on, 96, 97, 103,

106; interest in CBS, 106; cartoons, 116; contract with Korda, 133; contract with Wanger, 139; rejects Goldwyn picture, 158; defendant in *Paramount* case, 170-71; sells film package, 188; wartime earnings, 202; finances independent production, 205; refuses play dates for *Verdoux,* 214; in Great Britain, 221; postwar earnings, 224; consent decree, 226; mentioned, 40, 63, 65, 66, 85, 125, 139, 147, 168, 223
Pathé Exchange, Inc., 63
Pathé Frères, 6
Pathé News, 168
Peck, Gregory, 238
Peron, Eva, 233, 234
Peyser, Seymour M., 237
Philips, William, 65, 67, 117, 125-26, 130
Phillips, Nizer, Benjamin & Krim, 233
Phoebus Films, 166
Photophone Sound System, 79
Picker, Arnold M., 237
Pickfair, 33, 138, 183
Pickford, Mrs. Charlotte, 12, 15-16, 29
Pickford, Jack, 43
Pickford, Mary: pre-UA career, 11, 14-17, 26; investigates merger rumors, 12; achievements of, 14-16, 91-93, 240; on UA founding, 26; weds Douglas Fairbanks, 32-33; divorces Owen Moore, 33; opinion of McAdoo, 35; production financing, 37, 39; goodwill tours abroad, 40; on foreign distribution fee, 42; helps form Associated Authors, 43-44; attitude toward outside product, 45; earnings, 50, 72, 94; invests in Art Finance, 56; on proposed MGM merger, 61-62; invests in UA Theatre Circuit, 64; characterization of Goldwyn, 69-70; on Warner merger, 73; wins Academy Award, 80; decline as actress, 91-93, 124; divorces Fairbanks, 93, 94; on Schenck's management, 116, 121-22, 127; elected vice president, 127; forms Pickford-Lasky Productions, 131; management of UA, 136-40; opinion of Disney pictures, 137; on Goldwyn-Korda stock option, 144-55 *passim;* on Capra deal, 176-77; rupture with Chaplin, 194-97; suit to change bylaws, 196-97, 201; Selznick lawsuit, 201, 207-209; financing

Pickford, Mary (*cont.*)
 demands, 205-206; puts company up for
  sale, 215, 230-32; prematurely announces
  president, 215-16; brings in McNutt
  group, 232-33; sells stock, 237; men-
  tioned, 4, 5, 10, 13, 21-29 *passim*, 40,
  125, 130, 136, 140, 142, 150, 153, 155,
  159, 234, 235, 239, 241
Pickford-Fairbanks Studio, 67-68
Pickford-Lasky Productions, 131
Pinewood Studio, Ltd., 154, 198
Pommer, Erich, 166
Pooling arrangements, 225
Popeye cartoons, 116
Powell, Michael, 186
Preminger, Otto, 238, 239
Pressburger, Arnold, 189
Price, Oscar, 24, 29, 34, 35
Price discrimination, 103
Price fixing, 225
Principal Theaters, Inc., 227
Producers Distributing Corporation, 76
Production: companies in 1908, 5; practices
  of MPPC, 6-8, 23; rise of feature films, 8-
  10; quotas, 30, 35; acquisition of *Broken
  Blossoms*, 30-31; shortage, 30-31, 42-46,
  131-36, 174, 216-19, 229, 235; purchase
  of *Romance*, 34; of sound pictures, 75-78,
  80; strength of majors, 96; as affected by
  Depression, 106; facilitated by option
  contract, 106; formation of Walter
  Wanger Productions, 138-40, 174-76; cur-
  tailed by currency restrictions, 165; promoting Good Neighbor Policy, 168-69; de-
  crease in, 170; of *To Be Or Not To Be*,
  172-74; formation of United Artists Productions, 175-76; acquisition of Paramount package, 187-89, 202; rise of independent, 189-91, 229; of telefilms, 225.
  See also star system
—costs: affected by feature films, 5; affected
  by star system, 5; in relationship to Chaplin's distribution contract, 54; effect of
  sound on, 97; as affected by stars' salaries, 105-107; during World War II, 170;
  Arch of Triumph, 217; *The Birth of a Nation*, 21; *Broken Blossoms*, 31; *Dorothy
  Vernon of Haddon Hall*, 39; *The Great
  Dictator*, 164; *Hell's Angels*, 110; *His
  Majesty, the American*, 39; Hopalong

Cassidy westerns, 188; *Intolerance*, 24;
  The Love Flower, 39; Mickey Mouse cartoons, 116; *Pollyanna*, 39; *Robin Hood*,
  39; *Romance*, 34; Silly Symphony shorts,
  116; *The Struggle*, 87; *The Three Little
  Pigs*, 116; *The Trail of the Lonesome
  Pine*, 139; *Walter Wanger's Vogues of
  1938*, 174; *Way Down East*, 39; *The
  Westerner*, 158; *Whoopee*, 106
—financing: Paramount's method of, 9;
  First National's method of, 11; method
  for independents, 11, 191; of Pickford,
  16-17, 37; of Chaplin, 18; of Fairbanks,
  21, 37; of Griffith, 23-24, 36-37; difficulties in early years, 26, 35-39; attitude of
  banks toward majors, 35-36; attitude of
  banks toward independents, 35-36, 39,
  44, 216; block booking as a means of, 36,
  101; by Wall Street, 36, 56, 67; as affected
  Allied Producers, 43; of Associated Authors, 43-44; Chaplin's opinion of financing others, 56; by Art Finance, 56-57; of
  Goldwyn, 60; by Art Cinema, 66-68, 84,
  85-86, 93, 117-18; Schenck's plan for, 87,
  116-17; of Twentieth Century, 120; of
  Selznick, 136, 179, 181, 184; as cause of
  strife, 138, 206; investment in independents, 140, 173, 191-93, 203, 217; of
  Walter Wanger Productions, 140, 174-76;
  of Korda, 145-46, 154; by majors for independents, 205; Hughes producers fund,
  218-19; from Heller, 235; Krim-Benjamin
  policy of, 237-38
Propaganda, 166, 167, 168-69, 220
Prudential Assurance Co., Ltd.: finances
  London Films, 145; London Films mortgage, 146; protects Korda's interest, 149;
  settlement with Korda, 154; takes control
  of Denham, 154; sells Korda interest in
  stock, 186; mentioned, 147, 148, 199
Purviance, Edna, 45

Quota Act, 132
Quota laws, 132, 166, 167, 223
Quota pictures, 132, 134

Radio City Music Hall, 134, 138
Radio Corporation of America, 78-79
Radio-Keith-Orpheum: formed by RCA, 79;
  status in industry, 95; effects of Depres-

Radio-Keith-Orpheum (*cont.*)
sion on, 96; theater holdings, 97; cartoons, 116; Disney deal, 137; Schaefer becomes president, 152; defendant in *Paramount* case, 171; finances independents,
205; acquired by Hughes, 218; in Great
Britain, 221; *Paramount* consent decree,
226; mentioned: 66, 119, 136, 147, 169,
181, 188, 219, 223, 241

Raft, George, 120

Raftery, Edward: opinion of Code of Fair
Competition, 104; threatens action against
Code Authority, 108-109; elected to executive committee, 127; complaints
against Goldwyn, 158-59; named president, 184; justifies acquisition of inferior product, 193; opinion of Chaplin
suit, 194; opinion of Rank, 198, 200; calls
for production financing, 205; resigns,
215

Rank, J. Arthur: expresses interest in joining UA, 198; growth of motion picture
empire, 198-200; Korda's description of,
199-200; attempts to crack American
market, 200, 221-23; retaliates against
American companies, 222-23; mentioned,
154, 229, 241

Rankin, John E., 214

Rathvon, Peter, 219

Ray, Charles, 43, 45

Reeves, Alfred, 147, 153

Reich Film Law, 167

Reliance-Majestic, 23

Reliance Pictures, Inc., 117, 123

Republic Pictures, 222

Rex Pictures, 7

Rialto theater, 65

Rinehart, Mary Roberts, 57, 60

Rin Tin Tin, 118

Riskin, Robert, 176

Rivoli theater, 65

RKO. *See* Radio-Keith-Orpheum

RKO Pathé Studio, 136

Roach, Hal, 153, 162, 174

Roadshowing, 46-47, 51, 64

Robertson, John, 43

Robinson, Edward G., 118

Rogers, Charles "Buddy," 190, 206

Rogers, Charles R., 190

Rogers, Ginger, 138, 213

Rogers, Lela, 213

Roosevelt, Franklin Delano, 84, 97, 99, 100,
118, 120

Rosenblatt, Sol A., 99, 100, 107, 108-109

Rothschilds, 147

Rowland, Richard A., 4, 14, 162

Runs, 102, 225

Russell, Jane, 203, 204

Sarnoff, David, 79

Saville, Victor, 145

Savini, Robert M., 112

Schaefer, George, 150, 152

Schenck, Joseph M.: resolves loan problem,
44; pre-UA career, 52-54; named chairman, 54; becomes a partner, 54-56; forms
Art Finance, 56-57; forms Feature Productions, 56-57; proposes merger with
MGM, 61-62; forms UA Theatre Circuit,
64-65; distribution contracts, 66; forms
Art Cinema, 67-68; named president, 68;
organizes UA Studio, 68-69, 125; salary,
71; proposes merger of UA companies,
71-73; proposes merger with Warner, 71-
73; hires Swanson, 84; opinion of UA
partners, 85, 89, 127, 151; hires Griffith,
85-86; plans for production financing, 87,
116-17; achievement, 94, 109, 110, 123-
24; protests to Code Authority, 104, 105;
handling of Hughes pictures, 112; fights
Fox-West Coast, 113; helps finance Reliance, 117, 123; investment losses, 118;
forms Twentieth Century, 118-20; proposes capital structure reorganization,
121-22; resignation, 122-25; named chairman of Twentieth Century-Fox, 126; accused of misfeasance, 128-30; opinion of
Korda, 133-34; on Goldwyn's grievances,
150-51; brought in as arbitrator, 215;
mentioned, 83, 93, 142, 159, 232, 240,
241

Schenck, Nicholas, 52, 61, 68

Schlesinger, Leon, 116

Schulberg, Benjamin P., 25-26

Schwartz, Charles, 157, 158, 176, 194

Screen Actors Guild, 99

Sears, Gradwell L.: heads domestic distribution, 184-85; acquires Paramount pack-

Sears, Gradwell L. (*cont.*)
age, 188; denounces Pickford streamliners, 206; named president, 216; fights
producers' revolt, 216-19; advises dissolution, 229
Security-First National Bank of Los Angeles, 172, 191, 216
Selig Polyscope Company, 6
Selwyn, Arch, 59
Selznick, David O.: first distribution contract, 135, 177; pre-UA career, 136; forms
Selznick International, 136; partnership
negotiations, 176, 181-84; gives MGM
Gone With the Wind, 177-79; second distribution contract, 179; opinion of UA
distribution, 179-80; dissolves Selznick
International, 180-81; given special terms,
184; directs reorganization, 184; forms
Vanguard Films, 185; sells properties to
Twentieth Century-Fox, 187; charges concerning inferior product, 187-88; Chaplin suit, 187, 193-94, 208-209; resumes
production, 202-203; agrees to Pickford
financing, 206; hopes for *Duel in the Sun,*
207; ejected from company, 207-10; set-
tlement, 209-10; forms Selznick Releas-
ing Organization, 210; mentioned, 138,
153, 157, 163, 168, 186, 187, 188, 201,
216, 241
Selznick, Lewis, 9
Selznick, Myron, 136
Selznick International Pictures, Inc., 140,
180-81
Selznick Releasing Organization, 210
Semenenko, Serge, 215
Sennett, Mack, 10, 17-23 *passim,* 34, 45
Shaw, George Bernard, 33
Shearer, Norma, 136, 177
Sheldon, Edward, 34
Sherman, Harry, 188
Sherman Antitrust Act, 7, 79, 225, 228
Shinn, Everett, 59
Shubert, Lee, 65
Sidney, Sylvia, 140
Silverstone, Murray: testimony against
Schenck, 130; Goldwyn's presidential
choice, 143; supported by Goldwyn, 150-
52; made general manager, 151; formu-
lates profit-sharing plan, 152-54; negoti-
ates for *Gone With the Wind,* 177-78; re-
signs, 182-83; mentioned, 128, 129, 145,
153, 154, 176
Silverstone Plan, 152-54, 155, 157, 158, 186
Sinatra, Frank, 238
Skirball, Jack, 205
Skouras, Spyros, 235
Smadja, Charles, 237
Small, Edward, 117-18, 153, 162, 174, 188
Sound, 75-80
Spiegel, Sam, 235
Spirling, Milton, 205
Stack, Robert, 175
Stanley Corporation, 64, 72
Star system: effects on economics of indus-
try, 4-5, 14-17; first stars, 5; effects on
MPPC, 8; Laemmle as innovator, 8;
threatened by merger, 11-12; Pickford's
career, 14-17; Chaplin's career, 17-18;
Fairbanks' career, 18-21; failure of stage
actors, 20-21; D. W. Griffith's career, 21-
24; Talmadge's career, 52; Swanson's
box-office appeal, 57-58; effects of Code
of Fair Competition on, 98-99; Code
Authority investigation of, 105-107; provi-
sions of option contract, 106; Wanger as
star maker, 138; mentioned, 63, 96
Steuer, Max, 157, 159
Stevens, George, 205
Stewart, Anita, 194
Stone, Andrew, 190
Strand theater, 64
Streamliners, 174, 206
Stromberg, Hunt, 189, 190-92, 203, 205
Sully, Beth, 32
Sully, Daniel J., 32
Supreme Court, 103, 109, 171, 225-26, 229
Swanson, Gloria: becomes a partner, 57-58;
career as independent, 82-84; sells stock,
88; mentioned, 10, 66, 72, 123
Swanson Producing Corporation, 58, 83
Sweet, Blanche, 10

Tally, Thomas L., 11, 12
Talmadge, Constance, 10, 52
Talmadge, Natalie, 52
Talmadge, Norma: promoted by Schenck,
52; profits, 72; retirement, 81-82; men-
tioned, 10, 66, 93

Taylor, Robert, 213

Technicolor, 116

Television: cause of break with Disney, 137; growth of, 202, 224; acquisition of Warner film library, 239; mentioned, 229

Terra Film Verleih, 167

Thalberg, Irving, 136, 139, 194

Thanhouser Film Corp., 7

Theater Owners Chamber of Commerce, 99

Thomas, J. Parnell, 212, 213

Tobis, 79

Tobis-Klangfilm, 167

Todd, Michael, 239

Tourneur, Maurice, 16, 34

Towne theater, 227

Tree, Sir Herbert Beerbohm, 20

Triangle Film Corporation, 9, 18-19, 20-21, 23, 24

Tri-Ergon, 79

Twentieth Century-Fox: merger, 125-26; as defendant in *Paramount* case, 171, 226; buys Selznick properties, 187; named party to Chaplin suit, 193-94; wartime earnings, 202; in Great Britain, 221; mentioned, 129, 130, 194, 235

Twentieth Century Pictures, Inc.: formation of, 119-20; distribution terms, 120; financing of, 120; access to studio stars, 120; stock dispute, 120-22, 127; merger with Fox, 125-26; mentioned, 123, 124, 131, 159, 241

Two Cities Films, Ltd., 222

UFA, 95, 166

United Artists Corporation: formation, 12-14; origins, 25-27; capital structure, 27-28, 30, 124, 235; corporate structure, 27-29, 142-43; proposed MGM merger, 61-62, 124, 195; proposed Warner merger, 71-73, 124; reconstitutes board, 127-28; reorganization, 151-54; attempted sale of, 215; goes public, 239; acquired by Transamerica Corporation, 240; evaluation of, 240-41

—stockholders: founders, 27-29; Schenck, 54; Swanson, 58; Art Cinema, 69; Goldwyn, 70; Korda, 134-35; Selznick, 183-84

—managements: Price, 29; Abrams, 35; Schenck, 54, 68; Lichtman, 127; Pickford, 136; Giannini, 140; Raftery, 184; Sears, 216; McNutt, 232; Krim-Benjamin, 233

—position in industry: relationship to majors, 65-66, 96, 109, 161, 227-28; treatment at the hands of MPPDA, 104-107; treatment by Code Authority, 104-109; defendant in *Paramount* case, 171, 226-28; as leading distributor of British films in U.S., 220

United Artists Corporation, Ltd.: formation, 40-41; acquires theaters, 128-30; distributes quota pictures, 132; relation to Goldwyn-Korda stock option, 147; relations with Rank, 200; postwar conditions of, 221-23; sells shares in Odeon, 222

United Artists Export, Ltd., 168

United Artists Productions, Inc.: takes over Wanger properties, 175-76; Bagnall in charge of, 185; purchases Paramount package, 188; participates in Cagney pictures, 191, 192; participates in Stromberg pictures, 191-92; sells off pictures, 224

United Artists Studio: organized, 68; proposed amalgamation of, 71, 195; wires for sound, 77; home of Art Cinema, 85; Twentieth Century purchases, 120; real estate ownership, 125; Goldwyn becomes owner of, 125; home of Wanger Productions, 140; name changed, 157; mentioned, 67, 71, 118, 123

United Artists theater, 227

United Artists Theatre Circuit: Chaplin's opposition to, 64; relationship to UA, 64-65, 129; profits, 72; wires for sound, 77; imbroglio with Fox-West Coast, 113; suit with UA, 128-30; severs relations with UA, 130

United States *vs.* Paramount, et al. *See Paramount* case

United Studios, 52

United World Pictures, 233

Universal Film Manufacturing Company, 7, 9

Universal Pictures: converts to sound, 77; position in industry, 96; effects of Depression on, 96, 103; theater holdings, 97, 103; defendant in *Paramount* case, 171; finances independent production, 205; in Great Britain, 221; mentioned, 35, 76, 104, 105, 106, 132, 169, 188, 194, 199, 233

Valentino, Rudolph, 56, 66
Van Beuren's Esop's Fables, 116
Vanguard Films, Inc., 185, 193-94, 201
Veiller, Bayard, 59
Vidor, King, 34, 81
Vitagraph Company of America, 6
Vitaphone Corporation, 76
Von Sternberg, Josef, 57, 189
Von Stroheim, Erich, 83

Waldorf statement, 214
Wallis, Hal, 205
Walter Wanger Productions, Inc.: forma-
  tion of, 140; financing of, 140; closed
  down, 174-75; name changed to United
  Artists Productions, 175; value of reissue
  rights, 188; mentioned, 191
Wanger, Walter: pre-UA career, 138-40;
  forms Walter Wanger Productions, 140;
  contract terms, 140; stock company, 140;
  settlement, 175; mentioned, 153, 172, 188
Ward, Fannie, 9
Wardour, 132
Warner, Albert, 75
Warner, Harry, 75, 118
Warner, Jack, 75
Warner, Sam, 75
Warner Brothers: proposed UA merger
  with, 71-73; theater holdings, 72, 97; purchases First National, 72-73; purchases
  Vitagraph, 75; as innovator of sound, 75-
  77; forms Vitaphone, 76; profits during
  sound revolution, 78; place in industry,
  95; effects of Depression on, 96; cartoons,
  116; rejects Goldwyn picture, 157-58; in
  Paramount case, 171, 226; in Great Brit-
  ain, 199, 221; wartime earnings, 202; fi-
  nances independent production, 205;
  postwar earnings, 224; film library acquired, 239; mentioned, 66, 118, 120,
  124, 125, 182, 184, 193, 194, 217, 227
Warner theater, 76
Wayne, John, 238
Weber and Fields, 20
Wells, H. G., 144
West, Roland, 57
Western Electric, 75-78 *passim*
Westinghouse, 79

Whitney, Cornelius V., 13
Whitney, John Hay, 136, 149-50, 168-69,
  180-81
Wilcox, Herbert, 132, 133
Wilson, Woodrow, 24
Withey, Chet, 34
Woods, Frank, 20, 43-44
Woolf, C. M., 154
World Film Corporation, 9
World War I, 220
World War II: effects on foreign markets,
  164-70; effects on domestic market, 170;
  creates raw film stock shortage, 170; ef-
  fect on Korda, 172-73; causes decline in
  production, 174; effects on independent
  production, 190; creates boom in domes-
  tic market, 194, 202
Wright, Loyd, 136, 153, 194
Wyler, William, 205, 238

Young, Robert R., 235
Youngstein, Max E., 237
Yousling, George, 216

Zanuck, Darryl: career at Warner, 118;
  forms Twentieth Century, 118-19; characterization of, 120; stock dispute, 120-22,
  125; negotiations with Fox, 125-26; mentioned, 123, 124, 127, 135-36, 159
Ziegfeld, Flo, 106
Zoning, 102
Zukor, Adolph: as protagonist in struggle
  for industry control, 5; forms Famous
  Players, 8-9; joins Paramount, 9; forms
  Famous Players-Lasky, 10; deposes Hodkinson, 10; controls market with stars, 10;
  abandons theater personages, 10, 20-21;
  introduces block booking, 10-11; hires
  Pickford, 14-17; forms independent unit
  for Pickford, 16; forms Artcraft, 16;
  forms production unit for Fairbanks, 21;
  signs Griffith, 24; lures Hart from UA,
  24; accused by FTC, 26; goes into exhibition, 26, 63; sells *Broken Blossoms,* 30-
  31; lures Griffith from UA, 49-51; hopes
  for Fairbankses return, 51; quarrel with
  Valentino, 56; parts with Griffith, 85;
  mentioned, 14, 27, 96, 139

DESIGNED BY IRVING PERKINS
COMPOSED BY FOX VALLEY TYPESETTING, MENASHA, WISCONSIN
MANUFACTURED BY MALLOY LITHOGRAPHING, INC., ANN ARBOR, MICHIGAN
TEXT IS SET IN TIMES ROMAN, DISPLAY LINES IN STYMIE MEDIUM

Library of Congress Cataloging in Publication Data
Balio, Tino.
United Artists.
Bibliography: p. 289-292
Includes index.
1. United Artists Corporation. I. Title.
PN1999.U5B3   791.43′06′579494   75-12208
ISBN 0-299-06940-0